Natural Resources and
Violent Conflict

Natural Resources and Violent Conflict

OPTIONS AND ACTIONS

Ian Bannon
Paul Collier
editors

THE WORLD BANK
Washington, D.C.

© 2003 The International Bank for Reconstruction and Development /
The World Bank
1818 H Street, NW
Washington, DC 20433
Telephone: 202-473-1000
Internet: www.worldbank.org
E-mail: feedback@worldbank.org

ISBN 0-8213-5503-1

Cover photos: Inset—© Peter Turnley/CORBIS
             Background—© Adalberto Rios Szalay/Sexto Sol

Library of Congress Cataloging-in-Publication Data *has been applied for.*

Contents

BOXES

FIGURES

TABLES

Preface

RECENT RESEARCH UNDERTAKEN BY THE World Bank and others suggests that developing countries face substantially higher risks of violent conflict and poor governance if they are highly dependent on primary commodities. Revenues from the legal or illegal exploitation of natural resources have financed devastating conflicts in a large number of countries across regions. When a conflict erupts, it not only sweeps away decades of painstaking development efforts but also creates costs and consequences—economic, social, political, regional—that live on for decades. The outbreak of violent domestic conflict amounts to a spectacular failure of development—in essence, development in reverse. Even where countries initially manage to avoid violent conflict, large rents from natural resources can weaken state structures and make governments less accountable, often leading to the emergence of secessionist rebellions and all-out civil war.

Natural resources are never the sole source of conflict, and they do not make conflict inevitable. But the presence of abundant primary commodities, especially in low-income countries, exacerbates the risks of conflict and, if conflict does break out, tends to prolong it and makes it harder to resolve.

Reflecting a growing interest in the links between natural resources and conflict and the World Bank's evolving conflict agenda—which is placing greater emphasis on preventing conflicts—in 2002, the World Bank's Conflict Prevention and Reconstruction Unit and the Development Research Group began to define a research project to address this link. As the Governance of Natural Resources Project took shape, the discussion moved toward practical approaches and policies that could be adopted by the international community. While there is much that individual developing countries can do to reduce the risk of conflict—by addressing genuine grievances in their societies, adopting economic and social policies that are more inclusive, and improving transparency and accountability—there is also a need to articulate a convincing and practical agenda for global action. As members of the international community working to build a world that is safer and free of poverty, we share a global responsibility in assisting developing countries to ensure that revenues from the exploitation of natural resources do not exacerbate the risk of conflict.

This book presents the papers commissioned under the Governance of Natural Resources Project. When we commissioned this work, we asked the researchers to focus on the practical aspects from a global governance perspective—to focus on "what we can do collectively." The papers offer a rich array of approaches and suggestions that are feeding into the international policy debate and that we hope will lead over time to concerted international action to help developing countries better manage their resource wealth and turn this wealth into a driver of development rather than of conflict.

The Governance of Natural Resources Project and the publication of this book have been made possible through the generous support of the government of Norway, which is funding the project through the Norwegian Trust Fund for Environmentally and Socially Sustainable Development. We are very grateful for this support and encouragement. We also wish to thank the Agence Française de Développement (AFD), especially Pierre Jacquet (AFD executive director and chief economist), Serge Perrin, and the rest of the staff of AFD, not only for hosting the workshop that launched the project in Paris in December 2002 but also for their continued interest, support, and encouragement.

The project has received strong support and valuable inputs from a wide range of stakeholders. We especially want to thank the participants of the launch workshop for their valuable contributions and interest in this work. In addition, we are grateful to many others who sent us comments and suggestions. We also wish to thank our colleagues at the International Monetary Fund, especially Masood Ahmed, Martin Fetherstone, Nancy Happe, and Anton Op de Beke, who took an early interest in the project and have offered valuable suggestions along the way.

Within the Bank, the project has been a collaborative effort between the Conflict Prevention and Reconstruction Unit and the Development Research Group, with valuable and continuous support from the Oil and Gas Group, especially from Charles McPherson. We have also benefited from advice and guidance from many staff in the Bank, especially Nicholas Stern, Robert Bacon, Kerstin Canby, and Havard Hagre. A big thanks also to the authors of the research papers, who produced excellent chapters, despite having to work under very tight deadlines. Finally, a special thanks to Kazuhide Kuroda, not only for his conceptual and substantive contributions to the project but also for his tireless efforts to put it all together.

Ian Bannon

Contributors

Ian Bannon is manager of the Conflict Prevention and Reconstruction Unit, in the Social Development Department of the World Bank.

John Bray is a political risk specialist with Control Risks Group, the international consultancy. He has extensive experience in working with companies across the Asia/Pacific region, South Asia and East Africa. His professional interests include the politics of business and human rights, and anticorruption strategies for both the public and the private sectors. His recent publications include *Facing Up to Corruption: A Practical Business Guide* (London: Control Risks, 2002).

Paul Collier was director of the World Bank's Development Research Group until March 2003. He is currently director of the Centre for the Study of African Economies, University of Oxford, and senior adviser to the Vice President of the Africa Region in the World Bank.

Corene Crossin is the campaigns researcher at Global Witness (a nongovernmental organization that highlights the connection between natural resources exploitation and human rights abuses) and works on the governance of natural resources and transparency. She has recently worked on a World Bank initiative on "conflict timber" and the relationship between forests and violent conflict in Sub-Saharan Africa.

Patrick Guillaumont is founder and president of the Centre d'Etudes et de Recherches sur le Développement International (CERDI), a professor at the Université d'Auvergne, and a member of the Committee for Development Policy at the United Nations. He has written about 20 books and numerous papers on development economics, several of them focused on the consequences of export instability and on the policies implemented in response to this instability.

Sylviane Guillaumont Jeanneney is with CERDI, is a professor at the Université d'Auvergne, and is also a member of the Conseil de Surveillance of Agence Française de Développement. She has contributed numerous papers to journals and written several books on development issues, especially monetary policy and exchange.

Gavin Hayman is the lead campaigner and investigator for Global Witness and has been working on oil revenue misappropriation and corporate malfeasance since 2001. He is also an associate fellow of the Sustainable Development Programme at the Royal Institute of International Affairs, where he has written extensively on various environmental crime and commodity tracking issues.

Philippe Le Billon is an assistant professor at the Liu Institute for Global Issues, University of British Columbia, Canada. He has worked with the Overseas Development Institute and the International Institute for Strategic Studies (IISS) on war economies and the regulation of extractive industries in conflict areas. He recently authored *Fuelling War: Natural Resources and Armed* Conflicts (IISS/Oxford University Press). He can be contacted at philippe.lebillon@ubc.ca.

Leiv Lunde is a partner and senior policy analyst with ECON Centre for Economic Analysis (www.econ.no), based in Oslo. Lunde is a political scientist with broad experience in research and policy analysis in areas such as environmental policy, development cooperation, humanitarian policy and conflict prevention, and corporate social responsibility. From 1997 to 2000, Lunde served as state secretary for international development and human rights in the Norwegian Ministry of Foreign Affairs.

Mai Oldgard holds an M.Sc. from Copenhagen Business School, where she specialized in corporate social responsibility (CSR) and corporate governance. At ECON Centre for Economic Analysis, she specializes in issues such as CSR challenges to the oil and insurance industries, and has coordinated a major scenario project on the future of the Norwegian energy industry.

Michael Ross is an assistant professor of political science at the University of California, Los Angeles (UCLA). He received his Ph.D. from Princeton University and has been a Visiting Scholar at the World Bank. He has an ongoing project on "the resource curse" and has most recently written the paper "How Does Natural Resource Wealth Influence Civil Wars?" Most of his publications and working papers are available at www.polisci.ucla.edu/faculty/ross.

Trifin J. Roule is an assistant editor of the *Journal of Money Laundering Control* and consults on government and nongovernmental projects on money laundering, terrorist finance, and illicit resource extraction.

Philip Swanson is a senior economist in the Paris office of Oslo-based ECON Centre for Economic Analysis. He specializes in development issues, with a focus on energy, health, and corporate social responsibility. He has written papers exploring the links between natural resource revenues and governance.

Simon Taylor is cofounder of Global Witness (www.globalwitness.org), a nongovernmental organization whose work is to highlight the links between the exploitation of natural resources and human rights abuses. Most recently, he colaunched with George Soros the "Publish What You Pay" campaign.

Jonathan M. Winer is an attorney at the firm of Alston & Bird in Washington, D.C., where he practices international financial services regulatory law. He is a former U.S. deputy assistant secretary of state for international law enforcement. In that position, he worked on such cross-border illicit commodities as diamonds, firearms, money (for laundering), narcotics, and stolen cars. He can be reached at jwiner@alston.com.

Acronyms and Abbreviations

AUC	United Self-Defense Forces of Colombia
CCAMLR	Convention on the Conservation of Antarctic Marine Living Resources
CFF	Compensatory Financing Facility
CCSRP	Committee for the Control and Supervision of Oil Resources
CFC	Chlorofluorocarbon
CITES	Convention on International Trade in Endangered Species of Fauna and Flora
COTCO	Cameroon Oil Transportation Company
CPIA	Country Policy and Institutional Assessment
CTR	Commodity-specific tracking regime
ECGD	Export Credit Guarantee Department (United Kingdom)
ECOMOG	ECOWAS Monitoring Group
ECOWAS	Economic Community of West African States
ELN	National Liberation Army, Colombia
EU	European Union
FAO	Food and Agriculture Organization of the United Nations
FARC	Revolutionary Armed Forces of Colombia
FATF	Financial Action Task Force on Money Laundering
FLEG	Forest Law Enforcement and Governance
FLEGT	Forest Law Enforcement, Governance, and Trade
FLN	National Liberation Front, Algeria
FSAP	Financial Sector Assessment Program
FSC	Forest Stewardship Council
GAM	Gerakan Aceh Merdeka

GBIF	Global Biodiversity Information Facility
GDP	Gross domestic product
GeSI	Global e-Sustainability Initiative
HIPC	Highly Indebted Poor Countries
IFC	International Finance Corporation
IMF	International Monetary Fund
INTOSAI	International Organization of Supreme Audit Institutions
ITTO	International Tropical Timber Organization
LDC	Least developed country (United Nations grouping)
MIGA	Multilateral Investment Guarantee Agency
MMSD	Mining, Minerals, and Sustainable Development
MPLA	Popular Movement for the Liberation of Angola
MSC	Marine Stewardship Council
NEPAD	New Partnership for Africa's Development
NGO	Nongovernmental organization
NPFL	National Patriotic Front of Liberia
OECD	Organisation for Economic Co-operation and Development
PEFC	Pan European Forest Certification Council
RCD	Congolese Assembly for Democracy
ROSC	Reports on the Observance of Standards and Codes
RUF	Revolutionary United Front, Sierra Leone
SLORC	State Law and Order Restoration Council
SOFAR	State Oil Fund for the Azerbaijan Republic
SPLA	Sudan People's Liberation Army
TOTCO	T'Chad Oil Transportation Company
UN	United Nations
UNDP	United Nations Development Programme
UNEP	United Nations Environment Programme
UNITA	National Union for the Total Independence of Angola
WTO	World Trade Organization

CHAPTER 1

Natural Resources and Conflict: What We Can Do

Ian Bannon and Paul Collier

CIVIL WARS BESTOW MOST OF THE suffering on noncombatants, who tend to have little say in whether the conflict is initiated or if and when it is settled. As the conflict rages, incomes tend to plummet, mortality rises, and diseases spread. A generation's worth of education can be lost as education systems collapse for all but the privileged few. Civil wars are not temporary glitches in an otherwise smooth development path—the direct and indirect costs during the conflict are typically so high that even when post-conflict progress is dramatic and sustained, it will take countries a generation or more just to return to prewar conditions. This is because many of the costs of the war continue to accrue long after the fighting has stopped: the peace dividend proves elusive as the government finds it difficult to cut military spending; violent crime tends to explode, affecting people and the investment climate; capital flight continues and private investors, local and foreign, remain skittish; the prevalence of epidemics and disease remains higher than before the war; and human and social capital, destroyed or frayed during the war, can take decades to recover. Although there may be a few cases where a successful rebellion has ushered in social progress or led to the downfall of an oppressive and predatory regime, the majority of civil wars produce a spectacular failure of development. For the affected country, civil war represents development in reverse.

The costs of conflict, however, do not stop at the borders of the unlucky country. Civil wars also affect the country's neighbors and the global community. The costs suffered by other countries in the region may be as large as those suffered within the country, as the effects of the war spill across borders. The most obvious impact is through the

1

creation of large numbers of refugees, who impose a heavy economic burden on the host country and, because of their conditions on arrival and the crowded and unsanitary conditions in camps, exacerbate the risks of infectious diseases such as malaria, tuberculosis, and HIV/AIDS. A civil war in the neighborhood also leads countries to raise their defense spending, often generating a regional arms race. Conflict also disrupts regional trade and discourages foreign investors, who tend to regard the whole region as risky, even after the war has ended.

Civil war is also bad for the global community, especially in terms of three "global bads": drugs, AIDS, and terrorism. The cultivation of hard drugs requires territory outside the effective control of government. One consequence of conflict is that large rural areas tend to fall outside government control, making it difficult, if not impossible, to mount effective eradication measures. Conflict is an important vector of HIV/AIDS. Prevalence rates tend to be higher in conflict countries due to the more risky sexual behavior of combatants, coupled with their living conditions, mobility, age, and isolation from family and communities (Elbe 2002). The large and often massive movements of population induced by conflict favor the spread of AIDS, complicating the efforts of the international community to control the pandemic. By creating territory outside the control of a recognized government, conflict also provides terrorist organizations the safe haven they need to flourish and mount their attacks.

Understanding the Drivers of Conflict

Although, like Tolstoy's unhappy families, every conflict is unique in its own way, conflicts appear to embody recurring factors, which are often surprisingly strong. If reducing the risk of conflict is both necessary and possible, before we can propose measures to reduce the incidence of conflict we need to understand what makes countries vulnerable. Many models attempt to explore the factors that affect the risk of conflict (see, for example, Elbadawi and Sambanis 2002; Hegre and others 2001). In this chapter we review the results of the Collier-Hoeffler model and their findings on the links between natural resources and conflict (Collier and Hoeffler 2003). After testing for a number of factors, Collier and Hoeffler find that three are significant—the level of income per capita, rate of economic growth, and structure of the economy, namely, dependence on primary commodity exports. Doubling per capita income roughly halves the risk of a civil war. Each additional percentage point of growth reduces the risk by about 1 percentage point. The effect of primary commodity dependence is nonlinear, peaking with exports at around 30 percent of gross domestic product (GDP). A country that is

Figure 1.1 Natural Resources and Conflict Risk in
Low-Income Countries

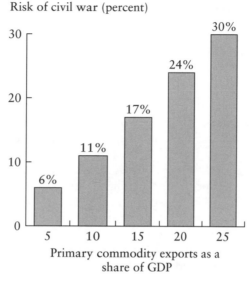

Risk of civil war (percent)

Primary commodity exports as a
share of GDP

Source: Based on Collier and others (2003).

otherwise typical but has primary commodity exports around 25 percent of GDP has a 33 percent risk of conflict, but when such exports are
only 10 percent of GDP, the risk drops to 11 percent (figure 1.1) Ethnic
and religious composition also matters. Societies in which the largest ethnic group accounts for 45 to 90 percent of the population—which Collier
and Hoeffler term "ethnic dominance"—have a risk of conflict about
one-third higher. Other than in the case of ethnic dominance, ethnic and
religious diversity actually reduces the risk of rebellion. Once a country
has had a civil war, its risk of renewed conflict rises sharply, although
this risk fades gradually over time at about 1 percentage point a year.

   The tools of war need to be financed, making civil war an expensive proposition. Governments have established defense sectors and
funding sources that support them, but to assemble, equip, and maintain a fighting force, the rebel group must find a regular source of
income. Before the end of the cold war, rebel groups typically were financed by one of the superpowers or by proxy regional powers. With
the end of the cold war, rebel groups have had to look for alternative
funding sources. So irrespective of the motivation of the rebellion, the
rebel group must also become a business organization. Its main and
pressing challenge is to secure funds in order to wage war. If it cannot overcome this financing problem, the rebel group will wither
away or be capable of only limited and low-level violence—more of

an irritant than a serious threat to an established government. Much of the economic analysis of rebellions tends to look for economic objectives, whereas much of the political literature generally ignores finance as a constraint. Yet finance is critical.

Natural Resources and Conflict: What Is the Link?

Unless a successful rebel organization is bankrolled by another country or an extensive and willing diaspora, it must generate income by operating some business activity alongside its military operations. The question then becomes the type of business activity in which a rebel group is likely to be competitive. Unfortunately, the obvious answer is that the rebel groups' only competitive advantage is their large capacity for organized violence and mayhem. Since, for military reasons, rebel groups tend to be based in rural areas, they turn to business activities such as various forms of extortion and the exploitation and trade of primary commodities.

Where rural areas produce primary commodities with high economic rents, generally for export, it is a relatively simple matter for rebel groups to run an extortion racket, levying protection charges on producers or carrying out some of the trade themselves. The best-known examples are the conflict diamonds of Angola and Sierra Leone. Alluvial diamonds are particularly well suited as a business line for rebels because the technology is so simple that the group can directly enter the extraction process and diamonds are a small, high-value commodity that is easy to hide and transport and has a readily accessible international market. As Michael Ross discusses in chapter 2, a number of other commodities such as coltan, drugs, gold, and timber have, at various times, been linked with civil wars in developing countries. In the case of high-value agricultural exports, the rebel group is not directly involved in production but levies informal taxes on producers and traders. The most spectacular example is that of illegal drugs, which, because of their illegality, are very high value. But even lower-value export crops are sometimes the target of rebel extortion—the Revolutionary United Front in Sierra Leone started by levying informal taxes on coffee and only shifted its activities to diamonds once it was well established.

Some extractive industries require sophisticated technology, generally supplied by a multinational company. This, too, provides opportunities for extortion. Rebel groups can target foreign companies and threaten expensive infrastructure, such as an oil or natural gas pipeline. As pointed out in chapter 2, a particularly remarkable recent development is for rebel groups to raise finance by selling the advance rights to the extraction of minerals that they do not control, but that they intend to control. This method of financing the tools of war through the sale of extraction rights is what Ross terms "booty futures."

Violent secessionist movements are statistically much more likely if the country has valuable natural resources, with oil being especially dangerous. Examples include Aceh (Indonesia), Biafra (Nigeria), Cabinda (Angola), Katanga (ex-Congo), and West Papua (Indonesia). There is some evidence that rebel leaders greatly exaggerate the likely gains from controlling the resources. This exaggeration is in part strategic, as secessionist leaders simply seize on the resource issue to build support for their movement. For example, leaders of the GAM (Gerakan Aceh Merdeka) rebellion in Aceh propagated the notion that secession would turn the province into another Brunei. Ross (2002) estimates that this was more than a tenfold exaggeration. But leaders themselves may also succumb to the glamour of the riches to be had from natural resources and overestimate the likely windfalls.

The discovery of a new natural resource or a higher endowment of a known resource greatly increases the risk of conflict in low-income countries, especially if the resource is oil (figure 1.2). In many such instances, ethnic cleavages can appear to cause the rebellion. In most societies, wherever a valuable resource is discovered, some particular

Figure 1.2 Risks from Natural Resources

Additional Risk of Civil War When the Natural Resource Endowment Is Double the Average

Effect of Oil on the Type of War: Risk that the War Is Secessionist

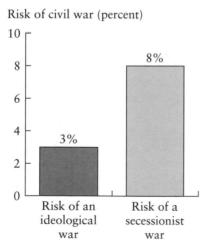
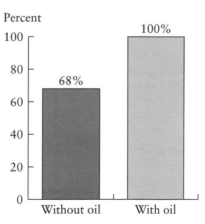

Source: Based on Collier and others (2003).

ethnic group is living on top of it and has an incentive to assert its rights
to secede. All ethnically differentiated societies have a few romantics
who dream of creating an ethnically "pure" political entity, but the discovery of resources has the potential to transform such movements from
the romantic fringe into an effective and violent secessionist movement.
Although this type of secessionist movement appears ethnically based
and cloaks its justification in the rhetoric of ethnic grievances, it would
seem a mistake to consider ethnicity or religion as the driver of conflict.

Poor governance and corruption can also exacerbate secessionist
tendencies, especially if the secessionist group has a fighting chance of
wresting control of a valuable natural resource. Where a region sees
what it considers its resources stolen by a corrupt national elite com-
fortably ensconced in the capital, the prospect of gaining control over
the natural resource revenues and using them for the benefit of the local
ethnic majority can be a powerful driver for a secessionist movement.

Kidnapping for ransom targeted at foreign extractive companies
also can be a profitable business. In the 1990s kidnapping became the
third largest source of financing for Colombia's two rebel groups
(National Liberation Army and Revolutionary Armed Forces of
Colombia), after drugs and extortion. Kidnapping netted the Colombian guerrillas an estimated $1.5 billion during 1991–99, and these
revenues have been rising. In 1999 the two groups are estimated to
have received a combined $560 million from extortion and kidnapping
(Pax Christi Netherlands 2001, pp. 33–34). A large number of kidnap
victims are employees of foreign extractive industries. Oil companies
are especially frequent kidnap targets, and in some regions kidnapping
has become a regular routine for them. Rebel groups may also target
foreign tourists for kidnapping, as has happened in the Philippines.
Following each successful kidnapping, rebel recruitment soars, presumably because young men anticipate large payoffs. In Colombia
rebel groups have combined with urban-based criminals to create a
market in kidnapped people. Criminals undertake the kidnapping, selling the victim to the rebel group, which then demands ransom.

Just as markets have emerged in some developing countries to trade
kidnap victims, markets have emerged in developed countries to supply
ransom insurance. Kidnap insurance, although understandable from a
personal or business sense, has the perverse effect of reducing the incentive to protect workers from kidnapping, increasing the size of ransom payments, and lowering the transaction costs for the rebel group.
In Colombia rebels are reputed to have, at times, gained access to insurance company data and thus been able to determine whether the actual or intended victim has kidnap insurance (Pax Christi Netherlands
2001, p. 30).

Wars also appear to have been lasting longer. The expected duration of conflict is now more than double that of conflicts that started prior to 1980 (Collier, Hoeffler, and Söderbom 2001). We do not know why this is the case, but one possible explanation is that it is now easier to sustain a conflict than it used to be. Even without support from a superpower or from a neighboring government, it is possible to find alternative sources of revenue with which to equip and sustain rebel movements.

Once conflict breaks out, it tends to make matters worse through its effect on the structure of the economy. Many natural resource exports are relatively unaffected by conflict because they have high rents or operate in enclave-type settings, with minimal backward or forward linkages with the rest of the economy. Contrast this with manufacturing or service activities such as tourism, which tend to have low margins and are easily disrupted by conflict. Moreover, economic policies and institutions, which are key to economic diversification, deteriorate markedly during the conflict and take a very long time to recover. As a result, countries are likely to find themselves even more dependent on natural resources than before the conflict started. This makes conflict much harder to resolve and, when resolved, raises the risk of a return to war.

A Call for Global Action

More than a billion people live in low-income countries that have been unable to put in place and sustain policies and institutions that would allow them to join the group of more developed middle-income nations. These countries have generally been mired in economic decline and dependent on primary commodities. This group faces a high risk of civil war, which, if it materializes, sets them on a path of reverse development. Close to 50 armed conflicts active in 2001 had a strong link to natural resource exploitation, in which either licit or illicit exploitation helped to trigger, intensify, or sustain a violent conflict. In other countries with low-intensity conflict or collapsed states, corrupt officials and their opponents, often involved with organized crime and terrorist networks, siphoned off revenues from natural resources. In addition to sustaining conflict and undermining governance, resource exploitation has contributed to famines, the spread of diseases, population displacement, and serious environmental damage. Abundant natural resources, which should be a blessing for a low-income country, in most cases make poor people poorer.

The adverse effects of natural resource endowments flow through a variety of channels, but most of these are amenable to policies and concerted global action. Some of the actions needed to avoid civil wars must come from the governments of developing countries themselves— for example, by making greater efforts to adopt economic policies and institutions that can stimulate growth and reduce poverty, improve governance and transparency, and redress reasonable grievances. Some measures, however, require concerted global action.

Building a more peaceful world is not just a matter of encouraging tolerance and consensus. It should involve a practical agenda for economic development and the effective global governance of the markets that have come to facilitate rebellion and corrupt governance. In the remainder of this chapter, we consider measures that can be regarded as part of a global development agenda and measures that are more appropriately viewed as part of the global governance of natural resources and its link to conflict.

The Development Agenda

Successful development is the best protection against civil war. In particular, raising and sustaining economic growth, diversifying the economy, and assisting countries to cope more effectively with commodity price shocks can all help to reduce the risk of conflict in low-income countries.

Raising Economic Growth. Faster economic growth would reduce the risk of conflict by raising the level of income and, indirectly over time, assisting diversification. The key issue is how to raise growth. There is a broad consensus that three instruments—domestic policies, international aid, and access to global markets—are all effective in raising growth.[1] The precise way in which they operate is subject to debate, but there is no significant disagreement on the merits of market access. Some analysts argue that aid and policies complement each other, with aid becoming more effective as policies get better and, conversely, policy reform being more effective as inflows of aid become larger. Other analysts argue that the beneficial effects of aid and policy are independent. The common ground is that, where policies are reasonable, aid is effective and that, where policies are not reasonable, policy improvement will enhance growth. The intention is not to enter into these arguments here but merely to assert that the old dictum of "good policies supported by generous aid and access to markets" remains an effective longer-term strategy for preventing conflicts.

Diversifying out of Trouble. One obvious way to reduce countries' dependence on natural resources is to help them to diversify their economies. Countries with a more diverse base of exports are better protected from the adverse effects of price fluctuations and less prone to the resource curse. On average, developing-country exports are no longer predominantly primary commodities. But this average masks a skewed pattern—at one extreme, the successful developers that have achieved astonishingly rapid diversification and, at the other, a group of low-income countries that have been left behind by development and marginalized from world markets. The fact that the former group has succeeded shows that it is possible for the marginalized to do the same; however, diversification may not always be a realistic or even a desirable option—Botswana is a landlocked desert with few options other than diamonds. For such countries, the priority should be to make natural resource endowments work effectively for development, as Botswana has managed to do. But for many countries, diversification is surely a viable option.

Three factors significantly reduce a country's dependence on primary commodities: growth, aid, and policy. On average, growth diversifies an economy, which reduces the risk of conflict in addition to the direct contribution of growth to risk reduction. This does not imply that all policies that promote growth promote diversification, but there is some presumption that the inducement of growth will normally assist diversification. Aid significantly reduces primary commodity dependence. This may be partly a result of "Dutch disease," which, by increasing the availability of foreign exchange, leads to appreciation of the exchange rate and thus reduces export incentives. Aid may also improve infrastructure—transport, power, telecommunications—which can help to lower business costs and improve the international competitiveness of activities that do not rely on high location-specific rents for their profitability. Good economic policy also significantly promotes diversification. Collier and Hoeffler (2003) measure this using the World Bank's Country Policy and Institutional Assessment (CPIA) ratings. On average, an improvement of 1 point in the CPIA—roughly equivalent to the difference between African and South Asian policies—would reduce primary commodity dependence from 15.2 percent of GDP to 13.8 percent.

As pointed out in chapter 2, OECD (Organisation for Economic Co-operation and Development) countries can also help natural resource–dependent, low-income countries to diversify by removing tariff and nontariff barriers on value added goods. OECD countries place no tariffs on imports of unprocessed oil and minerals, but exporters quickly run into tariffs and nontariff barriers if they wish to add value to these raw materials.

Reducing Exposure to Price Shocks.   Many of the problems caused by resource dependence come from the volatility of international prices.

Primary commodity prices are highly volatile so that countries that are heavily dependent on primary commodities periodically suffer from crashes in export prices. Studies show that commodity price shocks tend to promote corruption, weaken state institutions, and create a host of budget and management problems (see chapter 2). This is, in part, because shocks produce a multiplier contraction in output and severe fiscal pressures that do not disappear when prices recover. Recent research finds that when these shocks are large, they severely damage medium-run growth—each dollar of export income lost generates a further two dollars of output contraction (Collier and Dehn 2001). There is also some evidence that much of this lost growth is never recovered. Hence, negative price shocks may induce episodes of rapid and persistent economic decline that increase the risk of conflict.

Governments of low-income, shock-prone countries face macroeconomic management problems on a scale that developed countries have not seen since the 1930s. Yet their plight has received scant attention from donors. Shocks caused by natural disasters—earthquakes, hurricanes, floods, droughts—typically produce a massive and generous donor response, often overcompensating for the shock itself. Price shocks, such as the one being experienced by coffee producers today, although often much more devastating, have historically triggered no significant donor response. Until recently, the international community had two instruments to address the problem: the Compensatory Financing Facility (CFF) of the International Monetary Fund (IMF) and the Stabex Facility of the European Union (EU). For different reasons, neither of these worked well, and they are both dormant. The CFF was a nonconcessional borrowing facility, yet it is usually unwise for a country to borrow commercially at the onset of a severe negative shock. Stabex disbursements were so slow that they tended to be procyclical, arriving during the following price upturn.

Even the governments of developed countries, with sophisticated teams of experts, would find the management of such large shocks extremely difficult. Developing-country governments usually lack the expertise and political leeway to implement contractionary policies effectively. There is therefore a case for global action to cushion such shocks and assist countries to improve their risk management or transfer some of this risk. International financial institutions, especially the IMF and World Bank, could consider redesigning existing tools or developing new mechanisms to reduce the impact of price shocks. Beyond cushioning price shocks, there is also reason to reduce them where possible. Attempts to control commodity prices have failed repeatedly, and there seems to be little reason to propose them once again. However, the trade policies of countries in the OECD (Organisation for Economic Co-operation and Development) can exacerbate volatility for other countries. When OECD governments increase their subsidy to domestic producers in order to cushion them from a fall in the world price of an agricultural commodity, the effect is to amplify price shocks for the rest of the world. The cushioning that such subsidies provide to domestic OECD producers comes at the cost of increasing the price volatility for producers in low-income countries—precisely those that can ill-afford negative shocks and have few ways of softening the fall in prices.

The Governance of Natural Resources

Many low-income countries depend on primary commodities for their export and fiscal revenues. On average, such dependence is associated with increased risk of conflict, weak governance, and poor economic performance. However, the average conceals extremely wide variation. In 1970 Botswana and Sierra Leone were both low-income countries with substantial diamond resources. Over the next 30 years diamonds were central to the economic and social collapse of Sierra Leone—its per capita income is now much lower than it was in 1970, and the country has sunk to the bottom of the Human Development Index. By contrast, diamond resources were critical to Botswana's success in becoming the fastest-growing economy in the world and a middle-income country. Hence, although on average primary commodities have been a bane on development, they can also drive successful development. The natural resource curse is not destiny. The challenge, at both the national and international levels, is to adopt policies that better harness this potential.

The vast majority of resources that sustain and fuel civil wars depend on access to the global economy—to its markets, its financial intermediaries, its brokers, its investors, and the foreign companies that often extract a developing country's riches. This is not to decry the impact of globalization and add to the litany of negative effects ascribed to it. On the contrary, while globalization provides rebels with new opportunities, it also makes them more vulnerable to international pressure—more than would have been possible when rebellions were proxy wars of the superpowers—provided the international community is willing to exert it. The remainder of this chapter sketches out broad areas where global action would be effective, while the other chapters in this book explore each area in greater depth.

Who Gets the Money? Increasing Transparency of Natural Resource Revenues.   Although these proposals for global action are directed primarily at the international community, governments of low-income, resource-rich countries should also have a strong interest. They are often under threat from rebel groups financed by natural resource revenues and would obviously benefit if these funding sources were choked off. But these governments need to show that their natural resource revenues are well used. As discussed, rebel movements, particularly those seeking to secede on the back of natural resources, are greatly bolstered by the presence of a corrupt elite that siphons off the revenues rather than a government that uses them transparently to raise living standards across the board. The government's best defense is likely to be credible scrutiny of the revenues that it receives, how they enter the budget, and how they are spent. There are two serious obstacles, however, even when governments aim to be accountable. First are the sheer magnitude of resource revenues and the scale of the rents relative to the size of the country's economy. Governments in low-income countries, with poor institutional capacity and little tradition of accountability and public scrutiny, face enormous problems in absorbing and effectively tracking large revenue flows. This is not to exempt or excuse corruption in resource-abundant countries but merely to indicate the scale of the pressures and hence temptations involved. Second, in many instances it is not enough for resources to be accounted for and relatively well used—the government is not fully trusted and so will need to convince doubters by establishing a credible independent process of verification. These two factors suggest that even countries wanting to do the right thing need help, which, if successful, may exert pressure on those governments that do not manage their resource wealth effectively.

One possible way to address these issues in an integrated way is to develop an international template for the acceptable governance of natural resource revenues to which a resource-rich government could choose to subscribe. Such a template would have five elements. First, the host government would require international companies in the extractive industries to report payments so as to allow appropriate scrutiny and international comparability. Such reporting could either be to the general public, as envisaged in the Publish What You Pay campaign discussed by Philip Swanson, Mai Oldgard, and Leiv Lunde in chapter 3, or to an independent entity such as the international financial institutions. Second, the government itself would require national resource extraction companies, whether private or government owned, to report on the same basis. Third, the government would undertake to report its receipts from all of the above sources and ensure that they are easily tracked as they pass through the budget. Fourth, an independent entity, such as the international financial institutions, would collate the reported information, attempt to reconcile payments and receipts, integrate the figure for net government revenues with standard budget information on revenues and expenditures, and publish the results on an annual basis. A natural division of labor would be for the World Bank to collate, reconcile, and aggregate the data from companies and for the International Monetary Fund to integrate the net revenues into the budget data it already scrutinizes under its arrangements or Article IV consultations. Fifth, the government would designate and, if necessary, establish credible domestic institutions of scrutiny—such as parliamentary committees or ad hoc entities, including civil society organizations, as in Chad—to which the international financial institutions could report the information in a form that would be readily intelligible.

Where Does It Come from and Who Buys It? Shutting Rebel Organizations out of Markets.   The Kimberley Certification Process Scheme is designed to make it increasingly difficult for rebel organizations to sell rough diamonds in global markets. The process, which took only two years to establish (a comparatively short time for a global initiative), is an important first step. As Corene Crossin, Gavin Hayman, and Simon Taylor discuss in chapter 4 and appendix 4.1, significant technical and operational issues remain to be addressed, and it is too early to judge whether the Kimberley process will be successful and sustained. However, it is an encouraging sign that this type of global action is indeed possible.

If the Kimberley process proves ineffective, the present private voluntary agreement will need to be reinforced by intergovernmental legislation and probably provide for enforceable sanctions. However, the existence of the private agreement shows that all parties have recognized the need for effective action and deserve the opportunity to demonstrate success. Moreover, if the Kimberley process is successful, it could form the model for the governance of other commodities for which there is significant inadvertent funding of conflict.

Realistically, the effect of better regulation of commodity markets is not to shut rebel organizations out of markets altogether. Efforts such as the Kimberley process for rough diamonds, chain-of-custody tracking arrangements for illegal logging, and other schemes discussed in chapter 4 can be effective even if rebels are still able to sell the commodities they extort from local producers, as long as they can sell these illegal commodities only at a deep price discount. In this respect, a key global action is to monitor and evaluate the Kimberley process, while developing and implementing certification and tracking schemes for other commodities.

Going after the Money: The Finance of Illicit Commodities.   A practice that financed several rebel organizations in the 1990s is the sale of booty futures, whereby a rebel organization receives finance in advance in return for an entitlement to natural resource extraction in the future should the rebellion succeed. Reputable companies rightly view this practice as unacceptable; nevertheless, it happens on the fringes of the corporate world. As Philippe Le Billon discusses in chapter 6, there is a strong case for making such transactions criminal in the company's home country, analogous to the OECD agreement to criminalize international bribery.

Extortion and kidnapping have also become an important source of financing for rebel movements, and, as discussed earlier, the financial flows involved can be considerable. Although companies should be discouraged from operating in such conditions, the insurance industry has developed products offering ransom insurance. The overall effect of this is evidently to increase ransom payments, and there is a good case for banning ransom insurance. OECD governments could also undertake and live up to a commitment that public money will not be used to pay ransom to rebel movements and, correspondingly, that extortion payments will not be treated as tax-deductible business expenses. There is also a strong case for OECD countries to consider antidrug policies that reduce financial flows to rebel groups.

Tightening Scrutiny on Illicit Payments.   The proposed template is intended to ensure that legitimate payments from companies to governments are properly accounted for and used. Illicit payments by natural resource extraction companies to bribe people of influence are a different problem. The OECD agreement to criminalize such payments is a start, but bribes to officials can be disguised as "facilitation payments" to companies controlled by their relatives, and so complementary efforts are required. Some resource extraction companies, in line with OECD Guidelines for Multinational Enterprises, have now undertaken not to make facilitation payments. It would be desirable to make greater efforts to encourage adoption by non-OECD countries (chapter 6) but also to encourage the industry to determine precisely what is the boundary between legitimate and illegitimate payments and to embed this in corporate rules of behavior.

There is also an important role for the international banking system. The family of President Abacha was able to deposit in reputable international banks sums vastly in excess of his presidential salary, evidently illegally siphoned off from Nigerian oil revenues. Banks now have somewhat greater responsibility to know their clients and to report suspect receipts. There is also increasingly greater cooperation in securing the repatriation of corrupt money. However, there is scope for much tighter reinforcement of antibribery legislation on the part of the international banking system. As Jonathan Winer and Trifin Roule propose in chapter 5, the Financial Action Task Force should consider extending its recommendations to the exploitation of drugs or any other form of trade in illicit natural resources.

In some cases, even the best scrutiny and information on the dealings of corrupt officials and politicians will have no effect. Leaders and politicians may be impervious to moral pressure or wield sufficient power to place them above their own national law. In such cases the international community has some responsibility to impose penalties that target the guilty party and his or her associates without inflicting suffering on the society. The United Nations has been developing smart sanctions that offer some scope for such a targeted approach to penalties. These types of sanctions should be strengthened and internationally supported.

Attracting Reputable Companies to Risky Environments.   At present, some low-income countries face severe difficulties in attracting reputable resource extraction companies to exploit their resources. When reputable resource extraction companies withdraw from difficult environments as a result of greater international public scrutiny, they may well be replaced by companies that are less reputable or less vulnerable to international pressure or shareholder concerns. In this case, global efforts would be counterproductive. As John Bray discusses in chapter 7, survey evidence suggests that the two main impediments deterring good companies from entering very risky environments are the risk to their reputations and the political risk of unreasonable treatment. The template described in this chapter has the potential to address both of these risks.

One advantage of the Chad-Cameroon pipeline model of improved governance of natural resource revenues is that it provides international companies with a degree of reputational protection. The international financial institutions in effect certify a governance structure as acceptable. The introduction of a more standardized template for appropriate governance, and its adoption by governments interested in attracting reputable companies, would provide a much higher degree of reputational cover. Such a template also has the potential to address political risk. At present, the insurance entities that supply cover for political risks, such as the World Bank Group's Multilateral Investment Guarantee Agency (MIGA), have to assess each governance situation entirely on an ad hoc basis. Where governments subscribe to the good governance template, this would be pertinent information for MIGA and other insurers and could considerably facilitate their willingness to provide cover.

Note

1. An additional issue, not discussed here, is whether the way of raising growth inadvertently increases the risk of conflict. Collier and Hoeffler (2003) find that policies that raise growth rates do not directly increase the risk of conflict.

References

The word "processed" describes informally produced works that may not be commonly available through libraries.

Collier, Paul, and Jan Dehn. 2001. "Aid, Shocks, and Growth." Working Paper 2688. World Bank, Development Research Group, Washington, D.C., October. Available at www-wds.worldbank.org/servlet/WDSContentServer/WDSP/IB/2001/11/06//000094946_01102304052049/Rendered/PDF/multi0page.pdf. Processed.

Collier, Paul, and Anke Hoeffler. 2003. "Aid, Policy, and Peace." Forthcoming in *Defense and Peace Economics.*

Collier, Paul, Anke Hoeffler, and Mans Söderbom. 2001. "On the Duration of Civil War." Policy Research Working Paper 2681. World Bank, Development Research Group, Washington, D.C. Available at www.econ.worldbank.org/resource/php. Processed.

Collier, Paul, V. L. Elliott, Håvard Hegre, Anke Hoeffler, Marta Reynal-Querol, and Nicholas Sambanis. 2003. *Breaking the Conflict Trap: Civil War and Development Policy.* Washington, D.C.: World Bank.

Elbadawi, Ibrahim, and Nicholas Sambanis. 2002. "How Much Civil War Will We See? Explaining the Prevalence of Civil War." *Journal of Conflict Resolution* 46(June):307–34.

Elbe, Stefan. 2002. "HIV/AIDS and the Changing Landscape of War in Africa." *International Security* 27(2):159–77.

Hegre, Håvard, Tanya Ellingsen, Scott Gates, and Niles Petter Gleditsch. 2001. "Toward a Democratic Civil Peace? Democracy, Political Change, and Civil War, 1816–1992." *American Political Science Review* 95(1, March):33–48.

Pax Christi Netherlands. 2001. *The Kidnap Industry in Colombia: Our Business?* Utrecht. Available at www.paxchristi.nl/kidnappingincolombia.pdf.

Ross, Michael L. 2002. "Resources and Rebellion in Aceh, Indonesia." Paper prepared for the Yale–World Bank project on the economics of political violence. University of California Los Angeles, Department of Political Science, November 7. Available at www.polisci.ucla.edu/faculty/ross/ResourcesRebellion.pdf. Processed.

CHAPTER 2

The Natural Resource Curse: How Wealth Can Make You Poor

Michael Ross

SINCE THE MID-1990S THERE HAS BEEN a growing body of research on the causes of civil wars. One of the most surprising and important findings is that natural resources play a key role in triggering, prolonging, and financing these conflicts. This report summarizes the main findings of recent scholarship on the role of natural resources in civil wars and discusses some policy options.

The natural resources that cause these problems are largely oil and hard-rock minerals, including coltan, diamonds, gold, and other gemstones. Sometimes other types of resources are also at fault—notably timber. And if drugs are considered a natural resource, they too have played an important role in several conflicts. Table 2.1 lists 17 recent conflicts that are linked to natural resources. In eight of these, gemstones are one of the resources; in six, the resource is oil or natural gas; in five, it is some type of illicit drug; and in three cases, it is timber. In most of the conflicts, multiple resources play a role.

Resource-related conflicts may pose special problems for the states of Africa. Of the 17 resource-related conflicts in table 2.1, nine are in Africa. Moreover, conflicts in Africa, of all the world's regions, show the most worrisome trends. Between 1992 and 2001 the number of armed conflicts outside of Africa dropped by half, yet the number of conflicts in Africa stayed roughly the same (table 2.2). Moreover, within Africa, armed conflicts have grown more severe. During the 1970s and 1980s, half of all intrastate conflicts in Africa could be classified as civil wars—that is, they generated at least 1,000 battle-related deaths each year. In the 1990s two-thirds of Africa's intrastate conflicts were civil

Table 2.1 Civil Wars Linked to Resource Wealth, 1990–2002

Country	Duration	Resources
Afghanistan	1978–2001	Gems, opium
Angola	1975–2002?	Oil, diamonds
Angola (Cabinda)	1975–	Oil
Cambodia	1978–97	Timber, gems
Colombia	1984–	Oil, gold, coca
Congo, Rep. of	1997	Oil
Congo, Dem. Rep. of	1996–97, 1998–	Copper, coltan, diamonds, gold, cobalt
Indonesia (Aceh)	1975–	Natural gas
Indonesia (West Papua)	1969–	Copper, gold
Liberia	1989–96	Timber, diamonds, iron, palm oil, cocoa, coffee, marijuana, rubber, gold
Morocco	1975–	Phosphates, oil
Myanmar	1949–	Timber, tin, gems, opium
Papua New Guinea	1988–	Copper, gold
Peru	1980–95	Coca
Sierra Leone	1991–2000	Diamonds
Sudan	1983–	Oil

Note: Separatist conflicts are listed in italics.

Table 2.2 Armed Conflicts in Africa and the Rest of the World, 1989–2001

Year	Africa	Rest of world
1989	14	33
1990	17	32
1991	17	34
1992	15	40
1993	11	35
1994	13	29
1995	9	26
1996	14	22
1997	14	20
1998	15	22
1999	16	21
2000	15	19
2001	14	20

Source: Adapted from Wallensteen and Sollenberg (2000).

Table 2.3 Civil Violence in Africa by Decade, 1970–99

Period	Minor conflict[a]	Intermediate conflict[b]	Civil war[c]
1970–79	5	2	7
1980–89	8	0	8
1990–99	6	1	14

a. A minor conflict produces at least 25 battle-related deaths per year and fewer than 1,000 battle-related deaths over the course of the conflict.

b. An intermediate conflict produces at least 25 battle-related deaths per year and an accumulated total of at least 1,000 deaths, but fewer than 1,000 in any given year.

c. A civil war produces at least 1,000 battle-related deaths per year.

Source: Data are taken from Gleditsch and others (2001).

wars. Africa had seven civil wars in the 1970s, eight in the 1980s, and 14 in the 1990s (table 2.3).

Before proceeding, it is useful to clarify two facts. First, natural resources are never the only source of a conflict. Any given conflict is brought about by a complex set of events; often poverty, ethnic or religious grievances, and unstable governments also play major roles. But even after these factors have been taken into account, studies consistently find that natural resources heighten the danger that a civil war will break out and, once it breaks out, that the conflict will be more difficult to resolve. Second, natural resource dependence never makes conflict inevitable. Resource wealth raises the danger of civil war, but for every resource-rich country that has suffered from violent conflict, two or three have avoided it. Better policies may help to reduce the likelihood that resources will generate conflict and to direct resource wealth instead to education, health, and poverty reduction.

This chapter presents an overview of what recent scholarship can tell us about the role that natural resources play in civil wars. It suggests four main pathways through which resources lead to armed conflict: their effects on economies, their effects on governments, their effects on people living in resource-rich regions, and their effects on rebel movements. It offers some examples of each dynamic and discusses ways in which the international policy community could intervene to counteract these effects.[1]

Resource Dependence and Economic Performance

Resource dependence tends to make countries more susceptible to civil war through two economic effects: a reduction in growth and an increase in poverty.

Economic Growth

It may seem paradoxical that a "gift" from nature of abundant gem-stones, gold, or oil tends to cause economic distress. Yet study after study has found that resource-dependent economies grow more slowly than resource-poor economies.[2] A recent report by the World Bank, for example, looks at the economic performance in the 1990s of countries that have large mining sectors (World Bank 2002).[3] It finds that in countries with medium-size mining sectors (between 6 and 15 percent of all exports), gross domestic product (GDP) per capita *fell* at an average rate of 0.7 percent a year over the course of the decade. In countries with large mining sectors (between 15 and 50 percent of exports), GDP per capita dropped an average of 1.1 percent a year, while in countries with very large mining sectors (over 50 percent of exports) GDP per capita dropped a remarkable 2.3 percent a year. Collectively these mining states saw their GDP per capita fall 1.15 percent a year—a drop over the course of the decade of almost 11 percent (World Bank 2002; see also Ross 2002c).

This is a catastrophic record on economic grounds alone. But it also has implications for the susceptibility of these states to civil war: recent scholarship shows that when a country's growth rate turns negative, a civil war is more likely to break out (Collier and Hoeffler 2001; Hegre 2002). In the three years leading up to the war in the Democratic Republic of Congo, for example, GDP growth averaged –5.56 percent; in the three years before the Congo Republic's civil war, growth was –1.94 percent; on the eve of Liberia's civil war, growth averaged –1.34 percent (figures are from World Bank 2001).

Poverty

A country's reliance on nonfuel mineral exports—and possibly oil exports as well—also tends to create atypically high poverty rates. One reason for this pattern is that resource-rich governments do an unusually poor job of providing education and health care for their citizens. Ross (2001b) finds a strong correlation between greater dependence on oil and mineral exports and higher child mortality rates: for each increase in minerals dependence of five points, the mortality rate for children under the age of five rose 12.7 per 1,000; for each five-point increase in oil dependence, the under-five mortality rate rose 3.8 per 1,000.[4]

Again, this pattern is intrinsically worrisome, but it also has consequences for a state's susceptibility to violent conflict. The greater a country's poverty, the more likely it is to face a civil war (Collier and Hoeffler 2001; Elbadawi and Sambanis 2002; Fearon and Laitin 2002).

It is not surprising that people are more likely to rise up against their government when their economic predicament is bad and getting worse. Rebel groups find it easier to recruit new members when poverty and unemployment are widespread, since the prospect of combat and looting seems more attractive by comparison.

A glance at the world's most oil-dependent states, and most mineral-dependent states, illustrates these patterns. Table 2.4 lists the world's 20 most mineral-dependent states. Remarkably, the World Bank classifies

Table 2.4 Resource Dependency: Nonfuel Mineral–Dependent States and Oil-Dependent States

	Minerals		*Oil*	
Rank	*State*	*Dependence*	*State*	*Dependence*
1	Botswana	35.1	**Angola**[a]	68.5
2	**Sierra Leone**[a]	28.9	Kuwait	49.1
3	Zambia[a]	26.1	United Arab Emirates	46.3
4	United Arab Emirates	18.2	**Yemen**[a]	46.2
5	Mauritania[a]	18.4	Bahrain	45.7
6	Bahrain	16.4	**Congo, Rep. of (Brazzaville)**[a]	40.9
7	Papua New Guinea	14.1	Nigeria	39.9
8	**Liberia**[a]	12.5	Oman	39.5
9	Niger[a]	12.2	Gabon	36.1
10	Chile	11.9	Saudi Arabia	34.3
11	Guinea[a]	11.8	Qatar	33.9
12	**Congo, Dem. Rep. of**[a]	7.0	**Algeria**	23.5
13	Jordan	6.3	Papua New Guinea	21.9
14	Bolivia[a]	5.8	Libya	19.8
15	Togo[a]	5.1	**Iraq**	19.4
16	Central African Republic[a]	4.8	Venezuela	18.3
17	**Peru**	4.7	Norway	13.5
18	Ghana[a]	4.6	Syria	13.5
19	Bulgaria	4.0	Ecuador	8.6
20	**Angola**[a]	3.6	Bhutan	6.8

Note: Bold signifies a civil war since 1990. Mineral dependence is the ratio of non-fuel mineral exports to GDP. Oil dependence is the ratio of oil, gas, and coal exports to GDP. Figures are for 1995.

a. Defined by the World Bank as a highly indebted poor country.

12 of the 20 as "highly indebted poor countries"—the most troubled
category of states—even though they earn large sums of foreign exchange from the sale of their resources. Since 1990, five of them have
had civil wars. Table 2.4 also lists the world's 20 most oil-dependent
states. Here, too, the record is grim. Three of the top six states are
classified as highly indebted poor countries, and, once again, five of the
20 suffered from civil wars in the 1990s.[5]

What Can Be Done?

The international community could take two types of measures that
would help resource-rich economies. These suggestions and the others
in this chapter are preliminary ideas only, designed to stimulate further
analysis and discussion.

Promote Diversification through Trade Liberalization. One way to
reduce the dependence of governments on resource revenues is to help
them to diversify economically. States with more diverse exports are
better protected against international market fluctuations and are less
prone to the resource curse. For oil and mineral exporters, one obvious route to diversification is to develop downstream industries, which
can process and add value to raw materials. Many downstream enterprises use large numbers of low-wage workers and, hence, offer special
opportunities to the poor.

Yet downstream industries in oil- and mineral-dependent states
rarely succeed. One reason is that the advanced industrial states
place higher tariffs on processed goods than on raw materials to
protect their own manufacturing firms against competition. The states
in the Organisation for Economic Co-operation and Development
(OECD) place no tariffs at all on the import of much unprocessed oil
and many minerals, including aluminum, copper, crude oil, lead, nickel,
tin, and zinc. Yet if oil- and mineral-rich countries wish to add value
to these raw materials and export them in refined or processed
form—such as aluminum kitchenware, copper wire, or plastic resins—
they quickly run into OECD tariffs and nontariff barriers (table 2.5).
By removing the tariffs and nontariff barriers to value added
goods, the OECD states could help the resource-dependent states to
diversify.

Find Better Ways to Reduce Revenue Volatility. Many of the
problems caused by resource dependence come from the volatility of
resource revenues. For the last century, the international prices for
primary commodities—including oil and minerals—have been more

Table 2.5 Mean OECD Tariffs on Processed and Unprocessed Extractive Products

Product and description	Tariff
Copper	
Copper ores and concentrates	0.00
Wire of refined copper, if maximum cross-sectional dimension exceeds 6 millimeters	4.06
Tubes and pipes of refined copper	4.12
Cooking or heating apparatus used for domestic purposes	3.98
Aluminum	
Aluminum ores and concentrates	0.00
Unwrought aluminum (not alloyed)	4.10
Wire of aluminum, if maximum cross section exceeds 7 millimeters	6.13
Table or kitchenware of aluminum	5.83
Lead	
Lead ores and concentrates	0.00
Refined lead	1.88
Lead tubes, pipes, and fittings	3.90
Nickel	
Nickel ores and concentrates	0.00
Nickel bars, rods, and profiles (not alloyed)	0.33
Tubes and pipes of nickel (not alloyed)	0.31
Cloth, grill, and netting of nickel wire	0.77
Tin	
Tin ores and concentrates	0.00
Tin rods, bars, profiles, and wire	0.36
Tin tubes, pipes, and fittings	0.40
Zinc	
Zinc ores and concentrates	0.00
Refined zinc (containing by weight 99.99 percent or more of zinc)	1.80
Zinc bars, rods, profiles, and wire	3.84
Zinc tubes, pipes, and pipe fittings	3.92
Petroleum	
Petroleum oils, crude oil	0.00
Petroleum resins, coumarone, indene, or coumarone-indene resins, and polyterpenes	7.00
Woven fabrics made from high-tenacity yarn of nylon or other polyamides or of polyesters	8.47
Polyethylene (used for grocery bags, shampoo bottles, children's toys)	6.87
Polymers of vinyl chloride (PVC plastic)	7.52
Polycarbonates (used for light fittings, kitchenware, and compact disks)	7.84

Source: UNCTAD-TRAINS database (United Nations Conference on Trade and Development Trade Analysis and Information System); available at www.unctad.org/ trains/index.htm [consulted June 1, 2001].

volatile than the prices for manufactured goods (Grilli and Yang 1988). Since 1970 this volatility has grown worse (Reinhart and Wickham 1994). This means that when countries become more dependent on oil and mineral exports they also become more vulnerable to economic shocks.[6] Studies show that revenue shocks tend to promote corruption, weaken state institutions, and create a host of budget and management problems. In theory, governments should be able to buffer their economies against these market shocks by setting up stabilization funds and, perhaps, savings funds. Yet in practice these funds are often poorly managed and wind up doing more harm than good (Ascher 1999; Davis and others 2001). Policymakers should consider better ways for governments to smooth their revenue flows— not, perhaps, through stabilization funds but through other devices, such as long-term contracts and insurance mechanisms. This is a critical area for additional research and policy innovation.

Resource Dependence and Governance

Natural resource dependence also has an impact on governments. A strong and effective government should be able to offset some of the economic and social problems caused by resource dependence. But resource dependence tends to influence governments themselves, making them less able to resolve conflicts and more likely to exacerbate them. This occurs through three mechanisms: corruption, state weakness, and reduced accountability.

Corruption

The first mechanism is government corruption. There is strong evidence that, when a government gets more of its revenue from oil, minerals, and timber, it is more likely to be corrupt. Part of this problem is due to the sheer volume of resource revenues: governments can absorb, and effectively track, only limited amounts of money. Resource wealth often floods governments with more revenue than they can manage effectively. Another part of the problem comes from the volatility of resource revenues: sudden ebbs and flows of revenues tend to overwhelm normal budgeting procedures and can weaken state institutions.[7]

There are, unfortunately, many examples of resource-linked corruption. In the case of a major oil-exporting African country, almost $1 billion reportedly disappeared from the government's accounts in 2001 due to corruption. Fiscal discrepancies over the previous several years represented between 2 and 23 percent of the country's GDP. Most of these losses were linked to the country's dependence on oil. Large fractions of the signing bonuses for oil contracts disappeared, and the state oil company was criticized for managing the country's oil receipts through "a web of opaque offshore accounts," even though local law requires that the funds be handled by the central bank (Cauvin 2002; also see Global Witness 2002).

Weak Government

Natural resource wealth, ironically, can weaken governments—making them less capable of resolving social conflicts and providing public goods like health care and education. This can happen in two ways. One is by weakening the state's territorial control. If a country has a resource that is highly valuable and can be mined with little training or investment—such as alluvial gemstones and minerals like coltan and tanzanite—it will be difficult for the government to provide law and order in the extractive region. This opens the door for criminal gangs, warlords, and rogue military officers, who may eventually grow strong enough to challenge the government (see Reno 1995, 1998; Ross 2002b).

A second way this occurs is by weakening a state's bureaucracy. Some scholars have found that, when governments raise their revenues from oil instead of taxes, they fail to develop the type of bureaucracy that can intervene effectively in social conflicts. The result may be a heightened danger of civil war (Beblawi 1987; Fearon and Laitin 2002; Karl 1997; Mahdavy 1970).

Unaccountable Government

The third effect is reduced government accountability. Governments that get their income from natural resources become less democratic—and hence less accountable—than countries that rely on other sources of revenue, such as taxation. One reason for this pattern is that when governments have an abundance of revenues they tend to use them to quell dissent—both by dispensing patronage and by building up their domestic security forces. Indeed, oil- and mineral-rich governments generally spend unusually large sums on their military forces (Ross 2001a).

A second reason is corruption: instead of serving all citizens equally, corrupt governments tend to favor the wealthy, since the poor cannot afford to pay the necessary bribes. A third way is through the involvement of the military. In some states, resource industries are controlled by the military, giving the military more independence from, and greater influence over, the civilian government. In Indonesia, for example, the military has a large stake in many forest concessions and collects fees from oil, gas, and mineral companies. Since this money goes directly to the military, it does not pass through the central government's normal budgeting procedures, and the legislature has no influence over how it is spent. The result is that certain resource sales make the military less accountable to the legislature, undermining Indonesia's fragile democracy.

Once again, the harm that resource dependence does to democracy is intrinsically deplorable, but it also can make states more vulnerable to civil war. Several studies find a link between a government's accountability and the likelihood that it will suffer from a civil war.[8] Governments that are less than fully democratic are less able to resolve the grievances of their citizens and hence may be more prone to outbreaks of violent conflict.

It is easy to see how the effects of resource dependence on economies and governments can reinforce one another, creating a trap. Economic stagnation tends to destabilize governments. When governments are unstable, corruption can flourish. Corrupt governments cannot manage their economies well or properly counteract economic stagnation. Many countries have fallen into these kinds of traps; sometimes the outcome is a downward spiral that eventually leads to civil war—for example, in Algeria, the Democratic Republic of Congo, Liberia, and Sierra Leone.

What Can Be Done?

Perhaps the most important international response is to promote revenue transparency, both at the international and domestic levels.

Make Payments from Transnational Companies Transparent. Governments misuse the revenues they get from natural resources in part because the quantities are so large, and the government collects them in ways that are difficult for their citizens to track. Many of these funds wind up in off-budget accounts or the pockets of government officials and are never heard of again. The Publish What You Pay campaign has called attention to this problem and developed a strategy to persuade companies to disclose fully all payments they make to host governments. Chapter 3 offers a careful and comprehensive assessment of this issue.

Full disclosure of all resource revenues would be a major step toward curtailing corruption in the resource sector. But it is critical that a disclosure regime be comprehensive and mandatory. A partial regime may be worse than none at all: imagine, for example, that responsible companies decide to disclose all payments they make to host governments and, as a result, they are no longer able to work in countries with high levels of corruption. If the responsible companies are then replaced by other firms, which do not comply, the outcome is even worse: irresponsible firms are free to work with unscrupulous governments, and responsible firms are driven out of high-risk countries altogether.

Increase Domestic Financial Transparency.   Even if all foreign firms comply with a full disclosure rule, it would not be sufficient to sever the connection between resources and conflict. Determined governments will find ways to circumvent disclosure requirements, for example, by replacing royalty contracts with production-sharing contracts, where disclosures might mean little, or by working with domestic intermediaries instead of foreign companies.

Full *domestic* transparency—an independently audited account of all government revenues, including resource revenues—would place greater pressure on governments to reduce corruption and spend their funds accountably. The World Bank, International Monetary Fund, and World Trade Organization, export credit agencies, and the major bilateral donors may be able to bring about progress in this area, particularly if they work collectively.

Resource Abundance and Secessionist Movements

Resource wealth tends to promote civil wars through a third mechanism, by giving people who live in resource-rich areas an economic incentive to form a separate state.[9] Table 2.6 lists nine secessionist civil

Table 2.6 Mineral Resources and Secessionist Movements, 1949–Present

Country	Region	Duration	Resources
Angola	Cabinda	1975–	Oil
Congo, Dem. Rep. of	Katanga/Shaba	1960–65	Copper
Indonesia	West Papua	1969–	Copper, gold
Indonesia	Aceh	1975–	Natural gas
Morocco	West Sahara	1975–88	Phosphates, oil
Myanmar	Hill tribes	1949–	Tin, gems
Nigeria	Biafra	1967–70	Oil
Papua New Guinea	Bougainville	1988–	Copper, gold
Sudan	South	1983–	Oil

wars in regions that have abundant mineral resources.[10] These resource-inspired insurrections have several common elements. One is that, before the resource was exploited, people in these regions had a distinct identity—whether ethnic, linguistic, or religious—that set them apart from the majority population.

Another is the widespread belief that the central government was unfairly appropriating the wealth that belonged to them and that they would be richer if they were a separate state. Finally, in most cases, local people bore many of the costs of the extraction process itself—due to land expropriation, environmental damage, and the immigration of labor from other parts of the country.

The case of Aceh, Indonesia, offers a good illustration.[11] In many ways, Aceh—a province on the northern tip of the island of Sumatra—was an unlikely place for a separatist rebellion. Aceh played an important role in throwing off Dutch colonial rule in the 1940s and establishing the Indonesian republic. Although the Acehnese consider themselves ethnically distinct from the rest of Indonesia's population, they adhere to the same religion (Islam) and generally speak the national language (Bahasa Indonesia). Aceh had one of the highest rates of economic growth of any province in Indonesia in the 1970s and 1980s; by the late 1990s Aceh was at or above the national average in per capita income and in most welfare categories.

Yet a secessionist movement was formed in Aceh in 1976, just as a large natural gas facility was beginning its operations. The facility generated local resentments in at least four ways: the site's construction displaced hundreds of families and several entire villages; the area's development created a wave of immigration and subsequently an anti-immigrant backlash; the discharge of chemicals, plus periodic gas leaks, caused health problems among locals; and the influx of revenues, and the large police and military presence, led to exceptionally high levels of corruption. But the most important source of discontent was the belief that the jobs and the revenues from the natural gas plant were not being adequately shared with the people of Aceh. The separatist movement, popularly known as GAM (Gerakan Aceh Merdeka), seized on this issue. GAM propaganda suggested that, if independent, the Acehnese would become wealthy like the citizens of Brunei, the tiny oil-rich sultanate on the island of Borneo. Although small at first, GAM eventually won widespread support among the population, partly due to the brutality and ineptitude of the government's anti-insurgency campaign.

These essential features—an ethnically distinct population that bears too many of the costs of resource extraction and enjoys too few of the benefits—are repeated in most of the other cases and set the preconditions for a long and bitter civil war.

What Can Be Done?

Resource-inspired insurgencies are never inevitable. Often the underlying grievance—that resource revenues are not being shared equally—has merit, and addressing it through negotiations can avert conflict. Better transparency may also help.

Preventive Diplomacy. If a conflict can be anticipated, it can be prevented—at least part of the time—with preventive diplomacy. We know enough about resource-inspired secessionist movements to forecast where they are likely to occur. We also know that once they begin they are exceptionally difficult to stop.[12] Preventive diplomacy could make a real difference.

The civil war in Sudan, for example, might have been averted through wise diplomacy at a critical moment. The war began in 1983 when Sudanese President Numeiry took a series of measures that upset the delicate balance between the predominantly Muslim north and the heavily Christian and Animist south. Among these measures was his decision to place newly discovered oil in the country's south under the jurisdiction of the north and to build an oil refinery in the north instead of the south. The Sudan People's Liberation Army (SPLA) subsequently complained that the north was stealing the resources of the south, including oil; demanded that work cease on a pipeline to take oil from the south to the refinery in the north; and, in February 1984, attacked an oil exploration base, killing three foreign workers and bringing the project to a halt (Anderson 1999; O'Ballance 2000). Instead of responding to the SPLA's demands, however, the government waged a campaign of astonishing brutality. To date, the conflict has killed an estimated 2 million people.

Private resource firms can also help to prevent conflict in high-risk regions. A good example is the strategy that BP has adopted in the Indonesian province of West Papua, a resource-rich region with a long-running—and highly popular—separatist movement. BP is now in the midst of exploiting a vast natural gas field off the Papuan coast and building a $2 billion onshore facility. This is precisely the kind of project that is likely to produce new grievances and add fuel to the separatist movement. BP has made an admirable effort, however, to anticipate this danger by engaging in widespread community consultations to minimize the costs placed on local peoples, by promoting community-based programs to help distribute the benefits of development in sensible ways, and by not allowing the Indonesian military to station troops at the facility, so as to avoid the provocations and human rights abuses carried out by the military at some of Indonesia's other major extraction sites.

Increase Transparency. Better transparency in resource revenues might also help to avert these conflicts. Citizens typically have little idea how much money resource projects generate; this makes them susceptible to exaggerated claims that their resources are being "stolen" by the central government.

In Aceh, Indonesia, the separatist movement frequently made fanciful claims about the income that was generated by the natural gas facility—for example, that an independent Aceh would have the same per capita income as Brunei.[13] These fabrications were widely believed because the Indonesian government had long concealed and misused resource revenues, making the Acehnese justifiably suspicious of the government's assurances. Greater domestic transparency might have prevented the propaganda of a small separatist group from gaining credibility and, ultimately, from triggering a conflict that is now in its third decade.

Rebel Financing

There are hundreds, perhaps thousands, of rebel organizations around the world at any given time. Yet only a handful grow large enough to challenge the armed forces of a sovereign government. Why are these groups successful, while most other groups fail?

There is good evidence that rebel financing is a large part of the answer. To assemble and sustain a fighting force of hundreds or thousands of soldiers, a rebel group needs a regular source of income.[14] Before the end of the cold war, successful rebel groups in the developing world typically were financed by one of the great powers. Since the cold war ended, insurgent groups have been forced to find other ways to bankroll themselves; many have turned to the natural resource sector (Keen 1998).

In Angola, for example, UNITA (National Union for the Total Independence of Angola) was backed by South Africa and the United States for most of the 1970s and 1980s. But the end of the cold war, and the end of apartheid in South Africa, left UNITA with no outside sponsors. As a consequence, it began to rely much more heavily on diamond revenue to support itself (Le Billon 2001). Similarly, in Cambodia the Khmer Rouge had long been financed by the Chinese government. But at the end of the 1980s the Chinese government curtailed its support, which led the Khmer Rouge to adopt a strategy of selling timber and gemstones to gain funding (Le Billon 2000; Thayer 1991).

Why natural resources? There are probably two reasons: the extraction of natural resources can produce unusually large profits (that is, rents), and their production is tied to a specific location and cannot be easily moved. These characteristics make natural resource firms—particularly mineral firms—unusually susceptible to looting, or extortion, on a sustained basis. If rebels instead try to loot or extort money from manufacturing firms, the firms either move to a safer area or are forced out of business. But mining firms cannot move, and they often earn enough money to pay off rebel groups and still earn a profit. These characteristics—plus the location of most resource industries in rural areas, remote from government centers—make resources an ideal source of income for rebel groups.

Rebels raise money from resources in three main ways: through the direct looting and sale of resources, through the sale of resource futures, and through extortion and kidnapping.

Direct Resource Looting

Many rebel groups have financed themselves by selling natural resources. In general, these are resources that can be easily exploited by small numbers of workers with little training and little or no investment, such as coltan, gemstones, or timber. Since the late 1980s, there have been seven prominent examples:

• Angola's UNITA over the course of the 1990s sold hundreds of millions—perhaps even several billion—dollars worth of diamonds (Le Billon 1999).

• Afghanistan's Northern Alliance in the 1990s financed itself through the sale of $40 million to $60 million of lapis lazuli annually (Rubin 2000).

• A variety of groups in Myanmar, associated with the Kachin, Shan, and Wa peoples, sustained their armies in the 1970s and 1980s by selling jadeite, opium, rubies, sapphires, and timber (Lintner 1999; Smith 1999).

• Cambodia's Khmer Rouge at its peak in the early 1990s earned between $120 million and $240 million a year from the sale of rubies and timber (Brown and Zasloff 1998; Le Billon 2000).

• A range of armies in the Democratic Republic of Congo—both foreign forces and domestic militias—have systematically looted the country from the beginning of the current conflict, in 1998, to the present; among the looted goods have been coffee, coltan, diamonds, gold, and timber (see UN Panel of Experts 2001).

• In the early 1990s in Liberia, Charles Taylor's National Patriotic Front of Liberia was thought to be earning some $75 million a year from taxing the sale of cannabis, diamonds, iron ore, rubber, and timber (Ellis 1999).

- In Sierra Leone in the mid-to-late 1990s the Revolutionary United Front (RUF) sustained itself largely by producing between $25 million and $125 million in diamonds a year (UN Panel of Experts 2000).

Sale of Future Rights to War Booty

A less common—but possibly more dangerous—type of resource transaction is the sale of future exploitation rights to the spoils of war. The seven examples in the previous subsection cover the sale of resources already captured by the rebels. However, sometimes combatants sell exploitation rights to natural resources that they do not yet control, but that they hope to capture in battle. Since these transactions are for the sale of *future* exploitation rights, they might be called "booty futures." They are similar to other types of commodity futures. But while normal markets for commodity futures—like the Chicago Board of Trade—are formal, regulated, centralized at a single location, and have many buyers and sellers, the wartime market for booty futures is informal and often covert, has no fixed location, and includes a relatively small number of actors. It operates only in Africa, at least so far.

The booty futures market can help to solve the financing problems that prospective rebel movements often face, provided they wish to do battle in a resource-rich country. If an aspiring rebel group has no money, but stands a chance of capturing valuable resources in combat, it can sell off the future right to exploit the resources it hopes to capture, either to a foreign firm or to a neighboring government. The rebels can then use this money to pay soldiers and buy arms and thus gain the capacity to capture the promised resource.[15]

The market for booty futures is in some ways more dangerous than the standard market for conflict diamonds and other wartime commodities, since the booty futures market tends to benefit the weakest combatants. When combatants in a civil war sell natural resources that are under their control, this indicates that they are in a relatively strong military position, since they control a valuable piece of territory. But if they must sell resource futures, this implies that they are in a weak position, since they have not yet captured the resource whose value they hope to exploit.

The sale of booty futures is a tool of the weak against the strong: it helps to fund groups that are too poor or too feeble to capture territory on their own and might otherwise be forced to surrender. It hence tends to fund the initiation of civil wars that might otherwise never begin or to lengthen wars that are on the verge of ending. The sale of booty futures is also dangerous because it has self-fulfilling properties. If the rebel group is unable to sell the future right to exploit the resource, it might not have the funds it needs to capture the resource itself. Selling the future right to the resource makes its seizure possible. Without the futures market, the rebel offensive—and perhaps the conflict itself—would be less likely.

Not only can the trade in booty futures help to initiate conflicts, it also can lengthen preexisting conflicts. If either side in a civil war is near defeat, and is fighting for control of resource-rich territory, it can try to sell off the future right to exploit the resources it hopes to capture or retain on the battlefield. Again, the sale of booty futures can have self-fulfilling properties: the sale of future rights enables the army to capture or hold the resource itself. Instead of being defeated or forced to the negotiating table, the army is able to continue fighting—thus lengthening the war.[16]

In the 1997 civil war in Congo-Brazzaville, the private militia of former president Denis Sassou-Nguesso was funded, in part, by the sale of future exploitation rights to the Congo's extensive oil reserves. On the eve of the conflict, Sassou received substantial assistance from a European oil company. Some reports suggest that he received $150 million in cash; others state that the company helped him to purchase arms (see "Angola Aids Congo" 1997; Galloy and Gruénai 1997). These funds enabled him to defeat the incumbent president, Pascal Lissouba, following a four-month war that destroyed much of Brazzaville and cost 10,000 lives. These booty future swaps—and similar trades in Angola, the Democratic Republic of Congo, Liberia, and Sierra Leone—in each case have helped to initiate a war or prolong one that appeared to be ending (see Ross 2002a).

Extortion and Kidnapping

Under certain circumstances, rebels can earn large sums by extorting money from, and kidnapping the workers of, resource firms. Although extortion and kidnapping are endemic in conflict zones, a major resource industry can make these activities more profitable.[17] Extortion and kidnapping have been important features of the Colombian civil war, and they also played smaller roles in the wars in Aceh, Indonesia, and in Sudan. In Colombia and Sudan, the targeted resource was oil—or, rather, a long oil pipeline that ran through contested territory. In Aceh, it was a natural gas facility. In Colombia, oil must be transported to the coast from the unstable interior through pipelines that are hundreds of miles long. In 2000 the pipelines were bombed 98 times. Colombia's rebel groups have used these attacks to extort an estimated $140 million annually; this windfall has enabled one group, the National Liberation Army (ELN), to grow from fewer than 40 members to at least 3,000 (Dunning and Wirpsa 2002). Colombia's rebel groups have also turned kidnapping into a major industry. According to a government study, between 1991 and 1999 they earned a remarkable $1.5 billion from kidnap ransoms; many victims were associated with the oil industry (Pax Christi Netherlands 2001).

What Can Be Done?

Three initiatives could help to curtail the use of resources to finance rebel armies: a regime to control the flow of conflict commodities, a ban on resource futures, and restrictions on ransom payments.

Control Illicit Resource Flows.   A major effort to restrict the trade in "conflict diamonds" was launched in May 2000, at a conference in Kimberley, South Africa. The Kimberley Certification Process Scheme entails an agreement by the diamond industry to trade only diamonds that can be certified as originating from legitimate sources.[18] It is too early to know how well this process will work.

Even if it works as planned, the Kimberley process addresses only one of several conflict commodities. Other types of precious stones—jadeite, lapis lazuli, rubies, and sapphires—have also been used to finance recent conflicts. So have coltan and timber. All of these resources are highly "lootable"—that is, they can be extracted by unskilled workers and have high value-to-weight ratios. A comprehensive regime to ban the trade of all conflict commodities would have to address these goods as well. Although the trade in conflict commodities may never be eliminated, their price can be reduced considerably—thereby reducing the flow of funds to rebel groups.

An alternative strategy would target the financial flows generated by the trade in conflict commodities, instead of the commodities themselves. As Winer and Roule suggest in chapter 5, enforcing restrictions on money transfers in some ways may be easier than enforcing restrictions on the resources themselves.

Ban Booty Futures.   The United Nations Security Council has taken measures against the sale of natural resources by rebel forces in Angola, the Democratic Republic of Congo, Liberia, and Sierra Leone. But the booty futures market creates problems that cannot be solved by ad hoc, country-specific sanctions. Sometimes the sanctions come too late: the sale of booty futures can help to initiate a civil war, while the Security Council typically intervenes only after wars have been going on for months or years. The sanctions may also be directed against the wrong party: they typically apply to rebel groups, not governments— but in Angola, Republic of Congo, the Democratic Republic of Congo, and Sierra Leone, the government at least attempted to tap the booty futures market when rebels were approaching victory. A blanket prohibition on the sale of future rights to war booty—and strict sanctions against any commodity sold through such a contract—would be far more effective.

Restrict Ransom Payments.   Anytime a ransom is paid to a kidnapper, it produces obvious short-term benefits but much larger, hidden, long-term costs. The obvious benefit is the release of the kidnap victim; the hidden cost is the encouragement it gives to all organizations that specialize in kidnapping, now and in the future. Kidnapping is like any other type of business: if it is sufficiently profitable, old kidnapping organizations will expand and new kidnapping organizations will arise. In some countries, such as Colombia and the Philippines, the kidnapping industry has grown to an alarming size. To take away the incentive that groups have to kidnap workers in the resource industry, there should be international restrictions on ransom payments. These should include prohibitions on the sale of insurance against kidnapping, which tends to make ransom payments swifter and easier and may reduce the incentives for potential victims to take precautions.

Conclusion

This chapter reviews what scholars have learned about the role that resources play in conflict. It suggests that resource dependence can promote civil war through four types of effects: by harming a country's economic performance; by making its government weaker, more corrupt, and less accountable; by giving people who live in resource-rich regions an incentive to form an independent state; and by helping to finance rebel movements.

It also discusses a series of measures that could help to stop these patterns—measures that include removing OECD trade restrictions, reducing the volatility of resource revenues, increasing the transparency of resource payments to governments, undertaking preventive diplomacy, restricting the trade of conflict commodities, banning the sale of future rights to war booty, and restricting the payment of ransom to kidnappers. These measures are discussed in a preliminary manner to stimulate further debate and study.

Many of the countries suffering from resource-based conflicts are stuck in low-level development traps. In these countries—most of them in Africa—poverty, weak and corrupt government, and violent conflict reinforce one another. Left to their own devices, these countries will generate extraordinary hardships for their own citizens and, ultimately, for the international community. Strong measures, like the ones discussed here, can help them to break out of this trap.

Many of the policies discussed here can work only if they are enacted at a global level. Issues such as trade barriers, transparency, and the monitoring of conflict commodities can be addressed only through comprehensive, multilateral agreements. In some cases, partial or voluntary measures may do no good at all or even make things worse. For example, if some oil companies publish what they pay and others do not, we may find the most transparent and responsible companies driven out of corrupt, high-risk environments and less responsible firms moving in. If some firms try to behave ethically by refusing to pay kidnap ransoms, while others continue to pay them, employees of the ethical firms will be penalized, and the net effect on the kidnapping rate will probably be negligible. In both examples, ethical behavior is penalized and the underlying problems remain unsolved.

As difficult as stopping civil wars may be, it has grown easier in the last 10 years. The funding that natural resources provide to governments and rebels locked in combat can be stopped; the funding that the great powers once provided to combatants could not. A decade ago, before there was much of an Internet, financial transparency was a weak tool; now it is a strong one. The international policy community has a unique opportunity—and hence, a unique responsibility—to take action.

Notes

1. Important studies that touch on the role of natural resources in civil wars include Buhaug and Gates (2002); Collier and Hoeffler (1998, 2001); De Soysa (2002); Doyle and Sambanis (2000); Elbadawi and Sambanis (2002); Fearon (2002); Fearon and Laitin (2002); Hegre (2002); Keen (1998); Reynal-Querol (2002); Ross (2002a, 2002b).

2. See Gylfason (2001); Leite and Weidemann (1999); Manzano and Rigobon (2001); Sachs and Warner (2001). Ross (1999) offers a review of this literature.

3. This study looks only at nonfuel minerals—that is, not oil or natural gas.

4. Minerals and oil dependence was measured as the ratio of exports to GDP.

5. Resource dependence may also produce "Dutch disease" effects, but it is not evident that these make states more susceptible to civil war.

6. The nationalization of foreign oil and minerals firms in the 1950s, 1960s, and 1970s has also made states more vulnerable to economic shocks. Before nationalization, foreign corporations often captured and repatriated a large

fraction of any resource rents, including those created by resource shocks. This drain of wealth was much resented by developing-state governments. Yet, ironically, the repatriation of resource windfalls provided these governments with the unintended benefit of insulating state institutions from the volatility of international commodity markets. By expropriating foreign corporations— at a time when resource prices were growing even more variable—resource-exporting governments unwittingly exposed themselves to large market shocks.

7. Gelb and Associates (1988), for example, find that the oil booms of the 1970s generally were associated with a sharp drop in the efficiency of public investments, which indicates that corruption levels were rising. Similarly, Collier and Gunning (1999) find that commodity booms in developing states, for a wide range of products, were associated with a subsequent fall in investment efficiency. Ross's (2001c) study of the Indonesian, Malaysian, and Philippine timber sectors reports that rising timber prices led to heightened levels of corruption and the dismantling of institutions that had earlier protected the forest sector from misuse. Marshall (2001) reports evidence of unusually high rates of corruption in the minerals sector of many countries. Several statistical studies find the same pattern. Sachs and Warner (1999) find a strong correlation between resource dependence and a widely used measure of corruption; Gylfason (2001) and Leite and Weidmann (1999) produce similar results.

8. See Hegre (2002) for a careful discussion of this issue.

9. Important analyses of this problem include Collier and Hoeffler (2002); Fearon (2002); Le Billon (2001).

10. Since any region might be perceived as having some type of resource, I have limited this list to regions with significant oil or mineral industries in operation, or under development, at or near the time when the civil war began. Examples can also be found in wealthy states: Collier and Hoeffler (2002) describe the case of Scotland, where a peaceful independence movement emerged in the early 1970s following a sharp rise in the value of North Sea oil.

11. This account is based on Ross (2002d).

12. According to Fearon (2002), separatist insurgencies over natural resources tend to last longer than any other type of civil war.

13. This claim was exaggerated by more than an order of magnitude, even under the most generous assumptions; see Ross (2002d).

14. This argument is developed by Collier and Hoeffler (2001).

15. On the growing importance of private military firms, see Singer (2001).

16. The sale of booty futures is not an entirely new phenomenon. In 1960 the Katanga rebellion in the Democratic Republic of Congo, led by Moïse Tshombe, was bankrolled by a European mining firm; in exchange, the firm apparently sought future mineral rights. See Gibbs (1991). During Algeria's war of independence, a European oil company reportedly supplied money

and arms to the National Liberation Front (FLN) in exchange for future "considerations." See Le Billon (2002).

    17. Kidnappings are often carried out by other types of criminal organizations as well, including paramilitary groups and rogue police units.

    18. For an excellent account of the Kimberley process, see chapter 6.

References

The word "processed" describes informally produced works that may not be commonly available through libraries.

Anderson, G. Norman. 1999. *Sudan in Crisis*. Gainesville: University Press of Florida.

"Angola Aids Congo to Corral UNITA." 1997. *Johannesburg Mail and Guardian*, October 17.

Ascher, William. 1999. *Why Governments Waste Natural Resources: Policy Failures in Developing Countries*. Baltimore, Md.: Johns Hopkins University Press.

Beblawi, Hazem. 1987. "The Rentier State in the Arab World." In Hazem Beblawi and Giacomo Luciani, eds., *The Rentier State*, pp. 49–62. New York: Croom Helm.

Brown, MacAlister, and Joseph J. Zasloff. 1998. *Cambodia Confounds the Peacemakers*. Ithaca: Cornell University Press.

Buhaug, Halvard, and Scott Gates. 2002. "The Geography of Civil War." *Journal of Peace Research* 39(4):417–33.

Cauvin, Henri E. 2002. "IMF Skewers Corruption in Angola." *New York Times,* November 30, p. A6.

Collier, Paul, and Jan Willem Gunning, eds. 1999. *Trade Shocks in Developing Countries*. New York, N.Y.: Oxford University Press.

Collier, Paul, and Anke Hoeffler. 1998. "On Economic Causes of Civil War." *Oxford Economic Papers* 50:563–73.

————. 2001. "Greed and Grievance in Civil War." World Bank, Washington, D.C. October 21. Processed.

————. 2002. "The Political Economy of Secession." World Bank, Development Research Group, Washington, D.C.; University of Oxford, Centre for the Study of African Economies, June 30. Available at www.ifc.org/ogmc/pdfs/Paul-Collier.pdf. Processed.

Davis, Jeffrey, Rolando Ossowski, James Daniel, and Steven Barnett. 2001. *Stabilization and Savings Funds for Nonrenewable Resources: Experience and Policy Implications*. Occasional Paper 205. Washington, D.C.: International Monetary Fund.

De Soysa, Indra. 2002. "Paradise Is a Bazaar? Greed, Creed, and Governance in Civil War, 1989–99." *Journal of Peace Research* 39(4):395–416.

Doyle, Michael, and Nicholas Sambanis. 2000. "International Peacebuilding: A Theoretical and Quantitative Analysis." *American Political Science Review* 94(4):779–801.

Dunning, Thad, and Leslie Wirpsa. 2002. "Andean Gulf? Oil and the Political Economy of Conflict in Colombia and Beyond." University of Southern California, Los Angeles, California, May 31. Processed.

Elbadawi, Ibrahim, and Nicholas Sambanis. 2002. "How Much War Will We See? Estimating the Prevalence of Civil War in 161 Countries, 1960–1999." *Journal of Conflict Resolution* 46(3):307–34.

Ellis, Stephen. 1999. *The Mask of Anarchy: The Destruction of Liberia and the Religious Dimension of an African Civil War.* New York: New York University Press.

Fearon, James D. 2002. "Why Do Some Civil Wars Last So Much Longer Than Others?" Stanford University, Department of Political Science, Palo Alto, Calif., July 12. Available at www.stanford.edu/group/ethnic/workingpapers/dur3.pdf. Processed.

Fearon, James D., and David D. Laitin. 2002. "Ethnicity, Insurgency, and Civil War." Stanford University, Department of Political Science, Palo Alto, Calif., May 7. Processed.

Galloy, Martine-Renee, and Marc-Eric Gruénai. 1997. "Fighting for Power in the Congo." *Le Monde Diplomatique* (November). Available at mondediplo.com/1997/11/africa2.

Gelb, Alan, and Associates. 1988. *Oil Windfalls: Blessing or Curse?* New York: Oxford University Press.

Gibbs, David N. 1991. *The Political Economy of Third World Intervention: Mines, Money, and U.S. Policy in the Congo Crisis.* Chicago: University of Chicago Press.

Gleditsch, Nils Petter, Håvard Strand, Mikael Eriksson, Margareta Sollenberg, and Peter Wallensteen. 2001. "Armed Conflict 1946–99: A New Dataset." Paper presented at the World Bank–University of California, Irvine conference on civil wars and post-conflict transition, University of California, Irvine, May 18. Processed.

Global Witness. 2002. *All the Presidents Men.* London. Available at www.globalwitness.org.

Grilli, Enzo R., and Maw Cheng Yang. 1988. "Primary Commodity Prices, Manufactured Goods Prices, and the Terms of Trade of Developing Countries: What the Long Run Shows." *The World Bank Economic Review* 2(1):1–47.

Gylfason, Thorvaldur. 2001. "Natural Resources, Education, and Economic Development." *European Economic Review* 45:846–59.

Hegre, Håvard. 2002. "Some Social Requisites of a Democratic Civil Peace: Democracy, Development, and Armed Conflict." Paper presented to the American Political Science Association 2002 Annual Meeting, Boston, Mass., August 29–September 1. Available at www.cidcm.umd.edu/dcawcp/dcwcp1.pdf. Processed.

Karl, Terry Lynn. 1997. *The Paradox of Plenty: Oil Booms and Petro-States.* Berkeley: University of California Press.

Keen, David. 1998. *The Economic Functions of Violence in Civil Wars.* Adelphi Paper 320. London: International Institute of Strategic Studies.

Le Billon, Philippe. 1999. "A Land Cursed by Its Wealth? Angola's War Economy (1975–1999)." UNU/WIDER Work in Progress 23. United Nations University, World Institute for Development Economics, Helsinki. Processed.

———. 2000. "The Political Ecology of Transition in Cambodia 1989–1999: War, Peace, and Forest Exploitation." *Development and Change* 31(4): 785–805.

———. 2001. "The Political Ecology of War: Natural Resources and Armed Conflicts." *Political Geography* 20(June):561–84.

———. 2002. "Fueling War: Natural Resources and Armed Conflict." International Institute of Strategic Studies, London, May 28. Processed.

Leite, Carlos, and Jens Weidmann. 1999. "Does Mother Nature Corrupt? Natural Resources, Corruption, and Economic Growth." IMF Working Paper WP/99/85. International Monetary Fund, Washington, D.C. Processed.

Lintner, Bertil. 1999. *Burma in Revolt: Opium and Insurgency since 1948,* 2d ed. Chiang Mai, Thailand: Silkworm Books.

Mahdavy, Hussein. 1970. "The Patterns and Problems of Economic Development in Rentier States: The Case of Iran." In M. A. Cook, ed., *Studies in Economic History of the Middle East,* pp. 428–67. London: Oxford University Press.

Manzano, Osmel, and Roberto Rigobon. 2001. "Resource Curse or Debt Overhang?" NBER Working Paper 8390. National Bureau of Economic Research, Cambridge, Mass. Processed.

Marshall, Ian E. 2001. *A Survey of Corruption Issues in the Mining and Mineral Sector.* Report 15. London: International Institute for Environment and Development, Minerals, Mining, and Sustainable Development Project.

O'Ballance, Edgar. 2000. *Sudan, Civil War, and Terrorism 1956–1999.* New York: St. Martin's Press.

Pax Christi Netherlands. 2001. *The Kidnap Industry in Colombia: Our Business?* Utrecht. Available at www.paxchristi.nl/kidnappingincolombia.pdf.

Reinhart, Carmen, and Peter Wickham. 1994. "Commodity Prices: Cyclical Weakness or Secular Decline?" *IMF Staff Papers* 41(2, June):175–213.

Reno, William. 1995. *Corruption and State Politics in Sierra Leone.* New York: Cambridge University Press.

———. 1998. *Warlord Politics and African States.* Boulder, Colo.: Lynne Rienner.

Reynal-Querol, Marta. 2002. "Ethnicity, Political Systems, and Civil Wars." *Journal of Conflict Resolution* 46(1):29–54.

Ross, Michael L. 1999. "The Political Economy of the Resource Curse." *World Politics* 51(2, January):297–322.

———. 2001a. "Does Oil Hinder Democracy?" *World Politics* 53(3, April): 325–61.

———. 2001b. *Extractive Sectors and the Poor.* Washington, D.C.: Oxfam America. Available at www.oxfamamerica.org.

———. 2001c. *Timber Booms and Institutional Breakdown in Southeast Asia.* New York, N.Y.: Cambridge University Press.

———. 2002a. "Booty Futures: Africa's Civil Wars and the Futures Market for Natural Resources." University of California, Los Angeles, Department of Political Science, July 24. Processed.

———. 2002b. "Comments on *Treasure or Trouble: Mining in Developing Countries.*" University of California, Los Angeles, Department of Political Science, Processed.

———. 2002c. "How Does Natural Resource Wealth Influence Civil War?" University of California, Los Angeles, Department of Political Science, July 24. Processed.

———. 2002d. "Resources and Rebellion in Indonesia." University of California, Los Angeles, Department of Political Science. Processed.

Rubin, Barnett R. 2000. "The Political Economy of War and Peace in Afghanistan." *World Development* 28(October):1789–803.

Sachs, Jeffrey D., and Andrew M. Warner. 1999. "Natural Resource Intensity and Economic Growth." In Jörg Mayer, Brian Chambers, and Ayisha Farooq, eds., *Development Policies in Natural Resource Economies,* pp. 13–38. Cheltenham, U.K.: Edward Elgar.

———. 2001. "The Curse of Natural Resources." *European Economic Review* 45(May):827–38.

Singer, P. W. 2001. "Corporate Warriors: The Rise of the Privatized Military Industry and Its Ramifications for International Security." *International Security* 26(3, Winter):186–220.

Smith, Martin. 1999. *Burma: Insurgency and the Politics of Ethnicity,* 2d ed. New York: St. Martin's Press.

Thayer, Nate. 1991. "Rubies Are Rouge." *Far Eastern Economic Review,* February 7, pp. 29–30.

UN Panel of Experts. 2000. *Report of the Panel of Experts Appointed Pursuant to Security Council Resolution 1306 (2000), Paragraph 19, in*

Relation to Sierra Leone. S/2000/1195. New York: United Nations Security Council, December 20.

———. 2001. *Report of the Panel of Experts on the Illegal Exploitation of Natural Resources and Other Forms of Wealth of the Democratic Republic of Congo.* S/2001/357. New York: United Nations Security Council, April 12.

Wallensteen, Peter, and Margareta Sollenberg. 2000. "Armed Conflict, 1989–99." *Journal of Peace Research* 37(5):635–49.

World Bank. 2001. "World Development Indicators 2001." CD-ROM. Washington D.C.: World Bank Group.

———. 2002. *Treasure or Trouble? Mining in Developing Countries.* Washington, D.C.: World Bank Group.

CHAPTER 3

Who Gets the Money?
Reporting Resource Revenues

Philip Swanson, Mai Oldgard, and Leiv Lunde

THIS CHAPTER LOOKS AT THE REPORTING of resource revenues that host governments receive. Reporting as used here includes formal reporting of revenues to a particular body, audits and reconciliation procedures, as well as requirements to make information on such revenues publicly available (although information reported to a government body or other party is not always made public). Almost by definition, reporting concerns commodities that are legally traded. Here we focus on the oil and minerals sectors, while diamonds, timber, and several other commodities are covered to a lesser extent.

Reporting is a means to achieve transparency, which itself is a precondition for curbing corruption, mismanagement, and diversion of funds. The assumption is that strong reporting practices should increase transparency and oversight of financial flows, which in turn should reduce the possibilities and temptations for misappropriation. It is also assumed that strong reporting practices and transparency could provide host-country publics with an important part of the information they need to monitor the way their government uses the revenues it accrues. However, public knowledge of the full amount of revenue available to the government (or its elites) will not, on its own, pressure a government to make better spending choices; information on spending and probably a minimum of organized political opposition must also be available for this to happen. Nevertheless, public knowledge of potential income should make it more difficult for elites to divert large amounts of such revenue from the central budget, meaning that, in theory, more could be available across-the-board for public programs such as health and education.

A major problem is that host governments often have incentives not to reveal the extent of their resource revenues. Moreover, the leverage of the international community in this regard is probably limited. This is because large resource revenues usually give host governments the ability to reject assistance attached to conditions they do not like. If the host government is not providing information about the resource-related revenues available to it, an important indirect way of viewing these flows is to look at the payments that resource extraction companies make to the government. For this reason, nongovernmental organizations and others focus primarily on company reporting.

The first section explores what is known about the reporting systems of governments in developing countries. The second section briefly covers what is known about how oil companies report the payments they make to host governments. It draws primarily on work by Global Witness and the Publish What You Pay campaign. The third section reviews several additional issues related to host-government reporting: in particular, whether states tend to report resource revenues more accurately when they are treated as general revenues or when they are placed in a separate fund; whether some particular government functions are associated with poor reporting (with a focus on the role of resource parastatals); whether the quality of revenue reporting is influenced by revenue volatility; whether the quality of reporting varies by type of resource; and the effect of having a country's military forces directly accrue resource revenues. The fourth section looks at recent international initiatives that could be relevant for increasing the transparency of resource revenue flows. The initiatives covered are divided between those relevant primarily for host-government reporting and those relevant primarily for company reporting, although there could be overlap in some cases. The last section offers policy recommendations for global action.

Reporting Resource Revenues

This section examines what is known about how the flows of natural resource revenues are reported. It focuses on reporting by host governments. However, it also looks at reporting by extraction companies as an indirect way of estimating revenues received by host governments.

Reporting by Host Governments

Host countries receive revenue from resource extraction and exports in a number of ways. The most important of these usually are payments by private extraction companies, including taxes, royalties, and one-off or periodic payments, such as licensing or concession fees, signature bonuses, and other bonuses related to a particular stage in a project. The following are examples of payments that international companies make to host governments in the oil and gas sectors:

• Payments to central and federal governments, such as ministries of finance, the revenue authority, and the central bank, including taxes, royalties, dividends, signature bonuses, and profit share
• Payments to regional and local governments, including development funds and regional taxes
• Payments to other government agencies, including customs duties, fines (for example, to environmental agencies for spills and emissions), costs for studies (payable to government institutes or laboratories), and port fees
• Payments to state companies, including tariffs to pipeline monopolies; payments to utilities, railway, and air transport state monopolies; and drilling contracts
• Payments in kind (barrels of oil equivalent) for royalty, profit, and equity share
• Payments for the acquisition of shares in state companies, for example, through government privatization, including the purchase of bonds issued by state companies
• Payments related to joint ventures with state oil companies, including profit and dividend payments to the state company (including money remitted from ventures executed in other countries) and contributions for capital expenditures.

Other revenue flows can be provided via state-owned resource extraction companies, which may be partners in joint ventures with foreign firms, especially in the oil and mining sectors. Joint venture projects can imply income for the government that is not derived from payments by private or foreign companies.

Reporting Procedures in OECD Countries. Revenue reporting procedures are generally well documented and transparent in countries of the Organisation for Economic Co-operation and Development (OECD). For example, a recent, publicly available review by the United Kingdom's National Audit Office notes, "There are clear reporting lines through which the U.K. Oil Taxation Office provides Inland Revenue senior management with regular accounts of progress against targets"

(U.K. National Audit Office 2000, p. 4). In turn, Inland Revenue has procedures by which it must report to Parliament and publish information related to all revenue collected. Safeguards within the Inland Revenue system include separation of assessment and collection responsibilities between different offices within the tax authority. Such an arrangement "minimizes the risk of collusion between the taxpayer and the Inland Revenue and the risk of misappropriation of tax receipts by those responsible for making assessments" (U.K. National Audit Office 2000, p. 17). U.S. and Norwegian procedures are similarly well documented and transparent.

The OECD notes that, in its member countries, "the fiscal practices that promote integrity and accountability have been the subject of considerable discussion in recent years and there has been much progress in defining appropriate practices." Examples include the OECD's Best Practices for Budget Transparency and the IMF's (International Monetary Fund's) Code of Good Practice on Fiscal Transparency. However, the OECD notes, "In troubled countries, fiscal frameworks may not incorporate even the most rudimentary principles for effective public management for both revenues and expenditures" (OECD 2002b, p. 15).

Reporting Procedures in Developing Countries. In general, little public information is available about the way in which developing-country host governments report revenue from their extraction and export of resources. Furthermore, the collection and reporting of resource revenue in such countries are poorly covered in the academic literature. Based on what has been written, however, reporting procedures, where they exist, often are rudimentary, perhaps deliberately so. In some cases, this may be due to lack of knowledge about best practice, but in others it may be part of a general tactic to avoid accountability. The observations of Ascher (1999) for the logging sector also probably apply to revenue reporting in most high-rent natural resource sectors in developing countries: "Apparently weak enforcement 'capacity' is as much a choice as a 'given,' and lack of enforcement capacity is often part of the strategy of resource maneuvers." Moreover, governments have reduced the public awareness of such maneuvers "by suppressing information, as in the minimal reporting requirements for timber companies in Indonesia, or by making financial transactions and accounting so opaque that monitoring becomes virtually impossible, as in the case of the Nigerian and Mexican oil companies" (Ascher 1999, p. 259).

Unfortunately, Ascher and other authors we have reviewed do not provide specific examples of these minimal procedures, where they exist. Nor does the literature covering resource exploitation and revenue flows describe the procedures for reporting. Most research in this area focuses on the macroeconomic and corruption effects that large rents can have on the developing-country host government and, related to this, on how revenues are spent. The literature on logging, for example, focuses on the failures of forestry policy that have led to illegal logging or allowed logging concessions to be underpriced. The literature on diamonds focuses on the trade in conflict diamonds, which usually are diamonds that have been mined and traded outside host-government official control.

Other sources of information also have limitations. For example, international oil and mining companies presumably are in a better position than most to know about the internal reporting procedures of host governments. However, discussions with a number of company representatives shed little light on the issue and left us with the impression that companies have little incentive to find out—or admit to knowing about—the internal procedures followed by host governments once companies have made their payments.[1]

Information obtained via cooperation between developing-country host governments and international financial institutions probably has been limited by the fact that large resource revenues usually have given countries the ability to avoid cooperation that could impose difficult conditions, for example, examination of their revenue-reporting procedures.

Public expenditures reviews and other economic and sector work carried out by the World Bank provide overviews of controls in some developing countries. However, such work generally has not been performed in resource-rich countries. According to the IMF and World Bank websites, within the last five years such reviews were rarely conducted for countries that Global Witness lists as having resource-related governance problems. Nevertheless, there are notable exceptions, such as the public expenditures review for Kazakhstan, completed in 2000–01; assistance given to Azerbaijan's Oil Fund; and involvement in creating procedures for reporting oil revenue for Chad as part of the Chad-Cameroon Petroleum Development and Pipeline Project.[2]

A handful of other public and private studies and international development projects have provided glimpses into the reporting structures of a number of other countries, although this has not been an important focus of such studies. Such glimpses reveal procedures that often are rudimentary.

Most of the systems about which we have significant knowledge are those that have been imposed relatively recently by the international community on governments still in the early or expectant stages of resource revenue wealth—that is, on governments not yet in a position to refuse aid conditionality. Such procedures have not yet been adequately tested in practice.

Reporting by Companies

If the host government does not provide information about its resource revenues, an indirect way of viewing these flows is to look at the payments that resource extraction companies make to the government. In theory, disaggregated records of payments by companies to individual governments could be reaggregated to provide an overview of the amount of money being made available. In practice, this is difficult for several reasons.

The existence of collective action problems among companies means that, in practice, host governments can put a great deal of pressure on companies (especially in the oil industry) not to reveal such information, often citing "commercial confidentiality" agreements. In the face of host-government opposition, companies are not inclined to reveal information that may cause them to lose government favor and thus their comparative advantage with respect to rival firms.

In addition, as many international oil companies have pointed out, transparency of payments by international companies would provide only part of the picture. It would not necessarily cover the often-significant revenue flows through government-owned extraction companies. This is especially the case with joint ventures where the government-owned extraction company is not paid directly by the foreign company but receives a share of the resources or revenue of the joint venture. In practice, most companies report only what is required by regulators in their host and home countries.

Confidentiality Provisions in Contracts.   Many companies in the oil sector have signed contracts with developing-country host governments or state oil company partners that have confidentiality clauses. Such clauses often include requirements not to reveal tax and other payments that have been made to the host government.

A survey of four OECD jurisdictions (Alaska, Alberta, Norway, and the United Kingdom) and three non-OECD jurisdictions (Angola, Myanmar, and Nigeria) finds that OECD countries do not prohibit the disclosure of payments to the host government; this occurs only in non-OECD countries. According to OECD (2002b, p. 18), "This suggests that there are ways of protecting the legitimate interests of both business and governments while not compromising revenue transparency and accountability."

Global Witness has urged companies to form a common approach to ensure that confidentiality clauses address legitimate commercial concerns only and do not cover basic payments to the state. The elimination of nondisclosure clauses would make it more difficult for companies to justify not publishing the amounts they pay to host governments. However, it may not be enough to counter the apparently strong incentives some host governments have for keeping payments secret and for putting pressure on companies to do so. BP reportedly came under very strong pressure from the Angolan government even though the information on payments it released in early 2001 apparently did not fall under its confidentiality clauses.[3]

Confidentiality clauses also exist in the mining sector, although this industry appears to be making relatively more progress than the oil sector in dealing with the issue. For example, mining groups under the Mining, Minerals, and Sustainable Development (MMSD) Project have worked with Transparency International to increase the transparency of agreements between mining companies and governments, and MMSD has discussed creating an international database of members' payments (MMSD 2001).[4]

Reporting to Host Governments.   Companies in most extractive industries usually are required to report some information to the host government in order to allow it to calculate taxes due. Although the information required varies by industry and country, it generally includes information on production, sales, costs, and profits. However, host governments in developing countries rarely make such information publicly available.

There are a number of commercially available sources of information on fiscal arrangements in the oil, gas, and mining sectors of various countries, including developing countries, where much of the world's resource extraction activity takes place.[5] Such sources often specify the basis on which tax and other payments are calculated, but not the reports that must be filed. Moreover, they rarely provide information on the negotiated terms of a particular production-sharing agreement. Nevertheless, information on supposedly secret contracts often can be obtained through private consultancies.

Government websites in OECD countries, such as the website of the U.S. Mineral Revenue Management Service, often list reporting requirements for companies, including downloadable versions of forms that must be filed.[6] Examples of this practice are rare in developing countries.

Some countries (mostly in the OECD) require companies to file financial information on a regular basis with an official government information register, for example, the Registrar of Companies in the United Kingdom or the Brønnøysund Register Centre in Norway. Such information is used by government bodies and is often accessible by the public.

The Registrar of Companies website contains links to more than 50 similar registers worldwide.[7] Although most are in OECD countries, several are in developing countries, including a few countries identified as having difficulty tracking resource revenues. Moreover, although reporting requirements for many OECD countries include company annual returns and tax payments, public reporting procedures in most non-OECD registers are limited to company contact details and other basic, nonfinancial information.

Reporting to Home Governments. In its report *All the Presidents' Men,* Global Witness provides a brief overview of reporting requirements in the United Kingdom and United States for the overseas operations of companies registered in those countries (Global Witness 2002). The United Kingdom only requires each company to provide the total amount of "overseas taxation" paid, which is not broken down by country. In cases where the company has set up subsidiary oil companies for operations in a particular country, payments to that country can be calculated as long as all subsidiaries for the particular country are accounted for. However, not all companies operating in the same country will necessarily operate via separately listed subsidiaries. In Norway requirements are similar to those in the United Kingdom. In the United States, the Securities and Exchange Commission requires its listed companies to keep track of payments by foreign companies for its internal records and for inspection by U.S. regulators but does not require such records to be published or otherwise made publicly available.

The main initiative in the area of company reporting of revenue payments is the Publish What You Pay campaign, which is spearheaded by the nongovernmental organization Global Witness and by George Soros. In recognition of the collective action problems faced by the oil companies, the Publish What You Pay campaign is calling on home-country governments to require "their" companies to reveal payments. The suggested mechanism is for developed-country governments to require their stock exchanges to demand regular issuance of such information as a condition for listing.

According to Global Witness, the Publish What You Pay campaign has focused on the vehicle of stock market listings because many confidentiality agreements reportedly have an opt-out clause if information is required by regulators. For example, according to Publish What

You Pay, Article 33(2) of the Standard Deep Water Production-Sharing Agreement in Angola states, "Either party may, without such approval, disclose such information to the extent required by any applicable law, regulation, or rule (including, without limitation, any regulation or rule of any regulatory agency, securities commission, or securities exchange on which the securities of such Party or any of such Party's affiliates are listed)."[8]

As long as all major stock exchanges were involved, it would be difficult for companies to change jurisdictions; otherwise, there would be a risk of transferring the collective action problem from companies to stock markets. However, switching stock exchanges to avoid reporting conceivably could reflect badly on companies worried about their image of corporate social responsibility.

The main criticism of the stock market tactic is that it may not affect the handful of relatively technically advanced state-owned companies operating internationally but headquartered in developing countries. At a minimum, however, it could hinder their ability to raise capital in important Western markets. Global Witness argues that the problem of firms without public listings is likely to be minor and could be addressed as it arises.

The Publish What You Pay campaign appears to be gaining momentum. Although not everyone has endorsed the stock market regulation approach, support is at least growing for the general idea of more transparent company reporting, and such momentum could stimulate other creative tactical options.

Additional Issues Related to Government Reporting

This section examines a number of potentially important issues and their possible impact on the quality of government reporting of natural resource revenue flows, including general revenues versus off-budget funds; particular government functions, including the impact of resource parastatals; revenue volatility; and variation in reporting quality by resource type.

General Funds Versus Off-Budget Accounts

Off-budget accounting is fairly common in developing countries, but "what distinguishes economies with high resource endowments from those not having such wealth is the large volume of fiscal flows that are sent through these channels" (OECD 2002b, p. 18). Logically, controls on off-budget accounts are likely to be weaker than controls on central budgets simply because it is easier to keep track of one account than many. Moreover, as case studies in the forestry sector indicate, resource revenue "maneuvers" often are carried out off-budget precisely to decrease the chance of detection (Ascher 1999).

Available evidence also indicates that off-budget flows lack transparency. For example, several African case studies performed by the International Budget Project conclude that off-budget revenue flows in Nigeria are significant but that, due to inadequate accountability for such funds, no systematic information is available on their magnitude or on their intended or actual use.[9] Moreover, many off-budget funds cannot be audited because they fall outside the mandate of the Auditor General. According to Fölscher (2001), no known rules govern deposits into and withdrawals from various accounts and funds. Similarly, more than two-thirds of expenditures in Angola take place outside the formal budgetary system, making their composition difficult to determine (IMF 1997).

At the same time, the regular budgets in many resource-rich developing countries also lack transparency. For example, the International Budget Project report finds no law specifying the format of Nigeria's central budget, the documents that need to accompany the budget, or how and when budget information is to be disseminated. Moreover, the legal framework does not provide for public participation in the budget process and does not support transparency and accountability (Fölscher 2001).

Ascher, who compiled a number of case studies on natural resource policy failures covering a wide variety of resources and countries, concludes that revenue flows through the central budget are likely to be more transparent than off-budget flows. He points out that, while we have "no way of knowing, a priori, whether the scoundrels who wish to manipulate off-budget slush funds are better or worse than the scoundrels who wish to manipulate the central budget for objectionable ends . . . the latter type of scoundrel is more likely to be taken to task for his or her sins" (Ascher 1999, p. 255).

Resource revenues can enter off-budget accounts via state-owned extraction companies as well as through private firms. However, foreign resource extraction firms cannot always be sure that the accounts into which they pay their taxes flow to the general budget or remain outside the budget. For example, a mining company in Central Asia, following instructions from the Minister of Finance, reportedly paid funds into a particular bank account only to discover that this was a private account owned by the country's president (MMSD 2001).

Large and nontransparent off-budget flows are tempting targets for embezzlement. Given the high correlation between resource wealth and internal violence (chapter 1), it is not surprising that another major destination of off-budget resource flows is the military. Moreover, off-budget funds may be used to finance developmental or prestige projects of questionable economic or social value that may not be expected to stand up to the relatively greater scrutiny of the central budget process.

Trust Funds. Foreign banks sometimes set up off-budget trust funds to help repay loans using future oil or other commodity revenues as collateral. Reportedly, a significant portion of the money from oil sales by the Angolan state oil company, Sonangol, goes directly into these trusts without passing through the central budget. The banks, understandably, have demanded such arrangements as security for their loans. However, the government provides little public information about the flows through such funds. Since such a large portion of Angola's annual income apparently passes through them, Global Witness has called on banks to publish details so that there can be some outside scrutiny of the amounts involved (Global Witness 2002).

Resource Stabilization and Savings Funds. A number of resource-rich countries have created special funds to receive a portion of natural resource windfalls. Such funds usually are intended to promote macroeconomic stability or to save part of the windfall for the future. Most funds have been set up for oil, but at least one has been related to minerals—Chile's copper fund—and a number of relatively minor funds have been related to agriculture, such as Colombia's coffee fund.

In general, resource funds have received mixed reviews on macroeconomic grounds and in terms of promoting transparency. For example, according to Davis and others (2001a),

> Governance, transparency, and accountability may well be undermined by an oil fund. By their very nature, oil funds are usually outside existing budget systems and are often accountable to only a few political appointees. This makes such funds especially susceptible to abuse and political interference. Reporting and auditing requirements for the funds are often loose, and their lack of integration with the budget makes it more difficult for both Parliament and the public to monitor the use of public resources as a whole.

Many funds claim to take the Norwegian State Petroleum Fund as an example, while ignoring the important fact that the fund functions as a government account under the control of the Ministry of Finance. Davis and others (2001a) attribute the success of the State Petroleum

Fund to Norway's implementation of sound and transparent macro-economic policies.

A study of resource funds in Alaska, Chile, Kuwait, Norway, Oman, and Venezuela agrees that a resource fund "cannot be a substitute for sound fiscal management and that its success or failure can be attributed as much to fiscal discipline as to the fund's management" (Fasano 2000, p. 19). Stabilization funds have been more successful in countries with a strong commitment to fiscal discipline and sound macroeconomic management. Thus both the studies by Davis and others (2001a) and by Fasano (2000) emphasize the importance of concentrating on fiscal discipline and avoiding the "distraction" of potentially problematic funds.

Caspian Revenue Watch takes a slightly different approach; it assumes that, in some countries at least, it probably will be easier for civil society watchdogs and others to monitor revenue flowing into a specific fund than to monitor revenue going into the general budget.

Government Functions

A number of different actors can be involved in the control and reporting of revenues derived from natural resource extraction. The main ones usually are the Ministry of Finance, the relevant sector ministry, and often a parastatal extraction company. Others include the Office of the President or other powerful politicians or committees that have control over revenue flows.

Typically, the larger the rents involved in the resource, the more the various government actors may try to gain control of their collection and distribution. Rent seeking on the part of individuals or companies wishing to acquire logging concessions, for example, usually leads to what Ross (2001) calls "rent seizing" on the part of officials—that is, attempts to appropriate the right to allocate the economic rents to various private and public interest groups in return for political or other favors. In this way, politicians try to maximize the value of their allocation rights by making them as direct, exclusive, and discretionary as possible. The organization that distributes the extraction rights may not always be the one through which the resulting resource revenues flow.

Available evidence is probably not sufficient to allow generalizations about whether particular state actors are better at reporting resource revenues than others, although reporting is likely to be worse the farther one gets from the Ministry of Finance. Many of Ascher's case studies in minerals, oil, and timber involve efforts by the technocratic experts of the Ministry of Finance to rein in the resource flows of line ministries and parastatals that, in turn, try to obscure such flows for their own organizational or personal ends. Such off-budget organizations often depend on the protection of powerful politicians, who also may benefit from the resource revenues. For example, former Indonesian president Suharto reportedly used off-budget funds generated by the state oil company, Pertamina, and later by the Forestry Ministry's reforestation tax to fund questionable prestige and development projects.[10] The Finance Ministry was able to rein in Pertamina and redirect its revenue flows through the treasury only after 1979, following Pertamina's bankruptcy due to uncontrolled overborrowing on international markets (Ascher 1999).

The use of state enterprises in the extractive sectors appears to pose particular problems for the transparency of natural resource revenues. With respect to the oil sector in OECD countries, state-owned enterprises enlarge the scope for nontransparency of public accounts (OECD 2002b). In non-OECD countries, where overall fiscal controls generally are less transparent, the potential for opacity of revenue transfers is likely to be greater.

A potential problem is that parastatal companies typically are not integrated into the government in the same way as a line ministry and thus are not likely to come under the same general reporting procedures and controls. An additional problem is that extractive parastatals are likely to operate in remote areas, which poses difficulties for auditing and control. Related to this, at least for mining and oil and gas operations, the technical nature of parastatal activities can make it difficult for government auditors to calculate real costs and profits accurately. For example, after the Pinochet government regained control of the copper industry in Chile, it took the government several years to understand the industry and its accounts well enough to reestablish significant revenue flows through the central budget (Ascher 1999). The government eventually put severe limits on the copper company's activities, including its ability to invest, in order to "keep the scope of Codelco operations within the capacity of the government to monitor and control." Noting other examples, such as the oil industries of Mexico, Peru, and Venezuela, Ascher (1999) comments that it is common for state enterprises to be transformed from accomplices in off-budget financing to undercapitalized victims of the efforts of budget authorities to tax and control.

One reason it may be difficult for central budget authorities to keep adequate control over the finances of state-owned oil companies is that the market does not require these companies to provide transparent information. For this reason, state enterprises operate more transparently when they are involved in joint ventures with international companies than when they operate alone, largely because such relationships require more rigorous accounting procedures (Ascher 1999).

Revenue Volatility

Whereas high rents can provide incentives to take a long-term, sustainable approach to natural resource management, rent volatility may create incentives to waste. This is because resource rents can be expected to fall again in the future, and politicians and other parties may wish to take as much advantage as possible from a temporary windfall. Moreover, as Ross (2001) points out, the security in office of politicians overseeing the distribution of resource rents may have an important impact, with less secure officeholders having a greater incentive to divert more revenues to themselves while they remain in power, because they may not be around for the next windfall.

Ross bases his observations on the timber industry, particularly in the Philippines, the Malaysian states of Sabah and Sarawak, and Indonesia. Although volatility of commodity prices and revenue is similar in the mining, oil, and timber sectors, the same forces may not be at work. Given the scale of the initial investments involved, the mining and oil sectors are forced to take a longer-term approach than the timber sector.

Nevertheless, because of the exceedingly high rents involved, oil and mineral commodity booms may create incentives for governments to decrease the transparency of revenue flows. However, it is not clear in the case of minerals and oil that the problem is volatility as much as it is simply high rents. In general, mineral- and oil-dependent countries go through a cycle of increased incentives against transparency in times of commodity boom, followed by a period of efforts to rein in spending and control over revenues when commodity prices fall (Karl 1997). In the case of diamonds, the stabilizing role De Beers traditionally plays as the buyer of last resort may make revenue volatility less of an issue.

Another aspect of this problem relates to the so-called "Dutch disease." A number of countries have set up stabilization funds to deal with the volatile nature of revenue from particular natural resources. However, the use of stabilization funds can add to a country's fiscal management problems if not accompanied by sound fiscal practice.

Variation in Quality of Reporting by Type of Resource

Although there have been studies on the impacts of different commodities on issues such as the incidence of civil war,[11] there does not seem to have been a study yet comparing the quality of reporting in the various resource sectors. Yet the issues surrounding reporting may be somewhat different in different sectors.

In the forestry sector, tax rates often are set too low, not enforced, or not collected due to illegal logging. The diamond sector has experienced similar problems, with small, private sector operators not reporting their revenues. Moreover, in both sectors extraction often takes place in remote regions where government authorities have limited control, further compounding the lack of transparency. In both sectors, leakage of revenues before the money reaches a state agent may be a bigger problem than leakage after it has been collected. Also, because these industries tend to be dominated by the private sector, often by small operators, they tend to be less likely than the oil and gas sectors to face the reporting problems related to state-owned companies.

Because it is more difficult to engage in illegal or unmonitored extraction in the technically more complex metals mining and oil sectors, there is generally less scope for revenue leakage before reaching the state. However, the monitoring abilities of state auditors can be an issue. Moreover, these industries are more likely to have to deal with the potential reporting difficulties involved with state-owned companies.

Accrual of Resource Revenues by the Military

There are a number of cases in which a host country's military has directly accrued resource revenues outside the central budget process. This has involved the mining and oil sectors in Chile and Indonesia as well as timber concessions in a number of Southeast Asian countries.

The military has played a strong role in Indonesia's petroleum sector. The first head of Pertamina, General Ibnu Sutowo, also controlled one of its predecessor companies. According to Ascher (1999, p. 61), "The heritage of Pertamina was a set of practices dedicated to augmenting the revenues of the armed forces and an instinct to keep the operations and financing secret." A key political challenge for President Suharto was to maintain support by the military, which had been instrumental in the downfall of Sukarno, his predecessor. Since Indonesia was trying to court donors, "an openly defense-heavy national budget would have looked very bad; international borrowing beyond agreed limits would have looked even worse . . . . Thus, as a way to finance the armed forces without the visibility of central government spending, a huge but unknown portion of Pertamina revenues went to the military" (Ascher 1999, p. 61).

Similarly, some 10 percent of Chilean Codelco's copper export revenues apparently continue to go directly to the Chilean armed forces. This arrangement, which was established by the Frei government of the late 1960s, may have accounted for about one-third of Codelco's "tax" obligations during the 1980s. The arrangement "reflected a political convenience for the president, congress, and the armed forces to have an automatic appropriation rather than having to debate and justify the full military budget each year . . . . Executives and legislators were no longer held accountable for this component of military spending" (Ascher 1999, p. 165).

In general, there is a wide body of research on the negative implications of earmarked funds for good governance. Essentially, earmarking means that society is not able to evaluate the marginal social benefits of all programs and rearrange spending as priorities change. Giving programs their own source of revenue makes them less accountable to society as represented by Parliament and central budget authorities. Lack of accountability by the military to the civilian authorities is particularly worrisome in this regard.

A related problem is the use of natural resources to fund rebel movements (and in some cases governments), usually involving resources that are technically relatively easy to extract, such as alluvial diamonds and timber. There is a growing body of research on the influence of such resources on the length and nature of civil conflicts in various developing countries and how they should be addressed.[12]

Initiatives That May Improve Transparency of Resource Revenues

This section describes important international public and private instruments and initiatives that could have a positive impact on the transparency of resource revenue flows.[13] The initiatives fall into two basic groups: initiatives primarily relevant for host-government reporting and initiatives primarily relevant for company reporting. There is some degree of overlap for several of the initiatives. Some also contain a role for companies' home governments, which in principle could be encouraged to influence companies based in their jurisdictions.

Initiatives Relevant for Host-Government Reporting

In this section, we consider three groups of initiatives aimed at promoting host-government reporting of the resource revenues they receive: several initiatives of the International Monetary Fund, the Forest Law

Enforcement and Governance ministerial process, and the efforts of the Caspian Revenue Watch.

IMF Initiatives.   Several IMF initiatives could be used to promote transparency of host governments' revenue flows from natural resource extraction and export. Most notable is the Code of Good Practices on Fiscal Transparency. Related to this are reports on the observance of standards and codes (known as ROSCs).[14]

The IMF's fiscal transparency code represents the first coherent attempt to set a framework of international standards for the conduct of fiscal policy (Petrie 1999). The IMF adopted the original fiscal transparency code in 1998, while the latest version (as of October 2002) dates from March 2001.[15] The fiscal transparency code can be used to evaluate a country's fiscal transparency. It includes a supporting manual, which provides guidelines for implementation, a questionnaire, and a summary self-evaluation report, all of which can be found on the IMF fiscal transparency website.[16]

The code defines fiscal transparency as "being open to the public about the structure and functions of government" (IMF 2001c). It provides a set of practices for making fiscal management transparent. Public availability is a key element. The code is based on the assumption that, over time, fiscal transparency will result in good governance, which leads to more equitable and efficient fiscal policies, which in turn are important for achieving macroeconomic stability and growth. The objectives of the fiscal transparency code are as follows (IMF 2001c):

• *Clarity of roles and responsibilities* is concerned with specifying the structure and functions of government, responsibilities within government, and relations between government and the rest of the economy.

• *Public availability of information* emphasizes the importance of publishing comprehensive fiscal information at clearly specified times.

• *Open budget preparation, execution, and reporting* cover the type of information that is made available about the budget process.

• *Assurances of integrity* deal with the quality of fiscal data and the need for independent scrutiny of fiscal information.

Each main principle embraces a number of specific principles and good practices.

Implementation of the code is voluntary. Although the IMF is encouraging its 184 member countries to improve fiscal transparency by meeting the requirements of the code, member countries are under no formal obligation to adhere to it.

The fiscal transparency code can be used as one step in the fiscal module of a ROSC. The ROSC is a joint effort by the IMF and World Bank to summarize the extent to which a country observes certain internationally recognized standards and codes. The IMF has identified 11 areas and associated standards, based in large part on the fiscal transparency code and on the Code of Good Practices on Transparency in Monetary and Financial Policies.

ROSCs are prepared and published at the request of a World Bank or an IMF member country, and countries are not under a formal obligation to request them. ROSCs can be used in policy discussions with national authorities and by the private sector (including rating agencies) for risk assessment. The information in a ROSC is extensive but varies by country.[17]

The fiscal transparency code makes specific recommendations on the publication of fiscal information. The following recommended practices are relevant to resource revenue transparency (IMF 2001c):

- The public should be provided with full information on the past, current, and projected fiscal activity of government.
- The budget documentation, final accounts, and other fiscal reports for the public should cover all budgetary and extrabudgetary activities of the central government, and the consolidated fiscal position of the central government should be published.
- The central government should publish full information on the level and composition of its debt and financial assets.
- A commitment should be made to the timely publication of fiscal information.
- The publication of fiscal information should be a legal obligation of government.
- Procedures for the execution and monitoring of approved expenditure and for the collection of revenue should be clearly specified.

Although the fiscal transparency code and fiscal ROSC do not specifically address resource revenue, they emphasize good practice related to all significant sources of revenue. Therefore, the more significant resource revenues are in a country's overall revenue picture, the more the ROSC is likely to focus on these revenues. For example, if revenues accrue to an extrabudgetary fund, a ROSC would highlight the need to make the operation of this fund transparent. In addition, the IMF's *Government Finance Statistics Manual,* which the fiscal transparency code recommends using, suggests how data on revenues from natural resources should be reported (IMF 2001b). Among other countries, Azerbaijan has prepared a ROSC, including the element of fiscal transparency. Box 3.1 shows some findings from the Azerbaijan

---

Box 3.1 The Azerbaijan ROSC

The ROSC refers to problems of tax administration and tax arrears of many large state enterprises, including SOCAR, the state oil company. The report from 2000 admits that transparency could be improved: "Although information is not secret, there does not seem to be a strong commitment to regularly publish fiscal data of a comprehensive nature."

According to IMF staff commentary, some of the top priorities for Azerbaijan are to "develop a medium-term budget framework to take into account future income from oil resources and to set development priorities [and] ensure that the operations of the Oil Fund will be transparent."

Source: IMF (2000).

ROSC that are relevant to the issue of transparency of natural resource revenues.

The impact of the fiscal transparency code and ROSC depends on the participation of member countries. In some cases, the IMF has put pressure on governments with an IMF program to undertake a ROSC, and in others it has placed some conditionality on ROSC recommendations. The problem is that countries with large resource revenues are, by definition, less likely to have an economic incentive to participate in IMF programs.

Even if a country undertakes a ROSC, publication is voluntary. As of April 2002, ROSCs had been completed for 76 countries (not necessarily including all modules). Of these, reports for 59 countries were published. The IMF notes that the bulk of ROSC modules completed since January 1, 2002, have been for transition, developing, and emerging market countries (IMF 2002). However, among the countries that published the module on fiscal transparency, the list of developing countries with significant natural resources is short. The IMF argues that publishing ROSCs should remain voluntary to increase cooperation and country ownership in the process.

As long as ROSCs are published, there should be opportunities for the public to use the information. According to the IMF website, ROSCs are "used to help sharpen the institutions' policy discussions with national authorities, and in the private sector (including by rating agencies) for risk assessment."[18] There is at least one confirmed example of the fiscal transparency code being used by nongovernmental organizations (the Institute for Democracy in South Africa and the Center on Budget and Policy Priorities in Washington, D.C., according to Fölscher, Krafchik, and Shapiro 2000). However, this was not related to transparency of resource revenues.

In theory, civil society can pressure governments to undergo a ROSC and to improve standards and procedures by using the outputs of a ROSC. However, even in cases where a government has decided to publish the report, the operations of civil society could be hampered if freedom of the press is inadequate. Since publication of the fiscal ROSCs clearly shows how well a country's practices are aligned with the fiscal transparency code, it theoretically provides an incentive to improve. Countries are encouraged to publish short updates every few years, although this is voluntary. A task force on implementation of standards has suggested using World Bank and IMF policy dialogue with countries to improve their standards as a more proactive approach (IMF 2001a). Again, this assumes that the country has an incentive to work with the IMF in the first place.

Important steps forward could be to increase the number of countries completing a fiscal ROSC, improve the ratio of published reports, and increase the number of recommendations implemented. Another would be to address resource revenues explicitly in the fiscal transparency code, as the importance of this issue is gaining recognition.

To sum up, the fiscal transparency code has both potential strengths and weaknesses:

- The code offers a practical and fairly detailed standard for fiscal transparency.
- The IMF may offer assistance to help countries to achieve transparency.
- Vesting these initiatives with the IMF makes sense because of its strong position both globally and at the country level.
- However, ROSCs are voluntary, and only a small number of resource-rich developing countries have undertaken them.
- Even after undertaking a ROSC, publication is not mandatory.

The Forest Law Enforcement and Governance Ministerial Process. In 1998 the G-8 launched an Action Program on Forests, which, together with the World Bank's Forest Governance Program, led to the East Asia FLEG (Forest Law Enforcement and Governance) ministerial conference in September 2001. An important goal of the FLEG process is to increase the amount of forest-related rent that accrues to the government and to prevent the illegal appropriation of such rent, including via illegal logging.

Box 3.2 Highlights of the East Asia FLEG
Ministerial Declaration

• Improve forest-related governance in order to enforce forest law,
improve the enforcement of property rights, and promote the independence of the judiciary
• Involve stakeholders, including local communities, in decisionmaking in the forestry sector, thereby promoting transparency, reducing
the potential for corruption, ensuring greater equity, and minimizing the
undue influence of privileged groups
• Review existing domestic frameworks for forest policy and institute appropriate reforms, including those relating to granting and monitoring concessions, subsidies, and excess processing capacity, to prevent
illegal practices.

The following is an indicative list of actions for implementation of
the declaration:

• Institute systems that encourage responsible behavior and deter
criminal and corrupt behavior (for example, salaries, codes of conduct)
• Provide consistent, accurate, and timely information to monitoring organizations
• Develop and implement a transparent and participatory approach
to the allocation of concessions.

Source: FLEG (2001).

The ministerial conference included participants from 20 countries,
representing governments, international organizations, nongovernmental organizations, and the private sector. It produced a statement expressing political commitment for action in the area of forest law
enforcement and governance at the national and regional levels (see
box 3.2 for highlights of the declaration).

More recently, ministers from several African countries have expressed interest in a similar initiative. The World Bank (with sponsorship from France, the United Kingdom, and the United States) has been
asked to convene an African FLEG ministerial process in 2003. Both
the East Asia FLEG and the Africa FLEG are continuing processes with
dedicated websites.[19]

Some of the commitments made in the East Asia FLEG declaration
are relevant to the issue of resource revenues—for example, the calls
for ensuring transparency and for reducing the incentives for corruption. Furthermore, the declaration covers numerous aspects that are
interlinked, such as property rights.

There appear to be no control mechanisms for enforcement or follow-up of the principles endorsed by East Asia FLEG. The website states that the ministerial declaration commits participating countries to "intensify national efforts and strengthen bilateral, regional, and multilateral collaboration to address violations of forest law and forest crime and create a regional task force on forest law enforcement and governance to advance the declaration's objectives."[20] A task force met in May 2002 and is due to meet again in 2003. It is unclear whether the declaration will be adopted. The impact of the Africa FLEG initiative is difficult to evaluate at this relatively early stage. It is noteworthy, however, that the FLEG process has expanded to include other geographic regions.

Therefore, the initiative's strong and weak points are as follows:

- It is the only initiative that requires host-country endorsement.
- It includes possibilities for civil society influence.
- It is still in the early stages, so its impact in practice is still unclear.
- It includes no mechanisms for monitoring implementation.
- The issue of revenue disclosure is not specifically addressed.

Caspian Revenue Watch. The Caspian Revenue Watch policy program is a relatively new initiative of the Open Society Institute, which in turn is a part of the Soros Foundation.[21] It was established to explore how revenues are being invested and disbursed and how governments and extraction companies are responding to civic demands for accountability in the region. It also contains a strong advocacy component, aiming to ensure that "existing and future revenue funds in the region be invested and expended for the benefit of the public, such as poverty reduction, education, and public health— through the promotion of transparency, civic involvement, and government accountability."[22]

Although the ultimate focus is on how revenues generated by natural resources can benefit development within the Caspian region, transparency of these revenues is very much highlighted. Moreover, transparency and accountability of resource revenues are specific objectives of Caspian Revenue Watch.

The Eurasia Policy Forum notes that the report that eventually will be issued will offer "in-depth analysis and policy recommendations useful to donors, national governments, nongovernmental organizations, and the media."[23] However, since neither the report nor the expected recommendations have been published yet, it is difficult to evaluate the impact of the program.

Caspian Revenue Watch focuses almost exclusively on flows going to natural resource funds rather than on flows moving through the central budget. On the one hand, a fund in a nontransparent system could facilitate the plundering of resource revenues. On the other hand, the spotlight provided by Caspian Revenue Watch could make it more difficult for this to take place. In general, however, it probably will be difficult to create an island of transparency in a system that lacks transparency overall. For this reason, Caspian Revenue Watch may wish to consider expanding its agenda to include the transparency of resource revenues in general, particularly through the central budget.

To sum up, the potential strong and weak points of Caspian Revenue Watch are as follows:

- The advocacy approach may help to raise awareness of transparency issues.
- A strong civil society "spotlight" on the funds could make them more difficult to plunder.
- If the existence of funds in nontransparent systems can actually increase transparency problems, Caspian Revenue Watch's advocacy of such funds may be problematic.
- Caspian Revenue Watch focuses on funds rather than the national budget.

Initiatives Relevant for Company Reporting

In this section, we consider initiatives and instruments aimed at promoting company disclosure of the payments they make to host countries.

OECD Guidelines for Multinational Enterprises. The OECD Guidelines for Multinational Enterprises are nonbinding recommendations that governments address to all companies based or operating in their jurisdictions. The guidelines form part of the OECD Declaration on International Investment and Multinational Enterprises, which has been agreed to by 33 OECD governments and several non-OECD governments (Argentina, Brazil, Chile, and Slovakia). Since their introduction in 1976, the guidelines have been updated several times, most recently in 2000 (OECD 2000). They take the form of recommendations divided into the following topics: disclosure, employment and industrial relations, environment, efforts to combat bribery, consumer interests, science and technology, competition, and taxation. The consultation process used to develop and revise the guidelines has been relatively open and includes input from several permanent advisory bodies that coordinate the positions of interested business and civil society groups.

What differentiates the OECD guidelines from other recent initiatives is that they have been adopted by governments, not just nongovernmental organizations and companies. Although companies do not endorse the guidelines, and observance is voluntary and not legally enforceable, signatory governments commit to encouraging compliance by "their" companies. Each adhering government is obligated to set up a national contact point, responsible for promoting the guidelines, handling inquiries about their application, and resolving disputes.

The OECD guidelines from 2000 recognize the importance of transparency and disclosure, but they do not specifically focus on disclosure of payments. The most relevant parts are as follows (OECD 2000):

• Enterprises should ensure that timely, regular, reliable, and relevant information is disclosed regarding their activities, structure, financial situation, and performance. This information should be disclosed for the enterprise as a whole and, where appropriate, along business lines or geographic areas. Disclosure policies of enterprises should be tailored to the nature, size, and location of the enterprise, with due regard paid to costs, business confidentiality, and other competitive concerns.

• Enterprises should apply high-quality standards for disclosure, accounting, and audit. Enterprises are also encouraged to apply high-quality standards for nonfinancial information including environmental and social reporting, where they exist. The standards or policies under which both financial and nonfinancial information are compiled and published should be reported.

Information should be disclosed along business lines or geographic areas, which could be highly relevant for reporting payments by a specific host country (although the term geographic area is somewhat vague and could be interpreted more broadly, for example, as a continent rather than a country).

The OECD guidelines potentially benefit from OECD's credibility and intergovernmental status. However, they are not as well known internationally as other global instruments (OECD 2001b, p. 4).

The OECD guidelines are unique among aspirational voluntary codes in having a mechanism to address breaches. National contact points are key actors in the mechanism to resolve disputes—for example, allegations brought by one party against another for failing to observe the guidelines. If a company proves uncooperative, the national contact point can resort to the scheme's greatest sanction, essentially "naming and shaming." In principle, this could be an important deterrent for companies. In practice, however, the scheme suffers from a lack of will on the part of most home governments to address the breaches of "their" corporations. The guidelines do not specifically mention payments to host governments, which means that most home governments will not act against companies that fail to publish such information.

The guidelines are not legally binding on companies, in contrast to, for example, the Convention on Combating Bribery of Foreign Public Officials in International Business Transactions, which, according to Mack (2002, p. 8), is "an example of how regulation can enhance the interests of the private sector as a whole by helping create a level playing field." Although governments may still be committed to encouraging observance, the real strength of mechanisms for adherence is questionable.

As is the case for a number of initiatives, the OECD provides a dynamic framework for developing and revising the guidelines. Moreover, their authority and credibility are potentially enhanced by the transparent and inclusive way in which they have been developed. This ongoing process could be used to facilitate further refinement and even strengthening of the guidelines.

Possible improvements to the existing framework could include offering more specific recommendations on company disclosure as well as specifying individual countries, instead of geographic location, as the unit of reporting.

Making the guidelines legally binding for companies does not appear to be a realistic option. Nevertheless, if the political will exists, one option is to negotiate a more selective version in which national governments commit themselves to enact relevant national laws, similar to the model of the OECD antibribery convention. At a minimum, individual home governments can draw on the guidelines in creating relevant national laws.

To sum up, the potential strong and weak points of the guidelines are as follows:

- They include the critical feature of (home) government commitment.
- They feature a mechanism for dealing with breaches.
- They may not be specific enough on the disclosure of payments.
- Many adhering governments may lack the political will to enforce them.

UN Global Compact. The UN Global Compact is a voluntary code of conduct first proposed by UN Secretary General Kofi Annan in a speech to the Davos economic forum in 1999.[24] Essentially, the secretary general warned that business leaders needed to take more substantial voluntary actions in the areas of human rights, labor standards, and environmental practices in order to counter the "enormous pressure from various interest groups" to include mandatory standards in these areas in international trade regime and investment agreements. The compact was subsequently fleshed out during a series of meetings between representatives of the United Nations, business, and labor. Its operational phase began in 2000.

The nine principles of the Global Compact cover the areas of human rights, labor, and the environment, areas in which universal values have already been defined by international agreements, notably the United Nations Universal Declaration of Human Rights, the International Labour Organisation Fundamental Principles on Rights at Work, and the (UN) RioPrinciples on Environment and Development. Each of the nine principles is explained and expanded on in a document available on the Global Compact website.[25]

The main requirement for participation is that companies provide a brief report once a year on concrete actions they have taken that have been inspired by one or more of the nine principles as well as any lessons they have learned from doing so. The main purpose of this reporting is to share lessons with other participants, including measures that work and those that do not. These postings are to be incorporated into an online database or "learning bank." Participating companies are strongly encouraged, but not required, to take part in various partnership projects organized by the Global Compact. In January 2002 the Global Compact Advisory Council was formed to strengthen the governance and integrity of the initiative.

A July 2002 progress report emphasizes four main areas of activity: global and national initiatives, policy dialogues, the learning forum, and public-private partnership projects (UN Global Compact 2002b, p. 4). These areas do not address transparency directly, but they do have implicit relevance for resource revenues. Policy dialogues may have some relevance for resource revenue, given that the first of these concerned the role of business in zones of conflict; moreover, the Transparency Working Group, which was convened as part of this dialogue, recommended that home governments "enable relevant regulatory agencies, if necessary through appropriate legislation, to require local and international companies to disclose taxes, royalties, and other payments or transactions made in host countries"; that businesses "enhance transparency through public disclosure of information not subject to confidentiality clauses (financial statements, principal transaction, etc.)"; and that businesses "work with host governments and stakeholders to reduce opacity in current confidential contracts to enable greater transparency and where appropriate monitoring arrangements, help lines, etc." Moreover, the Transparency Working Group noted that "most of the multiyear payments made directly to governments by foreign companies take place in the extractive industries" (UN Global Compact 2002a, p. 1). Another working group within the dialogue on zones of conflict is dedicated to revenue-sharing regimes, which deal with "negotiated agreements among companies, governments, and local communities to more equitably distribute the benefits from natural resource extraction" (UN Global Compact 2002b, p. 15).

The Global Compact attempts to improve company behavior through moral persuasion and engagement, providing the incentive of association with a prestigious institution. On the one hand, the Global Compact's association with the United Nations is an advantage, because its "convening power at the highest possible levels provides an unparalleled opportunity for dialogue and for identifying and implementing high-profile and high-impact activities." On the other hand, the UN association may carry a number of potential drawbacks, such as perceived bureaucracy and inefficiency. Although many UN bodies are involved,[26] the status of the compact within the United Nations is unclear. It neither was created by nor reports to the General Assembly, reporting instead directly to the Office of the Secretary General, apparently relying on his patronage for much of its authority.

The requirements to join the compact are not very strict. On the one hand, the opportunity to participate without a substantial commitment might encourage more companies to engage. On the other hand, it is relatively easy for companies to benefit from association with the Global Compact without complying with its recommendations. Nevertheless, after reviewing the governance of the Global Compact, the Advisory Council concluded, "The procedures for joining and participating in the Global Compact should remain un-bureaucratic and encourage the entry of new companies and civil society organisations" (UN Global Compact 2002b, p. 8).

The inclusive nature of the compact is reflected in the vagueness of the specific recommendations on transparency "if necessary through appropriate legislation." The impact of the constituent working groups thus depends on the priorities of the stakeholders involved.

The Global Compact and the Transparency Working Group within the zones of conflict dialogue appear to be ongoing processes that have the potential to focus more on revenue transparency issues in the future. The most recent meeting notes from the Transparency Working Group (from April 2002, posted on its website) state that it will "continue to explore ways and means to support the ongoing process for increased transparency at the sectoral levels such as efforts in the mining and petroleum-industry sectors, multilateral development bank efforts on good governance, and the World Bank's review of the natural-resource industry."[27] One possibility for having a greater impact on revenue transparency could be to expand the nine principles of the Global Compact (as opposed to those of the Transparency Working Group) to include points related to transparency.

To sum up, the UN Global Compact has potential strong and weak points:

• The Transparency Working Group provides specific recommendations on resource revenue transparency.
• The process is both inclusive and evolving.
• However, the actions proposed by the Transparency Working Group are not part of the principles that companies must endorse.
• Association with the Global Compact does not require much effort on the part of companies and is not actively vetted; nonetheless, this fact may encourage more companies to participate.

Global Reporting Initiative.   The Global Reporting Initiative provides guidelines for companies (and other entities) to report their economic, environmental, and social performance. The initiative was launched in 1997 by the Coalition for Environmentally Responsible Economies, responding to growing demands by stakeholders for "sustainability" information and to the ad hoc response of companies to such demands, making information difficult to compare across companies or over time. The Global Reporting Initiative "seeks to make sustainability reporting as routine and credible as financial reporting in terms of comparability, rigour, and verifiability."[28]

The Global Reporting Initiative developed its reporting guidelines after a consultative process involving different types of firms and stakeholders from around the world. This process is intended to be continuous. The latest version of the guidelines was issued in 2002.[29] In addition, the Global Reporting Initiative is involved in developing sector-specific supplements through initiatives such as the Mining, Minerals, and Sustainable Development Project.[30]

Use of the guidelines is optional and does not involve notifying the initiative. The Global Reporting Initiative recognizes that companies with little experience in reporting sustainability information may find it easier to introduce the standards gradually. Hence the guidelines include an annex on their incremental application. In addition, organizations are encouraged to add information beyond what is requested in the guidelines. Although the Global Reporting Initiative promotes independent verification and auditing—and provides an annex on verification—they are not a requirement. Neither does it audit organizations or accredit others to do so.

The guidelines emphasize that "the principles of transparency and inclusiveness represent the starting point for the reporting process and are woven into the fabric of all the other principles." The Global Reporting Initiative encourages transparency by promoting reporting. More specifically, it provides standards and identifies indicators that could help to clarify the flow of resource revenues (Global Reporting Initiative 2002):

- *EC8* breaks down the total sum of taxes of all types paid by country.
- *EC10* breaks down donations to community, civil society, and other groups in terms of cash and in-kind donations per type of group.
- *EC12* includes the total spent on the development of noncore business infrastructure, which is infrastructure built outside the main business activities of the reporting entity, such as a school or a hospital for employees and their families.

The guidelines are widespread and gaining increasing acceptance; they appear to be setting the standard for all social and environmental auditing schemes. Greater focus on reporting in general may eventually benefit the reporting of payments specifically related to natural resources. Companies are encouraged to prepare sustainability reports that are as complete as possible, which means not picking and choosing the parts of the guidelines to include. However, the Global Reporting Initiative does provide scope for gradual introduction, with the understanding that the company eventually will produce a "complete" report. Annex 3 of the 2002 guidelines provides advice on incremental application (Global Reporting Initiative 2002). However, no clear guidance is given about the delay allowed in reporting on particular indicators, such as EC8.

Many international companies today are motivated to publicize their positive economic impact on host countries. Far from fearing comparability, many now welcome the chance to demonstrate their advanced performance. However, the willingness to report may depend on the subject. For example, paying a large signature bonus may not be perceived as positively as building a hospital.

Resource companies may be discouraged from reporting payments when this is not a legal requirement, and some companies note that nondisclosure clauses in their contracts with host governments prohibit them from publishing information. Nevertheless, the ability to introduce the Global Reporting Initiative gradually and the voluntary nature of standards may make it possible for more companies to participate. The challenge is to ensure that EC8 is used. The impact of the Global Reporting Initiative on the transparency of resource revenue flows thus may be determined by the level of pressure on companies to publish a complete sustainability report.

EC8, the indicator related most directly to revenue transparency, concerns the total sum of taxes of all types paid broken down by country. The term "taxes" could include all payments made to governments, including facilitation payments, signature bonuses, and royalties. However, companies could interpret it differently as long as indirect taxes or payments are not specified.

The consultation process is intended to be continuous, and for the foreseeable future each revision is likely to increase the amount and detail of information required from reporting companies. Developments in the Global Reporting Initiative guidelines will be important for other forums as well.

One suggestion that could increase the impact of the Global Reporting Initiative on transparency of resource revenues is to define taxes and specifically note that disclosure should include all payments, including signature bonuses. Another suggestion is to tighten up the recommendations for implementation, for example, by setting a recommended time frame for inclusion of all relevant indicators, which would include EC8 in the case of natural resource extraction companies.

In summary, the Global Reporting Initiative has potential strong and weak points:

- It continues to set the standard for sustainability reporting.
- It mentions taxes specifically by country.
- Guidelines for gradual introduction of "full" Global Reporting Initiative reporting may give companies too much discretion, perhaps allowing them to avoid using EC8 indefinitely.
- EC8 refers simply to taxes, allowing companies to decide whether to report signature bonuses and other relevant payments.

Minerals, Mining, and Sustainable Development.   Mining, Minerals, and Sustainable Development was a two-year process that ended in May 2002 with a final report (MMSD 2002). Nine of the world's largest mining companies initiated the project through the World Business Council for Sustainable Development. The International Institute for Environment and Development managed MMSD, in collaboration with the Global Mining Initiative. The MMSD Project focused on research, a process of stakeholder engagement, and a program of information exchange.

The sustainable development principles that came out of the process cover economic, social, environmental, and governance issues. However, the project essentially produced a review of current issues and practices and did not propose guidelines that companies must endorse or implement. Because of time limits, the website notes that MMSD did not seek to "solve or even to address all of the issues that will ever be faced by the mining and minerals industries. At best, it provided a starting point for identifying different concerns."[31] One of its concrete activities was to lay the basis for the future development of a mining sector supplement to the Global Reporting Initiative guidelines. The report and other relevant material are available on the MMSD website, but the project's office is now closed and will distribute no further material.

The sustainable development principles state the need to ensure transparency by providing all stakeholders with access to relevant and accurate information. Box 3.3 presents some of the recommendations relating to resource revenue transparency.

The recommendations in the final report are more numerous and detailed and similarly call for the disclosure of payments from companies as well as transparency of revenues by host governments. The MMSD initiative featured a working group focused on understanding "the obstacles which have prevented some developing countries from using mineral revenues as an effective catalyst to economic and social development, the so-called resource trap."[32] Several working papers were distributed, and a workshop was conducted in 2001.

MMSD is distinctive in its commercial angle and its initiation by industry. This is evident in its focus on market mechanisms and enterprise issues such as corporate governance and corporate culture. This is likely to enhance its credibility among private sector stakeholders. Although the recommendations are relevant and quite specific, they are not a set of codes or principles that have been endorsed. Finally, the MMSD initiative was limited in time, although the Global Reporting Initiative website states that "we anticipate this work will continue beyond the release of the MMSD final report in April 2002."[33]

In summary, MMSD has potential strong and weak points:

- It addresses resource revenue transparency specifically.
- It was initiated by the mining industry itself, which probably gives it credibility in the sector as well as in the private sector in general. The key role of industry may set an important precedent.
- The framework does not commit firms to any actions.
- The initiative is no longer operational.

Global e-Sustainability Initiative. The Global e-Sustainability Initiative (GeSI) is a joint initiative of the International Telecommunications Union and the United Nations Environment Programme (UNEP). The GeSI website states that the initiative aims to create a forum for the information and communications technology sector that

Box 3.3 MMSD Suggestions Relevant to
Revenue Transparency

Attracting investment:

• All parties should encourage a clear public debate on a definition
of principles that balance fair protection for investors with a fair return
to host governments, including calculations of all revenue and indirect
payments.

Transparency in the management of mineral wealth:

• Governments and companies should more widely adopt the practice of open publication of the basic information about how much
wealth is generated, the amounts of revenue received by all government
departments, and how that money is spent.
• Industry organizations should consider, possibly in partnership
with an international organization such as the World Bank Group, taking the initiative to establish an international and public register of all
payments by mining companies to governments at all levels.
• Nongovernmental "watchdog" organizations could bring pressure to ensure that open publication regarding mineral wealth is realized.

Access to information:

• Corporations should work with the Global Reporting Initiative
or other international bodies to harmonize public reporting.
• The private finance community should take a stronger role in encouraging best practice in public disclosure.
• Establishment (through a body such as the Global Reporting Initiative) of criteria for a harmonized public reporting system would
include verification, which is agreed to by a multiple-stakeholder process.
Although such a system would of necessity be voluntary, as no international legal mechanisms exist to enforce it, more research could be conducted to explore whether and how an appropriate regulatory regime
might work or be established.

Source: Excerpts from MMSD (2002).

will "promote and support greater awareness, accountability, and
transparency."[34] The initiative is still in its startup phase, and little
material is available on its website.

Although the information and communications technology sector
does not include extractive companies, it uses some extractive resources

in the production of electronic devices. Coltan, for example, is an important component of mobile phones and computers. Coltan trade has attracted attention due to its link with the second Congolese war in the Democratic Republic of Congo. The United Nations Security Council published two reports in 2001 on this issue, while a UN panel of experts concluded, "The role of the private sector in the exploitation of natural resources and the continuation of the war [in the Democratic Republic of Congo] has been vital" (UN 2001, § 215). The final report from 2002 listed 85 companies that the panel of experts considered had violated the OECD Guidelines for Multinational Enterprises in their involvement in such activities in the Democratic Republic of Congo (UN 2002). A report by Fauna and Flora International and GeSI considers the issue of transparency of the coltan trade in the Congolese economy. GeSI members propose regulation of the coltan industry in order to promote sustainable development (Hayes 2002). Another relevant aspect of the GeSI is the forthcoming initiative to develop a telecommunications supplement within the Global Reporting Initiative, due in 2003.

Both GeSI and its initiatives concerning coltan and the Global Reporting Initiative telecommunications supplement are new, and their impact remains unclear.

In sum, the GeSI has potential strengths and weaknesses:

• The focus on major consumers of coltan rather than on mining companies could prove to be an important way of addressing the problem, providing lessons for other commodities.

• The initiative has not specifically addressed the issue of revenue transparency.

• Although telecommunications companies are consumers of coltan, they are not directly involved in coltan mining or processing or in transferring mining revenues to host governments. Thus they may have limited influence in this regard.

Publish What You Pay.   In June 2002 the nongovernmental organization Global Witness, together with George Soros and some 60 other partners, launched the Publish What You Pay campaign. The initiative follows from the oil campaign of Global Witness, which calls on oil companies to publish what they pay to host governments.[35] The various resource campaigns of Global Witness have documented the diversion of revenues from the extractive industries in a number of countries, including Angola, Cambodia, the Democratic Republic of Congo, and Liberia.

Global Witness argues that the voluntary approach has "proved problematic."[36] For example, companies unilaterally publishing their payments face reprisals, making it difficult for a company to act unless competitors are under the same obligation. Global Witness and the Publish What You Pay campaign argue that the way forward is for home-country regulators to require companies to report their payments. Specifically, Publish What You Pay is calling on home governments to require their securities regulators (for example, the Securities and Exchange Commission in the United States) to demand a disaggregated reporting of payments by the host country as a condition for stock market listing. According to Publish What You Pay, mandatory regulation would eliminate concerns about contractual confidentiality clauses preventing companies' disclosure of payment data, noting that some contracts (especially in Angola) specifically allow companies to opt out of secrecy obligations if they are required to report payments by regulators in other countries.

The campaign argues that regulation also would eliminate "double standards" of the way in which the same company reports about its operations in the developed world and in the developing world: "We are not calling on companies to disclose commercially confidential information, but rather to publish the same basic data on net payments made to government and other public authorities which they are required to disclose in many developed countries."[37] Examples of specific recommendations that Global Witness has made to oil companies and home governments are provided in box 3.4.

The Publish What You Pay campaign is the international initiative targeted most directly at the issue of transparency of resource revenue flows in the extractive industries, although its focus is on the payment (company) side of transactions. It advocates the use of a particular instrument—that is, mandatory requirements by securities regulators in home countries. The campaign appears to be gaining momentum. U.K. Prime Minister Tony Blair has publicly supported the concept on several occasions, and the head of the International Finance Corporation, Peter Woicke, endorsed the idea in a speech in September 2002.

A possible weakness of placing regulation in the hands of stock market authorities is that this could miss the important handful of technologically competent and internationally active companies based in developing countries (notably China and Malaysia) that do not have significant public listings. Such companies, which generally do not face the same "corporate social responsibility" pressures that many Western-based companies do from their customers and shareholders, conceivably could take business away from OECD-based companies in some cases.

Box 3.4 Recommendations of Global Witness

Recommendations for oil companies:

  • Render summary figures of taxes and other payments made to national governments publicly available for all countries of operation
  • Provide data locally in the national language of each country of operation as well as in the home language of the company
  • Publish the names and locations of registration of all subsidiary companies operating in each country
  • Embrace a unified stand on full transparency of payments to national governments
  • Adopt a policy of independent, transparent auditing of social programs.

Recommendations for national (home) governments:

  • Ensure that national oil companies adopt full transparency criteria on overseas operations
  • Insist that financial regulators of international stock exchanges legally oblige companies filing reports with them to disclose payments to all national governments in consolidated and subsidiary accounts
  • Insist that their export financing agencies practice full transparency as a condition for setting up credit agreements.

In summary, the Publish What You Pay campaign has both potential strong and weak points:

  • It is one of the most directly focused initiatives in terms of resource revenue transparency.
  • Its campaign approach has succeeded in raising public awareness of the issue.
  • The focus apparently would miss nonlisted companies, which disgruntled host governments could increasingly reward for their continued lack of disclosure. According to its supporters, however, this is likely to be a relatively minor problem that could be addressed as it arises.
  • It would capture only part of the picture, that is, payments by foreign companies, leaving out significant revenue flows via host government–owned oil companies, including, for example, joint ventures with foreign firms.

Policy Recommendations

Reporting of natural resource revenues is a means to achieve transparency, which itself is a precondition for improving governance by curbing opportunities for corruption, mismanagement, and diversion of funds. Reporting also provides civil society with an important part of the information it needs to hold government to account. Other important information includes how government revenues are spent—for instance, how spending on health and education corresponds to increases in oil revenues.

Ultimately, the host government should have the ultimate responsibility for providing its citizens with details of the revenues it receives from resource extraction and export. Unfortunately, there are often strong incentives for resource-rich host governments or elites in developing countries not to disclose information, and the international community often has limited leverage to force them to do so. For example, the threat of sanctions and conditionality is problematic, since natural resources provide host governments with an independent and comparatively large source of funds from a legally traded commodity. This is why it may be necessary also to look at the company side of payments to host governments. Nevertheless, the ultimate focus must continue to be on the (perhaps long-term) goal of host-country transparency.

Technical Assistance to Host Governments

At a minimum, the international community should step up efforts to provide host governments with technical assistance on reporting and tracking revenues. This will at least cover the cases where the main barrier is technical. It is also important to remember that most governments are not monolithic and that technical assistance in reporting and tracking revenue could strengthen the hand of individuals who are concerned with good governance.

Ample opportunities exist for such assistance and cooperation along both bilateral and multilateral avenues. Many donor countries already support capacity-building schemes—for instance, in national petroleum administrations—and such schemes could be modified to incorporate reporting and transparency aspects. UN organizations and multilateral development banks also run comprehensive public sector reform programs, many of which relate to natural resource sectors and ministries. International umbrella organizations such as the International Organization of Supreme Audit Institutions already manage capacity-building programs in relevant areas across developing and transitional economies. However, like World Bank–sponsored public expenditure reviews, such programs focus mainly on the expenditure and not the revenue side of public financial management.

Making Government Transparency a Condition for Receiving Certain Benefits

It is recommended that technical assistance include diagnostic use of the IMF's fiscal transparency code and reports on the observance of standards and codes. Although opportunities to apply pressure to use the fiscal transparency code are likely to be limited, developed countries could make publication of a ROSC a condition for receiving certain types of aid or export credits.

Since many resource-rich governments often borrow on commercial markets (presumably to avoid conditionalities associated with less expensive loans from multilateral development banks), encouraging international banks to make publication of a ROSC a condition for lending could be useful. This could be encouraged, for example, by the use of a voluntary "white list" of banks, as suggested in chapter 5.

Other more general conditionality approaches (beyond ROSC) may also be considered in bilateral (for example, the U.S. Foreign Appropriations Act, as proposed by Global Witness) or multilateral contexts, taking into account the incentive problems noted and the generally mixed experience with conditionality as a policy tool.

Coordinating Home-Country Reporting Rules for International Oil Companies

Due to the (at least short-term) barriers to improving reporting procedures of host governments, an alternative approach to bring more transparency to natural resource–related revenue flows is to focus on reporting at other points in the flow. For example, many of the financial *inflows* to governments can be revealed by looking at the financial *outflows* from the international oil and mining companies.[38]

Many host governments do not want companies to reveal how much they pay and may be in a position to penalize companies that do. This creates collective action problems, especially for voluntary regimes or campaigns to pressure individual companies to be good corporate citizens. This could even lead to responsible companies leaving a difficult country and being replaced by less transparent firms over which the international community has little influence. For this reason, Global Witness and a number of others have concluded that the voluntary approach to revealing payments probably will not work.

The Publish What You Pay campaign is calling for governments in developed countries to require stock exchanges to demand full disclosure of payments as a condition for company listings. A related approach is to amend existing reporting requirements in oil companies' home governments. Many home governments already require companies to make an aggregated statement of payments to foreign governments; the change would require them to disaggregate that reporting by country.

If mandatory reporting is attempted in an uncoordinated fashion, one could effectively transfer the collective action problem from companies to stock markets or home governments. This is why, whatever the tactical approach taken (for example, stock market listing requirements or other company filings), there should be a coordinated approach among home governments. The U.K. government's efforts to catalyze global action in the context of the Extractive Industries Transparency Initiative are an important step in this direction.

Such coordination could be attempted in more formal ways through the OECD or multilateral bodies like the United Nations or the World Bank. A model could be the antibribery convention and other similar OECD agreements that have obligated each member government to introduce certain common domestic legislation, thus leveling the playing field. Home governments could use the OECD as a forum to negotiate an agreement to introduce common legislation to level the playing field for company reporting. This would make changing home-country jurisdictions less tempting. Such an agreement would have to specify a clear and consistent approach regarding the nature and level of aggregation of payments to be disclosed.

A possible problem with mandatory company reporting is that it is unlikely to include companies from developing countries that could provide credible and less demanding alternatives to OECD-based companies. However, the OECD antibribery convention could provide a precedent, since several non-OECD countries participated in its negotiation.

Unfortunately, multilateral negotiations often are very time-consuming. Attaching a company reporting agreement to an existing instrument could allow it to take advantage of existing infrastructure and protocols, which potentially could speed the process of negotiation. Nevertheless, success ultimately will depend on the political will of the negotiators.

It is sometimes easier to get an agreement among a smaller group of key countries. Thus another interesting vehicle could be the G-8, which encompasses the home governments of almost all major OECD oil companies, in addition to Russia. Agreement within the G-8 probably could go much of the way toward solving the collective action problem or at least could provide political momentum to fast track an agreement among a larger group of countries, for example, through the OECD.

Whatever approach is taken, consulting and engaging companies are crucial. Such consultation already is occurring in several forums, not only in the context of initiatives mentioned here but also within the World Bank's extractive industries review. In addition, industry-internal processes on this issue are under way, including in the oil company umbrella organization, the International Petroleum Industry Environmental Conservation Association. Such initiatives should be encouraged.

Issuing Credible and Publicly Available Estimates of Host-Country Revenues

To be useful as a deterrent against mismanagement of funds, reported information should be made publicly available. Thus information provided to home governments by international oil companies ultimately must be aggregated and made available to host-country citizens. This could be done by a reputable nongovernmental organization or an international organization, perhaps via the Internet. Ideally, this would include summary tables allowing countries to be compared. Such information should also be made available in languages used by the citizens of key host countries.

While waiting for detailed information to be provided through company or host-country reporting, it may be possible to provide some independent revenue estimates for many host governments, for example, based on known production, average market prices, and some simple, conservative assumptions on the percentage of production that accrues to the government. In order to ensure credibility, the assumptions behind the calculations should be explained in detail and backed up by robust research. This does not mean that the method of calculation would have to differ by country; in fact, a simple, common approach may even be more effective.

The approach should be conservative, designed to ensure that, in most cases, actual revenues likely are higher than the estimates. The point is to show populations in nontransparent host countries the order of magnitude of their governments' income from the extraction and export of natural resources.

If a host government disagrees with the estimate, it must provide its own figures. But if a government claims that it did not receive as much as the estimate, the host-country public can legitimately ask why the government did not obtain at least the "minimum international standard rent" from exploitation of its resources.

Further useful information for host-country publics could be provided by including estimates of government health and education spending calculated by reputable international organizations such as the United Nations Development Programme or the World Bank. This would help to put revenues into perspective, allowing comparisons with domestic expenditures and with other countries.

Because of its credibility in collecting data on oil production and making the information publicly available, the International Energy Agency may be in a good position to play a key role, possibly in cooperation with other global organizations such as the World Bank.

Appendix: Four Case Studies

Botswana

Botswana is generally considered to be a rare success story among developing countries because of the way in which it has handled its natural resource revenues, which come principally from diamonds. (Diamonds currently contribute about a third of gross domestic product and about three-quarters of export revenues.) It is also one of the few developing countries for which procedures for collecting and reporting resource revenues appear to be publicly available.

Botswana has been a model from the standpoint of both economic policy—for example, the design of economic policies for avoiding the worst effects of "Dutch disease"—and public policy—the development of a relatively open approach to government and to the collection and reporting of natural resource revenues in particular.

According to the Botswana Ministry of Finance (n.d.), procedures for the collection and recording of resource revenues are available from the Government Printing Office.[39]

Revenue collection is decentralized in Botswana, with the various line ministries responsible for collection in their respective sectors. The Ministry of Minerals, Energy, and Water Affairs collects revenue in the diamond sector, including royalties and taxes on company profits, although the procedures are essentially the same for each sector:[40]

• Line ministries make periodic projections of the revenues they expect to collect on a monthly basis and submit these to the Accountant General in the Ministry of Finance.
• Line ministries deposit all revenue they collect into a single government treasury account in the Central Bank of Botswana. This is usually done on a monthly basis, although diamond revenues are collected quarterly.
• The line ministry sends the receipt of the central bank deposit to the office of the Accountant General at the Ministry of Finance, along with required documentation showing how this revenue was calculated.

Box 3.5 Constitutional Basis for the Role of the
Auditor General in Botswana

In discharging his duties under Section 124(2) and (3) of the constitution, the Auditor General shall satisfy himself that:

• All reasonable precautions have been taken to safeguard the collection and custody of public moneys and that the laws, instructions, and directions relating thereto have been duly observed.
• The disbursement of public moneys has taken place under proper authority and for the purposes intended by such authority.
• All reasonable precautions have been taken to safeguard the receipt, custody, issue, and proper use of public stores and that the instructions and directions relating thereto have been duly observed.
• Adequate instructions or directions exist for the guidance of officers responsible for the collection, custody, issue, and disbursement of public moneys or the receipt, custody, and issue disbursement of public stores.

Where he considers it necessary or desirable, he will examine the economy, efficiency, or effectiveness with which any officer, authority, or institution of government falling within the scope of his audit has, in the discharge of his or its official functions, applied or utilized the public moneys or public supplies at his or its disposal, and shall forward a report of his findings thereon to the minister.

Source: See the Auditor General's website: www.gov.bw/government/
office_of_auditor_general.html.

• The Accountant General reviews and records this information and sends it to the Auditor General (see box 3.5).
• The Auditor General audits the information, noting discrepancies between amounts originally estimated, actual amounts to be received, and amounts collected.
• The Auditor General submits regular reports to the Parliamentary Public Accounts Committee, which has ultimate oversight of government revenues.
• The Public Accounts Committee holds regular hearings, at which those responsible for estimating and collecting revenue in the various line ministries may be questioned regarding any discrepancies found.
• The Public Accounts Committee publishes regular reports on government accounts and the results of hearings.

Botswana is a rare case of a resource-rich developing country with reporting procedures that are publicly available. However, like most government documents in Botswana and other developing (and developed) countries, the procedures are not available over the Internet. Moreover, foreigners probably would require permission from the Office of the President in order to obtain a paper copy from the Government Printing Office. Given that Botswana appears to be relatively advanced in terms of transparency and availability of information, this provides some indication of the difficulty that probably would be involved in compiling a comprehensive list of government reporting procedures in developing countries, even where such procedures are publicly available.

Azerbaijan

The State Oil Fund for the Azerbaijan Republic (SOFAR) was established in August 2000 and is designed to receive most of the government's oil revenues. Information on the working of SOFAR is relatively readily available. Caspian Revenue Watch, an initiative of the Soros Foundation, has investigated the fund extensively and plans to publish a book on both the Azeri and Kazakh funds in the near future.[41] (Econ was able to review advanced copies of some of the chapters.) In addition, the fund has a reasonably informative website.[42] Finally, the World Bank and International Monetary Fund (IMF) worked closely with the Azeri government in setting up the fund, and have made several presentations about the fund, including to the recent Petroleum Revenue Management workshop hosted by the World Bank in October 2002.

Impetus for the creation of SOFAR apparently came from the desire of the government to protect its new oil-related income from political pressures to spend too quickly and to avoid "Dutch disease" (Wakeman-Linn, Mathieu, and van Selm 2002). The emphasis of the fund appears to be more on savings than on macroeconomic stability, since the inflow and outflow rules theoretically prevent it from being used to make up budget shortfalls.

SOFAR is supposed to receive all revenue related to the new, post-Soviet fields—that is, those currently being developed by international oil companies. This leaves revenue from fields originally developed during Soviet times for the state budget. The fund therefore receives proceeds from less than half of Azeri production, which in 2002 stood at about 300,000 barrels per day. However, the proportion received by the fund is likely to increase substantially after 2004, when production by international consortiums is expected to take off. It is perhaps for this reason that most international attention has been on SOFAR rather than on the central budget.

Figure 3.1 Lines of Accountability in the State Oil Fund of Azerbaijan

President	• Can establish and dissolve the Oil Fund • Issues decrees approving all rules of the Oil Fund • Appoints and can dismiss the Oil Fund's executive director • Chooses or approves the Oil Fund's auditor • Decides how to spend the Oil Fund • Appoints members to the Supervisory Council
Supervisory Council	• Defines the rules for compilation of reports on the use of SOFAR's assets • Reviews and comments on SOFAR's annual report, auditor's report, and proposed budgets • Supposedly meets quarterly but has met once • Is to be composed of representatives of government and community-based organizations, but no community-based organizations are currently represented • Can hold off-schedule meetings at the request of one-half of the members or SOFAR's executive director
Executive director of SOFAR	• Exercises operational management, hires staff, and develops annual investment strategy • Responsible for investment and management of SOFAR's assets • Together with Ministry of Economic Development, prepares the program for expenditures from the Oil Fund • Submits quarterly and annual reports, and estimates operational expenses to the president • Cooperates with the auditor selected by the president and publishes the results of the audit and annual report

Note: SOFAR = State Oil Fund for the Azerbaijan Republic.
Source: Tsalik (2003).

SOFAR has an executive director and a supervisory board (see figure 3.1). However, the president has virtually unfettered power to appoint and dismiss both. Thus, in practice, "the ultimate authority over all aspects of the Oil Fund's activities rests with the President, who is empowered to liquidate and re-establish the Fund, approve the Fund's regulations, identify its management structure, etc." (Petersen and Budina 2002).

Caspian Revenue Watch similarly notes that SOFAR is "subordinated directly to the President and lacks sufficient mechanisms for oversight." It points out that a major weakness in the governance structure is the fact that SOFAR has been established on the basis of a presidential decree, which in practice will probably limit Parliament's ability to play any political oversight role (Tsalik 2003).

Nevertheless, some financial oversight is provided by a requirement for the fund to be audited on an annual basis by a reputable international firm. The first audit was performed by Ernst and Young in 2001. The Azeri Chamber of Auditors also has the right to audit the fund. Despite low marks for oversight, most observers generally have given SOFAR high marks for transparency. SOFAR's annual report, which it publishes on its website, provides financial information that is "thorough, and includes breakdowns of all proceeds from each revenue channel." However, the fund has not lived up to its own rules for publishing quarterly reports (Tsalik 2003). Caspian Revenues Watch notes, "Adherence to SOFAR's regulations and disclosure requirements is one of the criteria for receipt of $200 million in loans through the IMF's Poverty Reduction Growth Facility" (Tsalik 2003).

Another major criticism has been the laxity of SOFAR's expenditure rules and the almost complete discretion this effectively gives the president to decide how the money should be spent. In general, Caspian Revenues Watch concludes that the fund's "lax rules leave too much to wise governance. While the current leadership may demonstrate a commitment to good spending, what guarantee is there that future presidents will do the same? The current rules, with their absence of checks and balances, leave too much to chance" (Tsalik 2003).

Angola

According to the Publish What You Pay campaign, the IMF's Angolan "oil diagnostic," which is being carried out under the Staff Monitoring Agreement signed between the Angolan government and the IMF, provides one of the few glimpses of Angola's internal reporting procedures. However, due to the conditions of confidentiality under which that project is being carried out, details of the procedures cannot yet be made available.

Despite Angola's oil wealth, its government borrowed heavily during the last decade, as a result of the long-running civil war, economic mismanagement, and low oil prices. Moreover, it borrowed at a premium on international markets, presumably to avoid possible conditions attached to IMF financing. A significant amount of future oil revenue reportedly has been used as collateral. However, this growing debt burden gave the Angolan government an incentive to call on the World Bank and IMF.

In April 2000 the IMF and Angolan government signed a Staff Monitoring Agreement, which would help it eventually to qualify for loans under the Enhanced Structural Adjustment Facility. The agreement included an "oil diagnostic" program to monitor the government's oil revenues between July and December 2000, by comparing export, tax, and other earnings from oil activities with deposits into the Central Bank of Angola. The program's limited scope meant that it could not investigate discrepancies found nor monitor how the income was spent. The program had to rely on the information that the Angolan government and the international oil companies were willing to supply.

The oil diagnostic included a review of the government's internal reporting procedures for its petroleum income. AUPEC, a natural resource tax consultancy connected to the University of Aberdeen, was hired to conduct this review. According to the project terms of reference (provided by AUPEC), project components include the following:

• Design, develop, and install a monitoring system that will give the government an ongoing accurate view of the revenues received
• Recommend institutional and regulatory improvements as well as other measures necessary to support sound management of oil revenues.

However, AUPEC notes that its findings on the project so far remain confidential, in accordance with the wishes of the Angolan government. In practice, this means that it has not been able to reveal what reporting procedures may be in place nor its recommendations to improve them.

At a workshop on Petroleum Revenue Management held at the World Bank on October 23–24, 2002, a member of the audience asked the Angolan ambassador to the United States when the Angolan government planned to publish the findings of the oil diagnostic. The ambassador replied that the government was still reviewing the documents. She further noted that the government planned to meet with KPMG, the main consultant on the project, in November 2002, after which the government "probably has plans to publish the report." As far as she understood, there were "no missing funds, [and] the main problem was with the reconciliation procedures."

According to the BBC, an internal report by the International Monetary Fund viewed by the news organization indicated that more than $900 million disappeared from Angolan government finances in 2001 ("IMF: 'Angola's Missing Millions'" 2002). According to the BBC, "There has been little progress in the areas of governance and fiscal transparency in Angola [and] lack of useful data made the monitoring of Angola's fiscal situation difficult." The document reportedly stated that the state-owned oil company, Sonangol, "assumed some time ago complete control of foreign currency receipts from the oil sector and stopped channeling them through the central bank as mandated by law." According to the BBC, some diplomats have allowed that "at

least some of the discrepancy identified by the IMF may be due to bad
accounting practices on the side of the government [but] ... certain
individuals may have taken advantage of the smokescreen provided
by slack financial management in order to divert funds into their own
bank accounts."

Chad

Most reporting requirements for host governments are likely to be
imposed internally, for example, by the country's own parliament. In
theory, reporting conditions may be imposed by outside parties, for example, as a condition for assistance. However, countries with significant
natural resource–related revenue flows generally will be in a position to
avoid such conditions because they have less need for the sort of loans
required by other developing countries. As Ross (2001, p. 201) points
out, "Conditionality works best when the recipient state is small, and
its government relies heavily on international donors; or when a larger
government is in crisis and has little choice but to accept the donor's
demands. In most other cases, governments find ways to evade or counteract the conditions they dislike."

The Chad-Cameroon Petroleum Development and Pipeline Project
may be one of the few examples of conditionality on a natural resource
development project. The IMF and World Bank have placed oversight
conditions on resource revenue flows in exchange for their assistance
in financing the government's portion of this project, which seeks to
develop oil fields in southern Chad for export via a new pipeline to
Cameroon's Atlantic Coast.

A number of companies reportedly had been looking at Chad's oil
potential for several decades, but had been put off by the severe, long-
term political difficulties and economic mismanagement in the country. ExxonMobil finally agreed to invest on the condition that the
Chad government sign an agreement with the World Bank and IMF
arranging for a large portion of the government's oil revenues to go to
priority development projects.

According to the World Bank, the Law on the Management of Oil
Revenue, developed with World Bank assistance and passed by the
Chadian Parliament in 1998, establishes "clear guidelines for the allocation, control, and oversight" of oil revenue (World Bank 1999). This
law requires 10 percent of revenue to go to a future generations fund,
while 80 percent of the remainder must be invested in health, education, and vital infrastructure. These flows are to be monitored by
Parliament, as well as an oversight committee that includes representatives of civil society (see box 3.6).

Box 3.6 Control and Monitoring Institutions in Chad

• The control of the mobilization and use of oil revenues will be carried out jointly or separately by the Financial Controller of Finance and Economy, the Committee for the Control and Supervision of Oil Resources (CCSRP), the General Accounting Office of the Supreme Court, and Parliament (Article 14).

• The CCSRP will include a representative of local nongovernmental organizations (Article 16).

• A decree will define the organizational modalities and the conditions of control and supervision implemented by the CCSRP (Article 19).

• The monitoring of the mobilization, allocation, and use of the oil revenues is ensured by periodic audits and reports submitted to the government, especially (a) annual audits of special accounts and savings accounts for future generations, (b) periodic management reports of savings accounts, (c) periodic reports of the CCSRP, and (d) reports on and audits of primary banks insuring the management of special accounts.

Source: Excerpts from Chad (1999).

The money covered by the monitoring arrangements includes both the Chadian government's share of oil production and taxes paid by the foreign oil companies on their shares. However, bonuses paid by the international companies were not originally included. This exception caused some difficulties for the project's image when it was revealed that the government used some $4.5 million of its $25 million signing bonus to purchase weapons. This event reportedly led to an acceleration of the establishment of the oversight committee, which originally had not expected to be in operation until 2004—the year in which the first royalties and taxes were expected to begin accruing to the government.[43]

It is probably too early to tell whether the arrangements put in place in Chad will be successful in maintaining the transparency of expected revenue flows. Moreover, it is unclear that the Chad model would work beyond cases where the expected economic benefits for companies are outweighed by an extremely difficult local political situation. In most countries, oil resources of this size (estimated at 1 billion barrels) probably would be enough to compensate an international oil company for most political difficulties. In such cases, the host government would be likely to have several potential company partners to choose from, placing it in a position to reject "difficult" conditions, such as cooperation with the IMF and World Bank. Nevertheless, Chad offers an important test case and learning experience, on which resource revenue management assistance programs with other governments might be built.

Notes

1. Interviews conducted with various oil companies on behalf of Econ by John Bray of Control Risks Group, October 2002.

2. The Publish What You Pay campaign website notes that recent governance problems related to resource revenue have been cited in Algeria, Angola, Azerbaijan, Cambodia, Chad, Republic of Congo, Democratic Republic of Congo, Equatorial Guinea, Gabon, Kazakhstan, Myanmar, Nigeria, Sudan, and Venezuela; see www.publishwhatyoupay.org/faq.shtml. On the Kazakhstan public expenditures review, see World Bank (2000b); on the pipeline project, see World Bank (1999, 2002).

3. The OECD notes that BP "had to work around the nondisclosure agreements they had signed with the Angolan government" (OECD 2002b, p. 21). According to Publish What You Pay, BP's announcement "brought threats of concession termination from the Angolan oil company Sonangol."

4. See Transparency International, the on-line research and information system on corruption: www.transparency.org/coris/.

5. See, for example, Barrows (various years); Institute for Global Resources Policy and Management (1997); Johnston (1994); Otto (1995).

6. See www.mrm.mms.gov.

7. See www.companies-house.gov.uk/. A list of links to other registers is available at ws6.companies-house.gov.uk/ias/world_sites_-_english.html.

8. See the Publish What You Pay campaign website: www.publishwhatyoupay.org/faq.shtml.

9. See the International Budget Project website: www.internationalbudget.org/.

10. The amount offered by the fund to those interested in reforestation was set too low to make it worthwhile to claim, so that, in principle, the funds could be used for other purposes.

11. For example, see Ross (2002).

12. For example, the World Bank's Economics of Civil Wars, Crime, and Violence Project (www.worldbank.org/research/conflict), Fafo Institute's Economies of Conflict Project (Swanson 2002), the London School of Economics' Oil and Conflict Project (www.lse.ac.uk/Depts/global/OtherProjects.htm), and the International Peace Academy's Economic Agendas in Civil Wars Project (Ross 2002).

13. More initiatives may deserve scrutiny in further stages of this project, including the International Organization of Supreme Audit Institutions (INTOSAI), currently hosted by Norway. INTOSAI is involved in capacity-building programs that support improvements in public sector financial surveillance across a wide range of developing countries. A present constraint similar to those pertaining to the World Bank's public expenditure reviews is that INTOSAI activities, reflecting supreme audit institutions, mainly target the expenditure side of domestic financial governance.

14. Two other IMF initiatives have some relevance to natural resource flows. The Guidelines for Public Debt Management include guidelines on transparency and accountability; however, these are based largely on the financial transparency code and the monetary and financial policies code. The Financial Sector Assessment Program (FSAP) is a joint effort of the IMF and the World Bank introduced in 1999 to "increase effectiveness of efforts to promote the soundness of financial systems in member countries." The aim is to assess the strengths and vulnerabilities of a country's financial system. This includes determining how key sources of risk are being managed, ascertaining the sector's developmental and technical assistance needs, and helping to prioritize policy responses. A ROSC is a key component of the FSAP. See the FSAP website: www.imf.org/external/np/fsap/fsap.asp.

15. The OECD has produced a similar and complementary document, "OECD Best Practices for Budget Transparency," issued in May 2001 (OECD 2001a). According to the OECD, the document could serve as a reference for both OECD and non-OECD governments.

16. See www.imf.org/external/np/fad/trans/index.htm.

17. Some ROSCs are published on the IMF's ROSC website: www.imf.org/external/np/rosc/rosc.asp.

18. See the ROSC website: www.imf.org/external/np/rosc/rosc.asp.

19. For East Asia FLEG, see lnweb18.worldbank.org/ESSD/essdext.nsf/14DocByUnid/962B305C44866A7985256BF700556307? Opendocument; For AFLEG, see lnweb18.worldbank.org/ESSD/essdext.nsf/14DocByUnid/56BBBD15FF947FE385256BF700553EF8?Opendocument.

20. See lnweb18.worldbank.org/ESSD/essdext.nsf/14DocByUnid/962B305C44866A7985256BF700556307?Opendocument.

21. The advisory group held its first meeting in February 2002.

22. See www.eurasianet.org/policy_forum/abeinthehouse.shtml.

23. See www.eurasianet.org/policy_forum/abeinthehouse.shtml.

24. See the UN Global Compact website: www.unglobalcompact.org.

25. See www.unglobalcompact.org.

26. Notably the Office of the High Commissioner for Human Rights, the International Labour Organisation, the United Nations Environment Programme, the United Nations Development Programme, and the United Nations Fund for International Partnership.

27. See www.unglobalcompact.org.

28. See the Global Reporting Initiative (GRI) website: www.globalreporting. org.

29. See the GRI website on sector supplements: www.globalreporting.org/ GRIGuidelines/Sector/index.htm.

30. See also the website on the Mining, Minerals, and Sustainable Development initiative: www.globalreporting.org/GRIGuidelines/Sector/Mining/ index.htm.

31. See the website under the International Institute for Environment and Development: www.iied.org/mmsd/.

32. See the website on the Mining, Minerals, and Sustainable Development initiative: www.globalreporting.org/GRIGuidelines/Sector/Mining/index.htm.

33. See the website on the Mining, Minerals, and Sustainable Development initiative: www.globalreporting.org/GRIGuidelines/Sector/Mining/index.htm.

34. See www.gesi.org.

35. The Global Witness oil campaign includes the groundbreaking reports, *A Crude Awakening* and *All the Presidents' Men* (Global Witness 1999, 2002).

36. For information on the oil campaign, see www.globalwitness.org/ campaigns/oil/regulation.html.

37. See www.publishwhatyoupay.org/faq.shtml.

38. However, international company payments will not cover all resource-related revenues to host governments—for example, they will not cover income from joint ventures to state-owned oil companies of the host government.

39. Econ did not have the opportunity to review the documents but received a briefing on their contents from the Accountant General (telephone conversation with Mr. Namogang, October 3, 2002).

40. There is one main mining company in Botswana: Debswana, a 50-50 joint venture set up in 1975 between De Beers and the Botswana government.

41. See the website of Caspian Revenue Watch, under Eurasia Policy Forum of the Central Eurasia Project, Open Society Institute: www.eurasianet.org/ policy_forum/abeinthehouse.shtml.

42. Available at www.minfin-az.com.

43. See www.worldbank.org/afr/ccproj/project/pro_document.htm.

References

The word "processed" describes informally produced works that may not be commonly available through libraries.

Ascher, William. 1999. *Why Governments Waste Natural Resources: Policy Failures in Developing Countries.* Baltimore, Md.: Johns Hopkins University Press.

Barrows. Various years. *World Petroleum Arrangements.* New York.

Botswana Ministry of Finance. n.d. *Financial Instructions and Procedures.* 2 vols. Gaborone: Government Printing Office.

Chad. 1999. "Chad's Law No. 001/PR/99, Governing the Management of Oil Revenues." Available at www.essochad.com/eaff/essochad/documentation/documentation_frame2.html. Processed.

Davis, Jeffrey, Rolando Ossowski, James Daniel, and Steven Barnett. 2001a. "Oil Funds: Problems Posing as Solutions?" *Finance and Development* 38(4, December). Available at www.imf.org/external/pubs/ft/fandd/2001/12/davis.htm.

———. 2001b. *Stabilization and Savings Funds for Nonrenewable Resources: Experience and Fiscal Policy Implications.* Occasional Paper 205. Washington, D.C.: International Monetary Fund, April. Available at www.imf.org/external/pubs/nft/op/205/.

Fasano, Ugo. 2000. "Review of the Experience with Oil Stabilization and Savings Funds in Selected Countries." IMF Working Paper WP/00/112. International Monetary Fund, Washington, D.C., June. Processed.

FLEG (Forest Law Enforcement and Governance). 2001. "Ministerial Declaration." Forest Law Enforcement and Governance East Asia ministerial conference, Bali, Indonesia, September 11–13. Available at lnweb18.worldbank.org/eap/eap.nsf/Attachments/FLEG_S9-2/$File/9+2+Ministerial+Declaration+-+FLEG.pdf. Processed.

Fölscher, Alta. 2001. *Budget Transparency and Participation: Five African Case Studies.* Cape Town: International Budget, Idasa Africa Budget Project. Available at www.internationalbudget.org/resources/africalaunch.htm.

Fölscher, Alta, Warren Krafchik, and Isaac Shapiro. 2000. *Transparency and Participation in the Budget Process. South Africa: A Country Report.* Washington, D.C.: International Budget.

Global Reporting Initiative. 2002. "GRI Sustainability Reporting Guidelines." Available at www.globalreporting.org/GRIGuidelines/2002/gri_2002_guidelines.pdf. Processed.

Global Witness. 1999. *A Crude Awakening.* London.

———. 2002. *All the Presidents' Men: The Devastating Story of Oil and Banking in Angola's Privatised War.* London. Available at www.globalwitness.org/campaigns/oil/index.html.

Hayes, Karen T. 2002. *Coltan Mining in the Democratic Republic of Congo: The Implications and Opportunities for the Telecommunications Industry.* Cambridge, U.K.: Fauna and Flora International.

IMF (International Monetary Fund). 1997. *Angola—Recent Economic Developments.* IMF Staff Country Report 99/112. Washington, D.C. Available at www.imf.org/external/pubs/ft/scr/1997/cr97112.pdf.

———. 2000. "Report on the Observance of Standards and Codes (ROSC), Azerbaijan Republic." Prepared by the Fiscal Affairs Department, Washington, D.C., November 13. Processed.

————. 2001a. "Assessing the Implementation of Standards: A Review of Experience and Next Steps." IMF Public Information Notice (PIN) 01/17. Washington, D.C., March 5. Available at www.imf.org/external/np/sec/pn/2001/pn0117.htm. Processed.

————. 2001b. *Government Finance Statistics Manual.* Washington, D.C., December 19. Available at www.imf.org/external/pubs/ft/gfs/manual/index.htm.

————. 2001c. *Manual on Fiscal Transparency.* Washington, D.C., March 23. Available at www.imf.org/external/np/fad/trans/manual/intro.htm#P20_3386.

————. 2002. *Quarterly Report on the Assessments of Standards and Codes.* Washington, D.C.: Policy Development and Review Department, June. Available at www.imf.org/external/pubs/ft/stand/q/2002/eng/062102.htm.

"IMF: Angola's 'Missing Millions.'" 2002. *BBC,* October 18. Available at news.bbc.co.uk/1/hi/world/africa/2338669.stm.

Institute for Global Resources Policy and Management. 1997. *Global Mining Taxation Comparative Study.* Golden, Colo.: Colorado School of Mines, Institute for Global Resources Policy and Management.

Johnston, Daniel. 1994. *International Petroleum Fiscal Systems and Production Sharing Contracts.* Tulsa, Okla.: PennWell Books.

Karl, Terry Lynn. 1997. *The Paradox of Plenty: Oil Booms and Petro-States.* Berkeley: University of California Press.

Mack, Andrew. 2002. *The Private Sector and Conflict.* New York: UN Global Compact. Available at 65.214.34.30/un/gc/unweb.nsf/content/privateSector.htm [downloaded October 2002].

MMSD (Mining, Minerals, and Sustainable Development). 2001. "Meeting Report on Corruption Issues in the Mining and Minerals Sector." Berlin: International Institute for Environmental Development, September 7. Available at www.iied.org/mmsd/mmsd_pdfs/corruption_issues_report.pdf. Processed.

————. 2002. *Breaking New Ground: The Mining, Minerals, and Sustainable Development Final Report.* Berlin, May.

OECD (Organisation for Economic Co-operation and Development). 2000. *The OECD Guidelines for Multinational Enterprise.* Revision 2000. Paris.

————. 2001a. *Best Practices for Budget Transparency.* PUMA/SBO(2000)6/FINAL. Paris: Public Management Service, Public Management Committee, May 15.

————. 2001b. "Summary Report of the Roundtable Discussion." OECD Roundtable on Global Instruments for Corporate Responsibility, Paris, June 19. Processed.

————. 2002a. *Moving toward Healthier Governance in Host Countries: The Contribution of Extractive Industries.* Paris: OECD Directorate for

Financial, Fiscal, and Enterprise Affairs. Available at www.oecd.org/pdf/
M00026000/M00026525.pdf.

———. 2002b. "Multilateral Enterprises in Situations of Violent Conflict and
Widespread Human Rights Abuses." Working Paper on International Invest-
ment 2002/1. OECD Directorate for Financial, Fiscal, and Enterprise Affairs,
Paris, May. Available at www.oecd.org/pdf/M00030000/M00030496.pdf.
Processed.

Otto, James, ed. 1995. *The Taxation of Mineral Enterprises*. Boston, Mass.:
Graham and Trotman/M. Nijhoff.

Petersen, Christian, and Nina Budina. 2002. "Governance Framework of Oil
Funds in Azerbaijan and Kazakhstan." Presentation to the workshop on petroleum revenue management, World Bank, Washington, D.C., October
23–24. Processed.

Petrie, Murray. 1999. "The IMF Fiscal Transparency Code: A Potentially
Powerful New Anti-Corruption Tool." Paper presented at the ninth International Anti-corruption Conference, Durban, October. Processed.

Ross, Michael L. 2001. *Timber Booms and Institutional Breakdown in Southeast Asia*. Cambridge, U.K.: Cambridge University Press.

———. 2002. *Oil, Drugs, and Diamonds: How Do Natural Resources Vary
in Their Impact on Civil War?* New York, N.Y.: International Peace
Academy, Project on Economic Agendas in Civil Wars, June 5.

Swanson, Philip. 2002. "Fuelling Conflict: The Oil Industry and Armed
Conflict." Paper prepared for the project Economies of Conflict: Private
Sector Activity in Armed Conflict, Fafo Institute, Programme for Interna-
tional Co-operation and Conflict Resolution, Oslo, Norway. Processed.

Talisman Energy. 2002. Presentation to the workshop on petroleum revenue
management, Washington, D.C., October. Processed.

Tsalik, Svetlana. 2003. *Caspian Oil Windfalls: Who Will Benefit?* Forthcoming report. New York: Caspian Revenue Watch, Open Society Institute.

U.K. National Audit Office. 2000. *Inland Revenue: Petroleum Revenue Tax:
Report by the Comptroller and Auditor General*. London: Stationary
Office. Available at www.nao.gov.uk/publications/nao_reports/00-01/
00015.pdf.

United Nations. 2001. *Report of the Panel of Experts on the Illegal Exploitation of Natural Resources and Other Forms of Wealth of the Democratic
Republic of Congo*. 12.04.2001. New York.

———. 2002. *Final Report of the Panel of Experts on the Illegal Exploitation
of Natural Resources and Other Forms of Wealth of the Democratic
Republic of Congo*. 15.10.2002. New York.

UN Global Compact. 2002a. "Recommendations of Transparency Working
Group to Address Problems in Zones of Conflict. Global Compact Policy
Dialogue." New York. Available at www.unglobalcompact.org (down-
loaded October 2002). Processed.

————. 2002b. *Report on Progress and Activities.* New York, July.

Wakeman-Linn, John, Paul Mathieu, and Bert van Selm. 2002. "Azerbaijan and Kazakhstan: Oil Funds in Transition Economies: Revenue Management." Paper presented to the workshop on petroleum revenue management, World Bank, October 23–24. Processed.

World Bank. 1999. "Chad: Management of the Petroleum Economy Project." Project Appraisal Document Report 19427-CD. Washington, D.C., December 29. Available at www.worldbank.org/afr/ccproj/project/tdpadmpe.pdf. Processed.

————. 2000a. "Indonesia Oil and Gas Sector Study." Report 20512-IND. World Bank, Energy and Mining Sector Unit, East Asia and Pacific Region, Washington, D.C., June. Available at www-wds.worldbank.org/servlet/WDSContentServer/WDSP/IB/2000/08/14/000094946_00072405363422/Rendered/PDF/multi_page.pdf. Processed.

————. 2000b. "Kazakhstan Public Expenditure Review." Report 20489-KZ. Washington, D.C., June 27. Processed.

————. 2002. "The Chad-Cameroon Petroleum Development and Pipeline Project." World Bank Group, Washington, D.C. Available at www.worldbank.org/afr/ccproj/project/pro_document.htm. Processed.

CHAPTER 4

Where Did It Come From?
Commodity Tracking Systems

Corene Crossin, Gavin Hayman, and Simon Taylor

THIS CHAPTER PROVIDES A BASIC UNDERSTANDING of the main elements of a generic commodity control system. It also seeks to compare and contrast the key features of existing international commodity-specific tracking regimes (CTRs) to allow for more effective controls in the future. The specific international CTRs examined cover diverse areas of regulation of trade in endangered and threatened species; governance of renewable resources like timber and fish; control of environmentally damaging chemicals, including hazardous chemicals, persistent organic pollutants, pesticides, and ozone-depleting substances; security-related commodities such as small arms and light weapons, diamonds, and radioactive material; consumable commodities regulated for health reasons, including meat and genetically modified organisms; and "ethical" sector products, including products manufactured in accordance with international labor laws preventing the use of prison labor and so forth. Although most of these commodities are not generally associated with conflict or poor governance, the development of CTRs provides useful lessons that can be applied in addressing the link between natural resources and civil wars.

There is no one-size-fits-all specification for a successful commodity control regime—details will vary depending on the nature of the commodity and the nature and status of the international legal instruments used to impose controls. Nevertheless, there are common elements in successful control regimes, such as transparency, accountability, and coordinated and timely flow through well-designed, shared formats.

There are also clear contextual issues to be taken into account when designing any commodity tracking system, such as how the agreed controls interact with multilateral trade agreements under the World Trade Organization (WTO).

Table 4.1 sets out the major international agreements imposing commodity control regimes and their associated administrative bodies. Drawing lessons from these regimes, we propose five basic elements of a sound generic tracking system alongside five contextual considerations.

The five necessary elements are common definitions and reporting requirements, efficient reporting structure and effective information exchange, commodity labeling and audited chain-of-custody arrangements, effective compliance and enforcement measures, and capacity building. The following list details each.

- *Common definitions and reporting requirements:* (a) Agreement on common definitions, standards, and reporting requirements is essential for coordinated action. (b) Clear goals and targets for regulation must be identified. (c) Involvement of national, international, and interregional stakeholders, including the private sector, civil society, and relevant nongovernmental organizations, is necessary to promote the legitimacy of control measures. (d) Agreement should be international in scope and intent; that said, national and regional measures might be a good stepping-stone to wider international cooperation.

- *Efficient reporting structure and effective information exchange:* (a) Coordinated information exchange, such as harmonized and accessible databases and intelligence-sharing agreements, must exist. (b) Data sharing should be facilitated by cooperative arrangements with relevant national and international parties and international standards bodies. (c) Clear national and international management structures are needed to ensure that everybody knows what they should be doing. (d) Clear national contact points should also exist so that everyone can check that everybody else knows what they are doing.

- *Commodity labeling and audited chain-of-custody arrangements:* (a) Chain-of-custody and labeling arrangements are the core of any tracking regime. Commodities must be accompanied by information that allows them to be clearly distinguished and identified in the international marketplace. (b) Labeling requirements, if not strictly executed, simply serve to launder illicit material; credible audit procedures or third-party certification provide confidence that only compliant products gain access to restricted markets and that internal procedures can be trusted.

Table 4.1 Major Commodity Tracking Regimes

Commodity	Major tracking regime regulations	Governing institution(s)
Diamonds (rough)	Kimberley Certification Process Scheme	Kimberley process secretariat, with voluntary chain of warrantees by the World Diamond Council
Endangered species	1973 UN Convention on International Trade in Endangered Species of Fauna and Flora (CITES)	CITES secretariat, with trade monitoring assistance from the World Conservation Monitoring Centre
Fish	Numerous regional management agreements including the 1980 Convention on the Conservation of Antarctic Marine Living Resources (CCAMLR)	Specific fisheries commissions govern regional management. The Marine Stewardship Council runs an independent certification system to promote sustainable fisheries. The Food and Agriculture Organization has negotiated several codes of conduct, including the 2001 International Plan of Action to Prevent, Deter, and Eliminate Illegal, Unreported, and Unregulated Fishing
Genetically modified organisms	2000 Cartagena Protocol on Biosafety to the 1993 Convention on Biological Diversity, supplemented by the European Community Regulation 258/97 (Regulation of Novel Foods and Novel Food Agreements, 2001/18/EC)	Convention on Biological Diversity secretariat
Hazardous waste	1989 Basel Convention on the Control of Transboundary Movements of Hazardous Waste and Their Disposal	Basel convention secretariat

(Table continues on the following page.)

Table 4.1 (continued)

Commodity	Major tracking regime regulations	Governing institution(s)
Hazardous chemicals	1998 Rotterdam Convention on the Prior Informed Consent Procedures for Certain Hazardous Chemicals and Pesticides in International Trade	Rotterdam convention secretariat (although agreement not yet in force)
Livestock (meat)	Various regional agreements, most notably the EC Regulation 820/97 establishing a system for registering bovine animals and labeling meat products	Specific information-gathering bodies like the European Commission Animal Movement System
Ozone-depleting substances	1987 Montreal Protocol on Substances That Deplete the Ozone Layer to the 1985 Vienna Convention for the Protection of the Ozone Layer	Montreal protocol secretariat
Persistent organic pollutants	2001 Stockholm Convention on Persistent Organic Pollutants	Stockholm convention secretariat (although agreement not yet in force)
Small arms and light weapons	Various regional agreements and a forthcoming UN Firearms Protocol	No central international body to monitor flows in small arms and light weapons
Timber	No international convention establishing a global tracking system for timber, although CITES covers the products of a limited number of threatened tree species. A first attempt at tracking shipments between producer and consumer countries has been negotiated between the United Kingdom and Indonesia.	The Food and Agriculture Organization, the UN Forum on Forests, and the International Tropical Timber Organization all publish statistics on various aspects of the timber business, and numerous independent certification bodies exist, most importantly the Forest Stewardship Council

Note: This table does not include other stakeholder institutions such as national enforcement bodies, civil society organizations, nongovernmental organizations, and international organizations relevant to the operation of many tracking systems, such as the World Customs Organization.

- *Effective compliance and enforcement measures:*[1] (a) Clear compliance measures at the international level, such as conditional market access and trade measures, are necessary to eliminate free-riding states. (b) Dispute resolution procedures are needed to prevent unilateral actions. (c) Appropriate enforcement measures at the national level are necessary to deter evasion of national controls that implement the CTR. (d) Ideally, a CTR should generate incentives to comply and incentives for industry to monitor its own behavior, especially through conditional market access.
- *Capacity building:* (a) Any effective scheme should acknowledge differences in ability to comply with and enforce provisions, equity issues in compliance, and ability to take steps to build the capacity of national authorities, especially given the idea of shared but differentiated responsibility of producer and consumer states. (b) Conditionality on development assistance can be used as a lever to improve compliance, especially where noncompliance jeopardizes economic stability and poverty reduction targets.

In addition, there are five contextual considerations: detailed understanding of the commodity chain, dynamics of market supply, dynamics of demand, political and institutional context, and harmonization with existing international law. The following list details each in turn.

- *Detailed understanding of the commodity chain:* (a) Control systems should be tailored to the specific way in which a commodity is accessed, processed, transported, and sold. (b) Enforcement and compliance processes need to understand the complex relationship between licit and illicit markets and between suppliers of raw material and producers of final products as well as the role of ancillary specialist services.
- *Dynamics of market supply:* (a) Information such as property and access rights in producer countries is an important element of market supply. (b) The economics of legitimate and illegitimate access, including harvesting and capital costs, is another.
- *Dynamics of demand:* (a) Demand is related to the nature of the consumer market, including the degree of fragmentation of end users and the elasticity of demand for specific final products. (b) Public education has a role in promoting appropriate consumption policies.
- *Political and institutional context:* (a) Understanding is needed of the political, economic, and social circumstances of producing, processing, and consuming countries. (b) It is important to avoid bureaucratic satisficing (that is, the tendency of all institutions to meet their own immediate needs while failing to address the forces creating problems).

- *Harmonization with existing international law:* (a) Are new control systems compatible with existing control regimes? (b) Are they compliant with the WTO? If not, is a challenge likely?

If political will exists, it is perfectly possible to establish a successful CTR based on these elements subject to contextual considerations. The 10 elements can also provide a basic framework for building new CTRs. The paper begins by examining the five basic elements of a good generic tracking system by drawing on the experiences of the control regimes listed in table 4.1. It then broadens the perspective to examine the five wider contextual matters to be considered in the design or reform of any given CTR. A set of conclusions is presented to facilitate further discussion.

Comparison of the Five Necessary Elements with Existing CTRs

This section describes our five essential elements of an effective CTR and compares and contrasts the operational lessons from existing control regimes.

Element 1: Common Definitions and Reporting Requirements

As the majority of tracking systems need to follow transboundary commodity flows, it is preferable that a commodity agreement be established on an international level. Although this seems obvious, there are clear examples where commodity tracking efforts have been hamstrung by lack of effective coverage. For example, the Montreal Protocol on Substances That Deplete the Ozone Layer only instituted a global requirement for licensing of trade in ozone-damaging substances some 10 years after the protocol was originally negotiated. This allowed "virgin" ozone-depleting substances to be easily passed off as recycled material (which was not controlled by the protocol) because it was impossible for an importer to check the provenance of specific shipments with an exporter.

The absence of agreed international controls on forestry means that national controls are not reciprocated or respected by trading partners. Hence, once illegal timber has left a producer country, it will not be detected or sanctioned elsewhere. As a result, although rough estimates suggest that about 60–70 percent of the tropical timber imported into the European Union (EU) may be sourced illegally, the member states do not assist exporter countries by impounding shipments or even questioning their origin (European Union 2001).

Likewise, there is no coherent international tracking system to trace flows of either small arms and light weapons or radioactive material. Instead, those jurisdictions attempting to trace the movement of either commodity must adopt time-consuming and cumbersome methods to request information from a range of agencies, departments, and manufacturers within individual states along suspected supply routes. Although this is feasible, but highly inefficient, for the most important radioactive materials, it is less viable for the radioactive materials used in medicine or for small arms. Such systems are also porous because a lack of clearly defined responsibilities makes accountability difficult.

Some CTRs, like the Basel Convention on Transboundary Shipments of Hazardous Waste, have failed to specify clear definitions of the fundamental concepts on which CTRs are to be based. The Basel convention does not define "hazardous waste" but, rather, creates a mechanism to determine when a given waste can be considered hazardous.[2] In this regard, the convention is very much the product of the circumstances surrounding its negotiation in the 1980s[3] and of the innately diffuse nature of waste generation. According to this approach, a waste is hazardous if it is generated by certain processes or contains certain constituents (specified in Annex I of the convention) or if it possesses certain characteristics, such as being explosive. This deliberate avoidance of an explicit definition was intended to provide a degree of flexibility within the convention but confounds effective implementation, as different national interpretations reflect different environmental and economic priorities. For example, what may be considered hazardous in terms of domestic disposal may not be treated so for export. One company's waste stream may be another's recycling opportunity. Thus it is easy to describe highly toxic waste streams mistakenly as raw materials, resources for recycling, or bogus commercial products like fertilizer (see, for example, Wang 1996, p. 679). Definitional problems are amplified where no predefined category of commodities exists, as with attempts to distinguish between products produced by forced labor, including child labor, and goods produced through legal labor practices.

It is also necessary to have clear definitions of when products opt out of a tracking system. For example, attempts to control the ivory trade in the 1980s under the Ivory Export Quota System under the UN Convention on International Trade in Endangered Species of Fauna and Flora (CITES) were a disaster, not least because minimally modified or slightly carved raw ivory was exempt from the quota system.

Thus poached ivory was crudely carved or modified to avoid trade restrictions. Similarly, disagreement exists on the exact meaning of small arms—a major reason why there is still no international convention controlling supply and trade. The Kimberley process covers "rough diamonds" but does not specify when such commodities become finished diamonds and are no longer tracked.

If a lack of consensus prevents international agreement, then multilateral or regional arrangements provide a useful interim opportunity for partners to cooperate. This may include agreements on collaboration between customs officials, law enforcement agencies, export and import regulations, recognized and verifiable certification and chain-of-supply documentation, information sharing, and capacity building (especially in the case of developing countries). For example, the April 2002 memorandum of understanding signed between the Indonesian and United Kingdom governments on forest law enforcement cooperation provides for a test case on cooperation between a major producer and consumer of tropical timber on comparing import and export data. The memorandum also allows for focused technical assistance and capacity building for the government to gather trade statistics and oversee export licensing. Similarly, there are several regional agreements on the control of small arms and light weapons whose measures could be merged to create a more comprehensive global tracking system.

As with small arms and light weapons, regional agreements may be a good interim solution for illegal logging. A crucial first step would be to undertake bilateral cooperation between producer and consumer countries to enforce domestic legislation in both. If not in existence, legislation should be passed in producing countries to outlaw illegal logging. Consumer countries should recognize this legislation, and a bilateral agreement between the two countries should ban the trade in illegal timber. These bilateral agreements would form a body of international law that, in turn, could form the basis of a future multilateral international agreement.

Element 2: Efficient Reporting Structure and Effective Information Exchange

Unless partners efficiently and accurately report key information and share intelligence in a way that facilitates enforcement, commodity tracking becomes an exercise in moving paper. Clear international and national management structures and contact points are needed, as well as coordinated facilities for information exchange and cooperation, such as accessible databases and intelligence-sharing agreements.

The trade controls imposed by an Appendix II listing under the CITES—one of the first CTRs proposed by the international community—provide a good example of an inefficient structure. Appendix II procedures cover species that are not necessarily threatened with extinction now but may become so unless trade in them is subject to strict regulation. Range-states of that species must issue an export permit based on a nondetriment finding that importers are obliged to accept. Given the minimal information on the status of species within most developing countries, such permits are issued freely with minimal due diligence, and consuming countries have no reason to refuse such imports. Also, once issued, licenses are not rechecked with exporters and are easily modified to incorporate new items. Thus, despite moving around lots of papers and occupying lots of bureaucratic time, trade in most species under CITES has been relatively unrestricted, with range-states left operating national controls independently of one another, without any international assistance or expert oversight.[4] These problems have gradually been addressed by various oversight mechanisms, discussed under element 4.

National institutions may be similarly dysfunctional and work at odds with each other. One example is the way in which the Indonesian Ministry of Industry and Trade issues timber-processing licenses without consulting the Ministry of Environment, which issues the permits for cutting. As a result, processing capacity in the country is almost twice the legal annual allowable cut.

Administrative functions need not be centralized in one body (indeed, national governments are always wary of creating creatures they cannot control), but there have to be clear reporting responsibilities within any jurisdiction in which relevant information may reside. For example, it is unclear whether the Kimberley process' lack of a dedicated secretariat will be compensated for by clear national harmonization and data exchange structures to allow cross-checking and verification of shipments. It has been left entirely up to national participants to develop mechanisms to ensure that all diamond buyers, sellers, and exporters keep accurate records of the names of buying or selling clients and what diamonds are bought and sold in their jurisdiction (appendix 4.1). Information is made available to an "intergovernmental body or other appropriate mechanism" only on a quarterly basis for imports and exports and on a semiannual basis for production. A question mark therefore exists over whether the information that is collected will be actionable. The current EU initiative to track the movement of livestock suffers similar problems, with a lack of coherence between national standards and the bookkeeping systems of individual member states.

CTRs should also gather sufficient data to allow distinctions between products and include comprehensive review procedures to provide feedback to policymakers on compliance with, and the impact of, international controls. In addition to material directly relevant to the type, origin, and destination of specific shipments, data on prices, volume, and values of licit and illicit markets, gaps in commodity data between trading partners, stockpiling of data, registration details and capacities of processing and treatment centers, national implementation, policing efforts, and offenses detected should be recorded. No CTR currently comes close to such standards, although CITES reporting is perhaps the most comprehensive after a series of reforms designed to address previously poor implementation.

The Basel convention shows a particularly moribund standard of reporting, due to the absence of a definition of hazardousness and few guidelines on what should be included in national reports. Thus, although its secretariat collects information, the data submitted by national authorities cover widely disparate types of waste, collected over different time periods, and using divergent nomenclature. Data for 1997 show a 10–15 percent difference between total quantities of waste reported as exported and those reported as imported (Basel Secretariat 1999). Recorded imports from countries in the Organisation for Economic Co-operation and Development (OECD) to other countries are, at least, 10 times higher than recorded exports from OECD countries, raising a substantial question about the integrity of data. Details of how and where such wastes are to be treated were absent in 45–60 percent of the cases—despite the convention's prior-informed-consent procedure for handling waste. Similarly, among non-OECD countries, those importing waste reported a volume of trade twice as large as exporting countries. In these cases, 70–85 percent of reports failed to specify how these imports were handled.

Similarly, data on the international timber trade preclude the rational assessment of threat and the identification of illegal trade (see appendix 4.2). As the International Tropical Timber Organization notes, "Production statistics . . . are often weak or nonexistent. The primary problem in many producer countries is the lack of a comprehensive forest out-turn measurement system as well as any kind of regular industrial survey to obtain production figures" (ITTO 1999). Consumer countries are usually unable to distinguish the processing of types of timber: "Many make errors or omissions in providing trade data . . . [and] also have serious problems in their customs statistics" (ITTO 1999). No facility exists for producer countries to request information on the volume of imported material being declared to a consumer country's authorities for taxation purposes; moreover, if illegal exports are detected, they cannot be sanctioned in consumer countries.

There is no quick fix to bring together disparate reporting regimes, scattered information, and dysfunctional institutions, apart from reverse-engineering existing agreements. A process of incremental reform is required that involves all stakeholders at every level, interagency cooperation, and the establishment of clear operational guidelines on the form and content of required information through convention secretariats. Guidelines must set achievable deadlines and specify the minimum degree of detail and format of reports. Ideally, submission of regular reports should be mandatory, with penalties for noncompliance. Guidelines must also be flexible, since reporting will work best when it is part of existing national economic and social accounting processes.

Memoranda of understanding between the World Customs Organization and the secretariats of the Basel convention and CITES and between Interpol and the secretariats of the Basel convention and CITES have recently been signed to improve coordination between relevant intergovernmental bodies.[5] Similarly, in developing EU initiatives to track the flow of genetically modified organisms, there has been discussion of linking unique identifiers to facilitate the search for information through the Montreal protocol's Biosafety Clearing House and the OECD's BioTrack System.

Revisiting the CITES Appendix II example, a number of reforms have improved coordination and oversight outside the mechanisms originally enshrined in the treaty. The significant trade imposed under a revision to Article 4 of the convention has partially addressed the coordination of range-state permits by providing expert advice on species status through its periodic review of heavily traded species. The process then enlists consumer states in observing global trade quotas, which also relieve range-states of the burden of making nondetriment findings on a case-by-case basis. The 1992 U.S. Exotic Wild Bird Conservation Act introduced the concept of "reverse listing," meaning that a species is protected unless it can be proved that trade will neither deplete the species nor harm the welfare of individuals in trade. The EU's new wildlife control legislation system has altered the standard operating procedures of the convention to require an import quota for any shipment of Appendix II species into Europe, thus requiring harder evidence that an export will not harm the population of the species in question.

Harmonized Reporting. As the number of commodity tracking systems has multiplied, the amount of reports and information required has grown dramatically. This has placed a particular burden on developing countries with limited funds and capacity to complete reports.

In early 2001 the Environmental Management Group of the United Nations Environment Programme (UNEP) agreed to establish a subgroup dealing with the harmonization of information and reporting among the commodity control regimes instituted by its numerous multilateral environmental agreements.[6] In particular, the Subgroup on the Harmonization of National Reporting was concerned with examining ways of realizing the full value of data gathered by overcoming problems of limited access and a lack of comparability of information. The benefits of streamlining CTRs were suggested to include the following:

• Provision of more accurate and detailed information needed to determine the volume, severity, and nature of illegal trade
• Reduced duplication of efforts between organizations and member states
• Assistance to other parties to implement provisions by giving details on lessons learned, case studies, and experiences
• Improved efficiency in the use of information technology and communications
• Improved cooperation and analytical capacity
• Increased ability to use and develop clearinghouse mechanisms to trace commodity flows.

UNEP ran four national pilot projects to test different methods and develop guidelines for harmonized reporting. The results of the pilot scheme were presented at the Earth Summit in Johannesburg in 2002. At the time of writing, no follow-up harmonization initiatives have been announced for multilateral environmental agreements on biodiversity.

Information overload is compounded by overlapping reporting requirements under different, but related, international agreements. For example, there are parallels between CITES, the Convention on Migratory Species, the Convention on Wetlands, and the Convention on Biodiversity. There are also evident similarities between provisions under the Basel Convention on Hazardous Wastes and the Stockholm Convention on Persistent Organic Pollutants. Many countries— developed and developing—have expressed concerns over the burden of gathering and reporting information. It is widely acknowledged that improving the cooperation between secretariats and setting common standards for gathering and reporting information are fundamental to the effectiveness of commodity tracking systems.[7]

The Food and Agriculture Organization (FAO) of the United Nations, the UN Economic Commission for Europe, the European Union, and the International Tropical Timber Federation have begun to streamline international reporting procedures, submitting joint questionnaires to national forest administrations in April-May 1999. The effort saved by eliminating duplicate reporting practices is to be put into gathering international data on price, industry structure, secondary-processed products, and undocumented production and trade.

A further initiative that may strengthen biodiversity-related commodity tracking schemes is the Global Biodiversity Information Facility (GBIF), an intergovernmental body created with the aim of increasing access to global biodiversity information. The GBIF will create an Internet-based catalogue of species and harmonize databases and search engines. The diagram in figure 4.1 illustrates how harmonized information and reporting and linked inter-regime databases (such as that to be created by the GBIF) may facilitate efficient commodity tracking.[8]

Pilot programs would be an excellent method of testing the feasibility of procedures to streamline information. Lessons from pilot schemes, such as under the recent Stockholm convention, provide clear signposts

Figure 4.1 Measures to Build Bridges between Related Tracking Systems

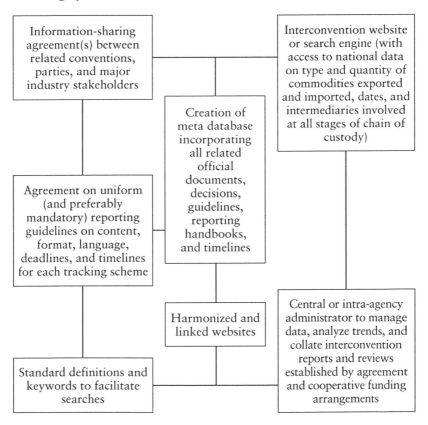

Source: Authors.

to how broader schemes should operate and indicate how and where national capacity building should take place (element 5).

Customs Codes. Improved coordination between trade tracking systems may also involve expansion of the World Customs Organization's Harmonized System of Customs Coding, which uses a six-digit number to identify traded goods. So far, the system has failed to keep up with an ever-expanding body of CTRs, as it is only revised and updated periodically (a complete revision takes about seven years). At present, the primary purpose of the harmonized system is to determine trade statistics—it is not designed to be a tracking device.

The statistical information that harmonized codes provide can assist in constructing patterns in the volume of goods exported, transported, and imported. When measured and analyzed against trading data supplied by national authorities and industry, anomalies and gaps can be identified that may indirectly indicate points of illicit commodity flows. The U.S. single product code for the Patagonian toothfish,[9] for example, has helped to distinguish between legitimate and illegitimate sources of a wide range of products made from the fish. Harmonized system codes are, however, easy to falsify, and it is possible to describe the same product in a number of different ways (for example, the ozone-damaging pesticide methyl bromide has at least four separate and equally convincing classifications), so cross-checking is necessary, and over-reliance on coding is best avoided.

Role of Information Technology. There is immense untapped potential for information technology to provide better-quality information for efficient commodity tracking. The analytical capacity of convention secretariats is hampered by a lack of software tools for modeling, time-series, and trend analysis and for Geographic Information Systems analysis. Greater investment in building technological capacity, as well as in harmonizing convention websites and databases, would provide a solid foundation for tracking commodities covered by more than one international or multilateral agreement.[10] As discussed below, technology may also improve the tracking of a commodity through various stages of production.

The analysis of trade records and the integration of data from different national and international authorities with "drill down" software that checks for irregularities and discrepancies should be central to any form of intelligence-led policing. Simple and cost-effective versions of such software need to be developed explicitly for developing countries. Internet access is often necessary for quick and regularized exchange of enforcement information, but many government departments in the developing world are not Internet enabled or restrict access to high-level officials who fail to transmit information down the line.

Extensive new technologies can make a big difference to national and international enforcement efforts. Compliance and inspection methodologies such as vessel monitoring systems, fine-scale satellite monitoring of forestry concessions, and forensic analysis of wildlife traffic have considerable potential to achieve economies of effort and lower monitoring costs. Despite this enormous potential, systems will be developed only if policy needs for their use are clearly identified. At present, technological developments precede policy rather than being driven by it, suggesting the need to promote directly the development of new enforcement methodologies and forensics.

Element 3: Commodity Labeling and Audited Chain-of-Custody Arrangements

Clearly, the core of any CTR is the ability to trace commodities and to distinguish approved materials for accounting and inventory control. Labels, certificates, or markings should supply important information about the origins of a commodity, how it has been produced, and who has been involved in the chain of supply. Chain-of-custody certification takes such labeling a step further by monitoring the commodity flow itself to ensure that commodities bearing a label have been produced from certified sources including monitoring at the point a raw product is extracted or mined, receipt at first measurement of the raw commodity, checks at delivery points, verification at each stage of processing or production, and tracking of movement through brokers, wholesale dealers, exporting and importing agents, and retailers. Procedures will inevitably differ depending on the commodity. Nevertheless, it is still possible to establish minimum requirements for chain of custody that may be used as a template for implementing chain-of-custody certification processes. Chain-of-custody certification may be built into commodity tracking systems that use product labels to differentiate products from verifiably legal or sustainably managed sources.

The reliability and integrity of any chain-of-custody system will depend on the transparent and independent auditing of procedures. Centralized and transparent monitoring is clearly essential; oversight should not be dispersed among various units, as separate audits of each link in the marketing chain create problems of varying methodology and investigative gaps. Similarly, it would be very difficult for consumer countries to cooperate with producers to check custody arrangements if information were not centralized.

Certification procedures also require an effective means of issuing and verifying the licenses or certificates, which implies separate systems for administration and monitoring. Such systems require significant investment in new monitoring capacity, as the commodity chain provided by articles like shipping waybills lacks adequate information. Such procedures may involve the use of tagging, bar coding, and transponder technologies and registers of approved traders and processing facilities. Currently, there are no generic "legality" certification tools for most CTRs, although some chain-of-custody standards such as an ISO 9000 mark exist. Thus, when Swedish flat-packed furniture giant IKEA wanted to make sure that all its timber was legally sourced, it had to develop its own system.

Such methods may imply significant reform of legal and administrative arrangements in the producer countries, possibly encouraged by donor pressure. Often matters relating to export controls are the responsibility of finance or trade ministries, whereas the monitoring of resource extraction falls under ministries of the environment or natural resources.

Consumers, retailers, and importers of the products need to be educated to look for and demand the license or certificate and to refuse products without certification. Central and local government procurement programs can also play an important role in leading these markets and rewarding compliance.

The Kimberley process has perhaps the most advanced regime in this regard. Its core provision for tracking rough diamonds is that individual shipments must be sealed in tamper-proof containers accompanied by an official certificate of origin. Certificates are forgery-resistant documents that identify a shipment of rough diamonds as being in compliance with the requirements of the certification scheme. Nevertheless, certain activities, described as "high risk" by diamond industry experts, such as the flow of diamonds from the mine to the first export point, are subject to recommended controls. Similarly, the scheme "encourages" participants to ensure that mining companies maintain effective security standards so that conflict diamonds do not contaminate legitimate production and "recommends" that a participant establish a license or registration scheme for all diamond buyers, sellers, exporters, agents, and courier companies. Figure 4.2 illustrates how these elements and considerations may be integrated into an effective certification-based CTR.

Both the timber and fisheries sectors lack systems that focus on the legality of material alone, but both sectors have market-driven labeling schemes, such as those of the Forest Stewardship Council (FSC) and the Marine Stewardship Council (MSC), identifying *sustainability*

Figure 4.2 Common Elements of Effective Certification
Tracking Systems

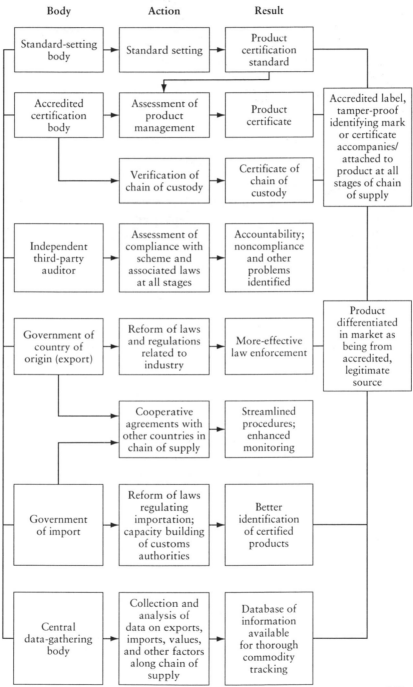

of production, which should imply legality as well. The main point of the system is that use of the MSC logo is permitted only where there has been independent verification that the product originated from an MSC-certified fishery. A chain-of-custody certificate provides this verification. The chain-of-custody certifier requests documentation relating to that supply chain and usually visits randomly one or more points in the supply chain to verify the product stream. A certifier must consider all parts of the supply chain (from fishing vessel to end consumer) when assessing the supply chain against the MSC standard. The costs of certification are agreed between the certifier and the client and depend on the size and complexity of the supply chain.

The importance of closely following a commodity through each stage is acknowledged in the timber certification system set up by the Forest Stewardship Council (FSC). Under the FSC scheme, labeled operations must have "forest management certification," which implies that harvesting activities are sustainable and legal, and "wood product certification," which demonstrates that independent chain-of-custody procedures have tracked the wood harvested in certified forests through all stages of their transport, processing, and marketing. FSC is the only international timber certification scheme to require such chain-of-custody certification explicitly. Figure 4.3 illustrates the main stages of production covered by the FSC scheme.

Swiss logistics company SGS is promoting the establishment of a system of independent validation of legal timber based on the concept of independent monitoring and verification of land-use changes, timber flows, and resource management. This could lead to sustainability certification like that of the FSC, but it does not have to and can be used simply to demonstrate that production is legal and licensed. Box 4.1 explains the main components of the system. Steps 1 and 2, which would be compulsory, provide the independent validation of legal timber, whereas step 3 is voluntary and would provide a certificate of sustainable forest management.

Labeling as Laundering. Trade-permitting systems themselves are prone to fraud and, if drafted without due care, may serve more as a laundering facility than as an effective check on contraband. Lack of political will, bureaucratic inertia, limited information, and corruption are common problems in many government departments; hence, without separate checks, there is the danger that any marking or labeling system will simply create a better and more effective method of laundering contraband.

CITES has perhaps the most complex administrative and permitting system of the various CTRs, and this has provided many opportunities to subvert and abuse agreed controls. Mismanagement of the

Figure 4.3 Forest Stewardship Council Chain-of-Custody
Certification

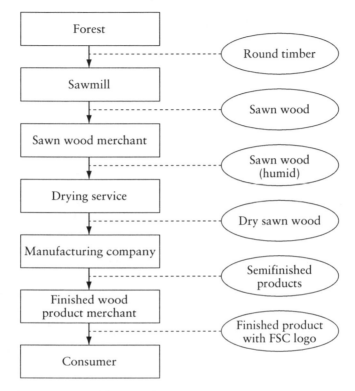

Note: FSC = Forest Stewardship Council.
Source: Authors.

permitting system has sanctioned activities that would not have been
allowed under a strict interpretation of the convention. As a result,
there may be little need to smuggle animals directly when permits can
be doctored or fraudulently declared to give shipments a false legitimacy. It is a simple matter, for example, to declare lesser-known endangered species improperly, especially if they have many look-alike
species or if illegally caught specimens can be labeled as "captive
bred." Smuggled animals or products can also be laundered as coming
from preconvention stockpiles or from noncontrolled populations.

   The notorious management quota system for African elephant
ivory in the 1980s serves as an example of how a system without independent checks on its integrity can facilitate illegal traffic. The combined effect of no controls over the volume of certificates issued and
the presence of large stockpiles of illegal material that could acquire
considerable additional value if they were certified led to a hopeless

Box 4.1   Independent Validation of Legal Timber

A stepwise, pragmatic approach is proposed to address the problems of illegal logging through the compulsory independent validation of legal timber, while providing a link or possibly integration with voluntary certification of sustainable forest management.

To illustrate this approach, a system of labeling sustainable timber is suggested in three steps: (a) timber from a legal origin, (b) validated legal timber, and (c) sustainably produced timber. Each step is conditional on a certificate issued independently by an accredited third-party verifier or certifier at different stages of the process.

The *certificate of legal origin* is the result of the successful verification— essentially through implementation of a log-tracking system—that the logs or timber products (a) were legally purchased from the rightful owner and have legally been sold and transferred down the chain of custody to the point of reference of the certificate and (b) conform to national or international product-specific regulations such as protected species or minimum diameters. The system would also periodically verify that duties have been paid and that allowed volumes of cut or quotas have been respected. Past, unsettled lack of compliance may block the whole process. In the suggested labeling system, compliant logs and timber products could be labeled as timber from a legal origin.

The *certificate of legal compliance* is awarded where forest management is found compliant with specified national legislation and regulations including the terms of the concession agreement or permit. This essentially refers to the preparation and implementation of the management and harvesting plans, including the forest inventories. Logs or timber products already certified as from a legal origin at this stage could be labeled as validated legal timber if the certificate of legal origin for the timber can be linked with a certificate of legal compliance for the forest yielding the timber.

The *certificate of sustainable forest management* refers to the certificate awarded or maintained as a result of successful auditing of forest management against the principles, criteria, and indicators of an international forest certification scheme such as that of the Forest Stewardship Council. It is suggested that logs or timber products already certified as being from a legal origin and originating from a forest certified both as legally compliant and, at this stage, sustainably managed could be labeled as sustainably produced timber. A certificate of chain of custody issued under the forest certification scheme would not be enough to replace a certificate of legal origin, whose scope is wider and which is based on advanced log-tracking systems.

Box 4.1 (continued)

Independent validation of legal timber covers the first and second steps—that is, verification of the legal origin of the timber and verification of the legal compliance of the timber source. From producer to consumer, the system of independent validation of legal timber has the potential to provide an effective tool to aid law enforcement by the government, a powerful market-based instrument both for producers (market access, fair competition) and for buyers (sound, transparent timber trade), and reliable information for all stakeholders, locally and internationally.

Source: See SGS proposal at www.sgs.com.

---

inflation of the system, with the end result that legal ivory trade amounted to under 20 percent of the total "legitimized" trade under the system (Barbier and others 1990).

To the extent that a tracking system relies on self-reporting as the principal means of monitoring, it will lack credibility with stakeholders and the public. Instead, it is preferable that regular independent third-party monitoring and auditing of systems should become an integral part of tracking systems to ensure that they are run according to their policy objectives. In the case of commodity tracking systems set up by industry and government partnerships (such as the Kimberley process), self-regulation should be avoided, as it lacks transparency. There is less temptation to turn a blind eye to violations when an independent party has the power to expose failings and gaps in a tracking system. For example, part of the FSC certification scheme's excellent reputation is due to the annual audits carried out by independent FSC-accredited bodies to assess observance of all stated principles and criteria of forest management.

A small degree of transparency and measures for independent monitoring were integrated into the Kimberley process after nongovernmental organizations strongly opposed self-regulation. The process now provides for a form of peer review in which a participant who considers another participant not to have adequate laws, regulations, rules, procedures, or practices to implement the scheme will inform that other participant through the office of the chair. However, such methods rely on one participant being sufficiently annoyed with another to call it publicly to account. Verification and review of complaints can take place only with their consent, and the membership and terms of reference of any agreed monitoring or verification mission are yet to be determined.

A lack of independent monitoring also undermines the effectiveness of the Basel convention. No impartial, independent mechanism yet exists for ensuring that consenting importing states have the capacity to dispose of waste in accordance with the convention. It is left to importing authorities to verify the adequacy of processing facilities.[11]

The presence of an external tracking organization can raise problems of national sovereignty and interference, and co-management of the process with the host country may sometimes be necessary. In Cameroon, a cooperative system operates where government enforcement and independent certifiers work in tandem. Another option is to develop a "super-agency" charged with specific responsibility for monitoring and certification and having a strong self-interest in ensuring that the system functions properly. However the auditing is carried out, an important point is that the entire procedure should be transparent.

Private companies such as SGS provide independent monitoring services, issuing documents allowing for the movement, sale, distribution, and export of forest products. This third-party service removes the certifiers of legal products from corrupting influences and precludes interference with the process from interministerial disputes or rivalries. If the third-party tracking organization discovers irregularities, it can then report them to government enforcement authorities for subsequent investigation. Separation of the law enforcement functions from the routine administration of forestry management is generally required for effective enforcement (element 4).

Even independently audited chain-of-custody schemes can suffer from evasion of rules; no system is infallible, and its integrity will always depend on the extent to which the chain of custody is monitored in practice. The point about the third-party approach is that it offers the possibility of monitoring at every stage and a transparent means of auditing these efforts. Along with any kind of certification where a market niche is established, it also benefits from a built-in incentive on the part of the operators to ensure that the system is fully implemented and to guarantee the integrity of the certificate.

Allied to these enforcement and monitoring reforms, processes can be set up to allow field observation and intelligence from local communities and nongovernmental organizations—assuming that the system is transparent enough for them to know what they are supposed to be monitoring. Networks of local and international nongovernmental organizations already exist in many producing countries, and donor countries have sometimes provided financial and technical assistance to help them to develop. The U.K. government, for example, funded the Environmental Investigation Agency to run training workshops in monitoring forest activities for local nongovernmental organizations and communities in Indonesia. The reform of property rights to devolve management of resources to local communities with a vested interest in their long-term security can also prove helpful.

Use of New Technology. As with data exchange, many technologies exist to help account for product inventory and trade. Also, as with data exchange systems, technological developments in tracking have tended to precede policy rather than to have been driven by it.

There are clear drawbacks to not employing technologically sophisticated tracking methods. For example, the outdated paper-based certificates or movement documents issued under CITES and the Basel convention are easily forged. Paper documentation, when not supplemented by electronic verification, is unreliable; falsification of CITES certificates is a common problem, particularly for high-value products such as caviar, as are the sale and theft of blank documents.

Table 4.2 gives examples of technology applicable to the monitoring of logs, although the methods are readily adaptable elsewhere and should be seen as complementary rather than exclusionary. The technologies listed are relatively self-explanatory: remote sensing and automatic cameras are clearly "large-scale" technologies that are not designed to measure individual logs but areas of operation and aggregate volume of traffic. Microtaggants are microscopic particles composed of layers of different colored plastics—millions of permutations are possible by combining several colors in different sequences. The coding sequences are then read with a X100 pocket microscope. Radio frequency identity tags can be read-only or read-write and can be programmed in the field or in advance. They are passive in that they transmit data only when "excited" by a signal from an appropriate reader. Reflectors are read by laser devices and may be of value to aerial surveillance teams trying to identify concession boundaries, log trucks carrying illegal loads, and the like, while satellite-based sensors can be read over enormous distances but are relatively cumbersome.

Element 4: Effective Compliance and Enforcement Measures

Compliance refers to a state's commitments under international law. Enforcement refers to a set of actions that a state may take within its national territory to ensure implementation of its international commitments, including adopting national laws and regulations, monitoring controlled activities, and deterring evasion of national regulations.

Countries often sign up for controls but fail to pass adequate laws or assign sufficient funds for their effective implementation. Responsibilities for implementation of controls may be assigned to an agency

Table 4.2 Forest Product Monitoring Technologies

Technology	Security and reliability	Practicality	Cost	Level of information
Microtaggant tracer paint and microscopes	Very high: virtually impossible to counterfeit; durable; identifies log origin from annual coupe; recommended by U.S. Forest Service for covert enforcement	Practical: easy to apply with spray gun; fastest-marking technique; one application for trees and cut logs; no use of sensitive electronic equipment; can be difficult to read in field; and wet or muddy logs may not take marker well; training required to read codes	Development and installation costs are high, but operating costs are low: $145 for an 8-ounce bottle of microtaggants in clear lacquer (1,000 applications); $30 for spray applicator; $20 for microscope	Very high: can be coded with the name of the concession, location of coupe, time of cutting, name of authorized paint users, issuing authority, and so forth
Chemical tracer paint	Medium: provides only custodial information, not origin; limited accountability controls; can give false readings if paint degrades or reacts	Practical: same as for microtaggant, but less training is needed	Low	Low: custodial information is limited to those allowed to use paint (assuming none is stolen, for example)

Method	Effectiveness	Practicality	Cost	Information
Bar-coded tags and scanners	Good: easily read; can be combined with microtaggant or chemical tracer paint for greater security	Practical: very easy to read, even from several meters; can link to automatic scaling system; can be difficult to apply; sensitive scanners may break down; tags can fall off or be cut out; metal staples can be fouled by milling equipment and vice versa; training is required for system use and data entry	Medium: $150 for standard application tool ($300 for pneumatic); $1,000 for automatic feed and paint application; $0.10 for a standard tag; $0.60 for a tag with paint application	Very high: as per microtaggant and may be linked to automatic scaling information
Radio frequency identification tags	Very good: tag is undetectable; accurate and reliable	Very practical: transponders very durable (more than eight years); codes can be reprogrammed; can be read remotely (and under water); direct interface with computers for data gathering; training in installation and reading required as well as equipment maintenance	Very high (but falling): $3,000 for applicator and reader; $800 for additional reader; $3–$8 per transponder in 100,000-unit volumes	Very high: as per microtaggant, but with direct computer link

(Table continues on the following page.)

Table 4.2 (continued)

Technology	Security and reliability	Practicality	Cost	Level of information
Brand hammers	Poor (fair if combined with documentation): easy to copy brand marks and hammers themselves	Fair: quick and easy to apply, but can be difficult in large piles of logs; cannot apply until tree is cut, so requires a system for standing inventory; difficult to read; minimal training	Very low	Poor: not site specific; concessionaire can use one hammer and forester or scaler can use another
CIRAD-Foret	Good: impossible to substitute logs in a shipment; can counterfeit forms and hammer marks to get through checkpoints but will be detected by audit	Practical: easy to learn and use as builds on existing skills	Low: scaling and grading already done, so added cost is only that of the forms and time taken to fill them out	High: form contains all the necessary information, but cross-checking and auditing required; log has form for matching serial numbers
Unique reflector identifiers	Very good	Poor but improving: technology is in infancy; reading is fast and accurate and can be achieved remotely (from air, for example); laser devices not yet robust enough for field use	High: $500 for laser measuring device; $0.75 per reflector in 100,000-unit volumes	Low (but improving): can be modified to incorporate memory cards and unique identifiers to store more that just location information

Ground video surveillance, cameras, and automatic activation devices	Good: signal can be transmitted to remote site to enforcement personnel	Not practical for monitoring movements of individual logs, but good for monitoring major transportation routes; can be activated by light, sound, or motion detectors; repeaters necessary if line-of-site to monitoring station not available; difficult to hide cameras for covert surveillance	High: $5,000 per unit; approximately $2,500 for repeater units	High
Satellite-borne sensors	Very good	Not practical for monitoring movements of individual logs but provides valuable information across whole concession; may be linkable to individual transponders in future	High but large-scale application	High over large scale
Genetic fingerprinting	Very good: chloroplast DNA cannot be faked	Not practical for monitoring individual logs; experimental but will be very useful if customs intercept unidentified timber	High (but falling); individual test requires specialist support	Low-medium; can trace origin of shipments to specific regions

that is already overloaded. Even where the rules on the books are adequate, lack of resources can cripple efforts to control environmental crime. Bureaucrats and enforcement agents are often poorly trained, underfunded, and inefficient. Customs, police, and other enforcement personnel may not be aware of the problem: customs staff tend to give a higher priority to other contraband such as arms and drugs, while the police tend to focus on robberies and violent crimes. Enforcement agents may have to endure hostile conditions or cover large geographic areas.[12] In addition, property rights for renewable resources may be unclear, as may be their actual value, meaning that the authorities may assign insufficient resources to their protection. Such capacity problems are becoming more evident given the increasing involvement of developing countries in many CTRs.

Regulatory failures involve inadequate regulations that fail to implement an environmental treaty properly, contain loopholes, or fail to deter (or even punish) evasion. Even when the rules themselves are adequate, institutional failures such as inadequate resources, untrained staff, or cumbersome administration may prevent the effective operation of controls.

Compliance Assurance.   Signatories to an agreement establishing a tracking system must transfer provisions into domestic law and apply sufficient resources for their effective administration and enforcement, but this rarely happens. States often have little incentive (or no mechanism) to police one another, meaning that implementation is left to national priorities at the expense of the global control regime. In the worst cases, noncompliance with, and free riding on, treaty provisions may undermine a treaty's sound implementation elsewhere. For example, in the ivory market, as the majority of the value was added to the product during its carving, the carving industry tended to settle in areas with the least restrictions. As restrictions were imposed on ivory-carving factories in Hong Kong (China), the industry shifted to Macau (China), then Singapore, then Taiwan (China), and finally the United Arab Emirates. Once carved, ivory was not subject to CITES procedures and could be traded relatively freely.

Gaps in implementation and enforcement are a near-universal theme of international policy discussion on CTRs. Significant implementation problems in commodity tracking by multilateral environmental agreements were highlighted at the Rio Earth Summit in Agenda 21; United Nations Development Programme and the Global Environment Facility's Capacity Development Initiative; the European Commission's Sixth Community Environmental Action Program; communiqués from the Montreal meeting of environment ministers of the Americas in March 2001; UNEP's February 2001 Montevideo III Program; UNEP's February 2001 Guidelines for Compliance and Enforcement in Multilateral Environmental Agreements; and the 1997 G-8 Ministers' Statement on Environmental Enforcement, International Cooperation, and Public Access to Information, held in Miami, Florida, United States.

A necessary minimum for the correct implementation of CITES is that national management and scientific authorities should be designated, trade in specimens violating the convention should be prohibited, and penalties and confiscation procedures should be specified. A large number of parties have been unable to fulfill these simple requirements: in 1994 of more than 80 parties to the convention, only one-fifth had adequate legislation for the implementation of CITES, while one-third had wholly inadequate legislation.

National data reports are often central to assessing compliance with international controls, but they are frequently late, incomplete, and sanitized. Taking CITES again, a report to the secretariat in 2000 highlighted that only about 40 percent of national data submissions were on time, while a significant number of parties failed to submit any annual report.

Noncompliance and inadequate implementation of CTRs are, perhaps, the biggest causes of tracking failures and system breakdown. Increased transparency of national reporting in many CTRs and diagnostic tools are needed to assess the quality of implementation and enforcement in partner countries. This, of course, is a sensitive area, as states understandably resist transferring any part of their sovereignty to an external or international body. Experience shows that national bureaucracies must have ownership of the development of legislation or they are unlikely to take action. Donor countries interested in legislative reform need to identify domestic constituencies for change and work with governments to improve judicial and administrative capacities.

There also needs to be a way to reward compliance and deter noncompliance. CTRs need to include measures to encourage compliance. In many cases, the reward will be financial, as revenue gathering improves. However, if states bear very different costs and see quite different benefits from a proposed measure, political will to implement and comply will differ widely. States with high costs and low benefits may well downgrade their implementation efforts, which may result in significant costs elsewhere by, for example, allowing the laundering of contraband.

Thus compliance procedures should allow for the independent assessment of problems and their amelioration. Such measures should provide an opportunity for settlement and assistance with capacity building. In particular, states reaping the benefits of controls should compensate those bearing the costs: developed countries should fund capacity-building programs in developing-country partners to the treaty. The multilateral fund of the Montreal protocol is perhaps the best successful example—contributions amounted to about $1.3 billion at the end of 2001.

The Significant Trade Process imposed under Article 4 of the CITES convention has partially addressed the failure of Appendix II listings procedure by providing independent expert advice on species status through its periodic review of heavily traded species. The process then enlists the help of consumer states in observing global trade quotas, which relieve range-states of the burden of making nondetriment findings on a case-by-case basis. The European Union's (EU's) new system of wildlife control legislation has altered the standard operating procedures of the convention to require an import quota for any shipment of Appendix II species into Europe, therefore requiring harder evidence that a given export will not have a harmful effect on the population of the species in question. The CITES secretariat now runs a Legislation and Compliance Unit, where legal and enforcement professionals provide real-time enforcement assistance to the parties and assessment of national compliance efforts. Activities include a rolling program of national legislation assessment, the issuance of CITES alerts to member states detailing actionable intelligence, cross-examination of permits and certificates, information outreach, and national missions for needs assessment or information verification.

A number of the major fisheries conservation treaties run schemes to detect and sanction reflagged vessels that may be free riding on catch controls. These mostly involve a register of noncontracting party vessels sighted in controlled waters, which face direct inspection if they put into the ports of contracting parties. Landings or transshipments from such offenders are banned unless the vessel can prove that controlled species on board were not caught in the regulatory area. In addition, some conventions also allow trade sanctions to be imposed on noncompliant states on the basis that they could not be exporting certain fish products unless they were catching them in an area controlled by the treaty.

Trade measures have proved an essential component in addressing noncompliant states. CITES, for example, has seen unilateral action under Article 14(1), which allows parties to undertake stricter domestic measures than are formally required under the convention to allow for targeted sanctions on noncompliant states including Bolivia, Democratic Republic of Congo, Greece, Italy, Thailand, and United Arab

Emirates (twice). Sanctioned parties must then agree to a compliance plan with the secretariat or a deputation of other parties in return for a phased withdrawal of trade sanctions.

Parties have also imposed trade controls on nonmembers to prevent them from free riding on the treaty and to encourage buy-in to CTR measures. Perhaps the most significant example was the Montreal protocol's trade restrictions on ozone-depleting substances and products containing such substances under Article 4. Although criticized as "trade war by environmental decree" by some developing countries, Article 4—in conjunction with the multilateral fund—has helped to drive the near-global ratification of the protocol. It was also one of the first treaties to include a specific noncompliance procedure; although slow in some instances, the model has been successful in expediting reporting requirements and promoting open dialogue and has since been widely copied.

It is worth noting that, in almost all cases, noncompliance procedures remain the creatures of the national parties—no CTR has delegated direct authority to sanction to an extraterritorial body.

Development Assistance Conditionality. Aid conditionality has also been used to generate domestic impetus for policy reform. This is not always an extraneous linkage of issues: proper management of natural capital such as the forest sector may be vital for state revenue and macroeconomic stability in developing countries. In Indonesia, the World Bank delayed a loan disbursement of $1.2 billion in mid-1999 (of which $400 million was forest related) because of illegal logging.[13] However, such methods have met with varying degrees of success, as a 1999 review comments, "The World Bank has approached the use of conditionality for environmentally oriented reform as a high-stakes poker game . . . the assumption implicit in this bargaining approach is that the borrower government is a unitary actor and that there is little genuine motivation for reform . . . . The twisting-arms approach by itself is of limited use even in achieving the limited goal of getting forest laws and regulations on the books" (Dubash and Seymour 1999, p. 14). A recent policy shift among Indonesia's Consultative Group donors has been to change the focus of treating illegalities from timber concessions to addressing the discrepancies between production and supply in the processing sector ("WB Leads Move" 2000).

National Enforcement. Effective national enforcement is predicated on the following:

- Designing and implementing a clear national control regime
- Undertaking effective national capacity building

- Targeting flagrant violators
- Increasing sanctions and introducing probation penalties
- Improving case processing times
- Encouraging compliance through positive incentives.

National legislation often needs to be reformed to include clear definitions of illegal activities, establish significant deterrent sanctions, and specify enforcement responsibilities at every stage of a commodity chain. Adequate resources must be committed to ensure effective enforcement. In cases where tax evasion occurs, improved enforcement may yield an immediate increase in revenues.

Lack of specialist knowledge and training may be addressed best by cascade, training-the-trainer programs followed by refresher courses, combined with the appointment of specialist prosecutors to cooperate with investigating officers. Frontline agents and specialist enforcement personnel should be put into early contact with each other and with their opposite numbers in other countries. Regularly updated national and international directories of enforcement expertise may facilitate contact.

Criminal profiling is vital for focused enforcement efforts. Risk analysis involves compiling records on importers and exporters and integrating this with actionable intelligence and enforcement actions to allow for the profiling of contraband, trafficking methods, and likely countries of origin. This process is reiterative—seizure and confiscation statistics from subsequent enforcement interventions should then be analyzed and the results fed back into the system to adjust profiles.

Special enforcement units have had a positive record in gathering intelligence, performing market surveillance, pursuing allegations of corruption, and prosecuting complex corporate investigations. South Africa's Endangered Species Enforcement Unit is a good example. The unit was founded by experienced officers from the rangeland crime division familiar with the need to penetrate networks, go undercover, gather intelligence, and conduct sting operations. Specialist units are likely to be most effective when run on a "stovepipe" arrangement, in which they are connected into the legal and administrative structure at a level sufficient to bypass regional and local "regulatory capture."

The model of bypassing existing bureaucracy can be taken further to create "super-ministries" such as the Kenyan Wildlife Service, whose broad remit and responsibilities, including almost all aspects of national park management, cooperative wildlife management, research, tourism, and infrastructure, allow for coordinated policies on wildlife protection. The result is a 24-hour operations room, a host of specialist units, a pool of paid informers, a network of honorary wardens to gather intelligence, and a highly motivated, well-paid staff.

Imaginative national and international enforcement programs are necessary, and adequate resources are required for their success. Actionable intelligence needs to be collected and disseminated, and enforcement needs to be targeted at weak points in global commodity chains. Regional enforcement cooperation agreements that allow for shared jurisdictional competence may also help to overcome the limitations of partitioning enforcement responsibilities between separate jurisdictions, especially where cross-border gangs are active and able to take advantage of territorial divisions. Perhaps the most innovative model is the 1996 Lusaka Agreement on Cooperative Enforcement Operations Directed at Illegal Trade in Wild Fauna and Flora, which makes extensive provision for shared, cross-border investigations into transnational wildlife poaching gangs in central and eastern Africa. The region's first multinational task force was constituted in 1999, with diplomatic status conferred on members to facilitate their work. The European Union's Europol Bureau may assume a similar role in helping to police some environmental CTRs across the EU, although its current mandate extends only to atomic and radioactive waste.

International Intelligence Coordination.   National intelligence on CTR violations needs to be collated and disseminated more efficiently to allow for coordinated enforcement between jurisdictions. Actionable information is often withheld in order to avoid embarrassing the countries involved or because of the perceived confidentiality of national enforcement processes. Information may be sanitized or sidelined into ritual exchanges at meetings rather than presented in an actionable way.

The CTR secretariats, relevant UN agencies, and transnational enforcement facilitation organizations like Interpol and the World Customs Organization all have a (coordinated) role to play in delivering better intelligence, information exchange, and training to their member states to improve CTR implementation and enforcement. That said, it is also important to understand the culture and the standard operating procedures of different organizations and where they fit into the picture. For example, Interpol passes information that "names names," whereas the World Customs Organization does not.

More international research is also needed on trafficking routes where nongovernmental organizations may be valuable partners. Trade Record Analysis of Flora and Fauna in Commerce, for example, acts as an occasional independent monitor, clearinghouse, and international research organization for information on wildlife trade (and some fisheries and forestry issues). Supported by the International Union for the Conservation of Nature, the World Wildlife Fund, and others, this is perhaps the most developed attempt to provide sustained intergovernmental support and intelligence to a CTR. Other non-governmental organizations like Global Witness, Global Survival Network, WildAid, and the Environmental Investigation Agency have also carried out extensive investigations into trade routes of particular forms of contraband.

Interagency Partnerships. Multiagency partnerships may also be necessary. The U.K. Metropolitan Police's Operation Charm has linked with the East Asian traditional medicine community and wildlife conservation nongovernmental organizations to educate traders and increase public awareness of the trade in endangered species through widely publicized enforcement actions, public information packs, and new forensic resources.

Clear processes can be set up to allow field observation and intelligence from industry informants, the public, and nongovernmental organizations to be relayed through appropriate government and enforcement agencies. Established networks of local and international nongovernmental organizations already exist and can be further promoted and developed.

Whether it is better to have a specialized unit or a multiple-agency partnership or simply to provide general training to all enforcement agents depends on the size of the available resources. Multiple-agency partnerships often lack dedicated budgets and tend to be highly dependent on the goodwill of the participants involved. When few dedicated resources are available, it may be better to concentrate them in a specialist unit to prevent dilution and loss of enthusiasm. Where larger funds are available, it may be possible to integrate an understanding of the basic principles and aims of specific CTRs into the curricula of law enforcement agencies and customs and to take a phased approach to capacity building through clustering and training-the-trainer programs.

Effective (Criminal) Sanctions. Penalties are often inadequate and may be treated more as operating costs for unscrupulous entrepreneurs than as a serious deterrent to market entry. Even when deterrent penalties are permitted in national legislation, they may not be applied by the judiciary, which is generally unaware of the aim and purpose of CTRs and the potentially devastating effects of their violation. A lack of awareness and cooperation among prosecutors and investigators may lead to loss of cases through technicalities. In addition, costs of enforcement tend to be "sunk" and are rarely recovered on successful prosecution of offenders.[14]

The use of criminal sanctions to deter some of the more serious CTR breaches on hazardous waste and endangered species has gained widespread international acceptance. The provision for criminal penalties has also been central to involving law enforcement organizations in such incidents. Where there are difficulties with pursuing criminal prosecutions—for example, where it is difficult to prove intent to violate laws or to acquire evidence of guilt to the criminal standard of "beyond reasonable doubt"—strict liability procedures may prove more effective. These sanction a company or an individual for failure to exercise due diligence and operate irrespective of fault or intention.

There may also be scope for the use of innovative extraterritorial and reciprocal enforcement legislation to allow for the effective sanctioning of deliberate evasion of CTRs outside the boundaries of a single nation-state. For example, in March 1998, the Norwegian government imposed the requirement that all Norwegian-registered companies or vessels operating in waters "outside the jurisdiction of any state" must obtain a one-year registration. Removal from the register—for contravening conservation or management measures laid down by regional or subregional agreements—also invalidates access to all quotas in domestic or cooperative fisheries.

The U.S. Lacey Act Amendments of 1981 contain a different sort of long-arm measure that makes it unlawful to "import, export, sell, acquire, or purchase fish, wildlife, or plants taken, possessed, or sold in violation of state or foreign law." It thus provides for extraterritorial action, but instead of making it an offense to violate U.S. law elsewhere, the act allows for laws violated elsewhere to be prosecuted in the United States. Such reciprocal measures may form the basis of future enforcement cooperation on many CTR issues.

Money laundering legislation may also provide for effective sanctions since finance often represents the soft underbelly of trafficking organizations. The main obstacle may be the collateral damage imposed on licit finance. Nevertheless, stricter controls on money transfers as part of the war on terrorism may provide for significant progress in this area.

Element 5: Capacity Building

Without consistent application and enforcement of regulations set down by commodity tracking agreements across all countries involved in the supply chain, it is unlikely the system will be effective. However, differing levels of administrative capacity exist in developed countries, transition countries, and developing countries. There are also serious equity issues in any CTR, particularly where poverty-stricken developing countries bear the burden of access restrictions for the common good.

The recent Stockholm convention contains detailed provisions to assist developing states in meeting common reporting and enforcement standards. The Global Environment Facility and UNEP are running pilot programs with 12 countries to develop national implementation plans for the management of persistent organic pollutants.[15] This is in line with Article 13, which establishes a financial support mechanism for developing countries and parties with economies in transition, and with Article 14, which entrusts the Global Environment Facility with the interim operation of the financial mechanism (until the first meeting of the conference of parties). Part of this project involves the elaboration of detailed action plans to identify the required national responses, processes, and measures to reduce the release of persistent organic pollutants. Activities include establishing inventories of persistent organic pollutants, identifying management options, and preparing schedules of estimated costs for remedial and management actions.[16]

The existence of a clear financial mechanism to build the compliance capacity of developing states is highly desirable. In Article 13, the Stockholm convention specifically requires developed parties to provide resources to assist in meeting the full incremental costs of meeting their obligations under the convention. This mechanism is more detailed in the Montreal protocol, where the 1990 London amendment instituted a multilateral fund to finance technology transfer and capacity-building programs.

Market-based certification programs should also consider equity issues. Frequently such schemes marginalize or exclude the small, community-oriented operations that should be encouraged for sustainable development. The Marine Stewardship Council, for example, has explicitly developed a community-based certification methodology to account for the small-scale, complex nature of some fisheries. At the same time, the MSC program is working to enhance the auditing and certification infrastructure in more remote fishing regions in Africa. Annual certifier workshops provide a forum for training and updating certification skills.

There are a number of methods to make capacity-building assistance more efficient. A cascade approach of training the trainers, for example, may give greater returns than broader but more shallow seminar programs. Similarly, if funding is limited, it may be most effective to set up a specialist administrative or enforcement unit and create a culture of empowerment and excellence. With larger funds, mainstreaming compliance into basic training for enforcement agents may be possible. Better use of existing technologies and forensics and the development of new enforcement tools should also be promoted to improve the efficiency of policing. Joint capacity-building missions that cluster relevant CTRs may allow quicker implementation and improve the ability to share the lessons learned between similar control problems. Clustering would also allow more effective regional studies of implementation as well as shared training.

Capacity building should not be limited to state agents. Public education efforts should be significantly increased to create a duty-of-care culture and to balance vested government and private sector interests. It is essential to have international control efforts be seen as justified and in everyone's best interests rather than have violations be seen as entrepreneurship.

Contextual Considerations

Our five basic elements should inevitably be adapted to specific circumstances and contexts. Some of the issues that are likely to have a significant impact on the success of a specific CTR are elaborated in this section. Specific technical, legal, institutional, and political circumstances will shape any CTR, and there is a need to understand the international market that underpins a specific commodity. Many CTRs are often dogged by an ad hoc and unsystematic approach where individual enforcement agencies attempt to target individual traffickers in contraband without reducing the size of the illegal market in which they operate. Without addressing demand and supply pressures that determine profit-making opportunities, other operators will expand or new operations will enter the market. Thus controls must go beyond simply increasing enforcement of national laws to address the international demand and supply of the commodity.

Consideration 1: Detailed Understanding of the Commodity Chain

Complicated networks link raw materials and producers to customers through a web of supplier relationships with the involvement of ancillary specialist services and other key actors such as legitimate businesses, government officials, and consumers. These interactions are critical in shaping a CTR regime. For example, in the case of diamonds, the global mining industry consists of three main sectors: mining, rough diamond trading, and cutting and polishing. A diamond tracking system must therefore take into account well-organized large companies,[17] uncontrolled smaller operations, and the hundred or so countries that participate in the exporting, cutting, and polishing of rough diamonds.

Mixing of commodities from different sources must also be considered in the design of a commodity tracking system. Just as conflict diamonds can easily be added to batches of legitimately mined diamonds if there are insufficient checks and monitoring of their precise origin, so illegally harvested timber can be mixed with legally produced timber—indeed, some logged-out forest concessions are on the books purely for this purpose. Similarly, potential mixing of genetically modified grains is routine in the United States but is problematic under proposed EU regulations, which require strict separation, testing, and labeling to control the importation and movement of genetically modified substances.

The dynamics of specific commodities are also central in understanding how (and indeed whether) to regulate a commodity. For example, concern has been raised that mining of coltan, a key component in chips for mobile electronic devices like cellular phones, in the Democratic Republic of Congo may have exacerbated regional conflict. Coltan has a long and complex commodity chain (illustrated in figure 4.4; see Volpi 2002). The fact that coltan mining in the Democratic Republic of Congo is highly fluid and chaotic—the country provides less than 4 percent of the world's supply—and the nature of the product—a component in a bigger chip that has to be processed several times before reaching the consumer—make chain-of-custody certification problematic. End-use consumer pressure is therefore unlikely to be effective as a driving force for change. Extraction from the Great Lakes region is likely to decrease in importance as new reclamation technologies are developed (the vast majority of the world's supply is sourced from treated tin mining slags and existing inventories). World coltan prices are falling, and capacitor manufacturers are increasingly turning to fixed-contract arrangements with large suppliers. However, there are only three large processing companies, so these are likely to be the most significant players in any potential control regime; they could be effectively engaged in screening suppliers. The additional sourcing costs could then be passed up the chain to consumers.

Where profits are high and risks low, it is clear that expertise in avoiding specific controls will develop gradually. Also restrictions or bottlenecks at certain points along international commodity chains allow for more classic "organized" criminals to evade specific CTRs, as with cross-border smuggling groups that specialize in avoiding border checkpoints. Thereafter, however, the contraband passes into very different channels of distribution. For example, Mexican and U.S. organized smuggling gangs may move endangered parrots, ozone-depleting substances, narcotics, and weapons together across the Rio Grande. Chinese nationals who specialized in "sanctions busting" for

Figure 4.4 Coltan Extraction Chain from Eastern Democratic
Republic of Congo

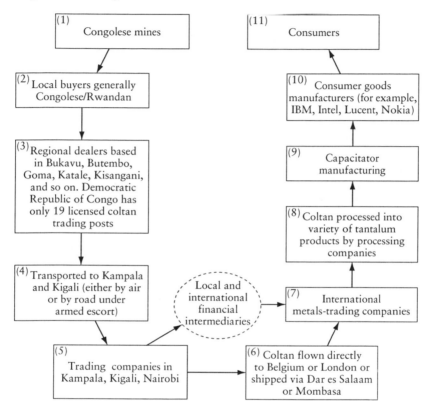

Source: Authors.

South Africa's apartheid regime also ran lucrative sidelines importing
stolen vehicles from the United Arab Emirates and exporting ivory and
rhino horns poached under South African sanction from countries like
Angola to the Far East.

It may even be possible to distinguish different criminal constituencies within a specific CTR. In the wildlife trade, for example, there are
clear differences between (a) low-volume, low-value "tourist" cases;
(b) high-volume, low-value opportunist smuggling; (c) high-volume,
high-value smuggling by organized criminal networks; and (d) low-
volume, high-value smuggle-to-order operations for collectors. In the
primate trade, tourists tend to buy protected species randomly; smuggling to order tends to involve high-value animals like orangutans
or chimpanzees that make good tourist attractions; and professional

smugglers tend to concentrate on supplying rhesus monkeys to the lucrative laboratory market by laundering wild-caught animals through captive-breeding facilities.

Considerations 2 and 3: Market Forces That Drive Enterprise Crime

Evasion of CTR controls is known as enterprise crime. Traditional law enforcement bureaucracies have been set up to tackle traditional predatory crime, which involves the involuntary redistribution of wealth through theft and robbery. In contrast, enterprise crimes are structured around consensual and mutually beneficial exchanges among producers, processors, retailers, and final consumers where supply and demand for services interact in a free-market relationship. Because there is no obvious victim to report a crime, the authorities are required to take a lead in investigating and prosecuting such offenses. If theft is involved, it is more often theft from the state than theft from an individual. Society as a whole is victimized—although the individuals trading in conflict diamonds may gain from their transactions, those commodities are funding belligerents. Trade in conflict timber not only funds national or regional destabilization but also damages the global environment.

The traditional "head-hunting" approach adopted by law enforcement agencies to tackle predatory crime does little to address the pressures of supply and demand that shape profit-making opportunities. Society as a whole is often unaware of its victimization, so regulators may not set appropriate levels of enforcement effort and restitution; regulatory institutions may even assume that because many problems related to enterprise crime are not directly quantifiable, they are not significant.

Indeed, commodity control regimes themselves may inadvertently create incentives for evasion of regulations by artificially altering supply and demand. Supply may be constrained to conserve a scarce environmental good such as an endangered animal population or because of the increased costs of complying with altered environmental regulations. Similarly, demand may be adjusted through policies like taxation to compensate for an associated cost or externality related to the production or consumption of particular commodities. Avoidance of these "restrictions" may bring significant profits.

In the case of the Montreal protocol, a lack of consideration of market forces and different phase-out schedules for ozone-depleting substances between the developed and developing world generated a significant black market. Although direct supply restrictions were put in place, demand was generally left to adjust to market forces (apart from bans on products like aerosols). Although the replacements for ozone-depleting substances themselves were often cheaper, significant capital costs were involved in prematurely retiring machinery dependent on ozone-depleting substances; thus a significant latent demand for ozone-depleting substances remained to service existing equipment in developed countries. At the same time, such materials were cheaply and freely available on developing-country markets. This demand was further exacerbated because, despite numerous technical innovations, one critical application did not emerge: there was no quick substitute for CFC-12, the most widely used chlorofluorocarbon (CFC) in small refrigeration and air conditioning. Replacing CFC-12 in car air conditioning initially cost around $250–$500, while a recharge cost around $50 in the black market. The demand for CFC-12 was particularly high in the United States (and Canada) because more than 90 percent of automobiles were fitted with CFC-dependent air conditioning, compared with about 10 percent in Europe. In 1995 some 110 million automobiles were using CFC-12; this demand was met by some 10,000–20,000 tons of illegally imported CFC-12, worth more than $100 million.

The illegal dumping of waste has increased as regulations governing the safe and proper disposal of hazardous waste tighten, increasing handling charges and decreasing the capacity for safe disposal at licensed facilities.[18] As illegal dumpers do not have to connect buyers and sellers in a clandestine market, but simply lose the material somewhere, waste dumping does not require specialists, and entry costs into the illegal market are low. In one New York police sting in 1992, undercover detectives, posing as illegal dumpers, went into the business of disposing of toxic waste from small businesses for $40 a barrel, but they found the competition so fierce that they had to lower their price (New York Times, May 13, 1992). The cost of legal waste disposal was about $570 per barrel.

The design of tax regimes may also affect incentives to evade CTRs. The stumpage tax on most timber harvesting, based on the value of logs at the stump (that is, the cost of extraction plus a reasonable profit margin), provides strong incentives for tax evasion by underreporting harvests, undergrading the quality of the timber harvested, or inflating costs to show zero profits. The Cambodian forest sector experienced all these problems in the 1990s. In 1997 authorized log production was about 450,000 cubic meters, while estimated total harvesting was 4.3 million cubic meters. Transnational subsidiaries may also "transfer price" timber shipments by underselling and undergrading timber shipments to their parent companies; the real value of the goods is then reaped higher up the corporate chain, often being deposited in tax havens. Transfer pricing on timber sales from Papua New Guinea in the 1980s was estimated at $5–$10 per cubic meter, resulting in losses of up to $30 million per year.

Sole emphasis on enforcement of existing regulations may ignore (or tacitly condone) the context of the wider system that generates such opportunities to offend. Thus, in addition to simply improving frontline enforcement, a coordinated approach to commodity controls must address the pressures of supply and demand that shape an illegal market. Enforcement agents can rarely address these factors themselves, yet they routinely have to deal with the results; therefore, enforcement agents and government officials should be locked in dialogue to maximize the efficiency of global controls.

Globalization of Trade.   As globalization vastly increases the volume and speed of goods and persons in transit, customs-led interdiction strategies look increasingly ineffective as a method of addressing evasion of CTRs. The problem of "trying to promote legal cross-border economic flows while simultaneously enforcing laws against illegal flows has been an increasingly awkward and delicate task and a growing source of frustration for law enforcement bureaucracies" (Andreas 2000, p. 4). Data from the U.S. Office of Drug Control for 1999, for example, indicate that more than 75 million passengers and crew arrived in the United States by air, in 900,000 aircraft; 9 million arrived by sea, using some 200,000 ships; and 395 million crossed land borders, in 153 million trucks, trains, buses, and cars; and there were 16 million cargo containers (White House 2000). London's Heathrow airport sees some 5 million shipments of airfreight, about 0.5 million tons, per year. Because of the high rent, traders in illegal commodities can afford to have large amounts seized.

Supply-Side Controls.   The supply of contraband can be adjusted by market intervention, such as altering the management structures or property rights that govern access to resources or subsidizing alternatives. Supply businesses also need to be given incentives to comply with international controls; monopoly and cartel arrangements may play an important role in ensuring that those in the marketplace have a vested interest in keeping competitors out. The diamond industry's reaction to conflict diamonds is another example of how self-interest can be an important element in the drive to establish an effective CTR. Without the active involvement of De Beers Consolidated Mines, which controls more than 70 percent of the global diamond trade, it is unlikely the Kimberley process would have progressed as far as it has in establishing an international diamond certification scheme.

Supplies of look-alike commodities also need to be addressed to prevent laundering. Trade controls may be key, but collateral damage on legitimate commerce may be an important constraint. For example, more than 20,000 of the species regulated under CITES are non-threatened orchids, which results in considerable bureaucracy and antagonism for both the CITES authorities and the orchid breeding industry.

Another key supply-side policy is to identify and eliminate surplus capacity. Much illegal logging stems from overallocation of logging concessions and processing licenses, frequently associated with corruption. As mentioned, the Indonesian forestry sector has a processing capacity that is almost double the size of legal supply. Aid conditionality on forest sector reform has only recently begun to move from getting "laws on the books" to addressing such issues. Subsidies to industrial fishing fleets have served to promote massive excess capacity and inflate demand for catches. In 1989, due to the excessive number of vessels and government support across the world, total subsidies and expenditure on fleet support cost $92 billion, while the total value of fish extracted was only $70 billion.

Demand-Side Controls.   Demand-side policies complement supply-side strategies by attempting to create incentives for enlightened self-interest by manufacturers. For example, dozens of voluntary certification programs have been developed to meet the demand for ethical products. In addition to the FSC and the MSC programs, another good example is the Indian Rugmark Program, which began in 1994 to identify Indian carpet manufacturers who avoided using child labor. The licensees themselves help to finance monitoring by paying 0.025 percent of the value of their carpets to the scheme, which then certifies their products subject to surprise inspections and cross-checking of export records.

Such certification systems will be even stronger if backed by an educated and informed public. In some cases, consumer demand has led CTRs, such as the regulation of trade in genetically modified organisms. Consumer pressure has apparently prompted the European Commission to design a stringent tracking system. Similarly, consumer pressure has driven some clothing and carpet manufacturers to impose International Labour Organisation standards on their own factories and their suppliers. In May 1998 Nike announced that it was imposing a minimum age of 16 for light manufacturing workers and 18 for footwear manufacturers. Reebok has implemented a system for monitoring and labeling soccer balls made in Pakistan to ensure that no underage workers are involved. Companies like Mattel and Wal-Mart have published policies stating they will not use child labor for the production or sale of their products.

Government and private procurement programs can complement certification schemes by creating demand for "ethical" products. The U.K. government, for example, is attempting to procure all its timber from legal or certified sources. A more general duty-of-care culture can also be fostered through "soft" regulatory mechanisms, such as due diligence schemes—often used in the antiques trade—that may help to provide for formal liaison between traders and law enforcement. Due diligence may be reflected in industry certification procedures, such as adherence to International Standards Organization programs like the ISO 14000 standards or the European Eco-Management and Audit Scheme, that classify an organization or company by its ability to manage all aspects of its business in an environmentally sound manner.

Lateral thinking is also necessary to convince insurance companies and banks to assess the legality of operations as part of their financial due diligence procedures. Investors, banks, and export credit agencies that have funded illegal activities or activities without due diligence could perhaps be targeted by tort litigation, money laundering, or proceeds-of-crime legislation. Due diligence procedures imposed by insurance companies concerned with potential cleanup liabilities, for example, have been one of the major drivers in compliance with U.S. Superfund hazardous waste legislation.

Considerations 4 and 5: Political and Legal Context of Regulations

Any CTR will be partly a product of the political, economic, and social circumstances of producing, processing, and consuming countries. In addition, prior legal precedent, developing international jurisprudence, and national case law all will profoundly affect the shape and methodology of specific control regimes. For example, attempts to control illegal fishing and impose access restrictions on fishing fleets have been hindered by the "freedom of the high seas." Within this broad context, the Convention on the Conservation of Antarctic Marine Living Resources (CCAMLR) Treaty that protects southern ocean resources has a number of unique features and must be understood against the background of the Antarctic Treaty System from which it emerged. In the Antarctic Treaty of 1959, the 12 potential claimants of portions of Antarctica[19] agreed to set aside their territorial claims in the interests of international harmony. Article IV of the treaty contains the central provision that decrees the mutual abeyance of parties' territorial claims and ambitions on the continent, although specifically without prejudicing their future positions on the issue. CCAMLR inherited this unresolved jurisdiction and consensus approach to decisionmaking from the Antarctic Treaty System, both of which have hindered subsequent attempts to crack down on illegal and unregulated fishing in the CCAMLR area.

Similarly, although the Basel convention requires setting up systems to ensure that participants "exercise due care" in the waste trade, no attempt is made to regulate its volume, organizational complexity, or geopolitical reach (Wynn 1989, p. 137). This approach sharply contrasts with the Montreal protocol where explicit controls on production and consumption of CFCs and other gases are central to international efforts to protect the ozone layer. "The inability of the developing countries to obtain a North-South ban in the context of the [initial negotiations surrounding] the Basel convention shaped the future development and tone of all subsequent negotiations," not least in shifting the axis of negotiation away from discussing the environmentally sound management of industrial processes. Indeed, "neither the third world nor the developed countries pressed for a definition that would address the major problem underlying the hazardous waste trade: the polluting and toxic nature of many industrial processes. Although NGOs [nongovernmental organizations] such as Greenpeace identified the existence of dirty industries as a significant problem to be addressed, the priority for developing countries was the issue of the hazardous waste trade itself" (Miller 1995, p. 97). Political recognition has only recently occurred that regulating transboundary movements should be part of a broader strategy of waste management to generate less waste and to uncouple industrial activity from environmental damage.

Lack of Government Transparency, Governance Failures, and Corruption.   Civil strife and breakdown of government have created conditions that allow illegal trade to flourish. Beyond simply rendering a government incapable of fulfilling its tracking obligations, ruling elites may actively abet such disorder to preside over massive public losses for their private gain.

Revenues from illegal logging, for example, may exacerbate national and regional conflict. In turn, the state of emergency from such conflicts may allow for the leakage of formal state revenues, which would be far more difficult in peacetime. Examples include Cambodia, where the timber trade funded the genocidal Khmer Rouge; the Democratic Republic of Congo, where the world's largest timber concession (about

33 million hectares) funds the incremental cost of neighbors' standing armies in the country; and Liberia, where almost $100 million in revenues and direct logs-for-arms swaps help to fund the government of Charles Taylor, posing a serious threat to regional stability. In each case, this "conflict timber" has been routinely imported into northern markets.

More generally, extractive activities such as logging are difficult to disguise, and illegal access is heavily reliant on corruption.[20] As the World Bank's recent review of its global forest policy observes, "Countries with tropical moist forest have continued to log on a massive scale, often illegally and unsustainably. In many countries, illegal logging is similar in size to legal production. In others, it exceeds legal logging by a substantial margin . . . poor governance, corruption, and political alliances between parts of the private sector and ruling elites combined with minimal enforcement capacity at local and regional levels, all played a part" (World Bank 1999, p. xii; "World Bank Sees Flaws" 2000).

This problem is not confined to developing countries, but the problems there are generally more evident and more serious because the salaries of enforcement officials and bureaucrats are often low, civil society is weaker, and transnational companies that offer inward investment are relatively more powerful. Allocation of licenses to exploit resources like timber can also be used as a mechanism for mobilizing wealth to reward political allies and provide patronage. Even in such highly corrupt situations, some rules must still exist, if only to allocate patronage to specific individuals or sectors of society. Enforcement, however, becomes an instrument to control the flow of illegal rents and ensure the patronage of clients.

Wider forces may also be at work in the failure of commodity controls. For example, the 1996 Commission of Inquiry into the Alleged Smuggling of and Illegal Trade in Ivory and Rhinoceros Horn in South Africa provided a wealth of detail about the South African apartheid regime's policy of destabilizing neighboring states funded through illegal trade.[21] Smugglers of illicit commodities such as currency, gemstones, ivory, rhino horn, and the drug mandrax had formed complicated networks involving senior government officials in surrounding states. Infiltration of these networks by South African intelligence operatives was thus an effective way of penetrating the machineries of these states in pursuit of regional political destabilization. From the late-1970s to the mid-1980s, South Africa's special forces ran large quantities of diamonds, ivory, rhino horn, and teak out of Angola and Mozambique and used the proceeds to fund the equipment and training of insurgents like the National Union for the Total Independence of Angola and Mozambique National Resistance.

If a tracking system is also intended to monitor commodity flows from conflict zones, intelligence gathering requires an entirely different level of involvement, commitment, and courage. Some enterprise crimes may also be inseparable from human rights abuses, especially those derived from place-based operations that directly affect the health and well-being of local populations.

Government Transparency.   Political, economic, and social features of the countries of origin or transit have a direct impact on how freely and effectively a tracking system will be able to function. In particular, monitoring will be stymied when confronted with uncooperative national governments that are reluctant to allow foreign interference in "sovereign" trade practices. For example, monitoring labor standards in some countries is frustrated by the reluctance of officials to permit external verification. In contrast, some countries, such as India and Pakistan, are more amenable to external observation of workplace practices. Monitoring of work practices in India is also assisted by civil society and nongovernmental organizations that conduct independent investigations.

World Trade Organization Implications.   Any restrictions on trade, including labeling requirements, tariffs and taxes, potential embargos, or other forms of discrimination, are potentially subject to the discipline of the various multilateral trade agreements administered by the World Trade Organization (WTO). Virtually all the CTRs mentioned in this chapter require parties to control or restrict trade in various ways, including imposing requirements for licensing requirements or requiring different forms of informed consent for trade to occur.

WTO jurisprudence shows a number of simple lessons from previous disputes and adjudications:

• The less trade-disruptive the measure, the lower the chance of a successful WTO challenge—a requirement simply for labeling or for a government procurement policy would be less likely to fail than a ban on imports.

• The more it can be shown that less trade-disruptive measures—such as preferential tariffs—have been attempted and have not proved effective, the greater the chance more trade-disruptive measures have of being found acceptable. This may even extend to non-trade-related efforts, such as capacity-building assistance to the exporting countries concerned.

• Similarly, the more precisely targeted the measure, the less the chance of a successful challenge. An embargo applied, for example, to an entire country's fish exports because some of them are believed to be illegal would be more vulnerable to a WTO challenge than an embargo applied only against products that could be proved to be illegal or not shown to be legal. In the latter case, adherence to an internationally accepted means of determining legality in this context—for example, a requirement for chain-of-custody documentation audited by an independent third party—would also help to justify the measure (as long as one's own industry is subject to the same requirements).

• The less discriminatory the measure, the lower the chance of a successful challenge to its operation. A very strong case could be made under the WTO if a country was applying more restrictive measures to imports than to its own production.

• The greater the effort to ensure that a measure is multilaterally acceptable, the less it is likely to be challenged.

Two important WTO rulings in this regard are the Mexico and United States tuna-dolphin dispute and the India, Malaysia, Pakistan, Thailand, and United States shrimp-turtle dispute, in which the United States banned imports of shrimp caught without the use of turtle excluder devices. In both cases, commodity import restrictions that were nominally intended to promote conservation were challenged and overturned as an invalid exception to Article XI(1) of the General Agreement on Tariffs and Trade, which prohibits quantitative trade measures.[22] In the tuna-dolphin dispute, one of the central reasons for rejecting the import restrictions was that the measure discriminated between similar products. The United States banned tuna from Mexico and used a retroactive standard (the dolphin kill ratio) as its reason, so it was impossible for Mexican fishermen to know in advance the standard that they had to meet. Similarly, the shrimp-turtle dispute was partially motivated by complaints that the sanctioning mechanism enacted by the United States looked only at relevant procedures at a national level, rather than at whether individual boats were using the devices. Thus a fisherman who was using a turtle excluder device but whose country did not have an official certification program (designed to certify that the vessel was meeting standards consistent with those required of domestic fishermen under the Endangered Species Act) would face an import ban on his products. In addition, fishermen from different countries were given a different length of time in which to comply with certification. Thus, although the appellate body recognized the U.S. sovereign right to use trade restrictions for environmental protection, the United States did not do so in a nondiscriminatory manner.

WTO jurisprudence highlights the need for flexibility when applying unilateral standards to other states and the need to apply any control measures or certification scheme with an even hand to prevent unjustified discrimination. There is sufficient flexibility on the impact of WTO agreements that it should be possible for many different types of trade-restrictive measures to be designed and implemented so as to survive a WTO challenge, provided they are not overtly protectionist or discriminatory.

Conclusions and Recommendations

If the political will exists, it is perfectly possible to establish a successful CTR based on our five basic elements, subject to the five contextual considerations discussed above. These 10 factors can also provide a basic framework for building new CTRs, including measures to control access to commodities like coltan and tanzanite.

In all cases, clear and effective national legislation detailing enforcement responsibilities and deterrent sanctions for crimes is necessary, as are transparent and effective international noncompliance measures to discourage free riders, while encouraging countries to share their problems openly. The need to focus on transit countries and the laundering of transshipments has also been raised. Controls and feedback structures should be engineered in a precautionary manner rather than the current "wait and see" attitude.

A central part of these processes should be direct access to enforcement experts at CTR meetings and when preparing control measures. There is also a strong case for setting up a specialist unit on enforcement and compliance in CTRs to institutionalize such expertise. Such measures may also serve to depoliticize the process of enforcement and compliance.

Evasion of CTRs is a consensual, economic crime where there are rarely victims to complain, so that the state must bear the burden of enforcement. CTRs must gather sufficient data in their basic operations to allow distinctions between products and should contain comprehensive review procedures to provide feedback to policymakers on compliance with, and the impact of, international controls. In addition to information directly relevant to the type, origin, and destination of specific shipments, there is a need to record price data on controlled commodities, the volume and values of licit and illicit markets, gaps in commodity data between trading partners, data on stockpiling, details on registration and capacities of processing and treatment centers, policing effort, and offenses detected. It is apparent in the work of Global Witness that widespread resource mismanagement has been facilitated by the extension of bureaucratic controls by central governments over resources, without the corresponding development of effective feedback and information systems.

In establishing any system of tracking, it is also necessary to keep in mind the international market incentives that drive opportunities to offend. Labeling sustainably produced timber and fish is unlikely to reverse rampant depletion if massive overcapacity exists within an industry. In such situations, simply head-hunting individual malfeasants will not touch the pressures of supply and demand that drive offenses.

Traffic in controlled commodities should be made "conditional" on the provision of adequate data sharing that it is within the boundaries specified by a specific commodity tracking regime. The burden on the state as direct sole manager of resources should be lessened through efficiently managing resource externalities in the collective interest and through individual or collective privatization, in which the resources are given to the owner who most values them. Placing management of resources in the hands of local collectives may be an effective way to address problems of both poverty and compliance with controls.

Computer and tagging technology can play a major role in efficient tracking and information exchange. For example, most corner grocery stores are able to keep a near real-time inventory of their merchandise through the use of bar codes, so there is almost no excuse for the primitive paper-only systems that are currently used for all international controls.

Lessons from first-generation commodity control agreements should now inform second-generation agreements. Assembling all 10 factors of a successful CTR implies a higher level of international cooperation than currently exists. This exercise may also involve building institutions that are not simply the creatures of their constituent governments and for governments to yield some of their sovereign authority.

Appendix 4.1. Diamonds

The primary purpose of the Kimberley Certification Process Scheme is to establish an international certification scheme for rough diamonds based primarily on internationally agreed minimum standards for certificates of origin and on national certification schemes.[23] It aims to protect the legitimate diamond industry and stem the flow of "conflict diamonds."[24]

The process acknowledges that an international certification scheme for rough diamonds will be credible only if all participants have established internal systems of control to eliminate the presence of conflict diamonds in the chain of producing, exporting, and importing rough diamonds within their own territories. Participants—states or regional economic organizations such as the European Union—are to establish internal controls to eliminate the presence of conflict diamonds from shipments of rough diamonds imported into and exported from their territory. This will include designating importing and exporting authorities, as applicable, to monitor diamond shipments and to ensure that all diamonds are imported and exported in tamper-resistant containers accompanied with Kimberley process certificates. Participants are obliged to amend or enact appropriate laws or regulations to implement and enforce the certification scheme and to maintain penalties for transgressions. They also are to collect and maintain relevant official production, import, and export data and to collate and exchange this information when necessary (Sections IV and V).[25]

In taking account of chain-of-custody monitoring requirements, the scheme defines country of origin as the country where a shipment of rough diamonds has been mined or extracted; whereas country of provenance is the last participant from where a shipment of rough diamonds was exported, as recorded on import documentation. The scheme recommends that the importing participant complete an import confirmation part for the certificate containing the following information: the country of destination, identification of the importer, the carat weight and value in U.S. dollars, the relevant Harmonized Commodity Description and Coding System, and the date of receipt and authentication by the importing authority.

Each participant is to ensure that a duly validated certificate accompanies each shipment of rough diamonds on export and import (Section II). The original of the certificate must be readily accessible for at least three years to facilitate the tracking of diamond flows.

To further filter out conflict diamonds, participants are to ensure that no shipment of rough diamonds is imported from or exported to a nonparticipant. Participants through whose territory shipments transit are required to ensure that the shipment leaves its territory in an identical state as it entered its territory (that is, unopened and not tampered with; Section III).

A degree of transparency and monitoring was integrated into the process after nongovernmental organizations voiced strong opposition to proposals that the regime be self-regulating. Section V provides for a type of peer review mechanism where a complainant who considers that another participant does not have adequate laws or procedures can inform that participant through the chair.

The scheme formally began in November 2002, but implementation had yet to begin at the time of writing. Will it be successful in tracking the flow of diamonds? Although the process has been an important first step, significant technical and operational issues remain to be addressed, including the following:

• Some "high-risk" activities, such as the flow of diamonds from the mine or field to the first export, are subject only to recommended controls.

• Participants are merely encouraged to ensure that mining companies maintain effective security standards to ensure that conflict diamonds do not contaminate legitimate production.

• It is only recommended that participants establish a license or registration scheme for all diamond buyers, sellers, exporters, agents, and courier companies.

• Instead of setting common minimum standards and procedures to meet, the process leaves many controls to be designed and implemented by national authorities (Section IV). Without independent, regular monitoring of all national systems, it will be very difficult to assess with certainty whether certificates are genuine or whether the process is halting conflict diamonds from entering international trade.

• The process has not adequately dealt with the uneven enforcement capabilities of participants. There is no initial mechanism to determine whether an applicant country is able to fulfill the requirements of the scheme. It is unclear how and when capabilities will be assessed and what measures will be introduced (if any) to redress imbalances.

• The period after rough diamonds enter a foreign port or final point of sale will be entirely self-regulated by the World Diamond Council system of warranties.[26] Participation in the World Diamond Council system is voluntary and may not be monitored independently. Unless there is independent, third-party monitoring of this and all other stages of the scheme, there is some doubt over the scheme's accountability and effectiveness.

• There is continued disagreement over how best to implement the scheme with respect to alluvial diamonds (diamonds washed onto riverbeds). Alluvial diamond fields tend to be widely scattered and difficult to monitor.

• There is as yet no international secretariat (or similar body) to administer the scheme.

- The process fails to specify or designate a database or central body to control and enable the sharing of vital statistical information. There is also a lack of detail on what information should be gathered by participants and when it will be shared and used. The proposed scheme recommends only that information be made available to an "intergovernmental body or other appropriate mechanism" on a quarterly basis for imports and exports and a "semiannual" basis for production.
- The process has not specified the consequences of noncompliance. It is unclear, for example, whether countries that contravene certification provisions will be excluded from trading with participants.
- Membership is voluntary, and some countries involved in the diamond industry have not participated in negotiations over development of the diamond-tracking system.
- It is unclear how existing stockpiles of rough diamonds of undetermined origin will be dealt with.
- The monitoring mechanism put in place by the Kimberley process is based on states reporting on other noncompliant participants. However, verification and review of a participant's activities can take place only with their consent, and the precise membership and terms of reference of monitoring or verification missions are yet to be determined. State sovereignty will potentially be a major block to the effective implementation and oversight of the scheme at the national level.
- There are no details on how or when participants should carry out self-assessment.

Whether the Kimberley process will be successful depends on whether these problems are properly resolved. Effectiveness will also be highly contingent on the legislative and administrative measures introduced at the national level to implement the scheme.

Appendix 4.2. Timber

Timber trade is characterized by endemic corruption, links to organized crime, and, in numerous instances, links to various warring factions. Despite this, consuming countries and multilateral agencies display a remarkable lack of concern for the illegal activities of logging companies. Timber is, of course, a legally tradable commodity. However, according to Friends of the Earth UK, based on 1999 figures, approximately 70 percent of tropical timber imports into the European Union are illegal. There is no reason to suppose that worldwide imports are much better.

There is currently no comprehensive global tracking regime for monitoring flows of timber, nor is there an international agreement or treaty specifically intended to control illegal logging. Efforts to track timber, therefore, rely on a series of voluntary schemes, most of which incorporate certification and classification procedures. These schemes are intended either to differentiate commodities that have been pro- duced in accordance with set criteria and indicators of legal and sus- tainable forest management or to classify timber-related organizations or companies by their ability to manage all aspects of their business in an environmentally sound manner (for example, in accordance with ISO 14,000).

International Initiatives

The international community has no legislative power, other than United Nations (UN) sanctions, to place an embargo on a producer's timber exports. The UN Security Council has taken this action only once. In 1992 it was recognized that the Khmer Rouge guerrillas in Cambodia were obtaining funding essential to their war effort by trad- ing timber with Thailand. The United Nations passed Resolution 792 banning exports of round logs from Cambodia, effective from January 1, 1993. As described below, the ban was effective in under- mining the financial basis of the Khmer Rouge but had several unin- tended consequences that need to be considered in future bans.

The G-8 has taken a strong stance on illegal logging, particularly the five-point Okinawa statement, and should provide direction to international action. Given the pace at which the forests are being destroyed, and the fact that armed conflict and criminality are both driving this destruction, members of the G-8 and the United Nations should consider more immediate and direct measures.

The Convention on International Trade in Endangered Species of Fauna and Flora (CITES) provides the only existing international framework for licensing imports and exports. Its relevance to logging is restricted, of course, to endangered or threatened species; 15 tree species are currently listed under CITES, although the World Conser- vation Monitoring Centre has identified more than 300 Asian and African species in trade. However, individual countries may unilater- ally list any species that they wish to protect on Appendix III, and then trade cannot proceed without an export permit. A CITES listing is, of course, a species-specific measure; nevertheless, it would give authorities in consumer countries the mandate to refuse shipments of certain precious wood species that may have been illegally obtained in producer countries. Given the speed and scale of the illegal timber trade, CITES should probably be considered an adjunct to more wide-ranging measures rather than a solution in itself.

A number of prominent, but disparate, international bodies are involved in creating forestry policy and guidelines. These are outlined briefly below. However, the various international institutions that discuss forestry issues do not yet have a specific mandate to take comprehensive action to combat illegal logging. These fora could be worthwhile arenas to exchange ideas, but they are unlikely to be active in reaching international agreements or coordinating action.

UN Forum on Forests

The United Nations (UN) Forum on Forests was established in 2000 to replace the Intergovernmental Forum on Forests created at the UN General Assembly Special Session ("Rio plus Five") in 1997. The predecessor of the Intergovernmental Forum on Forests was the Intergovernmental Panel on Forests, which submitted a report containing policy recommendations to the fifth session of the UN Commission on Sustainable Development. The Intergovernmental Panel on Forests was mandated to review implementation of the 1992 Earth Summit's forest-related decisions; international cooperation in financial assistance and technology transfer; research, assessment, and development of criteria and indicators for sustainable forest management; and international organizations and multilateral institutions and instruments. The report called for an intergovernmental dialogue on forest policy, despite the existence of issues where a consensus could not be reached, including financial assistance, trade-related issues, and whether to begin negotiating a binding convention. It also called for national action and international cooperation to reduce and eventually eliminate the illegal forestry trade. In 2000 the final report of the Intergovernmental Forum on Forests called for the creation of an intergovernmental arrangement on forests and the establishment of the UN Forum on Forests, acting as a subsidiary body of the UN Economic and Social Council. The UN Forum on Forests is to meet on an annual basis.

At its first meeting in 2001, the UN Forum on Forests adopted a multiyear program of work, which noted that an intergovernmental arrangement for global forest policy, over which member countries still differ, should promote the management, conservation, and sustainable development of all types of forests. There is no mention of illegal logging in the program, although this might be encapsulated in the provision noting the importance of good governance and an enabling environment for sustainable forest management.

The UN Forum on Forests is supposed to consider the prospects for a legal framework on all types of forests within five years. This would provide an obvious forum for global discussion of the issues raised by illegal logging and conflict timber. However, the participants at the forum remain divided over whether a forestry convention is needed, let alone over the need for measures aimed specifically at the forestry sector. Any discussion of a forestry convention should include on its agenda the issues of illegal logging and conflict timber.

Food and Agriculture Organization

The linkage between human development and sustainable management forms the cornerstone of the forestry mission of the Food and Agriculture Organization of the United Nations (FAO). Its Forestry Program seeks to "maximize the potential of trees, forests, and related sources to improve people's economic, social, and environmental conditions, while ensuring that the resource is conserved to meet the needs of future generations." The FAO Program on Forestry and Planning provides for the collection, analysis, and dissemination of information on numerous matters, including trade, production, and consumption. The FAO also works with other international bodies on forest policy. It chairs the Inter-Agency Task Force on Forests, which coordinates the work of other international organizations, and it is the lead organization in the UN Forum on Forests on rehabilitation of forest cover, technology transfer, and supply and demand analysis of wood and nonwood forest products.

The FAO's Forest Products Division provides technical, environmental, and economic advice and assistance in the harvesting, transport, processing, trade, and marketing of wood and nonwood forest products, including wood-based energy and the management and development of forest industries appropriate to the conditions of individual countries. The Forest Harvest, Trade, and Marketing Branch undertakes a wide range of activities, including monitoring and analyzing forestry and trade in forest products. It also prepares studies on tariff and nontariff barriers, reviews trade policies of relevance to marketing of forest products, and promotes the development of appropriate policies of relevance to trade in forest products. In addition, it works on schemes for timber certification from sustainably managed forests. No specific program at FAO is looking at illegal logging or corruption in the forestry sector.

International Tropical Timber Organization

Initial efforts at the International Tropical Timber Organization (ITTO), such as the establishment of a Market Information Service to assist trade monitoring, appear to be promising for cooperation in the tracking of forest products. It is hoped that the results from these types of technical capacity-building initiatives will feed into developing a consensus among members and overcome the previous inability to reach an accord on illegal logging.

The ITTO also announced its intention to promote sustainable timber trade. A mid-term review estimated the combined cost of institutional strengthening and capacity building as $22.5 billion (Adams 1997). Estimates may come out much lower, however, if the exercise concentrates on the relatively few major players in the global marketplace. There are only six big producers—Bolivia, Brazil, Cameroon, Gabon, Indonesia, and Malaysia, which together account for 60–80 percent of world markets. Overall, some 70–100 concession holders harvest around 25–30 percent of all the tropical timber entering the global market. Concentrating financial and technical assistance and monitoring on these concessions could reap early rewards.

That said, the ITTO—an organization funded by timber trading countries—is often used as a shield by producers trying to fend off more onerous initiatives such as Forest Stewardship Council certification and, possibly, international efforts to curb illegal logging. Furthermore, critics argue that the tropical timber industry is far better at negotiating solutions to problems of illegal logging than implementing any of the resultant recommendations.

Forest Stewardship Council

The Forest Stewardship Council (FSC) is an independent, nonprofit, and nongovernmental organization that administers the first and most authoritative forest-product certification scheme. It has developed global standards for forest management through consultation with stakeholders from social, economic, and environmental sectors.

Forest certification is the process whereby forestry operations are measured against the FSC's 10 principles and 56 criteria for good forest management. Independent, FSC-accredited certification bodies conduct thorough assessments according to the criteria requested by landowners. If the forests conform with FSC standards, a certificate is issued that allows the producer to sell FSC-certified wood and to use the FSC logo on its products. An award of a certificate is predicated on adherence to all applicable laws of the country, including international agreements to which the country is a party, as well as specific forest management plans. It also requires all prescribed fees, royalties, and taxes to be paid. Further, FSC Criterion 1.5 requires the forests under approved management to be protected from illegal harvesting, settlement, or other unauthorized activities. Also the FSC is the only international certification scheme to require chain of custody as an explicit component.

The FSC logo provides consumers with assurance that the wood they purchase is from sustainably and legally managed forests. While the certification process does add to the cost of production, the impact on the selling price is small. FSC certification has received recognition from major supply chains (first was U.K. 95+ Buyers Group) and a commitment to buying and selling of FSC-endorsed products. The marketing and selling of FSC products in Europe have been successful, as the market in this region is sensitive to nonsustainably produced timber. However, in Asia (particularly in Japan) consumers are not so discerning, and even in Europe and the United States demand for FSC products is not uniform. This problem can be addressed partly by better consumer education and information campaigns.

Rival industry-based or quasi-government certification schemes have been created to fill a growing demand for certified timber products. It is possible that the presence of other international certification processes will weaken the hold of FSC or confuse the marketplace.

Currently, there are more than 2,400 FSC-certified companies in 66 countries, and FSC-certified forests cover some 71 million acres globally. As impressive as the FSC scheme is, the majority of FSC-certified forests and companies are located in North America or Europe. The FSC scheme has little impact in Asia or Africa, where there are very few certified bodies—areas with the worst aggregate records for illegal and unsustainable forest management. Until there is greater global consumer demand for certified timber products, other methods of control and tracking need to be implemented to address illegal logging. Regional agreements to control the timber trade and schemes like the FSC are useful starting points, but to attack a global problem like illegal logging, a global solution is required.

Policy Recommendations

Policy recommendations fall into eight categories:

• *Greater transparency in global forestry operations*. This is essential to the prevention of illegal logging and should be applied to every stage of a logging operation. Allocation of concessions should be by competitive and technical tender, with the results widely publicized.

Concession boundaries, the allocation of cutting licenses, and forest revenues accrued to the state should all be publicly available.

• *Involvement of local communities.* If local communities had a share of the profits deriving from a logging operation, they would be inclined to protect their forest from outsiders, insist that it be managed sustainably, and, in short, be the best monitors of the operation. Local communities should be included in the decisionmaking process related to the use of forests.

• *Enhanced enforcement.* Forest management authorities may need external capacity building to fulfill their mandates. External monitoring—for example, in Cambodia and Cameroon—can enable national enforcement units to tackle situations that would ordinarily be too sensitive for that country's nationals. Donor countries need to work with governments to improve capacities to detect and suppress forest crime.

• *Creation of legality certification schemes.* The current lack of international legislation suitable for tackling illegal logging means that as soon as illegally obtained timber leaves the borders of the producer country, it is de facto immediately laundered into the legal timber trade. A certificate of legality could be awarded by the appropriate authority in the producer country and be subject to independent verification. In turn, the certificate would be recognized in the legislation of signatory consumer countries. All timber imports would need to be accompanied by this certificate, with other imports being impounded. Like all systems, this would be vulnerable to forgeries and evasion, but monitoring and enforcement should minimize this problem. Producer and consumer countries should begin to develop a certificate of legality for timber shipments, in order to distinguish between legal and illegal timber.

• *Improved chain-of-custody monitoring.* Tagging of timber, bar coding, and transponder technologies need to be used to establish chains of custody and prevent the mixing of legal and illegal material. Accurate systems of accounting and inventory control are imperative and will result in enhanced revenue collection. Simple computer packages should be developed to permit governments and enforcement agencies to track products from the forest to the marketplace.

• *Customs collaboration.* If customs officials were directed to look for illegal logs or timber, or required importers to declare the legality of its source, this would improve due diligence assessments by industry partners. At the moment, importers are largely unaware of and uninterested in the processes and authorizations required to export the timber. Shipping companies may unknowingly transport illegal timber or products. The exporting country would also be involved in the process since an export certificate may legitimize the shipment.

• *Consumer-country controls.* Consumer-country customs authorities might, for example, follow a "red-amber-green" approach to investigating illegal timber shipments. For instance, exports from countries with known illegal logging problems could be flagged for further inspection; information on the shipment could then be exchanged with national authorities in the producer country. For the purpose of ensuring an efficient customs management process, a standard certificate would be desirable.

• *International cooperation and legal reform.* Bilateral cooperation between producer and consumer countries is needed to enforce domestic forestry legislation in both countries. If not already in existence, legislation should be passed in producing countries to outlaw illegal logging. Consumer countries should recognize this legislation, and a bilateral agreement between the two countries should ban the trade in illegal timber. These bilateral agreements would form a body of international law that could form the basis of a future multilateral agreement.

Notes

1. Compliance refers to a state's situation with regard to its obligations under international law. Enforcement refers to a set of actions—such as adopting laws and regulations or arresting and prosecuting malfeasants—that a state may take within its national territory to ensure implementation of a specific CTR. In other words, compliance is used in an international context and enforcement in a national one.

2. The Basel convention defines "wastes" somewhat tautologically as substances that are disposed of.

3. That is, the necessity to get an agreement up and running quickly as arguments over the precise categorization of hazardous waste could have gone on for years.

4. Of over 25,000 species regulated under CITES, more than 90 percent are listed on Appendix II.

5. Interpol signed memoranda of understanding with the CITES Secretariat in 1998 and with the Basel convention secretariat in 1999.

6. This is in line with UN General Assembly Resolution 55/198 on enhancing complementarities among international instruments related to environmental and sustainable development. See www.unep.org/gc_21st/Documents/gc-21-INF-19/e-GC-21-INF-19.doc.

7. For example, the fifth goal of the CITES 2000 strategic plan (Strategic Vision through 2005) emphasizes the importance of cooperation and links

with UNEP and other biodiversity-related conventions. Further, the Nairobi Declaration on the Role and Mandate of UNEP (1997) identifies one of the core UNEP purposes as developing "coherent interlinkages among existing international environmental conventions." The European Environmental Agency is also working on a range of projects regarding harmonizing reporting requirements, including the compilation of a database listing all obligations (legal and moral) resulting from reporting requirements under a wide range of international agreements.

8. Developed from a diagram in Johnson and others (1998, p. 20).

9. A valuable, white-fleshed fish caught in the southern ocean area, also known as Chilean sea bass.

10. The Centre for International and European Environmental Research conducted research in 2000 on links between forest-related multilateral environmental agreements at global, regional, and national levels and recommended greater use of technology in ensuring harmonized and complementary reporting of forest-related obligations to international bodies.

11. Article 19, Basel convention.

12. This problem is especially common in fisheries and forestry operations. Data from EU enforcement of its common fisheries policy show that there are about 50,000 vessels spread across approximately 106 square kilometers of sea, or an average of one vessel per 20 square kilometers. EU enforcement authorities carried out 20,357 inspections in 1990. Hence, the average chance of inspection is once every two years.

13. Kyoto, January 31, 2000.

14. Data from the Brazilian forest sector for 1996 show that only about 26 percent of the cost of enforcement actions was covered by the fines awarded. See Amigos da Terra (1996).

15. Barbados, Bulgaria, Chile, Ecuador, Guinea, Lebanon, Malaysia, Mali, Micronesia, Papua New Guinea, Slovenia, and Zambia. Additional countries will participate in subregional consultations to share experiences and lessons of the pilot countries.

16. See www.unep.org/unep/gef.

17. De Beers Consolidated Mines, Alrosa, Rio Tinto, and BHP Billiton together mine approximately 76 percent of the world's rough diamonds.

18. This interaction between tightening regulations and crime was made very clear in a U.S. court case in July 2000 where a Detroit-based company was caught deliberately contaminating rivers with diesel fuel and other toxins with the aim of profiting by providing a clean-up service. If the regulations did not exist, the waste would not have been dumped in the river as a kind of environmental "protection racket."

19. Argentina, Australia, Chile, France, New Zealand, Norway, and the United Kingdom all claim a specific portion of Antarctica; the claims of Argentina, Chile, and the United Kingdom overlap. The United States and

the Soviet Union rejected these claims and argued that their own substantive presence in the region could constitute a future claim. Belgium, Japan, and South Africa constituted the other original consultative parties to the Antarctic Treaty System.

20. Corruption is different from facilitation payments. The former is a bribe to induce an official to do something that he/she should not do as part of his/her job (that is, to award a contract without an open tender); the latter is a payment to encourage an official to do something that he/she should already be doing.

21. The commission was presided over by Judge M. E. Kumleben under the auspices of the South African Truth and Reconciliation Committee.

22. Article XX(g) of the treaty allows exception to this provision for the purposes of "conservation of exhaustible resources" or environmental protection. However, the various dispute panels felt that such measures did not achieve these aims in a manner consistent with the objectives of the General Agreement on Tariffs and Trade.

23. Angola, Guinea, and Sierra Leone have national certification schemes and receive technical support from the High Diamond Council in Antwerp.

24. Conflict diamonds are defined as diamonds that originate from areas under the control of forces that are in opposition to elected and internationally recognized governments or are in any way connected to those groups.

25. The sections cited in this appendix are from the Kimberley process working document dated January 2002.

26. The World Diamond Council is an industry association formed by the World Federation of Diamond Bourses and the International Diamond Manufacturers Association to address the problem of conflict diamonds. In late March 2002, the World Diamond Council announced it would implement its own control system of warranties that would endorse every rough diamond transaction at international trade centers. The council claims its system will complement the Kimberley process regime, but it is unclear whether the schemes will be complementary or confusing.

References

The word "processed" describes informally produced works that may not be commonly available through libraries.

Adams, Michael. 1997. "Resources Needed but Directed Where?" *ITTO Newsletter* 7(3). Available at www.itto.or.jp/newsletter/v7n3/19.html.
Amigos da Terra. 1996. *Forest Management at Loggerheads*. 1996 Update Report on Illegal Logging in the Brazilian Amazon. São Paulo.

Andreas, Peter. 2000. "Contraband Capitalism: Transnational Crime in an Era of Economic Liberalization." Paper presented at the conference on international organized crime in the global century, International Organized Crime in the Global Era, Oxford University, July 5–6. Processed.

Barbier, Edward B., J. C. Burgess, T. M. Swanson, and David W. Pearce. 1990. *Elephants, Economics, and Ivory.* London: Earthscan.

Basel Secretariat. 1999. *Hazardous Waste by the Numbers. Press Kit for the Tenth Anniversary Meeting of the Basel Convention.* Fifth meeting of the Conference of the Parties, December 6–10.

Dubash, Navroz K., and Frances Seymour. 1999. "The Political Economy of 'Environmental Adjustment': The World Bank as Midwife of Forest Policy Reform." Paper presented at the conference International Institutions: Global Processes–Domestic Consequences, Duke University, Durham, N.C., April. Processed.

European Union. 2001. "Special Report: EU Illegal Timber Imports." *EU Forest Watch* (July-August). Compiled by Forests Monitor on behalf of Fern. Available at www.fern.org/pubs/fw/srsep01.pdf.

ITTO (International Tropical Timber Organization). 1999. *Annual Review and Assessment of the World Tropical Timber Situation 1998.* Yokohama.

Johnson, T., and others. 1998. *Feasibility Study for a Harmonized Information Management Infrastructure for Biodiversity-Related Treaties.* Cambridge, U.K.: World Conservation Monitoring Centre.

Miller, Marian. 1995. *The Third World in Global Environmental Politics.* Buckingham: Open University Press.

Volpi, M. 2002. "Is Greed or Grievance at the Root of the Current Conflict in the Democratic Republic of Congo?" M.Sc. Thesis, University of London.

Wang, Xi. 1996. "The International Control of Transboundary Illegal Shipment of Hazardous Wastes: A Survey of Recent Cases That Happened in China." In *Proceedings of the Fourth International Conference on Environmental Compliance and Enforcement, April 22–26,* Vol. II. Washington, D.C.: International Network for Environmental Compliance and Enforcement.

"WB Leads Move to Link Indonesia Aid to Forest Conservation." 2000. *Asia Pulse,* February 1.

White House. 2000. *National Drug Control Strategy: Annual Report.* Washington, D.C.

World Bank. 1999. "Forest Sector Review." Washington, D.C. Processed.

"World Bank Sees Flaws in Forest Policy." 2000. *Financial Times,* February 11.

Wynn, Brian. 1989. "The Toxic Waste Trade: International Regulatory Policy and Options." *Third World Quarterly* 11(3):120–46.

CHAPTER 5

Follow the Money: The Finance of Illicit Resource Extraction

Jonathan M. Winer and Trifin J. Roule

AN UNINTENDED CONSEQUENCE OF THE reduction in trade barriers and border controls is the increased use of the infrastructure of legitimate cross-border trade to move narcotics and weapons, smuggle persons, and transport the proceeds of crime from one country to another in violation of applicable national legal and regulatory barriers (see, for example, Findlay 1999; "Globalization of the Drug Trade" 1999). This is sometimes referred to as the dark side of globalization (see, for example, Litan 2001; Summers 2000). Central to this problem are abuses of the integrated system for global movements of funds, allowing people to store and transport monetized value almost anywhere (International Institute of Strategic Studies 2002). To combat these abuses, a series of international initiatives have been undertaken, beginning with the inclusion of anti–drug money laundering and law enforcement commitments in the 1988 United Nations (UN) Convention to Combat Illicit and Psychotropic Drugs (Vienna convention) and the creation of the Financial Action Task Force on Money Laundering (FATF) by the G-7 in 1989. They have since included the 1998 Organisation for Economic Co-operation and Development (OECD) Project against Illicit Tax Competition, the G-7 creation of the Financial Stability Forum in 1999, the 2000 UN Convention against Transnational Organized Crime (Palermo convention), the Council of Europe's GRECO Program to assess and implement mechanisms to prevent and prosecute corruption, and the creation of various regional bodies to engage in a process of mutual assessment as a means to achieve greater financial transparency.[1] Further related but separate initiatives to promote financial transparency have been undertaken by important self-regulatory organizations, such as the Basel Group of Bank Supervisors, in connection with its revised standards for assessing risk to bank capital, the International Organization of Securities Commissions,[2] and the Offshore Group of Bank Supervisors, among others. Finally, a coalition of private sector financial institutions, denominated the Wolfsberg Group, has established its own set of transparency standards, initially created in 2000 to prevent the use of their banks and brokerage firms to hide the proceeds of corruption and extended in late 2001 to prevent terrorist finance.[3]

The increasing integration of national financial payments and clearing systems into a global financial infrastructure has made it possible for changes in financial regulatory systems to be contemplated, mandated, and enforced at a global level, as the twin name-and-shame exercises initiated in 1999 by FATF and OECD have already demonstrated. In these exercises, countries with lax financial regulatory systems were warned that they could face loss of market access to major financial centers if they did not harmonize their standards for financial transparency with the requirements levied by the members of those organizations. Both FATF and OECD developed lists of jurisdictions deemed not to be in compliance with those standards. In each case, many of the targeted jurisdictions complained bitterly that the approach did not respect their sovereignty. However, in each case, jurisdictions threatened with being blacklisted adopted comprehensive domestic legislation, which on paper complied with the required norms almost immediately.[4]

The initiatives share many common elements. These include the need to know one's customers to ensure that they are not engaged in illicit activity; the need for financial institutions to share information pertaining to illicit activity with regulators, with law enforcement, and, when needed, with one another; the need to trace such funds; and the need of each country to assist all others in enforcing violations of their domestic laws. Principles initially used to combat drug trafficking and later extended to include all serious crimes and, recently, terrorist finance and corruption have now been extended to include many fiscal offenses, as countries have come to recognize that a beggar-thy-neighbor approach to tax violations threatens to beggar all jurisdictions.

To date, cross-border exploitation of illicit extraction represents an aspect of the illicit use of the global financial services sector that has received comparatively little attention. Existing financial transparency initiatives have not addressed the need to combat the flow of funds from abuses of natural resources in cases of conflict. Although such activity could often fall within the parameters of standards and regulations designed to address money laundering, terrorist finance, or corruption, the existing standards do not directly address the steps that a financial institution is supposed to take in handling what may be the proceeds of the sale of coltan, diamonds, oil and gas, tanzanite, timber, or similar commodities that warring political factions use to sustain conflict. The closest the current standards come to dealing with these issues are the requirements that financial institutions eschew the proceeds of corruption and that they respect UN sanctions. While both standards have existed in principle for a long time, enforcement is very recent and remains incomplete.

Access to the global financial services infrastructure is a critical element in sustaining resource-related conflict, as its use is usually required to transport and store the wealth of those who are using the natural resources they control to remain in power and fund conflicts. Indeed, these services are necessary to speed the transportation and investment of, and to provide security for, funds generated by the exploitation of resources by persons whose control of those resources is often very insecure. The power to control the resources may be the combatant's most important asset and the one that opposing factions can most easily capture. Thus the ability during conflict to strip assets quickly and convert them into money stored safely can become a critical element in building the capacity to sustain a military or political force.

Purely domestic mechanisms within a country in the midst of conflict are especially unlikely to be effective in countering illicit exploitation of natural resources. If there are to be any practical impediments to such exploitation, they must necessarily be built so as to strengthen the capacity of critical institutions situated *outside* the country at war. To be effective, rules limiting financial transactions involving illicit commodities must be enforced by persons and entities located not only locally but also at a distance from the conflict. Absent other systems of incentive and sanction, those persons and entities may have little immediate stake in cutting off trade associated with the conflict.

As the Kimberley Certification Process Scheme has suggested for diamonds, an adequate response to the exploitation of natural resources to sustain conflict will likely require new approaches to handling the movement of physical goods across borders.[5] To date, even the most developed states have had tremendous problems in combating cross-border smuggling, with substantial deficiencies evident even in the world's most important borders, such as that of the Schengen area in the European Union or the 2,000-mile-long U.S.-Mexican border. A system of adequate controls to segregate licit from illicit goods that move across borders remains an essential element of combating other critical global security problems, including drugs and arms trafficking and terrorism. The sheer investment in personnel, engineering systems, and the technology required to individually monitor and inspect goods in transit means that such initiatives will be long term in nature. By contrast, extending the new regimes covering the global financial services infrastructure explicitly to cover abuses of natural resources could take advantage of initiatives that are well under way and already beginning to have an impact in other areas important to global security. Although it may appear counterintuitive, the enforcement of documentary requirements and regulatory oversight over intangible goods (money) may be in certain respects relatively easier than the enforcement of such controls on tangible goods. Intangible goods require legal rules of recognition for validity: thus tightening such rules and insisting on their embodiment in the data-processing software necessary for electronic fund transfers have the potential to regulate and monitor all the funds that enter electronic payment systems.

The growing literature on the relationship between resource abuse and conflict includes many studies of how commodities such as diamonds, oil and gas, and timber have been used to fund corrupt political leaders and parties, armies, guerrilla groups, and terrorists (de Soysa 2001). The literature also provides insights into the economics of conflict and war. However, substantial gaps remain in articulating and assessing how the money has actually moved, the nature of the persons and institutions handling it, and the mechanisms used to launder the funds and avoid sanctions or other legal restrictions. This chapter seeks to provide an initial review of the financial infrastructure used to exploit natural resources linked to conflict.

The chapter first outlines a conceptual framework for viewing the financial infrastructure used in connection with violent conflict, corruption, and poor governance. It then turns to a series of case studies involving different forms of resource exploitation in connection with these phenomena and the mechanisms used to finance such exploitation. For each case study, the paper reviews the existing regulatory and enforcement capabilities within the affected jurisdiction or region and their adequacy in countering illicit resource exploitation. The paper then reviews the existing initiatives created to address illicit resource exploitation and their handling of the illicit money flows that arise from such exploitation. The paper seeks to address the implications of the typological similarities and differences in the financial mechanisms used to exploit different kinds of natural resources at different levels of conflict. It also explores potential synergies between existing financial transparency and anticorruption initiatives and their ability to be refocused to combat resource exploitation in areas of conflict. Finally, the chapter articulates a series of possible initiatives that could be undertaken to respond to the existing problems and capacity gaps by various institutions, including governments, international financial institutions, international organizations such as the United Nations, regional bodies, self-regulatory organizations, and parts of the private sector. This section identifies possible new initiatives under which oversight mechanisms could be created to discourage resource exploitation in areas of conflict.

Any effective response to the exploitation of natural resources in areas of conflict will require cooperation among a diverse set of global and regional institutions and entities. These include not just individual governments and international organizations but also international financial institutions, self-regulatory organizations, important nongovernmental organizations, and key elements of the private sector. The participation of all the legitimate stakeholders in the solution is likely essential for progress to be possible, let alone sustainable.

Definitions and Concepts

With the end of the cold war, policy analysts and academics initiated a concerted effort to account for the growing number of civil conflicts arising across the globe. Some widely held explanations for civil conflicts attribute the onset of civil strife to environmental stress, demographic pressure, and a variety of societal factors, such as religious and ethnic differences (see, for example, Homer-Dixon 1999; Snow 1996). Increasingly, the growth in conflicts has been attributed to groups determined to achieve a "payoff" for their efforts through the trafficking of illicit commodities. As Paul Collier concludes, some individuals can "do well out of war" (Collier 2000). Collier's conclusion can be extended beyond individuals to entire government agencies, especially security forces such as the military, police, and customs officials, organized criminal groups, terrorists, drug traffickers, and private security forces such as paramilitary groups and guerrilla organizations. However, scant literature is devoted to the financial networks that these groups use to exploit natural resources in times of conflict.

The exploiters of natural resources in areas of conflict generally rely on a common infrastructure for handling illicit proceeds. This includes the formal financial services system of local banks linked to foreign banks, alternative remittance systems such as *hawala* and *hundi* institutions, import-export firms that participate in false invoicing schemes, precious metal markets, and the use of trusts, international business companies, and nontransparent jurisdictions as mechanisms to hide funds. Such exploiters are themselves often interrelated. Governments of questionable legitimacy often have significant ties to criminal organizations, especially when both are involved in resource extraction. However, there are also important differences in the infrastructure that tends to be available to governments, criminals, terrorists, and private security forces. Accordingly, it may be useful to distinguish the principal types of exploiters in order to determine the financial infrastructure that is most relevant to their exploitation. It is also important to define the major differences between lawful and illicit resource extraction in order to articulate more precisely what is illicit than the general formulation "I know it when I see it."

Defining Legitimate Resource Extraction

Numerous legitimate governments license private sector entities to engage in resource extraction or, alternatively, engage in such extraction themselves. The extraction of commodities as a legitimate function of government commonly includes (a) fairness in bidding for sales or leasing, so that the government receives the maximum possible revenue for the resources sold; (b) transparency in the pricing and amounts of commodities sold; (c) conservation measures designed to minimize the permanent loss of the commodities and to maximize the length of the extraction period; (d) reinvestment in the means of production for extracting the resources, such as investments in pipes or drilling equipment for oil or replanting of trees in logging concessions; (e) restoration of the environment from which the commodities have been extracted, to minimize the environmental damage and to maximize the long-term economic value of the extraction area; and (f) deposit of the funds generated from the extracted resources in the state treasury, where they are then used to fund government operations.[6]

Defining Illicit Resource Extraction

Illicit extraction by governments features the converse of the principles of licit resource extraction. Ordinarily, illicit extraction involves (a) politicized or crony-based contracts for the sale of commodities, (b) limited or falsified information on pricing and quantities, (c) asset stripping with no regard to the future, (d) little to no investment in long-term production, (e) failure to restore stripped areas, and (f) disappearance of the revenues from the sale of the resources so that they cannot be traced, with minimal or no benefit to the state treasury. When all of these factors are present, a particular case of extraction is likely to be illicit.

Other cases may be less clear. For example, a government that issues contracts for the sale of commodities to insiders on a noncompetitive basis to permit kickbacks to corrupt officials may still insist on a portion of the revenues returning to the state treasury. Such routine corruption may undermine both the revenue base and the popular support for a government, but only the criminalized portion of the transaction might be characterized as illicit. The standard definition of corruption is the exploitation of public resources for private gain (World Bank 1997, p. 8). In practice, the determination of whether particular natural resources are public goods or available for private sale may be both uncertain and fluid, as was demonstrated in the many ambiguities that arose in the course of the privatization of state-owned oil and gas resources from the Soviet Union during the 1990s.

Accordingly, illicit resource extraction is here defined as the sale of natural resources from a country by means that avoid the payment of taxes to the national government in the host country or that violate UN resolutions. Thus, when taxes are properly paid on resources extracted at market prices for goods not subject to sanction, the sale is deemed licit.

Defining Conflict

Contemporary conflicts are most often intrastate, rather than between states, and involve aspects of both political and criminal violence; it is these forms of conflict that have been most linked to the exploitation of natural resources (Collier 2000). There have been numerous efforts to define "armed conflict."[7] This chapter uses as its definition "a contested incompatibility that concerns government or territory or both where the use of armed force between two parties results in at least 25 battle-related deaths and where at least one of the two parties is the government of a state." This definition fits nicely within a study whose focus is the contested incompatibilities of control over natural resources that have economic value to the person or entity controlling them and the mechanisms used to translate that value into wealth, store that wealth, and make that wealth available to strengthen the political control that the person or entity is seeking to exercise over government, territory, or merely the commodities themselves.

Defining the Entities Exploiting Illicit Commodities

Roughly speaking, at least four distinct types of entities systematically use the funds from illicit commodities to fund their security operations and control in areas of conflict. The four entities are governments, rebel groups, organized criminals, and terrorists. Although there are important differences among them and their relationship to the illicit commodities, the categories are not exclusive. Corrupt officials often form relationships with organized criminals, as do terrorists, in what

Michael Ross (forthcoming) has termed "cooperative plunder." Similarly, relationships between rebel groups and organized crime have existed in Angola, Congo, Kosovo, and the Philippines. Comparable linkages between organized criminal and terrorist groups have been prevalent in Colombia and Sri Lanka. Typically, in cases where governments are funded by illicit commodities, organized groups of criminals and terrorists that are funded by them also spring up, as government exploitation of illegal commodities is closely related to poor governance, popular unrest, and high levels of criminality and violence. Where governments, organized criminals, and terrorists are exploiting illicit commodities, there is greater risk of a secessionist movement or outright civil war, generating rebel groups funded by such commodities.[8]

Governments Financed by Illicit Commodities. Because governments financed by illicit commodities govern poorly and provide little in return from their resource exploitation to the people of the country, they are often not democratically elected regimes and retain power in part through the funds generated by commodity sales. Regimes in Cambodia and Myanmar, for example, have been subject to repeated rebellions, civil wars, warlordism, and guerrilla movements but have survived in substantial part by sharing the revenues of the sales of opium, precious stones, and timber with groups necessary to help them maintain their security (see Curtis 1998; Takano 2002). The Abacha regime in Nigeria similarly retained power and put down challenges in part by ensuring that oil revenue went to those factions of the military needed to sustain control (see, for example, Ihonvbere and Shaw 1998). Charles Taylor's Liberia remains perhaps the prime example of such exploitation and its impact on a region, as his exploitation of Sierra Leone's diamonds played a substantial role in sparking and sustaining a brutal civil war.[9] In other cases, countries may be democratic, but governance is weakened by the involvement of government in illicit commodities, which weakens law enforcement structures, reduces tax collection, and empowers corrupt officials and organized criminals.

Rebel Groups Financed by Illicit Commodities. The principal difference between rebel groups financed by illicit commodities and terrorist groups financed by illicit commodities is the nature of the forces (O'Neill and Meyer 2001). Rebel groups control territory and target government territory in military operations, while terrorists primarily target civilians. Long-term rebel activity in which illicit commodities sustained rebel military forces have included Angola, where the National Union for the Total Independence of Angola (UNITA) largely funded their war against the government through diamond revenues during 1992–2001; Sierra Leone, where the Revolutionary United Front similarly exploited diamonds throughout most of the 1990s; and Afghanistan, where the Taliban and the Northern Alliance each built their military operations on the exploitation of opium and precious stones.

Organized Crime Financed by Illicit Commodities. In poorly governed countries, criminal organizations can use payments to well-placed officials in order to secure revenue streams for themselves from the exploitation of natural resources. In such cases, the corrupt officials may receive payment, but the criminal organization, which manages most elements of the exploitation, retains the greatest share of the proceeds. In such countries, the governments formally oppose the asset stripping. Elements of the government may even be ineffectively trying to discourage it, but the capacity of the government to prevent the exploitation is weaker than the capacity of the criminals to carry it out. In such cases, the only persons within the country who benefit from the resource extraction are the criminals and those who have been corrupted by them.

Terrorists Funded by Illicit Commodities. While some aspects of terrorist finance remain uncertain, the reliance of a number of terrorist groups on trafficking in illicit drugs—chiefly coca and opium—is well documented.[10] Illicit drugs, like illicit sales of metals, oil and gas, precious stones, and timber, mostly move through the same transport systems and modalities as licit commodities. That is, terrorists, like governments and organized criminals, need to use the formal banking system to handle the proceeds of their illicit activity. To do so, they need to launder the revenues derived from their illegal activity, which they accomplish through similar techniques. These include the use of false invoicing, trusts, and international business companies; reliance on bank secrecy havens; and reinvestment of illicit funds in legitimate businesses. Unlike governments, terrorists also rely on black market money exchange systems, such as the black market peso exchange used by Latin America and the United States and the *hawala* system used by the Middle East, South Asia, and the rest of the world, to avoid having to move currency across borders and to retain value in their native currencies at home. For similar reasons, they also convert their funds into gold and gemstones, as both are anonymous commodities that are readily convertible into cash.[11] Terrorists generally fund their activities by providing security to farmers growing illegal coca or opium rather than engaging in more demanding forms of resource extraction. This limitation may be related to lack of opportunities to secure illicit control over licit commodities. Historically, terrorists have played an important role in sustained conflict in numerous countries, including Bolivia, Colombia, and Peru (coca), Afghanistan and Pakistan (opium), Kosovo (primarily opium), Lebanon (opium), and Myanmar (opium). Recently, important terrorist groups have included the Abu Sayyaf Group in the Philippines, Al-Qaeda in Afghanistan and Pakistan, the Kosovo Liberation Army, the Kurdish Workers Party in Turkey, Liberation Tigers of Tamil Eelam in Sri Lanka, and the Revolutionary Armed Forces of Colombia, each of which has funded their operations through the sale of narcotics.

Common Elements of Finance by Illicit Commodities

Money launderers, terrorist financiers, corrupt officials, and tax evaders have relied on a relatively standard set of tools to transfer, store, and conceal money generated domestically from government mechanisms in their home countries. Although many other tools are in the toolbox of illicit finance, the basics include the following.

To generate illicit proceeds:

• Work in collusion with purchasers of smuggled or illicit goods to prepare invoices that falsify the identification of importer, exporter, quality, or quantity of goods
• Unilaterally engage in invoice fraud, with false declarations of importer or exporter and quality or quantity of goods
• Collude with customs or corrupt officials to smuggle illicit goods from a country and then sell them to an independent no-questions-asked third party at a discount from market prices
• Provide a license for others to obtain illicit goods and sell them in violation of law, by providing safe haven for the illicit activity within a territory and receiving a kickback for providing this protection or opportunity
• Obtain cash in return for the illicit good and place it in a financial institution that either does not object to receiving the proceeds of illicit commodities or is in collusion with the seller.

To layer illicit proceeds in order to hide their actual ownership:

• Establish shell companies to engage in import and export transactions
• Create overseas trusts to shield the ownership of assets and to permit the assets to be managed by a trusted third party with a duty of secrecy to the owner of the assets
• Open bank accounts offshore in the name of other fictitious trading, investment, or service companies
• Hire local agents to act as nominees for shell companies and bank accounts held in the name of shells or fictitious companies

- Use underground or alternative remittance systems, including black market currency exchanges, to avoid cross-border currency controls
- Exchange one potentially traceable commodity, such as oil or timber, for another less traceable commodity, such as gold
- Sell a poorly traceable commodity, such as gold, in a major commodities market, such as Dubai in the United Arab Emirates or the Colon Free Zone in Panama
- Smuggle cash to another jurisdiction for placement in a willing financial institution.

To reinvest, use, or expend illicit proceeds:

- Use funds held at a foreign bank in a false name or company to purchase legitimate businesses and then use those legitimate businesses to generate new funds
- Purchase goods outside of the country with the illicit proceeds and then sell those goods inside the country to generate new clean revenues
- Receive payment domestically from a broker in local or hard currency at some discount in return for the broker making an offsetting payment in another jurisdiction
- Leave the funds in a foreign trust under the control of a local agent as an insurance policy against the day when the persons controlling the money need to flee their home jurisdiction.

Common Elements of Conflicts Financed by Illicit Commodities

A recent study by Michael Renner for the World Watch Institute (Renner 2002) describes a number of common elements in conflicts financed by illicit commodities. As described by Renner, essential components of conflicts financed by illicit commodities are (a) the availability of "lootable natural resource wealth," (b) licit or illicit taxation on resource extraction by various forces with uncertain legitimacy, (c) ability to keep revenue streams "off the books" and hidden from oversight, (d) enrichment of corrupt elites, and (e) use of extreme violence against civilians to establish and enforce control over resources through intimidation (Renner 2002, pp. 10–14). These criteria are strikingly reminiscent of those applicable to traditional, mafia-style organized crime and reflect the standard approaches to business still used by criminal organizations and terrorist groups wherever they operate. Thus the conflicts themselves feature precisely the elements of the critical legal, social, and economic infrastructure required by criminals and terrorists. It is logical that such conflicts generate organized crime and terrorism to accompany the exploitation of natural resources undertaken by governments and rebel groups, as each type of group takes advantage of common mechanisms to secure and harness the revenues extracted from the resources.

Existing Initiatives

International efforts to respond to abuses of commodities linked to conflict have run along a number of separate tracks, only some of which deal with financial aspects. Most of the initiatives fall into one or more of the following categories, each of which is reviewed briefly to assess the degree to which it has addressed financial flows and mechanisms associated with resource exploitation:

• Embargoes, in which the United Nations has agreed on measures to limit transborder transactions during the conflict
• Certification programs, in which goods are permitted to move across borders only if they meet certain documentation requirements
• Disclosure regimes, in which public or private participants in transactions involving a commodity linked to conflict must disclose certain information about any transaction for it to be lawful
• Anticorruption and transparency standards and norms, which may indirectly criminalize the activities of officials and private persons involved in various forms of commodity exploitation
• Antiterrorist standards and norms, which may lead to the regulation of financial mechanisms used by terrorists and by groups involved in the exploitation of illicit commodities.
• Anti–money laundering standards and norms, which may sanction countries that facilitate various forms of commodity exploitation
• Drug or crime control standards or norms, which establish broad international obligations to combat drug trafficking or organized crime by criminalizing certain forms of conduct, authorizing procedures for enforcement, requiring certain regulations, and mandating forms of international cooperation, including criminalizing and regulating the laundering of the proceeds of illicit transactions involving narcotics
• Private sector "seal" initiatives that establish minimum standards to which a business must agree to adhere in order to be certified as a member in good standing of the seal organization
• Name-and-shame exercises, both governmental and nongovernmental.

Each of these categories has areas of effectiveness and limits, and these, together with examples of each type of initiative, are discussed below.[12]

Embargoes

An ongoing conflict in which contesting military or security forces are operating within a territory is generally the prerequisite to the UN authorizing a broad regime of sanctions that covers a territory, with certain exceptions to allow for the imposition of sanctions on regimes that have initiated conflict and are deemed to be dangerous (such as Iraq). Sanctions regimes can be total or partial, short term or long term.[13]

The imposition of embargoes reduces access to markets, especially those in the most developed countries, which constitute the most sustained source of demand for the products of an embargoed country. In cases where there is a political consensus in support of sanctions, the loss of market access for both imports and exports can have an immediate and substantial impact on the civilian population of the targeted country, undermining political support over time for continuation of the conflict. Embargoes also may make it harder for people to export illicit natural resources, as buyers become scarce. By reducing demand, embargoes may accomplish their immediate objective: reducing the sources of funds for warring combatants. They may also have the secondary benefit of reducing the harvesting of the commodities.

Embargoes are only as good as the political consensus that sustains them. Black marketers, criminal organizations, corrupt officials, and legitimate businesses willing to ignore sanctions in favor of profits will routinely violate sanctions to the extent that broader regulatory and enforcement measures do not prevent them from doing so. Embargoes on countries selling goods such as oil and timber that have inelastic markets may increase the price on global markets for the banned commodity, rewarding those willing to violate the sanctions. Embargoes may also strengthen the relative political and economic power of those violating them, both within and outside the embargoed country, by giving those willing to break the law a market advantage over those abiding by the law. Civilian populations tend to experience the brunt of across-the-board sanctions, as local security forces requisition key commodities for themselves, focusing any market deprivations on the general population, which may then blame the sanctions rather than the government or local security forces for their suffering.

The imposition of sanctions on South Africa played a critical role, over time, in forcing the dismantling of apartheid and the creation of democracy in the country. Sanctions imposed on Serbia made a key contribution to the eventual displacement of the Milosevic regime. Indeed, some U.S. policymakers have argued that Milosevic's downfall was brought about by the impact of sanctions once funds controlled by Milosevic and held in financial institutions outside Serbia were identified and the sanctions began to impose constraints on the well-being of those within the regime.[14] By contrast, sanctions imposed on Iraq after the Gulf War did not bring about regime change or attenuate the power of Iraq's military ruler, as the Iraqi regime was able to sell enormous quantities of oil illegally despite the sanctions. Similarly, sanctions have done little to stop the conflict in the Democratic Republic of Congo. In neither case did the limitations on the sale of commodities stop the conflict or bring about regime change. In the South Africa case, the sanctions did not prevent the government from exporting large quantities of the country's most important commodity: diamonds. Serbia had no commodities to exploit. The comprehensive UN sanctions on Iraq and the Democratic Republic of Congo did not prevent security and military forces from selling enough commodities to sustain themselves irrespective of sanctions. There have also been extraordinarily few prosecutions or seizures of assets of entities or persons engaged even in systematic violations of sanctions, rendering enforcement risks low and enforcement action largely symbolic.

As has been commonly observed, broad sanctions imposing barriers on trade can reduce the funds available to regimes engaged in conflict but require active support from many, if not most or all, countries to be effective (Cortright and Lopez 2002; Hufbauer, Schott, and Elliott 1990). Such sanctions certainly have not prevented exploitation of natural resources when the legitimate market for the commodity is of substantial size and scope. Other limitations on effectiveness include the limited capacity of some governments and the impact of corruption and criminality in facilitating illicit activity.

Sectoral Embargoes. A small number of commodities are widely viewed to be incompatible with social stability in general and are subject to international embargo, with limited exceptions for commercial or military use. These mainly include illicit drugs, especially opium and coca derivatives, certain forms of weaponry, and some precursor materials that can be used to create weapons of mass destruction. Of these, narcotics and nuclear material controls are most relevant to this study, as each is a prohibited commodity.

Sectoral embargoes on illicit narcotics, military weapons, and the precursors of weapons of mass destruction have established global standards and norms that have, for all practical purposes, eliminated any lawful commercial market for these products. Those participating in buying or selling embargoed goods face substantial criminal as well as civil penalties in almost every country. Most countries cooperate well with one another in investigating violations of sectoral sanctions and, in general, are willing to extradite violators. Over time, most persons violating sectoral sanctions are punished, and most of the persons producing the illicit commodities find they can no longer remain in the illicit business.

Prohibitions may not eliminate substantial market demand for the commodities. To the extent such market demand continues, those willing to violate the legal norms are likely to have substantial economic incentives to engage in the prohibited conduct. Regions of conflict produce especially widespread violations of sectoral sanctions. Typically, such regions are located in countries or provinces that provide safe havens or impunity for those involved in illicit production, sale, and purchase of sanctioned goods. Indeed, sectoral embargoes tend to concentrate production in areas where governments, military forces, or other security forces can exploit illicit production. Sectoral sanctions also tend to reward those involved in black markets, increase the size of black markets, and over time create networks of private sector entities and corrupt officials participating in the illicit activity. Thus sectoral prohibitions can weaken governance by encouraging rent-seeking behavior and increasing the relative economic and political strength of criminals and criminal organizations.

International conventions universally regulate opium and coca derivatives, with the most important instrument being the Vienna convention, which prohibits the cultivation and production of these products as well as their transportation, purchase, sale, and financing. The convention has been the backbone of all subsequent international efforts to combat the sale of illicit drugs. Its signatories include almost every country in the world.[15] The requirements of the prohibition regime have driven signatories to build new anti–money laundering enforcement and regulatory regimes, capacities, and agencies. Many countries have created entire antidrug agencies to implement their obligations under the convention. Notably, the impetus for the creation of financial intelligence units and the Egmont Group also arose as one of many consequences of the convention's adoption. Drug money–laundering prosecutions and asset seizures are fairly common internationally, making drug trafficking and drug money laundering a business that has real rather than theoretic risks for market participants. The United Nations plays an important role in assessment and implementation of the prohibition regime through the UN International Drug Control Program and the annual meetings of the Commission on Narcotic Drugs in Vienna. Similarly, the many conventions covering nuclear weapons have created an international prohibition regime that is largely, although not universally, accepted. The conventions include the Treaty on Non-Proliferation of Nuclear Weapons, the Convention on the Physical Protection of Nuclear Material, and the Convention on Nuclear Safety, among others. These conventions generally prohibit the acquisition of nuclear weapons and relevant precursors by those who do not already have them. These control regimes criminalize or regulate relevant forms of commercial activity, both domestic and transborder, involving nuclear material and related items, with national adherence to the regimes monitored through the International Atomic Energy Agency, also based in Vienna. The relevant conventions and the International Atomic Energy Agency are focused on the control of particular substances and technologies, not on the financial aspects of nuclear smuggling. However, criminal involvement in nuclear smuggling has been separately addressed by the Palermo convention, which does cover money laundering.

Effective action against narcotics has required the development of anti–money laundering capacities that adhere to international standards. By contrast, control of nuclear material within the private sector has been largely effective irrespective of financial control mechanisms, with the notable exception of nuclear smuggling in which state actors have been the source of demand.[16] The international consensus that the material should not enter the stream of commerce for any entity other than a state has helped to maintain adequate controls. However, one additional and unique element of controls over nuclear material is the physical danger involved in smuggling radioactive substances, which both increases the barrier to entry in direct exploitation of the material (mining) and reduces the incentive to smuggle. Notably, even in this extraordinarily tough enforcement and regulatory environment, nuclear smuggling has remained an active, although comparatively infrequent, phenomenon.[17]

Certification Regimes

In at least a general sense, customs authorities have always relied on country-of-origin certification requirements, which, although often falsified or ignored, provide a baseline for the imposition of duties. Beyond the standard country-of-origin requirements levied by customs authorities, commodities long covered by international certification regimes have tended to fall into two categories: (a) commodities regulated because they are dangerous, such as weapons, both military and small, and technologies useful for military purposes as well as for standard commercial applications and (b) commodities regulated because they are deemed irreplaceable or "at risk" as a result of prior exploitation, such as endangered species. Recent efforts to create certification programs covering timber might also fall into the second category. However, a third category may also now exist: (c) commodities regulated because of their exploitation in connection with sustaining conflict. Diamonds were the first commodity subject to certification within this category, as a result of the Kimberley process. Tanzanite may be a second example if the Tucson protocols are implemented.

Goods moving in international commerce are generally required to bear country-of-origin certifications, using a standard form or certificate of origin adopted by the Customs Cooperation Council of the World Customs Organization in 1973. The standard form requires identification of the exporter and consignee, particulars of transport, description of the goods, and country of origin. Customs agencies have generally been the sole enforcers of such certifications. The limitations of individual customs agencies due to low pay, poor training, inadequate resources, and corruption inhibit effective enforcement of country-of-origin certifications in developing countries. Because the goods move across borders, these domestic weaknesses are exported with the goods, as certifications of origin are only as good as the enforcement mechanism in the weakest link in the customs chain. Customs certifications typically are accompanied by declarations of value. False declarations are endemic to international trade, especially as underinvoicing provides the opportunity to reduce taxes at the country of origin and tariffs at the country of destination. To date, there has been no systematic effort to tie certification schemes on a global basis to transparent payment mechanisms. Certification is required in several notable sectors: diamonds, endangered species, and firearms. We deal with each in turn.

Diamonds.   Since May 2000, representatives from 37 nations, the diamond industry, and a number of nongovernmental organizations have conducted negotiations (referred to as the Kimberley process, after the town in South Africa where the first meeting was held) to develop an international system of diamond certification. In March 2002, delegations reached agreement on a range of issues, including establishment of a database and standards for handling rough diamonds at each successive stage. Ultimately, the process failed to adopt one important element that had been recommended by a number of participants, namely, independent, effective monitoring of the regulations and control mechanisms that each nation is supposed to put in place so that a global system can go into effect. Very few countries have adequate measures in place. Consequently, the process relies primarily on voluntary participation and adherence by governments and industry; it lacks an international authority to monitor and enforce rules. The process entails recommendations, rather than binding controls, for how diamonds are to be handled from mining to export. Participation in the "chain of warranties" that follows the initial export is voluntary, and monitoring and enforcement are left to self-regulation. After the rumors that members of Al-Qaeda were attempting to exploit the loosely regulated tanzanite markets, American dealers in precious stones undertook initial steps to apply to tanzanite measures similar to those specified in the Kimberley process, although implementation has yet to take place ("Kimberley Process for Tanzanite" 2002). Neither the Kimberley process nor the Tucson protocols include any measures covering financial mechanisms.

Endangered Species. In 1975 the Convention on International Trade in Endangered Species of Wild Fauna and Flora (CITES) came into force, affording various degrees of protection to more than 30,000 species of animals and plants, whether they are traded as live specimens, fur coats, or dried herbs. There are currently 160 parties to CITES, which requires that the export of any specimen of a species included in its Appendix I require permission and the presentation of an export permit and that the import of such a specimen require permission, an import permit, and either an export permit or a reexport certificate.[18] CITES requires parties to criminalize trade in protected species and to maintain records of trade in the protected species.[19] The convention does not address financial mechanisms that may be used in such trade. The Palermo convention covers transnational criminal activity involving endangered species, however, including an obligation to regulate and enforce the laundering of the illicit proceeds of trafficking in such species.

Firearms. Although many countries have long required end-user certificates for weapons, a common certification approach was not adopted until the passage in June 2002 of the Protocol against the Illicit Manufacturing of and Trafficking in Firearms, Their Parts and Components, and Ammunition supplementing the Palermo convention.[20] The certification approach is similar to that of CITES, requiring import, export, and reexport certificates as applicable. Notably, the firearms protocol lies within the framework of a convention that criminalizes the laundering of the proceeds of any activity that violates its terms. Thus the firearms protocol is backstopped by the obligation to criminalize, regulate, and enforce violations of the protocol, which include all forms of illicit cross-border activities involving firearms. The firearms protocol also prompted the Customs Cooperation Council of the World Customs Organization to add particular categories of weapons and components to the harmonized system by which national customs agencies track goods in transit.

Strengths and Weaknesses. Certification regimes provide a level of harmonization and control over commodities requiring certificates. They provide a means by which well-intentioned entities and persons can choose to deal only in licit commodities, thereby creating market incentives for licit goods to be of greater value than illicit goods. The certification process simultaneously creates universal rules to distinguish licit from illicit activity and thus provides a basis for structuring national regimes and national regulatory and enforcement activity in support of national regions. Finally, the certification regimes provide an evidentiary trail for regulatory and enforcement activity, as abuses by corrupt officials and criminal organizations through unlawful issuance, forgery of certificates, or frauds are exposed.

Regimes requiring the certification of goods have not tended to create adequate verification mechanisms. None of the certification regimes has simultaneously provided for immediate integration of record keeping regarding certified commodities and the actual financial mechanisms (whether wire transfers or currency deposits) that accompany the physical movements of goods. The sectoral regimes have not been able to address problems of domestic capacity and corruption in areas of weak governance, with the result that links in the chain have facilitated considerable circumvention of the certificate process. Notably, enforcement activity against those involved in illicit buying and selling of prohibited commodities, including diamonds, endangered species, and firearms, remains relatively haphazard and often confined to a few jurisdictions. Financial institutions generally have little awareness of certification regimes, and financial regulators do not make their enforcement a visible component of anti–money laundering obligations.

Certifications have had an impact in every sector in which they have been adopted. However, limited capacity and corruption create substantial gaps in regulatory and enforcement activity, and criminal organizations structure their activities to circumvent certification programs. Certification regimes rely especially on the institutional competence and integrity of customs agencies, which are often deficient. These deficiencies worsen substantially where such competence and integrity are needed most—in areas of resource exploitation and in areas of conflict. To date, cross-fertilization between certification regimes and anti–money laundering regulations has been minimal. The Palermo convention requires anti–money laundering laws to cover all illicit proceeds.

Accordingly, the convention necessarily covers laundering of the proceeds of crimes involving certification abuses. However, there is no international mechanism to coordinate activity between those regulating and enforcing the laws governing money laundering or financial transparency and those seeking to enforce certification regimes.

Disclosure and Monitoring Initiatives

The United Nations, international financial institutions, and various nongovernmental organizations have undertaken a wide range of private sector disclosure and public sector monitoring initiatives in connection with the illicit exploitation of commodities.[21] These include all of the sectoral certification processes discussed above as well as various local mechanisms in other sectors, including timber and oil.

The Forest Crimes Monitoring Unit, established in Cambodia by the World Bank and the government and supported by the United Nations Development Programme (UNDP), the United Nations Food and Agriculture Organization (FAO), Australia, Denmark, and the United Kingdom. The unit is designed to assist the Cambodian government to combat forest crime. This unit includes a Forest Crime Monitoring Office in the Department of Forestry and Wildlife, a Department of Inspection in the Ministry of the Environment, and independent monitoring by Global Witness, whose efforts led to the initiative. A key component is the development of systems for tracking logs and cases of forest crime, which have improved accountability and transparency and led to a significant increase in enforcement actions. In an attempt to curtail illegal logging, bilateral agreements have been drawn up between Indonesia and its largest trading partners. The Indonesian government has signed an agreement with the British government under which the United Kingdom will move to ban the import of illegal Indonesian logs into Europe. This was driven by the large "green movement" in the United Kingdom, which also assisted in the "light-touch mechanisms" placed in the U.K. Pension Act. Extensive use of such agreements with other countries may result in a significant decrease in the export of illicit timber from Indonesia. International pressure has convinced Malaysia to join the International Tropical Timber Organization, which issues guidelines for the sustainable management of natural tropical forests. To date, none of these timber-related initiatives contains a financial monitoring element relating to formal or informal financial sectors.

Although other initiatives have been undertaken in the oil sector whereby private sector entities make various commitments to socially responsible extraction, the Publish What You Pay campaign, launched in June 2002 by George Soros and Global Witness, provides the first significant effort to focus attention on monitoring not only the purchase and sale of a commodity but also the funds used to pay for it. Notably, Publish What You Pay does not focus on the mechanisms by which illicit commodity sales move, but rather on the amounts, timing, and recipients of particular revenues paid by licit private sector companies purchasing energy. The information that could be developed from such a regime, in turn, would be available to assist regulators and law enforcement officials in determining whether a particular transaction not reported under Publish What You Pay may have been illicit in nature. Separately, the International Association of Oil and Gas Producers has established industry guidelines on issues such as environmental management and in November 2001 held an initial meeting in Houston to discuss corruption. Among the ideas discussed were proposals to share best practice in due diligence and training, both within the association and, ideally, with other industry associations (Bray 2002). Potentially, the initiative could propose standardizing the provision of information to the public that would facilitate the tracing of corrupt payments in the energy sector.

Anticorruption and Transparency Standards and Norms

During the late 1990s, anticorruption initiatives were being undertaken at a rapid rate, covering active and passive bribery.[22] These included regional conventions against corruption within the Organization of American States and the Council of Europe, each of which focused on criminalizing the taking of bribes, and a major global convention undertaken at the OECD, which focused on the making of bribes. The initiatives arose in an environment in which capital flows to emerging and developing countries had shifted markedly in favor of the private sector, rather than on a government-to-government basis. As a result, multinational corporations and financial markets generally became a more significant factor in transfers of capital than official assistance. Economic collapses in East Asia, Mexico, and Russia often revealed extreme corruption in financial and business sectors, even as they created substantial private sector losses. The Latin American malaise and the Asian economic flu, in turn, prompted the International Monetary Fund and the World Bank to focus on strengthening standards and norms not only in fiscal but also in regulatory areas. The regulatory standards emphasized documenting financial transactions involving governments—and account records at financial institutions generally—in order to facilitate prevention and punishment of corruption.

The OECD Convention on Bribery in Transnational Business Transactions was signed in 1997 and came into force in 1999. Under the terms of the convention, the OECD's 35 member countries have agreed to introduce laws similar to the Foreign Corrupt Practices Act enacted in 1977 in the United States to make it possible to prosecute companies that pay bribes abroad. Major elements of the OECD convention are the requirement to criminalize active bribery, to make bribes no longer tax deductible by corporations, to require companies and businesses to provide adequate recording of relevant payments, and to provide mutual legal assistance to facilitate inquiries into suspected breaches. Of particular importance to the issue of resource exploitation is the OECD convention's requirement to criminalize extraterritorial bribery. As a result, bribes paid by a person who is a citizen of a signatory country anywhere in the world are subject to prosecution. The OECD convention also provides for a process of mutual assessments as a mechanism to evaluate and improve compliance. The process of evaluation is critical, as no prosecutions of corrupt activity have been attributed to domestic laws enacted as a result of the convention. Enforcement of the OECD convention could also highlight where corrupt practices have led to resource exploitation and critical nodes by which corrupt payments have been made. Jurisdictions or institutions identified as nodes for handling funds relating to illicit exploitation of natural resources could be required to put greater due diligence mechanisms into place as a condition of market access for the jurisdictions and of licensing for the institutions.[23]

Antiterrorism Standards and Norms

After September 11, 2001, in an effort to assure UN support for combating terrorist finance schemes, the UN Security Council unanimously adopted Resolution 1373, a binding document that requires all 189 member states to do the following:

- Criminalize the use or collection of funds intended, or known to be intended, for terrorism
- Freeze immediately funds, assets, or economic resources of persons who commit, attempt to commit, or facilitate terrorist acts and entities owned or controlled by them
- Prohibit nationals or persons within their territories from aiding or abetting the persons and entities involved in terrorism
- Refrain from providing any form of support to entities or persons involved in terrorism
- Deny safe haven to those who finance, plan, support, or commit terrorist acts or provide safe havens.

The resolution requires member states to answer a series of queries and report their findings to the United Nations, but the UN cannot sanction member states for failing to comply with international standards for combating terrorist finance schemes.[24]

In April 2002 the Financial Action Task Force on Money Laundering published guidance specifying in some detail the criteria for detecting possible terrorist transactions. This guidance covered laundering of the proceeds of narcotics and other commodities as well as other forms of terrorist finance. It asked financial institutions to focus on the following:

- Accounts that receive periodic deposits and otherwise are dormant. Such accounts may prove to be "sleeper" accounts for later use by terrorists.
- Accounts containing minimal sums that suddenly receive deposits or a series of deposits followed by daily cash withdrawals that continue until the transferred sum has been removed.
- Refusals by a customer to provide adequate identification.
- Accounts for which several persons have signature authority when the persons appear to have no family ties or business relationship.
- Accounts opened by a legal entity or an organization that has the same address as another legal entity or organization but for which the same person or persons have signature authority, with no apparent economic or legal reason for the arrangement.
- The opening by the same person of multiple accounts into which numerous small deposits are made that in aggregate are not commensurate with the expected income of the customer.
- Use of mutual personal and business accounts to collect and then funnel funds immediately or after a short time to a small number of foreign beneficiaries.
- Foreign exchange transactions performed on behalf of a customer by a third party followed by wire transfers of the funds to locations that have no apparent business connection with the customer.[25]

These and the other mechanisms listed in the guidance have general applicability for money laundering and terrorist finance. They are not especially applicable to financial transactions involving commodity exploitation in which officials and private companies collude to place illicit funds under the name of front companies in a minimally regulated jurisdiction.

Anti–Money Laundering Standards and Norms and the FATF

The Financial Action Task Force (FATF) is an intergovernmental body whose purpose is the development and promotion of policies, at national and international levels, to combat money laundering. The FATF is a policymaking body that works to generate the necessary political will to bring about national legislative and regulatory reforms to combat money laundering. The FATF monitors members' progress in implementing anti–money laundering measures, reviews money laundering techniques and countermeasures, and promotes the adoption and implementation of anti–money laundering measures globally. In performing these activities, the FATF collaborates with other international bodies involved in combating money laundering. It does not have a tightly defined constitution or an unlimited life span. It reviews its mission every five years.

The FATF was established during the French presidency of the G-7 in 1989, in response to recognition of the threat that drug money laundering posed for their banking and financial systems. The FATF's initial mandate was to examine the methods used to launder drug proceeds and to develop recommendations for combating them. The 40 recommendations, developed during the first year, became the basis for what was then an innovative implementation system. The FATF, which had a tiny secretariat and was not a chartered international organization, but only a voluntary association, initiated a system for self- and mutual assessment. Under this system, each member would first assess its own compliance with the 40 recommendations. Then other members would visit the jurisdiction, question the authorities, and reach their independent determination of where the jurisdiction was failing to meet the recommended standards. This approach included several innovations. First was the notion that technical experts would develop standards that, over time, would bind their countries in compliance even without entering into a formally binding international agreement. Second was the concept of mutual evaluation, in which a country would submit to peer review as a means of improving its domestic capabilities.

The 40 FATF recommendations can be summarized as five basic obligations:

- Criminalize the laundering of the proceeds of serious crimes and enact laws to seize and confiscate them
- Oblige financial institutions to identify all clients, including all beneficial owners of financial property, and to keep appropriate records
- Require financial institutions to report suspicious transactions to competent national authorities and to implement a comprehensive range of internal control measures
- Put into place adequate systems for the control and supervision of financial institutions

• Enter into agreements to permit each jurisdiction to provide prompt and effective international cooperation at all levels, especially with regard to exchanging financial information and other evidence in cases involving financial crime.[26]

In 1996, under the U.S. presidency, FATF expanded its mission to cover money laundering involving all serious crimes, not just drug trafficking. It also agreed to take on new developments in money laundering, especially those involved with electronic funds transfers. It also broadened its authority to include efforts to change the behavior of nonmember jurisdictions. Accordingly, FATF developed a "black list" of other countries whose practices were deemed to facilitate money laundering and therefore were considered "noncooperative" with its objectives. The development of a black list reflected a dramatic change in approach, necessitated by growing recognition of the interdependence of the global financial infrastructure and the inability of any jurisdiction to protect itself in the face of bad practices in other jurisdictions. By 2000 FATF had developed its initial list of noncooperative countries and territories. To date, the threats of enhanced scrutiny or greater regulatory barriers have been used against a number of jurisdictions but imposed on none. The simple threat has been enough to cause essentially any country targeted with immediate action to change its laws, with Antigua, the Bahamas, Hungary, Indonesia, Israel, Liechtenstein, Russia, St. Kitts and Nevis, and Vanuatu, among others, all taking action in response to the threat of sanctions.

Neither FATF nor any of the regional bodies that replicate FATF standards and conduct mutual assessments[27] have focused on combating money laundering involving illicit commodities apart from narcotics. No attention has been given to the laundering of the proceeds of coltan, oil and gas, tanzanite, timber, or gemstones, except a few references to the use of diamonds and gold in connection with discussions of terrorist finance. Accordingly, FATF and other bodies have yet to develop typologies describing the mechanisms by which the funds from these commodities are handled. This is an informational, regulatory, and enforcement gap that no other international body has sought to fill.

Antinarcotics and Anticrime Standards and Norms

Only brief reference is made in this chapter to international instruments governing antinarcotics and anticrime and their relationship to the financial mechanisms used in resource exploitation. The two most important of these are the 1988 Vienna convention and the 2000 Palermo convention, each of which requires signatories to adopt anti–money laundering regulations and enforcement measures and to carry out mutual assistance to combat, respectively, the production and trafficking of illicit drugs and transnational organized crime. The Palermo convention implicitly criminalizes the laundering of all proceeds of illicit commodities extraction, as it covers all serious transnational crimes involving more than one person. It pays scant attention to extraction-related criminal activity, focusing largely on better-recognized crimes against private persons and private property such as trafficking in persons, trafficking in women for sexual exploitation, and trafficking in firearms. Notably, it also criminalizes the laundering of the proceeds of corruption.

Private Sector Seal Initiatives

Seal initiatives represent a method by which private sector institutions agree to abide by certain standards of corporate conduct in return for being placed on a white list that provides either practical or public relations benefits. Significant recent seal initiatives include the International Chamber of Commerce rules of conduct to combat extortion and bribery in international business transactions and the Wolfsberg principles.

International Chamber of Commerce Rules of Conduct. Rules developed by the International Chamber of Commerce in 1996 prohibit extortion and bribery for any purpose, a broader standard than the OECD convention's focus on public officials. The rules also call on governments to make their procurement procedures more transparent and to condition procurement contracts on abstention from bribery, including the requirement for antibribery certification from bidders. The International Chamber of Commerce's Standing Committee on Extortion and Bribery is charged with promoting the corporate rules of conduct; it could perhaps consider calling on major companies in the forest products industry to participate in its proceedings and develop a corporate code of conduct when bidding for concessions.

The Wolfsberg Principles. In October 2000, 11 leading international banks working with Transparency International announced agreement to a voluntary set of global anti–money laundering principles. Initially, the Global Anti–Money Laundering Guidelines for Private Banking applied solely to private banking, that is, to the accounts of the extremely rich—those with deposits of $3 million to $5 million—but the obligations they articulate have potentially broad applicability. The guidelines are as follows:

• Adopt client acceptance procedures so that the banks accept "only those clients whose source of wealth and funds can be reasonably established to be legitimate," including (a) taking reasonable measures

to establish the identity of its clients and beneficial owners before
accepting money; (b) demanding adequate identification before opening an account; (c) determining the source of wealth, the person's net
worth, and the source of the person's funds; and (d) requiring two persons, rather than just one, to approve the opening of an account

• Engage in additional diligence or attention in cases involving the
use of numbered or alternative-name accounts, high-risk countries,
offshore jurisdictions, high-risk activities, or public officials

• Update client files when there are major changes in control or identity

• Identify unusual or suspicious transactions, follow them up, and
then decide whether to continue the business relationship with heightened monitoring, end the relationship, or advise authorities

• Monitor accounts through some means

• Develop and implement a "control policy" to ensure compliance
with bank rules

• Establish a regular method of reporting on money laundering
issues to management

• Train bank employees involved in private banking on the prevention of money laundering

• Require the retention of bank records that might be material to
anti–money laundering matters for at least five years

• Establish an "exception and deviation procedure that requires
risk assessment and approval by an independent unit" for exceptions
to the previous nine principles

• Establish an anti–money laundering unit at the financial
institution.[28]

The signatories to the Wolfsberg principles did not create a mutual
assessment or other evaluative mechanism, relying instead on an
honor system whereby reputational injury was considered an adequate
disincentive to any failure by a member to meet its public commitments. In just two years, the Wolfsberg Group has extended its original mandate twice. In January 2002 it issued a set of principles on the
suppression of the financing of terrorism, and in September 2002 it issued a set of principles for correspondent banking, which has been one
of the areas of greatest vulnerability to money laundering for money
center banks. Major elements of the Wolfsberg principles for antiterrorism include the following:

• Require strict adherence to "know your customer" policies by requiring the proper identification of customers by financial institutions
and the matching of such identifications against lists of known or suspected terrorists issued by competent authorities having jurisdiction
over the relevant financial institution. This principle further includes

the requirement to implement procedures for consulting applicable lists, taking steps to determine whether its customers are on the lists of sanctioned persons or persons of interest to the government, and reporting to the relevant authorities matches from lists of known or suspected terrorists

- Identify high-risk sectors and activities
- Engage in heightened monitoring of unusual or suspicious transactions indicative of terrorist finance.

Major elements of the Wolfsberg correspondent principles for banking include the following:

- Make risk-based due diligence a component of evaluating all financial institution accounts to determine whether higher scrutiny should be given to their transactions because the jurisdiction in which they are based has inadequate anti–money laundering standards, has insufficient regulatory supervision, or presents a greater risk for crime, corruption, or terrorist financing
- Review the location of owners, the corporate legal form of the financial institution, the transparency of the ownership structure, as well as the involvement of high-level officials and their associates, termed "politically exposed persons," in their management or ownership
- Review the customer base of each financial institution to determine whether its clients may be at higher risk for money laundering or terrorist finance
- Create an international registry by which financial institutions can share information useful for conducting the due diligence specified in the principles.

Each of these sets of principles is potentially applicable to combating the financing of illicit commodities. The terrorist finance principles together create a framework by which governments or international bodies can match their customers against a government-endorsed list and then monitor or freeze their assets, as the government that regulates them may direct. The Panel of Experts on the Illegal Exploitation of Natural Resources and Other Forms of Wealth of the Democratic Republic of the Congo has created such a list, which highlights both the opportunities and the pitfalls of such an approach. The list named a number of persons and financial institutions as being in violation of international sanctions without, in many cases, providing any background on such violations, let alone evidence of them (UN Security Council 2000). Any list provided to financial institutions for heightened scrutiny or asset freezes must be subjected to a high standard of evidence to minimize violations of due process and personal rights. The correspondent banking principles potentially could be applied to customers in general, not just financial institutions. Thus financial institutions participating in the seal approach adopted by the Wolfsberg Group would be required to vet all new accounts for possible money laundering risk, including the laundering of proceeds from illegal extraction. In order for due diligence to include a focus on illegal extraction, substantial publicity and education would be required of regulators and financial institutions to identify "red flags" indicating such activity and specific examples of individuals or institutions laundering such funds.

Name-and-Shame Initiatives

The most prominent name-and-shame initiatives dealing with the inappropriate handling of transborder financial activity have included that of FATF, discussed above, and the OECD tax haven initiative, discussed here.

As of the late 1990s, the growing recognition that lack of transparency was creating substantial problems even for the most affluent countries began to embrace the area of taxes. OECD came to recognize that international tax evasion was linked to a host of other serious threats to the global system; in the words of its general secretary, "There are strong links between international money laundering, corruption, tax evasion, and other international criminal activities. These illegal activities are widespread and involve such sizeable sums that they can pose a threat to the stability of the global system of finance and even the global trading system" (Johnston 2000). In May 1998 OECD governments issued a report on harmful tax competition, which led to the Forum on Harmful Tax Practices, the Guidelines for Dealing with Harmful Preferential Regimes in Member Countries, and finally, a series of recommendations for combating harmful tax practices. The initiative adopted three FATF elements. First, it developed a set of agreed standards to combat a set of agreed problems; second, it put into place a system of multilateral assessment of each jurisdiction's implementation of the agreed standards; third, it agreed to "name and shame" nonconforming jurisdictions that would face loss of market access or other sanctions if they did not take action. In four years, the initiative has had substantial results, causing some targeted jurisdictions to change their laws immediately and most others to agree to complete doing so by the end of 2005. The OECD standards are similar to those of the FATF and the Wolfsberg Group, and their application to the financing of commodity exploitation would address a number of the mechanisms by which the proceeds of illicit extraction are converted from public to private ownership (OECD 2001):

• Ensure that information is available on beneficial (that is, actual) ownership of companies, partnerships, and other entities organized in the jurisdiction

• Require that financial accounts be drawn up of companies organized in the jurisdiction in accordance with generally accepted accounting standards and that they be appropriately audited
    • Put into place mechanisms for the jurisdiction to share informa-
tion pertaining to tax offenses with corresponding authorities in other
jurisdictions
    • Ensure that its regulatory and tax authorities have access to
bank information that may be relevant for the investigation or prosecution of criminal tax matters.

In particular, agreement to share information on the ownership of
companies, regardless of where they are located, to require appropriate audits of each company organized in a jurisdiction, to require such
audits to become available to the public, at least for publicly traded
firms, and to match tax information with bank information and the
records maintained by the business of its activities all have potential
applicability to efforts to punish those exploiting revenue streams from
illicit commodity extraction.

Gaps and Possible Institutional Responses

Today a patchwork of initiatives for monitoring illicit commodities
involves numerous institutions, none of which has broad jurisdiction over
the tracking of natural resource commodities and the proceeds of their
exploration. Moreover, none of the initiatives has sought to develop a
reporting or disclosure mechanism to create documentation that would
simultaneously track the physical transactions and movement of commodities and funds. The Publish What You Pay initiative would
provide a precursor to such tracking by providing documentation at
the front end of commodity transactions, such as oil and gas, that involve highly concentrated markets of both sellers and buyers. Similarly,
the Wolfsberg initiative, which includes an obligation to exercise
heightened scrutiny of large private bank accounts, could also provide
a structure applicable to tracking the funds generated by the sale of
natural resources. The existing Wolfsberg principles already require
participating institutions to impose higher levels of scrutiny on certain
types of transactions in some regions to determine whether they might
be the proceeds of corruption. Thus they could help to create greater
accountability over the illicit proceeds of commodity exploitation,
should typologies for such exploitation and "red flags" be developed to
indicate that illicit proceeds from commodity extraction are being
laundered.

Current capacity limitations exist at the national and international levels. Many national regulatory and law enforcement agencies deal poorly with money laundering and the smuggling of goods that are clearly illicit, such as narcotics. International organizations responsible for developing harmonized standards to combat such smuggling, such as the World Customs Organization and FATF, have tiny secretariats and limited resources. Regional law enforcement agencies, such as Europol for cross-border police investigations within the European Union and Eurojust for cross-border prosecutions of such crimes, remain in their infancy and, to date, have focused on traditional crimes such as the smuggling of drugs and people. Existing certificate-of-origin mechanisms are also in their infancy and face significant limitations in enforcement. The example of the Kimberley process is instructive. A certificate-of-origin system can be undermined by poor enforcement and circumvented by intricate international smuggling networks. Lax government controls in the major diamond-trading and -cutting centers and the opaque, unaccountable nature of the diamond industry have also been major obstacles in the struggle to root out conflict diamonds.

Other than diamonds, most types of natural resources linked to conflict are not the subject of internationally agreed standards. For example, no international rules or agreements presently address the issue of illegal logging and conflict timber. The UN Forum on Forests, for instance, does not have a specific mandate for such a purpose, although it could prove a useful forum for international discussion. A certification system might build on existing efforts by the Forest Stewardship Council to ascertain whether timber is being produced in a sustainable manner. The council effort, initiated in 1993, entails independent audits to verify compliance with a series of requirements. Of particular interest is its chain-of-custody certification, which seeks to trace the lumber or furniture on consumer store shelves all the way back to the forest where the trees were felled. Such a tracking system could determine whether timber had been produced in conflict situations but would need to be matched against financial transactions to determine whether the asserted facts contained on certifications are authentic. This form of matching system could also be used to trace diversions of commodities through middlemen participating in the transactions as well as to identify the physical and financial infrastructure (transportation vehicles, financial institutions) used to move the illicit commodities.

Some of these gaps might be filled by the creation of an international legal framework to cover the sale of natural resources used in conflict or accompanied by serious corruption. Such a framework would focus on establishing common tracking and disclosure mechanisms for the extraction and sale of certain categories of commodities and extend the principles for international cooperation against money laundering to that involving the proceeds of illicit extraction of natural resources. An intergovernmental mechanism may also be needed to exercise oversight over the implementation of such a framework and to integrate work undertaken by international financial institutions and development agencies by existing intergovernmental organizations such as the World Customs Organization, CITES, and Interpol. Such a framework and mechanism could cover a group of commodities, including gemstones, oil and gas, precious metals, and timber, and establish standard documentation and disclosure mechanisms that would be universally applicable. Just as the Vienna convention and the Palermo convention established national requirements for money laundering regulation and enforcement and judicial cooperation covering narcotics and organized crime, this framework and mechanism would focus on building a common approach to handling both the commodities and the funds they generate. The framework would resemble the recent Organization of American States firearms convention and the UN firearms protocol, as well as existing efforts by the World Customs Organization, by requiring standard documentation for the commodities covered, an approach outside the two UN conventions. Notably, the UN firearms protocol and existing certification requirements of the World Customs Organization focus on documenting licit movements of goods across borders, highlighting illicit activity in the process. The firearms protocol and the existing certification initiatives are to be implemented largely by the private sector. A framework covering both the movement of commodities-in-transit through certifications and the corresponding financial movements would rely not only on the private sector involved in handling the commodities but also on the financial institutions already laboring to deal with drug money laundering, terrorist finance, criminal money laundering, and the proceeds of corruption.

As this study suggests, there are very significant differences in the market structure for different commodities in different situations. The market for oil and gas tends to be concentrated, with few players. Tropical timber has some concentration of markets among the end users, but many players are capable of exploiting the timber. Coltan, diamonds, and tanzanite more nearly resemble timber than energy, with an extremely deconcentrated set of suppliers and an increasingly narrow band of purchasers as the products move to the end users. Accordingly, a framework covering all these commodities would need to focus on the potential choke points through which each type of commodity, and its financing, would be likely to pass.

Certain financial mechanisms used to handle the proceeds of illicit extraction are already being addressed by initiatives to handle money laundering and terrorist finance. These follow on FATF and OECD recommendations and have received International Monetary Fund and World Bank assistance. Offshore money laundering havens, jurisdictions offering nontransparent international business companies, and trusts that can be readily used as fronts are already under substantial pressure to replace their current laws with regimes that meet prevailing international standards. Geographic regions that remain largely uncovered by money laundering and financial transparency frameworks, especially the Middle East and most of Sub-Saharan Africa, will remain the object of ongoing efforts to bring about reform regardless of whether the financing of illicitly extracted natural resources is included within the scope of the reform efforts.

Other important financial mechanisms used to launder the proceeds of illicit resource extraction have yet to be subject adequately to international regulatory and enforcement standards or action. Some of these mechanisms, especially alternative remittance systems such as *hawala* and *hundi,* are now being developed to counter terrorist finance. Other mechanisms associated with illicit resource extraction, such as the use of gold and precious metals to launder proceeds, have not yet been subject to international disclosure rules. An effective response to illicit resource extraction requires coverage of high-value barter commodities. Developing a strategy to integrate such commodities in international financial transparency and disclosure mechanisms might properly be undertaken by an intergovernmental organization focused on combating the extraction of illicit resources.

Any intergovernmental organization mandated to combat illicit resource extraction must also work (a) to develop mechanisms by which the financial movements of the proceeds can be incorporated into the reporting of suspicious activity and due diligence requirements of existing frameworks and (b) to devise mechanisms for enabling international mutual legal assistance in connection with investigations of illicit extraction. Such an organization would need to assure compliance by the affected industries and promote a regulatory scheme that harmonizes international standards rather than impedes legitimate trade.

One alternative to creating a new intergovernmental organization would be for the G-8 to establish a steering group to review the recommendations made here and in the other papers in this study and to provide a consensus view of whether an international framework and intergovernmental organization are necessary or whether existing frameworks and organizations could be reoriented to deal with illicit resource extraction. For example, the World Customs Organization has extensive experience in developing standard certifications and perhaps could develop such certifications for commodities that require more detailed information on chain-of-custody and payment mechanisms. Similarly, the FATF might be asked to develop a set of typologies for the laundering of the proceeds of various commodities and to recommend procedures by which FATF members could implement appropriate regulatory and enforcement actions to cover funds generated by illicit resource extraction.

The Wolfsberg approach provides a possible third model for action. The G-8 could ask that all relevant international or intergovernmental entities with a role in combating illicit resource extraction meet with representatives of the major sources of demand in the relevant markets: oil and gas, timber, precious metals, and gemstones, together with major participants in the key transportation markets (ground, sea, and air) and the global financial services infrastructure. The mixed private sector, public sector group, which could also include nongovernmental organizations, may possibly establish principles for tracking the purchase, sale, and flow of those commodities and the associated financial mechanisms. An agreed plan of action could be reached, with designated responsibilities for follow-up by each participant and a timetable for completion of the mandated activities. The group would meet periodically to discuss implementation issues and to report back to the G-8 on progress. Successes could be followed by additional mandates, and alternative approaches could be developed to respond to inadequacies in the regime.

A related approach would involve the development of further seal for major market players among purchasers and sellers of commodities subject to illicit extraction. Such "white lists" could include commercial and government entities involved in commodity extraction as well as the transportation and financial infrastructures handling the commodities and the funds generated.

A necessary element of any approach will be continued research and analysis. This chapter provides only a partial overview of the mechanisms by which those engaged in illicit resource extraction handle the proceeds of their activities.[29] To date there have been no detailed studies of the financial mechanisms used by the purchasers and sellers participating in illicit resource extraction. Such studies would provide greater texture and depth to the observations and analysis put forth here and would require fieldwork in addition to this literature review.

With these options in mind, and setting important areas for additional research, the next section provides a series of recommendations that could be included within a basic framework for combating illicit resource extraction. The recommendations establish a basic framework designed for universal application, covering the criminal justice system and law enforcement, the financial system and its regulation, and international cooperation. The measures build on existing international obligations and are designed to focus on disclosure, accountability, and cooperation in cross-border trade and financial transactions without impairing the freedom to engage in legitimate transactions or threatening economic development.

Recommendations

The following constitutes a possible global framework for combating illicit resource exploitation. It should be seen as an initial set of suggestions to stimulate further analysis and review rather than as a finished set of guidelines for adoption in its current form.

General Framework

Each country should take immediate steps to ratify and fully implement all international conventions related to the oversight of illicit commodities. An effective oversight mechanism should include increased multilateral cooperation and mutual legal assistance in money laundering investigations as well as prosecutions and extradition in money laundering cases, where possible.

Role of Individual Firms in Combating Illicit Commodities

The role of individual firms in combating illicit commodities needs to be strengthened in the following areas: (a) rules for identification and record keeping; (b) measures to cope with the problem of countries with no or insufficient anti–money laundering measures; (c) measures to monitor, detect, and prosecute illicit trafficking; and (d) the implementation and role of regulatory and other administrative authorities.

Identification and Record-Keeping Rules. First, all industries should label the origination point of the product through a central database that includes the official or other reliable identifying document and should record the identity of their clients, either occasional or regular, when establishing business relations or conducting transactions. In order to fulfill identification requirements concerning legal entities, financial institutions should, when necessary, take measures (a) to verify the legal existence and structure of the customer by obtaining from a public register or the customer proof of incorporation, including information concerning the customer's name, legal form, address, directors, and provisions regulating the power to bind the entity and

(b) to identify and verify that any person acting on behalf of the customer is authorized to do. Second, firms should maintain, for at least five years, all necessary records on transactions, domestic or international, to enable them to comply with official requests for information. Such records must be sufficient to permit reconstruction of individual transactions so as to provide evidence for criminal prosecution if necessary. Financial institutions should keep records on customer identification (for example, copies or records of official identification documents like passports, identity cards, driving licenses, or similar documents), account files, and business correspondence for at least five years after the account is closed. These documents should be available to domestic authorities in the context of relevant criminal prosecutions and investigations.

To improve the diligence of firms, if a financial institution suspects that funds stem from a criminal activity, including the evasion of taxes due on the sale of natural resources, or represent the proceeds of any form of corruption, it should be required to report promptly these suspicions to the authorities.

Financial institutions should develop programs to assure proper oversight of commodities. These programs should include, at a minimum, (a) the development of internal policies, procedures, and controls, including the designation of compliance officers at the management level, and adequate screening procedures to ensure high standards when hiring employees, including reference to prevention and detection of transactions involving the proceeds of illicit resource extraction; (b) issuance of instructions regarding red flags for transactions or accounts that may involve the proceeds of illicit resource extraction; (c) an ongoing employee training program; and (d) an audit function to test the system.

Measures to Cope with the Problem of Countries with No or Insufficient Anti–Money Laundering Measures. Firms should ensure that the recommended principles are also applied to branches and majority-owned subsidiaries, wherever they are located, including in countries that do not apply or insufficiently apply these recommendations, to the extent that local applicable laws and regulations permit. When local applicable laws and regulations prohibit this implementation, competent authorities in the country of the parent institution should be informed that the financial institution cannot apply these recommendations.

Firms should give special attention to business relations and transactions with persons, including companies and financial institutions, from countries that do not or insufficiently apply these recommendations. Whenever these transactions have no apparent economic or visible lawful purpose, their background and purpose should, as far as possible, be examined, and the findings should be established in writing and be available to help supervisors, auditors, and law enforcement agencies.

Other Measures to Monitor, Detect, and Prosecute Illicit Trafficking. Countries should consider implementing feasible measures to detect or monitor the physical cross-border transportation of specific commodities. They should consider the feasibility and utility of a system where banks and other financial institutions and intermediaries report all domestic and international currency transactions above a fixed amount to a national central agency with a computerized database, available to competent authorities for use in money laundering cases and subject to strict safeguards to ensure proper use of the information.

Countries should further encourage firms to develop modern and secure techniques of commodity management, including increased use of checks, payment cards, direct deposit of salary checks, and book entry recording of securities to encourage the replacement of cash transfers.

Countries should take notice of the potential for abuse of shell corporations by money launderers and should consider whether additional measures are required to prevent unlawful use of such entities.

Implementation and Role of Regulatory and Other Administrative Authorities. The authorities supervising firms should ensure that the supervised institutions have adequate programs to guard against trafficking in illicitly extracted resources. These authorities should cooperate with and, on request, lend expertise to other domestic judicial or law enforcement authorities in money laundering investigations and prosecutions.

The authorities should establish guidelines to assist firms in detecting suspicious patterns of behavior by their customers. It is understood that such guidelines must develop over time, will never be exhaustive, and will primarily serve as an educational tool for the personnel of financial institutions.

The authorities regulating or supervising financial institutions should take the necessary legal or regulatory steps to guard against control or acquisition of a significant participation in firms by criminals or their confederates, including any person or entity found to have been involved in illicit resource extraction.

Strengthening of International Cooperation

International cooperation needs to be strengthened in the following areas: (a) administrative cooperation; (b) exchange of information relating to suspicious transactions; (c) cooperation in confiscation, mutual assistance, and extradition; (d) improved mutual assistance; (e) development of further standards; and (f) oversight. We offer recommendations for each of these in turn.

Administrative Cooperation. National administrations should consider recording, at least in the aggregate, international flows of commodities through a series of tracking measures, including Global Positioning System and import-export records from relevant states. Such information should be made available to an international oversight body.

International authorities, perhaps Interpol and the World Customs Organization, should be given responsibility for gathering and disseminating information to authorities about developments in combating the trafficking of illicit commodities. Central banks and bank regulators could do the same in their network. National authorities, in consultation with trade associations, could then disseminate this information to financial institutions in individual countries.

Exchange of Information Relating to Suspicious Transactions Involving Illicit Commodities. Each country should make efforts to improve a spontaneous or upon-request international information exchange relating to suspicious transactions and to persons and corporations involved in those transactions. Strict safeguards should be established to ensure that this exchange of information is consistent with national and international provisions on privacy and data protection.

Cooperation in Confiscation, Mutual Assistance, and Extradition. Countries should try to ensure, on a bilateral or multilateral basis, that different knowledge standards in national definitions—that is, different standards concerning the intentional element of the infraction—do not affect the ability or willingness of countries to provide each other with mutual legal assistance. The signing of memoranda of understanding in instances where treaties are not viable may be especially important for the oversight of illicit commodities. The use of GPS systems and import records from allied states could assist in the oversight.

International cooperation should be supported by a network of bilateral and multilateral agreements and arrangements based on generally shared legal concepts, with the aim of providing practical measures to affect the widest possible range of mutual assistance covering illegal natural resources.

Focus of Improved Mutual Assistance on Combating Illicit Commodities. Cooperative investigations among countries' authorities should be encouraged. There should be procedures for mutual assistance in criminal matters regarding the use of compulsory measures, including the production of records by financial institutions and other persons, the search of persons and premises, and the seizure and gathering of evidence for use in money laundering investigations and prosecutions and in related actions in foreign jurisdictions.

There should be authority to take expeditious action in response to requests by foreign countries to identify, freeze, seize, and confiscate proceeds or other property of corresponding value to such proceeds, based on the extraction or trafficking of illicit commodities.

To avoid conflicts of jurisdiction, consideration should be given to devising and applying mechanisms to determine the best venue for prosecuting defendants in the interests of justice in cases that are subject to prosecution in more than one country. There should also be arrangements for coordinating seizure and confiscation proceedings that may include the sharing of confiscated assets.

Countries should have procedures in place to extradite, where possible, individuals charged with crimes related to illicit commodities. Each country should legally recognize the extraction and trafficking of illicit commodities as an extraditable offense. Subject to their legal frameworks, countries may consider simplifying extradition by allowing direct transmission of extradition requests between appropriate ministries, extraditing persons based only on warrants of arrests or judgments, extraditing their nationals, and introducing a simplified extradition of consenting persons who waive formal extradition proceedings.

States, entities, or individuals found to be in violation of these recommendations should be subject to sanctions, including the freezing of financial accounts and travel restrictions.

Development of Further Standards. The Customs Cooperation Council, which is associated with the World Customs Organization, should be asked to review the certification form it uses to specify country-of-origin to determine whether it should contain additional information to facilitate identification and tracking of licit goods and financial payments and thereby distinguish them from illicit goods.

FATF should be asked to review its 40 recommendations to determine whether they provide an adequate basis for combating the laundering of the proceeds of illicit resource extraction and to develop recommendations or other mechanisms to improve the reporting of suspicious activities involving the proceeds of illicit resource extraction.

Transparency International and the Wolfsberg Group should be asked to determine whether they can agree on additional guidelines that could be used to assist financial institutions seeking to avoid being used to launder the proceeds of illicit resource extraction and related corrupt activities.

An ongoing consultative process should be created with the mandate to reach agreement on methods to improve reporting, disclosure, and tracking of natural resources in international trade, together with the financial aspects of the transactions. This process should be preceded by a special meeting of experts from relevant stakeholders, including representatives of other international and intergovernmental organizations, governments, resource extraction industries, nongovernmental organizations, and financial institutions to assess whether these or other standards could become the basis for a global framework to combat illicit resource extraction.

Oversight. Consideration should be given to creating an international organization or intergovernmental process that includes a secretariat to coordinate efforts to combat illicit resource extraction and to monitor implementation of this legal framework and related initiatives. Such an organization or process would also be responsible for administering the ongoing consultative process specified in the previous recommendation.

Appendix 5.1. Coltan and the Democratic Republic of Congo

Coltan is composed of a mixture of the elements columbium (or niobium) and tantalum, an extremely heavy element used throughout the electronics industry to carry a charge. The market price for coltan has ranged from $20 a pound in 1990 to $350 a pound in December 2000, retreating to prices of $100 to $120 per pound since then (Zajtman 2001). Coltan mining during the Congolese civil wars was undertaken by a number of different military forces. There are no official figures for the revenues derived from illicit coltan sales during the years of civil war, although one estimate places coltan revenues for the Rwandan army alone at $20 million a month in 2000 (Ware 2001).

Tantalum is an increasingly important component of high-end consumer electronics, especially automobiles, cellular phones, and computers. The demand prompted many international companies to import coltan from the Democratic Republic of Congo through Rwanda. The United Nations (UN) expert panel identifies 85 multinational businesses that it says violated ethical guidelines set down by the Organisation for Economic Co-operation and Development (OECD). They include banks as well as gem and mining firms based in Belgium,

Canada, Germany, the United Kingdom, and the United States (UN Security Council 2000; see also Montague 2002).

In addition to coltan, illicit trade in cobalt, coffee, diamonds, gold, and timber contributed to what is sometimes referred to as Africa's "first world war," in which the death toll approached 4 million in three years; of these, coltan is the most lucrative.[30] Rebel forces and armies from neighboring states funded their operations through full-fledged commercial operations in coltan, thus helping to prolong the conflict.

The Congolese civil war enabled cross-border security forces and businesses to play a critical role in resource exploitation. The coltan mining areas in the eastern region of the Democratic Republic of Congo have no significant roads and minimal employment opportunities other than mining. As a result, coltan mining was a central means of obtaining food and other supplies from the military forces occupying the area. Profits earned from Congolese coltan financed a large part of Rwanda's military budget. For example, according to the UN panel of experts, after Rwandan army soldiers took control of a mine near Kasese, they awarded a single firm the right to commercialize the ore. The company paid approximately $1 million per month to the Congolese Assembly for Democracy (RCD), a rebel movement. By 2001, the RCD controlled a near-monopoly on the exploitation of coltan through the firm, which reportedly paid the RCD $10 per kilogram of exported coltan until the RCD abolished the monopoly late in the year.

The UN expert panel has provided the most detailed information and analysis available on the logistical mechanisms used to exploit natural resources in the Democratic Republic of Congo (UN Security Council 2000). The panel's report describes the specific military forces controlling the coltan, individuals transporting it from eastern Democratic Republic of Congo, and various commercial middlemen and ultimate purchasers of the coltan. The mechanisms described include elaborate multiparty transactions involving false documents on country of origin. However, the report does not specify the financial mechanisms used to pay for the complex logistical transactions (UN Security Council 2000, par. 79–82). Notably, these are likely to involve not the Democratic Republic of Congo itself, but its neighbors. The country has not had a modern financial system for some time. According to the head of its central bank in late 2001, it is still common practice for those in business in the Democratic Republic of Congo "to eschew regular banking channels to transfer funds from, say, Kinshasa to Lubumbashi. Packing the cash in a suitcase and catching the next flight could save a wait of 30 days."[31] Throughout the civil war, the country continued to have access to international banks, both from local offices of major banks and from local banks that maintained correspondent accounts with major banks. With control of coltan, it is logical that rebel armies would repatriate excess funds to their home countries. Indeed, reports by both nongovernmental organizations operating in the Democratic Republic of Congo and the UN expert panel link neighboring officials with profiteering and suggest that they used banks in neighboring countries to handle the funds (see "Four Companies Named" 2000; UN Security Council 2000). Regional financial institutions also remained engaged in the Democratic Republic of Congo throughout the conflict, and some profited directly from it.

The Democratic Republic of Congo has no functioning government in the coltan-extracting areas. It is not surprising that the various military forces that controlled the mining areas applied no regulatory or enforcement measures except the use of force against their enemies. Regulatory or enforcement action would be possible only if the country's neighbors were to undertake such action. Instead, the neighbors sought to profit from the civil war. In general, these countries have poor regulation and enforcement of money laundering laws. The failure is one of both political will and institutional capacity.

Given the ongoing conflict, the Democratic Republic of Congo fails to meet the most rudimentary international anti–money laundering norms. Regulatory and enforcement gaps include the following:

• No meaningful measures by financial institutions to obtain information about the true identity of the persons on whose behalf an account is opened or a transaction conducted
• No requirements to report suspicious transactions
• No programs in financial institutions against money laundering, such as internal policies, procedures, and controls, or screening procedures to ensure high standards when hiring employees
• No measures to detect or monitor the physical cross-border transportation of cash and bearer negotiable instruments
• No laws banning the use of anonymous accounts or accounts in obviously fictitious names
• No barriers in practice to the laundering of funds by essentially any person for any purpose, other than the logistical barrier of placing funds in a banking system that is still based largely on outdated practices and technologies.

In 2002 the International Monetary Fund announced a program of technical assistance for the Democratic Republic of Congo, which includes reforms to the banking sector. Regardless of such reforms, the exercise of control over coltan mines by foreign security and rebel forces means that the Democratic Republic of Congo with the best of intentions will not be able, by itself, to discourage the exploitation of coltan.

Very little information is available specifying the particular financial institutions and financial mechanisms most involved in handling conflict coltan, although it is likely they are similar to those used in handling illicit diamonds and other commodities. The lack of information does not hide the basics of the trade, however, which involve (a) military forces (b) self-financing through (c) resource exploitation involving (d) the sale of coltan from local, low-paid miners to (e) intermediaries on the country's borders who, in turn, (f) sell the coltan to middlemen from more developed countries by making payment of electronic funds to (g) neighboring banks. In turn, these banks conduct transactions upstream with financial institutions based in major financial markets and downstream with local institutions created in the Democratic Republic of Congo to take advantage of the profits of the war. The breakdown in governance did not create a corresponding breakdown in the payments system. Instead, local, regional, and international financial institutions adapted to the conditions created by the war to continue to provide services, without regard to the provenance of the goods sold, the sellers of the goods, the buyers of the goods, or the source or purposes of the funds involved in the transactions. In short, rather than constituting a technical failure susceptible to technocratic solutions, the exploitation of coltan in the Democratic Republic of Congo represented an ongoing political problem arising out of decisions of parties throughout the region to exploit coltan and the Democratic Republic of Congo rather than to cut off the trade and finances used to maintain the war. Accordingly, even if the sensible suggestions for reform made by the UN panel of experts were put into place, regional agreement and regional corrective action are needed to address the financial mechanisms sustaining conflict in the Democratic Republic of Congo.[32]

Appendix 5.2. Narcotics and Terrorists

Since the decline of state sponsorship of terrorism, terrorist groups have increasingly turned to the sale of illicit drugs to finance their operations. Indeed, in 1994, Interpol's chief drugs officer, Iqbal Hussain Rizvi, observed, "Drugs have taken over as the chief means of financing terrorism" (*Reuters News Agency*, December 15, 1994). In every case where large quantities of illicit narcotics have been produced and transported to licit markets, the illicit drug activity, over time, has drawn terrorist organizations. Links between terrorist organizations and drug traffickers take many forms, ranging from facilitation, protection, transportation, and taxation to the terrorist organization itself trafficking in the drugs to finance its activities. Traffickers and terrorists have similar logistical needs to move illicit goods, people, and money, and relationships between them often benefit both. The military skills, weapons supply, and access to clandestine infrastructure possessed by terrorists can help traffickers to move illicit drugs. At the same time, drug traffickers can provide terrorists with both drug-derived revenues and expertise in money laundering. Moreover, both groups rely on corrupt officials to assist them in moving illicit goods, people, and money across borders. Both types of organizations tend to rely on a structure of cells to accomplish their goals, with the members of local cells responsible for carrying out operations on a day-to-day basis. Drug traffickers and terrorists also use similar financial mechanisms: bulk cash smuggling, front companies, and multiple bank accounts in the name of such fronts, together with alternative remittance systems (*hawala*) or black market currency exchanges.

Drugs have financed terrorist groups in many regions in conflict, including Europe, Latin America, the Middle East, South Asia, Southeast Asia, and the former Soviet Union. Major cases include the Shining Path in Peru from the 1980s through the 1990s, the FARC (Revolutionary Armed Forces of Colombia), ELN (National Liberation Army), and AUC (United Self-Defense Forces of Colombia) in Colombia from the 1980s to the present, Al-Qaeda and Kashmiri separatist groups operating in South Asia, the Tamil Tigers of Sri Lanka, Hezballah in Lebanon, members of the Irish Republican Army, the Basque Fatherland and Liberty Party, and the United Wa State Army in Myanmar, among others. Such groups tend to intensify their drug trafficking and their terrorist activities in parallel with intensified civil conflict.

The most successful use of narcotics to fund terrorist activities was overseen by the Al-Qaeda network, which received millions of dollars through the production and distribution of opium. Prior to the U.S.-led invasion of Afghanistan, the Taliban and Al-Qaeda produced thousands of metric tons of opium each year in 18 of the 31 Afghan provinces. Opium cultivated by Al-Qaeda has been smuggled through neighboring Central Asian states and transported to distribution networks in East Africa. Although the Taliban officially banned the cultivation of opium poppies in July 2000, a UN Security Council report finds that the move was aimed at boosting the price of heroin, while the Taliban retained large stocks of the drug to continue to supply the market ("Afghan Opium Threatens" 2001). The Taliban also taxed heroin laboratories and heroin and opium convoys passing through Taliban checkpoints, charging producers and smugglers 10–20 percent of the total value of the wholesale opium, with the tax collected by village mullahs for the leadership in Kabul. During the period of Taliban rule, the military and security forces of the Taliban and Al-Qaeda were intermingled. Because of the use of alternative remittance systems and an absence of oversight of financial transactions in Southwest Asia, it is not possible to trace opium profits from Afghanistan to particular Al-Qaeda operations.

In Colombia, the enormous profits created from the drug trade have enabled FARC to establish a vast and sophisticated military and financial network. This network was responsible for the sustained growth and success of FARC throughout the 1990s. The drug trade, combined with other sources of funds (kidnappings, road tolls, and robberies), has enabled the continued purchasing of large amounts of weapons, including sophisticated surface-to-air missiles as well as heavy weaponry and military vehicles (Kinsell 2000). With more than half of FARC's funds coming from the drug trade, some $250 million to $300 million annually, drug cartels have become FARC's partners in maintaining its capacity to operate against the government. FARC commonly purchases arms and equipment with large amounts of cocaine (Kinsell 2000). It is believed that FARC has an annual income of $500 million to $600 million (Klepak 2000).

While drug traffickers may receive the proceeds of drug sales at various stages of the chain of distribution, from opium or coca farmers all the way through small urban dealers, terrorist groups that control national territory receive funds almost entirely at the first stages of production—that is, at the location of extraction. These terrorist groups typically receive their share of narcotics funds in cash and then seek to avoid cross-border currency controls by placing the funds in local financial institutions that are willing to accept drug proceeds. Alternative remittance systems, such as *hawala* and black market pesos, become central to the placement function, permitting terrorist groups to move funds to where they need them. Other techniques for hiding drug funds often rely on barter, or substitute commodities, for cash, such as gold or precious gems. It is sometimes said that terrorist finance differs from money laundering in that terrorists take clean money and hide it to fund criminal activities, while money launderers take dirty money and hide it to fund lawful activities. In the area of terrorism funded by narcotics, however, the terrorists use precisely the same infrastructure for handling their funds as do drug traffickers. Systems that are open to drug money laundering prove to be equally as open to terrorist money laundering, except that the identity of the collusive parties may be colored by ideological overlays not present in the context of commercial drugs. The differences between money laundering by terrorist organizations in Latin America, Southeastern

Europe, and Southwest Asia are more the result of minor regional differences in mechanisms than of operational distinctions. With that in mind, the following financial mechanisms have been used to launder drug funds:

- Exploitation of poor governance to provide safe havens for those generating drug wealth in source countries and making payoffs to underpaid officials in such regions. This feature accompanies the use of narcotics funds by terrorists in Latin America (Colombia, Peru), the Middle East (historically, Lebanon), Southeast Asia (Cambodia, Myanmar, the Philippines), and Southwest Asia (Afghanistan, Pakistan).
- Reliance on ideologically sympathetic corrupt officials to facilitate the placement of drug funds for terrorist groups. This phenomenon has been especially important in Pakistan for both Al-Qaeda and various Kashmiri militant groups but may have played a role in the Andes (Colombia, Peru), Lebanon (Hezballah), and Southeast Asia (Cambodia, Myanmar).
- The use of long-established money laundering centers, such as Dubai, Indonesia, and Panama, for placement of funds, before moving them to jurisdictions that previously paid little attention to terrorism, such as Kenya, Malta, and Singapore.
- Reliance on nontraditional methods of transferring currency, including *hawalas* and cash couriers, and then infiltrating these funds into the formal financial system.
- Physical transportation through complacent or collusive banks or other financial institutions, typically located in developing countries adjacent to countries producing the drugs. For example, FARC is believed to have a series of such banks operating in Ecuador to facilitate the transfer of funds outside of Colombia. From there, FARC can manage its finances electronically, using computers and accessing its accounts online from the jungle. Arms shipments have frequently been arranged using this method, minimizing risk (Klepak 2000).
- Camouflage of terrorist finance through import-export businesses, such as buying and selling honey, fish, or grain.
- Collusion with otherwise legitimate businesses that work with collusive financial institutions to invest terrorist funds in legitimate real estate and business ventures (Klepak 2000).
- Investment of the proceeds of narcotics trafficking in real estate. Real estate investment is a traditional refuge for the proceeds of drug trafficking, and traffickers have controlled substantial elements of the urban construction of luxury hotels and resorts in neighboring countries.

Prior to the September 11 terrorist attacks, there were only minimal global efforts to target terrorist finance per se. Few countries had ratified the only significant international treaty covering the issue: the 1999 United Nations Convention for the Suppression of the Financing of Terrorism. As a result, the convention had yet to come into effect.[33] The principal anti–money laundering organizations, including the Financial Action Task Force on Money Laundering (FATF), had yet to take up terrorist finance in a meaningful way. After September 11, the FATF issued eight special recommendations on terrorist financing. These included (1) ratifying the 1999 UN convention, (2) criminalizing terrorist finance and money laundering, (3) freezing and confiscating terrorist assets, (4) requiring financial institutions to report suspicious activities related to terrorism, (5) calling for international cooperation and the sharing of information on terrorist finance and for countries to take measures to ensure they do not provide safe harbor to terrorist financiers, (6) taking measures to regulate alternative remittance systems, (7) taking measures to require financial institutions to include accurate and sufficient information on wire transfers to permit transactions linked to terrorism to be traced to their source, and (8) reviewing the adequacy of laws and regulations of nonprofit organizations, such as charities, to discourage terrorist finance.[34] These very general recommendations have yet to be implemented in the countries most central to the placement of terrorist funds or, in a meaningful way, in countries ideologically sympathetic to particular terrorist causes. Generally, they add little to existing requirements for enforcement of anti–drug money laundering, in effect adding terrorist finance to the preexisting framework for anti–money laundering regulation and enforcement established by the FATF over the previous 10 years. A few of the recommendations, however, are potentially significant, especially the recommendations to require registration of alternative remittance systems, regulation of nonprofit organizations, and adequate documentation of wire transfers. Notably, none of them addresses the relationship of terrorism to the exploitation of drugs or any other form of natural resource, focusing solely on the identity of the persons moving the funds (that is, terrorist groups).

The global effort to combat terrorist finance is still in its infancy, and there has yet to be any particular focus in regulatory or enforcement efforts on the relationship between the finance of terrorism and drug trafficking. To the contrary, enforcement efforts against narcotics and terrorism have tended in most governments to remain discrete, with limited cross-fertilization between those responsible for combating each problem. Although there is relatively limited information on how terrorists move the proceeds of narcotics to fund their operations, the information that is available suggests that terrorists use essentially the same infrastructure and armamentarium as do traffickers, from bulk cash to barter, from alternative remittance systems to front companies. They also use many of the same jurisdictions and even the same financial agents, relying on many of the same mechanisms to prevent the tracing of their funds back to their source. The effort to combat narcotics-financed terrorism, therefore, requires similar solutions as the effort to combat narcotics-financed crime and corruption more generally. These solutions begin with ensuring that formal financial institutions maintain barriers against money of uncertain provenance, monitoring those barriers, and sanctioning those that fail to maintain standards. Although such standards are increasingly being adopted, even in countries where corruption is endemic, too often they remain inspirational only. In countries where governance is weakest, and terrorists comparatively strong, such standards remain largely absent and, when present at all, systematically ignored. To date, despite the name-and-shame process for noncooperative countries and territories initiated by the Financial Action Task Force, sanctions have not actually been imposed on any country, as potential targets enact laws that bring them in formal compliance with international standards. It is too early to determine whether the new frameworks that were established in many countries during 2001 and 2002 will be enforced in practice. Without such enforcement in the jurisdictions where narcotics are placed, the targets of terrorism in other jurisdictions are likely to remain largely unprotected, absent controls on access from the poorly regulated or lax jurisdictions.

Notes

1. These include the Caribbean Financial Action Task Force (1990), the Asian-Pacific Group (1997), the Financial Action Task Force on Money Laundering in South America (2000), and the Financial Action Task Force on Eastern and Southern Africa (1999) to undertake assessments of anti–money laundering vulnerabilities and enforcement capacities. They also include Organization of American States conventions against money laundering (December 1995, amended October 1998), the European Union's First and Second Money Laundering Directives (1991 and 2001, respectively), and, to some extent, the work undertaken by the Basel Committee of Bank Supervisors in its current initiative (2000–03) to revise standards for the treatment of bank capital, which would include certain provisions pertaining to risks associated with lack of transparency.

2. Current membership includes the securities regulators and enforcement agencies of approximately 60 countries.

3. The Wolfsberg Group consists of the following leading international banks: ABN Amro, Banco Santander Central Hispano, Bank of Tokyo-Mitsubishi, Barclays Bank, Citigroup, Credit Suisse Group, Deutsche Bank, Goldman Sachs, HSBC, J. P. Morgan Chase, Société Générale, UBS AG. See www.wolfsberg-principles.com.

4. FATF is engaged in a major initiative to identify noncooperative countries and territories in the fight against money laundering. Specifically, this has meant the development of a process to seek out critical weaknesses in anti–money laundering systems, which serve as obstacles to international cooperation. The goal is to reduce the vulnerability of the financial system by ensuring that all financial centers adopt and implement measures for the prevention, detection, and punishment of money laundering according to internationally recognized standards. In June 2000, 15 jurisdictions (Bahamas, Cayman Islands, Cook Islands, Dominica, Israel, Lebanon, Liechtenstein, Marshall Islands, Nauru, Niue, Panama, the Philippines, Russia, St. Kitts and Nevis, and St. Vincent and the Grenadines) were named as having critical deficiencies in their anti–money laundering systems or a demonstrated unwillingness to cooperate in anti–money laundering efforts. In June 2001, FATF updated the list: four countries left the list (Bahamas, Cayman Islands, Liechtenstein, and Panama), and six were added (Egypt, Guatemala, Hungary, Indonesia, Myanmar, and Nigeria). In September 2001, two countries were added (Grenada and Ukraine), and in June 2002 four countries were removed (Hungary, Israel, Lebanon, and St. Kitts and Nevis).

5. See chapter 4 and appendix 4.1 for a description and analysis of the Kimberley process and www.kimberleyprocess.com.

6. Countries that exemplify this model might include Botswana (diamonds), Canada (timber), and Norway (oil). An oil counterexample is Angola. Iraq's handling of its oil sales includes both licit and illicit resource extraction.

7. A summary of many of the efforts is set forth in Geditsch and others (2001).

8. For definitional purposes, terrorists funded by illicit commodities are groups whose violence is directed principally at civilian targets and thus can be readily characterized as terrorist in nature, while rebel groups funded by illicit commodities are groups engaged in military activity directed against a government. In practice, the two categories are often difficult to distinguish.

9. United Nations (2000). According to recent press accounts, Taylor has facilitated terrorist finance through diamond smuggling involving agents of Al-Qaeda, taking bribes in return for providing safe harbor to financial officers of the terrorist organization. See Farah (2002).

10. Each year, the U.S. Department of State publishes an "international narcotics control strategy report" (for example, see U.S. Department of State 2001), which provides an overview of drug trafficking throughout the world.

In the course of its country-by-country assessments, it has provided extensive information on the use of narcotics proceeds by terrorist groups in each of the major illicit drug–producing areas. During the period of 1994 through 1999, there was no exception to this phenomenon: wherever substantial amounts of illicit narcotics were produced, terrorists or rebel groups were taking advantage of drug profits.

11. For terrorists, gold and gemstones have generally been vehicles for laundering money, rather than commodities to be exploited. Since the September 11, 2001, terrorist attacks, numerous public reports have highlighted these mechanisms.

12. The examples provided are illustrative rather than exhaustive.

13. Many other studies have undertaken considered reviews and assessments of the impact of sanctions on areas of conflict. See, for example, Cortright and Lopez (2002); Hufbauer, Schott, and Elliott (1990). Adequate consideration of this topic is beyond the scope of this chapter. The following brief discussion of sanctions is offered only as a summary relevant to financial mechanisms pertaining to illicit commodities transactions in zones of conflict.

14. Interviews of former U.S. ambassador for the implementation of the Dayton Accords, Robert Gelbard, November 2002, and of former U.S. special envoy to the Balkans, James O'Brian, March 2002, each by Jonathan Winer.

15. As of November 2002, 166 countries were signatories to the Vienna convention. Two notable exceptions remain Cambodia and Myanmar. See www.vienna.convention.at/.

16. We do not address illicit resource *purchases* by governments as a matter of government policy, which raise different issues from illicit resource *sales* by officials within a government acting in their individual capacity.

17. A U.S. Central Intelligence Agency chronology of nuclear smuggling from November 1993 through March 1996 lists more than 70 reported incidents involving nuclear material. See www.cia.gov/cia/public_affairs/speeches/archives/1996/go_appendixa_032796.html.

18. Article III, Regulation of Trade in Specimens of Species Included in Appendix I, CITES.

19. Article VIII, CITES.

20. The UN firearms protocol was, in turn, based on a ground-breaking regional convention, the Inter-American Convention Against the Illicit Manufacturing of and Trafficking in Firearms, Ammunition, Explosives, and Other Related Materials adopted by the Organization of American States, November 4, 1997, signed by 33 of the 34 member states. The Organization of American States firearms convention requires signatories not to export, import, or permit the transit of weapons except when the movement of the firearms is simultaneously lawful in the countries of export, import, and transit. The treaty mandated not only end-user certifications but also the labeling

of all firearms with unique markers at the time of manufacture and the time of import.

21. This section is included for the sake of a complete review that analyzes the financial aspects of commodity control regimes and is necessarily incomplete given the scope of the chapter. A more detailed and precise discussion of the reporting of resource revenues, especially in oil and timber, is set forth in chapter 4.

22. "Active" bribery is defined as the offering or making of a bribe by the person or entity seeking to influence official action; "passive" bribery is the request for or acceptance of a bribe by an official offering to take government action on behalf of a private interest.

23. OECD Convention on Combating Bribery of Foreign Public Officials in International Business Transactions. See www.oecd.org/pdf/M00017000/M00017037.pdf.

24. For copies of the reports of member states and related documents, see www.un.org/Docs/sc/committees/1373/.

25. For a complete description of FATF initiatives related to terrorist finance, see www1.oecd.org/fatf/TerFinance_en.htm.

26. The full text of the FATF's 40 recommendations is available at the FATF's website at www.oecd.org/fatf.

27. These are the Asia/Pacific Group on Money Laundering; the Caribbean Financial Action Task Force; the Council of Europe Select Committee of Experts on the Evaluation of Anti–Money Laundering Measures; the Eastern and Southern Africa Anti–Money Laundering Group; and the South American FATF. Only two regions—Central and Western Sub-Saharan Africa and the Middle East—remain largely outside the scope of these anti–money laundering institutions; each of these regions has little capacity to prevent the laundering of the proceeds of illicit activity, including those derived from commodity exploitation.

28. For a description of the Wolfsberg principles and related documents, see www.wolfsberg-principles.com.

29. Among the many gaps in this chapter is a discussion of the monitoring and tracking mechanisms put into place in countries such as Botswana and Norway that have avoided the resource curse.

30. The scope of the paper does not permit a review of the illicit commodities used by political officials in the Democratic Republic of Congo.

31. International Spotlight advertising supplement, *Washington Post* (purchased by the Democratic Republic of Congo), November 28, 2001, in a promotional article noting the country's intention to adopt a new electronic payments system in the near future.

32. According to the UN panel of experts, measures must be developed to deal with the revenues that would be lost for all the parties involved in illegal exploitation within the Democratic Republic of Congo, and these measures

would be effective only in the context of a regional political process. The suggested reforms include capacity building for Congolese institutions, including customs, tax authorities, and natural resource agencies. The panel also recommended restrictive measures, including freezing the assets of persons involved in illegal exploitation, barring select companies and individuals from accessing banking facilities and other financial institutions, and barring them from receiving funding or establishing a partnership or other commercial relations with international financial institutions. These recommendations suggest that financial mechanisms knit together illicit resource extraction within the country and broad access to the financial resources and institutions of developed countries.

33. On March 10, 2002, the UN convention reached the minimum number of ratifications (22) stipulated as necessary for it to come into effect. As a result, it went into effect on April 10, 2002. As of the end of March 2002, 132 countries had signed the convention, but just 24 had deposited ratification instruments with the United Nations.

34. Financial Action Task Force special recommendations on terrorist financing, October 31, 2001. See www1.oecd.org/fatf/TerFinance_en.htm.

References

The word "processed" describes informally produced works that may not be commonly available through libraries.

"Afghan Opium Threatens All Central Asia." 2001. *Agence France Presse*, September 16.
Braeckman, Colette. 2001. "Coltan: The New War Prize." *Le Soir*, March 27.
Bray, John. 2002. "Special Report: Progress Solid but Uneven in Fight against Corruption." *Oil and Gas Journal*, August 26.
Collier, Paul. 2000. "Doing Well out of War." In Mats Berdal and David Malone, eds., *Greed and Grievance: Economic Agendas in Civil War*. Boulder, Colo.: Lynne Rienner.
Cortright, David, and George A. Lopez, eds. 2002. *Smart Sanctions: Targeting Economic Statecraft*. Lanham, Md.: Rowman and Littlefield.
Curtis, Grant. 1998. *Cambodia Reborn? The Transition to Democracy and Development*. Washington, D.C.: Brookings Institution.
De Soysa, Indra. 2001. *Paradise Is a Bazaar? Greed, Creed, Grievance, and Governance*. Research Discussion Paper 2001/42. New York: World Institute for Development Economics, July.
Farah, Douglas. 2002. "Report Says Africans Harbored Al-Qaeda Terror Assets Hidden in Gem-Buying Spree." *Washington Post*, December 29.
Findlay, Mark. 1999. *The Globalisation of Crime: Understanding Transnational Relationships in Context*. Cambridge, U.K.: Cambridge University Press.

"Four Companies Named." 2000. *Africa Energy and Mining,* September 27.

Geditsch, Nils Petter, Havard Strand, Mikael Eriksson, Margareta Sollenbery, and Peter Wallensteen. 2001. "Armed Conflict, 1956–1999: A New Dataset." Paper prepared for the conference on identifying wars: systematic conflict research and its utility in conflict resolution and prevention, International Peace Research Institute; Uppsala University, Department of Peace and Conflict Research; and World Bank, Development Economics Research Group, Uppsala, June 8–9. Processed.

"Globalization of the Drug Trade." 1999. *Sources* 111 (April 4). Available at www.unesco.org/most/sourdren.pdf.

Homer-Dixon, Thomas. 1999. *Environment, Scarcity, and Violence.* Princeton, N.J.: Princeton University Press.

Hufbauer, Gary Clyde, Jeffrey J. Schott, and Kimberly Ann Elliott. 1990. *Economic Sanctions Reconsidered,* 2d ed. Washington, D.C.: Institute for International Economics.

Ihonvbere, Julius Omozuanvbo, and Timothy M. Shaw. 1998. *Illusions of Power: Nigeria in Transition.* Lawrenceville, N.J.: Africa World Press.

International Institute of Strategic Studies. 2002. "Transnational Control of Money Laundering." In *Strategic Survey 2001/2002.* Oxford, U.K.: Oxford University Press.

Jackson, Stephen. 2002. "Criminalised Economies of Rumour and War in the Kivus, DR Congo." Unpublished paper presented at the annual conference of the American Association of Anthropology, San Francisco, November. Processed.

Johnston, Donald J. 2000. "Introductory Remarks." Remarks of the secretary general of the OECD at the high-level symposium on harmful tax competition, June 29. Processed.

"Kimberley Process for Tanzanite." 2002. *Africa Mining Intelligence,* January 23.

Kinsell, Jeremy. 2000. "Unpublished Report on the FARC." University of Pittsburgh, August. Processed.

Klepak, Hal. 2000. "Why Doesn't the War in Colombia End?" *Jane's Intelligence Review,* June 1.

Litan, Robert E. 2001. "Economic: Global Finance." In P. J. Simmons and Chantal de Jonge Oudraat, eds., *Managing Global Issues: Lessons Learned.* Washington, D.C.: Brookings Institution.

Montague, Dena. 2002. "Stolen Goods: Coltan and Conflict in the Democratic Republic of Congo." *SAIS Review* 22 (1, Winter-Spring). Available at www.worldpolicy.org/projects/arms/news/22.1montague.pdf.

OECD (Organisation for Economic Co-operation and Development). 2001. *The OECD's Project on Harmful Tax Practices: The 2001 Progress Report.* Paris. Available at www.oecd.org/pdf/M00021000/M00021182.pdf.

O'Neill, Bard E., and Edward C. Meyer. 2001. *Insurgency and Terrorism: Inside Modern Revolutionary Warfare.* Dulles, Va.: Brasseys.

Renner, Michael. 2002. *The Anatomy of Resource Wars*. World Watch Paper 162. Washington, D.C.: World Watch Institute, October.

Ross, Michael. Forthcoming. "How Does Natural Resource Wealth Influence Civil War? Evidence from 13 Case Studies." *Journal of Conflict Resolution*.

Snow, Donald M. 1996. *Uncivil Wars: International Security and the New Internal Conflicts*. Boulder, Colo.: Lynne Rienner.

Summers, Lawrence. 2000. "International Financial Crises: Causes, Preventions, and Cures." 2000 Ely Lecture. American Economic Association, Nashville, Tenn. Processed.

Takano, Hideyuki. 2002. *The Shore Beyond Good and Evil: A Report from Inside Burma's Opium Kingdom*. Tokyo: Kotan Publishing.

United Nations. 2000. *Report of the Panel of Experts Appointed Pursuant to UN Security Council Resolution 1306*. New York, December.

———. 2001a. *Report by the UN Monitoring Mechanism on Sanctions against UNITA*. New York, October 12. Available at www.un.org/Docs/sc/committees/Angola/966e.pdf.

———. 2001b. *Report of the Panel of Experts on the Illegal Exploitation of Natural Resources and Other Forms of Wealth of the Democratic Republic of Congo*. 12.04.2001. New York.

UN Security Council. 2000. *Report of the Panel of Experts on the Illegal Exploitation of Natural Resources and Other Forms of Wealth of the Democratic Republic of the Congo*. New York, June.

U.S. Department of State. 2001. "International Narcotics Control Strategy Report." Bureau for International Narcotics and Law Enforcement Affairs, Washington, D.C. Available at www.state.gov/g/inl/rls/nrcrpt/2001/. Processed.

Ware, Natalie D. 2001. *ICE Case Studies* 10 (December).

World Bank. 1997. *Helping Countries Combat Corruption: The Role of the World Bank*. Washington, D.C.: World Bank Group.

Zajtman, Arnaud. 2001. "Ore Fuels West's High-Tech Gear." *AP Online*, April 9.

CHAPTER 6

Getting It Done: Instruments of Enforcement

Philippe Le Billon

"Let's choose to unite the powers of markets with the authority of universal ideals."

UN Secretary General Kofi Annan, Davos, 1999

"Well, if you know everything, then why don't you catch us?"

UN sanctions buster questioning a UN panel of experts 2000[1]

ACCESSIBLE AND INTERNATIONALLY MARKETABLE resources such as diamonds, oil, and timber—not to mention drugs—figured prominently in armed conflicts during the 1990s. Arguably, natural resources have provided the bulk of revenues that have financed wars in developing countries since the end of the cold war. For many armed groups, profiteering from resource exploitation has become an end in itself, with violence and the context of war providing the means and impunity to control resource revenues. Access to international markets has been crucial in allowing myriad armed groups and their business allies to prosper from criminally controlled but legally traded resources. Belligerents can benefit from resources in a number of ways, including the award of concession contracts to access resources; direct exploitation or partnerships; and taxation, protection schemes, or racketeering of resource companies, their subcontractors, or the local economy.

Given the devastation caused by civil conflicts, a broad set of reforms on natural resource governance is needed that places the basic needs and security of affected populations before the political agendas and profits of their domestic elites, businesses, and consuming countries.

In terms of development and conflict prevention, such reforms would cover issues of economic diversification and greater access to international markets, commodity price stabilization and buffer mechanisms, environmentally and socially sound management of resource exploitation, and accountability of resource revenue distribution.

In terms of conflict termination, such reforms should focus on curtailing the use of natural resources—or so-called conflict resources—to finance belligerents (see box 6.1). The economic value of these transactions may not always be large in global terms, but it is generally significant in local contexts and for business interests or criminal networks involved in laundering money.

This chapter examines international instruments of enforcement relating to the trade of conflict resources—conflict trade—with the

---

Box 6.1 Defining Conflict Resources

Conflict resources are natural resources whose control, exploitation, trade, taxation, or protection contribute to, or benefit from the context of, armed conflict.

Conflict goods are "nonmilitary materials, knowledge, animals, or humans whose trade, taxation, or protection is exploited to finance or otherwise maintain . . . war economies. Trade can take place by direct import or export from the conflict zone or on behalf of military factions (government and nongovernment)" (Cooper 2001, p. 27).

Conflict timber is "timber that has been traded at some point in the chain of custody by armed groups, be they rebel factions or regular soldiers, or by a civilian administration involved in armed conflict or its representatives, either to perpetuate conflict or take advantage of conflict situations for personal gain . . . . Conflict timber is not necessarily illegal, as the legality (or otherwise) of timber is a product of national laws" (Global Witness 2002, p. 7).

Conflict diamonds are "rough diamonds used by rebel movements or their allies to finance conflict aimed at undermining legitimate governments, as described in relevant United Nations Security Council (UNSC) resolutions insofar as they remain in effect or in other similar UNSC resolutions which may be adopted in the future, and as understood and recognized in United Nations General Assembly (UNGA) Resolution 55/56, or in other similar UNGA resolutions which may be adopted in future" (see www.kimberleyprocess.com).

objective of ending armed conflicts. It is rare for conflicts to be financed solely by conflict resources. Diaspora remittances, foreign support, looting of consumer goods, human trafficking, and embezzlement of humanitarian aid also provide revenue for combatants and the criminal networks with which they may be linked. Accordingly, this chapter covers only a few instruments within a broader array of policies and legal instruments that are aimed at controlling war economies in the interest of peace.[2] Furthermore, although recourse to violence must be condemned, international instruments of enforcement curtailing access to resource revenues for armed groups might, in some cases, be counterproductive if no effective alternative is provided to end oppression and injustice.

The main rationale behind instruments of enforcement is that the availability of resources to belligerents and competition over the control of their revenues generally prolong conflicts.[3] Natural resource revenues can support the weaker party and allow it to continue fighting and to maintain access to a source of wealth. Furthermore, as profits take priority over politics, the conflict risks becoming increasingly commercially driven, with the belligerents correspondingly motivated by economic self-interest. As such, controlling conflict resources can help to starve belligerents of revenues and promote peaceful modes of conflict resolution.

The relationship between resources and the duration and impact of armed conflicts is not straightforward, however, and instruments of enforcement need to take this into account if they are to be effective in promoting peace. On the one hand, resources can prolong and intensify armed conflicts by providing access to weapons and matériel. Fighting can be intensified where competition arises over control of areas of economic significance. This occurred in Sierra Leone over the best diamond areas and in Cambodia over log yards. Armed groups can also settle for a "comfortable stalemate" in which opposing parties can secure mutually beneficial deals to produce and market resources, thereby prolonging conflict. This relationship can, however, favor localized peace agreements and defections, when local commanders lower the intensity of conflict and even negotiate their individual disengagement without approval from their supposed leaders.

Resource revenues can also prolong conflicts by providing political networks of support, including commercially driven diplomacy. In Uganda, diamonds not only allowed the National Union for the Total Independence of Angola (UNITA) to buy arms but also attracted diplomatic and logistical support from regional political leaders (United Nations 2000b). On the other side of the Angolan conflict, the Popular Movement for the Liberation of Angola rapidly gained favor with major Western powers and their oil companies once it was established that UNITA had lost the elections and was unable to gain power through military means.

Finally, resource wealth can prolong conflict by weakening the prospects for third-party peace mediation. Access to resources can act as a divisive factor among international players. Bilateral actors are inclined to accommodate domestic interests in order to secure commercial benefits for their corporations. In addition, the ability of the belligerents to draw on private financial flows decreases the potential leverage that multilateral agencies (for example, the International Monetary Fund, the World Bank, and the United Nations) exercise through grants and loans. In many contemporary armed conflicts, private capital inflows have assumed greater importance than foreign assistance, especially in comparison with conflicts during the cold war era.

Although access to resource revenues can contribute to prolonging conflicts, curtailing belligerents' access to resource revenues does not automatically ensure that a war will be shorter or have a less harmful impact on populations. First, belligerents lacking access to resources may intensify predation and attacks on civilian populations. However, there does not seem to be a clear correspondence between access to resource wealth by belligerents and attacks on civilians. In theory, large-scale revenues can allow belligerents to shift from a war of terror targeting "soft targets" such as civilians to a conventional type of conflict more respectful of the laws of war. In practice, however, wealthy rebel groups such as the Revolutionary United Front (RUF) in Sierra Leone and UNITA have used widespread terror tactics against civilians.

Second, resources can allow a party to settle a conflict by winning the war. Massive oil revenues allowed the Angolan government to mount a decisive military campaign between 1999 and 2002 against UNITA, which was unable to exchange its significant stockpiles of diamonds for arms and logistical support. Ironically, UNITA's diamond wealth may have encouraged it to pursue a bold but ultimately self-defeating strategy of conventional warfare (Malaquias 2001).

Third, internal competition over resource revenues can also undermine the cohesion of armed groups and facilitate their fragmentation and ultimate demise. As a Khmer Rouge commander noted, "The big problem with getting our funding from business [rather than China] was to prevent an explosion of the movement because everybody likes to do business and soldiers risked doing more business than fighting."[4] In order to prevent such "explosion," or fragmentation, the Khmer Rouge fully supported soldiers and their families, tightly controlled cross-border movements, and supervised business dealings by local units.

Fourth, under certain circumstances, resources can provide an economic incentive for insurgents to defect to the government or negotiate for peace. Several Khmer Rouge commanders defected to the Cambodian government after being guaranteed amnesty and continued control over gems and timber resources. The caveat is that unsupervised or ill-considered wealth-sharing mechanisms can prolong wars rather than consolidate peace, even if they can tactically be used to bring belligerents to the negotiating table. A mechanism of economic "demobilization" and "supervision" during peace processes is proposed later in this chapter.

Finally, rebel groups exploiting natural resources are easily portrayed as mere bandits or criminals driven more by economic self-interest than by political ideals. This portrayal can lessen support from the population and allies. It can also facilitate the sanctioning and political isolation of rebel movements, like it did for the RUF, UNITA, and the Revolutionary Armed Forces of Colombia (FARC). However, this policy runs the risk of making a political resolution of the conflict more difficult than a military solution. Along with ignoring similar "criminal" practices on the part of government officials or paramilitary groups, this can prolong the conflict and fail to address its root causes.

For lack of international legislation, "conflict resources" are not always illegal—the commodities involved are legally traded on international markets and the economic activities involved are licit. Even trade with rebel groups can be considered legal under international law unless a United Nations or other sanctions regime and domestic legislation define it otherwise. Generally, conflict trade involves a mix of legal and illegal actors and activities, posing special challenges for the regulation of conflict trade, including the following:

- Defining legality, responsibility, and notions of complicity throughout supply chains and their connections to financial, transport, and insurance services
- Dealing with economic sectors in which the share of conflict resources may be minimal, resulting in not only a need for targeted regulations but also a frequent resistance to regulation on grounds of costs and inconvenience on the part of authorities and business interests
- Curbing financial access for belligerents while promoting economic activities benefiting populations and investments in the long term
- Intervening within an international political economy driven by "free trade" and private sector actors that are generally adverse to prescriptive regulations.

There is, however, an advantage to tackling otherwise legal trade and commodities. By increasing the risks of sanctions without increasing prices, regulation is likely to reduce the commercial viability of conflict trade. For example, interdiction policies on narcotics have largely failed to curb revenues, crime, and their impact on conflicts. Yet this failure has come precisely from the global nature of interdiction policies, in particular in importing countries. In a sector where all the supply is illegal, but demand is high and enforcement difficult, prices and profits are likely to rise. Unlike with narcotics, legal producers and importers shape the international price of otherwise licit natural resources. This points to a potential advantage of enforcement instruments aimed at controlling conflict trade, in that criminalizing specific suppliers within a broader market is less likely to inflate prices and thus to increase the profitability of illegal supply. This conjecture is, however, general in nature; agencies considering the application of enforcement instruments should take into account possible counterproductive results, particularly in terms of prices, profitability, and attractiveness for belligerents and criminal networks.

Institutional Structure of Enforcement Instruments

A broad range of instruments is relevant to conflict trade, with a variety of goals, targets, means, and scale of application. The most relevant ones have been specifically designed as international legal instruments, such as United Nations (UN) Security Council economic sanctions, but many others have been developed to address broader environmental and social issues or to respond to threats posed by transnational organized crime and international terrorism. States remain the most important actor in terms of legislation and enforcement. Yet intergovernmental organizations, private businesses, and civil society groups have played an increasing role in shaping a new generation of instruments and policies defining ethical norms and mixing voluntary compliance, market-based incentives, and independent monitoring. Given the blurring of boundaries in design and implementation, governance models for enforcement instruments to control the flow of natural resources are increasingly diverse. For example, nongovernmental organizations are now participating more in the design of mandatory instruments led by governments, while governments are participating in industry self-regulation schemes. Overall, however, these initiatives have been developed largely in response to pressure from civil society and advocacy groups.

The proliferation of actors involved in the governance of natural resources means that resource exploitation linked to human rights or environmental abuses is more likely to be detected than in the past. Violence is also less and less accepted as a means of political struggle, meaning that economic activities supporting violence are more likely to be denounced. Yet, although large extractive companies come under greater scrutiny, the complexity of commercial and financial operations, the use of independent brokers and offshore companies, as well as difficulties of access to many exploitation sites continue to leave too much room for conflict trade to operate. Furthermore, coordination is largely fragmented when it comes to effective decisionmaking and enforcement. International instruments largely continue to rely on national governments for enforcement, while the rise of voluntary measures by private actors risks weak self-regulation and ineffective enforcement.

Despite the diversity of governance models and fragmentation of enforcement instruments, some common issues can be identified. In particular, three key issues for the design of enforcement instruments to control natural resources related to conflict are the goals of the enforcement instrument, target and regulatory mechanisms, and scales of application.

Enforcement instruments relevant to conflict trade have two primary goals:

- To prevent resource exploitation and trade from financing war
- To motivate belligerents to resolve a conflict through nonviolent means.

In order to achieve these goals, instruments can target investments and technology transfer in resource exploitation and aim to prevent access to markets for conflict resources. Other measures can include the external control of resource areas and the destruction of resources—as is the case with drug eradication programs. These measures, however, are more properly viewed as military interventions rather than resource governance; this chapter examines such measures only in the light of peacekeeping deployment and the enforcement of economic sanctions.

Instruments of enforcement need to be based on criteria deciding which economic operations are licit and which are not. The incentive structure will depend to some degree on the target of the enforcement instrument:

- Resources identified as conflict-prone or as involved in fueling war are submitted to specific trade regimes (for example, certification of rough diamonds).

- Activities associated with conflicts and human rights abuses are prohibited (for example, prohibition of corruption or forced labor).
- Actors described as belligerents or war criminals are excluded from legitimate trade (for example, UN targeted sanctions on rebel leaders).

Regulatory instruments range from purely voluntary measures designed and adopted by resource businesses to mandatory regulations imposed by intergovernmental bodies under international law:

- Prescriptive legal instruments creating a disincentive for an offense (for example, mandatory sanctions)
- Market-based legal instruments creating an incentive for compliance (for example, tax rebates or market access and rewards linked to ethical business practices)
- Voluntary approaches creating an incentive for compliance (for example, corporate code-of-conduct and voluntary product certification)
- Normative pressure instruments (for example, advocacy campaigns by civil society groups).

Each instrument has its own advantages and disadvantages, which vary according to the type of target. It is often argued that voluntary instruments have the advantage of being internally defined by businesses and thus represent a greater ownership of policy and better adaptation to specific conditions than mandatory regulations. They can also offer the advantage of cutting across national jurisdictions and being global in scope when applied across a multinational company, its subsidiaries, and business partners. Yet voluntary instruments can be limited in scope—generally concentrating on core activities—and frequently lack accountability through independent auditing and enforcement. They are also unlikely to act as a deterrent, unless clearly linked to market incentives. Although generally slow and dependent on effective enforcement, mandatory regulations have undeniable advantages, considering that:

- Opportunistic belligerents and business people can be motivated solely by profits, whatever the cost to populations in conflict-affected regions.
- The absence of a level playing field within a sector or market places legitimate businesses following "pro-peace" best practices at a disadvantage compared with their less scrupulous competitors.
- A constraining "wartime" regulatory framework, such as trade sanctions, may motivate businesses to take a more active role in promoting peace.

   Mandatory and voluntary mechanisms are not mutually exclusive
and can usefully complement each other. There is some apprehension
on the part of some human rights organizations, however, that voluntary mechanisms somewhat reflect the weakness or complacency of
governments toward businesses and that voluntary mechanisms may
become a long-lasting alternative to binding and enforceable instruments. As the International Council on Human Rights Policy
(2002) argues in its review of the international legal obligations of
companies, voluntary mechanisms alone are insufficient. Not only do
legal instruments allow for consistent and fair judgments, but "even
where voluntary approaches are working, . . . anchoring these in a legal
framework is likely to enhance their effectiveness. And where voluntary
approaches are not effective, a legal framework provides powerful tools
and incentives for improvement."
   The most common form of international legal framework—
international treaties—frequently suffers from a lack of national
enforcement. Furthermore, as a result of negotiation and consensus
building, the offenses cited by such legal instruments are sometimes
ambiguous, while compliance measures are weak or left to national
authorities to define. It should therefore not be taken for granted that
a mandatory international instrument will prove more effective than
a voluntary one. Instruments mixing voluntary membership and mandatory compliance—through strong incentives to join, peer or independent monitoring, credible mutual enforcement, and threats to ensure
compliance, as in the Financial Action Task Force on Money Laundering (FATF)—may prove the most effective in the current international
environment.
   Finally, enforcement instruments can be designed and applied on
three main scales: national, regional, and international.
   National instruments are sponsored and enacted by one government
(for example, domestic legislation on customs, import-export regimes,
tax codes, company law, unilateral economic sanctions). They remain
the most widely applied and possibly the most robust means of combating conflict trade, including the national application of international economic sanctions. This strength comes from the sovereign
jurisdiction and judicial capacity of states within their national territory
and in international arenas. Controversially, national instruments can
also seek extraterritorial jurisdiction, as with U.S. unilateral sanctions
seeking extraterritoriality (for example, the Helms-Burton Act) and
U.S. courts accepting transnational suits (for example, the U.S. Alien
Tort Claims Act). However, the internationalization, growth, and mul-
tiplication of trading channels have complicated the task of national
authorities, while weak judicial systems, legal loopholes, or collusion

and economic self-interest seriously limit the effectiveness of domestic regulation in many countries. The transnational nature of the flow of conflict resources means that national strategies alone are inadequate and that regional or international enforcement instruments are required to fill this vacuum or limit collusion by domestic authorities.

Regional instruments, designed and enforced by regional organizations (and their member states) overseeing neighboring conflict-affected countries, have a strong potential. These regional actors are likely to be well informed about, and sensitive to, conflict trade as well as political dynamics in neighboring conflicts. However, like national initiatives, regional efforts may be constrained by limited capacity and complicated by local political or economic interests. Effective regional initiatives thus demand an assessment of national and local interests and agendas, as well as international support for capacity building.

International instruments, designed and enforced by international organizations (and their member states), represent an ideal given the global nature of conflict trade. However, international organizations may be prone to a time lag with respect to awareness of the significance and dynamics of conflict trade and may be delayed in taking adequate measures by other international issues. Furthermore, although an independent monitoring capacity is now emerging (that is, UN panels of experts investigating sanctions violations and war economies) international instruments continue to rely on national authorities for their implementation, and the record of enforcement is poor.

Regardless of the type of instrument considered, effective enforcement will depend on cooperation between different implementing agencies at various levels. Institutional structures of cooperation are essential, both horizontally within agencies dealing with similar matters (for example, financial regulation, customs, justice) and vertically (for example, national, regional, and international). Interpol, FATF, or the "fatal transactions" transnational advocacy network on conflict trade demonstrates the diversity of collaboration initiatives.

A comprehensive international regulatory instrument could be more effective than the current ad hoc approach of tackling this issue on the basis of individual actors or conflicts, commodities, or activities. Ideally, a comprehensive global instrument would deal not only with conflict trade in natural resources but also with other economic activities sustaining human rights abuses. Current international laws and principles as well as enforcement mechanisms provide a basis for such a global enforcement instrument. Elements constituting a comprehensive framework could include (but not be restricted to) targeted sanctions, economic protectorates and trust or escrow funds, certification regimes, and economic monitoring (see table 6.1). These enforcement

Table 6.1 Overview of International Instruments of Enforcement

Instrument	Goal	Institutional structure	Effectiveness	Future plans
Sanction regimes				
UN Security Council sanctions	Attenuate and resolve conflicts through economic leverage and criminalization	*Mandatory.* International law implemented by member states and targeting states, groups, or individuals	*Strong to medium*, if effectively enforced	More precisely targeted sanctions and effective criminalization of sanction busting by member states
Regional sanctions (for example, by ECOWAS)	Attenuate and resolve conflicts through economic leverage	*Mandatory.* Regional regulation implemented by member states and targeting states, groups, or individuals	*Medium*, function of implementation by neighboring-trading countries	Improved compliance and enforcement mechanisms by member states
UN panels of experts	Report on sanctions violations and war economies and recommend follow-up actions	*Voluntary.* Independent group of experts mandated by the UN Security Council and reporting to the UN Secretary General	*High* in terms of exposure and "naming and shaming"; *weak* in terms of enforcement via recommendations	Systematic use during sanction regimes; centralized support unit

(Table continues on the following page.)

Table 6.1 (continued)

Instrument	Goal	Institutional structure	Effectiveness	Future plans
Judicial instruments				
International Convention for the Suppression of the Financing of Terrorism	Prevent the financing of terrorism	*Mandatory.* Implementation by states overseeing activities of private sector and individuals	*Potentially strong,* function of relation to Al-Qaeda; *weak* for other types of terrorists (besides use by national authorities)	Possible application of the broad definition of terrorism to include all war criminals; development of relevant financial tracking mechanisms
International Criminal Court	Provide an international jurisdiction over war crimes, genocide, crimes against humanity	*Mandatory.* International tribunal	*Untested*	Possible extension of jurisdiction to financial accomplices of crimes covered by the statute
UN Convention against Organized Crime	Promote international legal standards on resource exploitation and trade	*Mandatory.* Implementation by states	*Untested*	Possible protocol on the illicit exploitation of and trafficking in natural resources

Certification regimes

Kimberley Certification Process Scheme	Prevent laundering of conflict diamonds in legitimate trade	*Mandatory.* International agreement by participating member states to be legally implemented by industry	*Weak,* until globally adopted and effectively monitored, which is unlikely	Extended globally to restrict market access for noncertified diamonds and provide independent monitoring
Timber certification (for example, forest certification schemes)	Achieve sustainable forest management	*Voluntary.* Adhesion to an independently monitored certification process	*Weak,* concerns only a minor share of the timber trade	Extended globally to restrict market access for conflict timber (noncertified)
Aid conditionality	Use economic leverage to improve governance by aid recipient	*Mandatory.* Suspension or cancellation of loans and grants by donor agency	*Untested,* problem of foreign policy focus on terrorism, function of significance of aid versus revenue	Integration of standards of resource governance in aid and trade agreements
Economic supervision	Supervise resource exploitation, trade, and revenue allocation during peace processes	*Mandatory.* Implementation by transitional authority mandated by resource project contract, peace agreement, UN Security Council	*Untested* in the context of a peace process (weak for Cambodia 1992–93)	Incorporation into peace negotiations, and UN peacekeeping and transitional authority mandates; possible future use in context of Sudan

(Table continues on the following page.)

Table 6.1 (continued)

Instrument	Goal	Institutional structure	Effectiveness	Future plans
Chad-Cameroon Petroleum Project	Monitor oil revenue allocation to promote development and avoid renewed conflict	*Mixed.* Domestic host-country legislation and international monitoring mechanism	*Potentially strong*, but untested in condition of normal oil revenue	Systematic use by World Bank and industry in petroleum project development in developing countries
Corporate conduct				
Global Mining Initiative	Identify and address environmental and social challenges facing the mining industry	*Voluntary.* Industry association and independent research	*Medium* normative impact; *untested* effectiveness, function of follow-up implementation by industry	Industry guidelines, continued dialogue with stakeholders
UN Global Compact	Adoption by business of UN principles on environmental, labor, and human rights	*Voluntary.* UN team facilitating dialogue, nonbinding principles	*Medium* in terms of visibility and dialogue; effectiveness remains to be seen	Long-term, value-based platform for dialogue, short-term outputs in corporate practices
OECD Guidelines for Multinational Enterprises	Improve the practices of corporations and offer "soft" regulatory channel	*Voluntary.* Set of guidelines, advisory commission, and national contact points for dissemination and soft regulation	*Weak* enforcement impact; *medium* normative impact	Strengthening of enforcement and increased adoption by non-OECD countries
Electronic industry and conflict coltan	Prevent the use of Democratic Republic of Congo conflict coltan in downstream industries	*Voluntary.* Warning and recommendations by industry associations	*Medium*, function of alternative sources of coltan and UN reporting	Continued avoidance until the issue is cleared up

instruments, and others, are discussed in detail later in the chapter. However, there are major political, legal, and practical obstacles to the development of a global instrument. Politically, a great diversity of states and nonstate actors needs to come to a consensus, and issues of state sovereignty, trade freedom, and North-South relations are likely to pose major difficulties. Legally, complex issues need to be addressed, including jurisdiction over individuals and organizations (for example, corporate liability), circumstances of application (for example, level of repression or state of war), and definition of offenses, degree of complicity, and sanctions. Enforcement faces numerous practical obstacles, ranging from policing a vast informal trade to tackling the vested interests and confidential practices of powerful businesses and state officials. As a result, the institutional structure of enforcement instruments is likely to remain dominated by existing multilateral sanctions regimes and national legislation on money laundering as well as by ad hoc initiatives bringing together industries, governments, and civil society organizations to devise mixed regulatory regimes on a commodity or activity. Although generally motivated by and targeted at the worst abuses of human rights such as conflict trade, these initiatives should be encouraged to deepen their analysis of and response to broader issues of economic and social governance.

Existing Instruments of Enforcement

This section examines enforcement instruments relevant to controlling the transborder trade in natural resources that finances armed conflicts. It focuses on international legal instruments but also considers examples of enforcement instruments that have been applied to resource governance but that are not legal rules under international law (that is, rules designed for authoritative interpretation by an independent judicial authority and capable of enforcement by the application of external sanctions). The analysis also touches on national instruments that are relevant to international trade in resources. National instruments in some cases can be highly relevant; for example, of all the individuals who are currently facing criminal charges in relation to conflict trade, only one is charged with violating international legislation, in this case a UN arms embargo.

The following instruments are examined in terms of goals, institutional structure, and, to the extent feasible, effectiveness:

- Trade sanctions
- Judicial instruments

- Certification instruments
- Aid conditionality and economic supervision
- Corporate conduct instruments
- Advocacy nongovernmental organizations and the media
- Other transboundary resource and environmental governance instruments.

Trade Sanctions

International trade sanctions represent one of the most powerful instruments of enforcement bearing on transborder trade in conflict resources. Although trade sanctions can directly affect the flow of resources and therefore stop resources from financing war, they have been used largely as a coercive measure and as a means of gaining economic leverage over exporting countries to serve the interests or objectives of sanction-imposing countries. The United States, in particular, has repeatedly used this instrument in foreign policy. Exporting countries have also used trade sanctions to send a political message and to achieve economic leverage over importing countries, most noticeably in the case of the 1973 oil ban imposed by the oil-producing Arab nations on trade with the United States. This section deals with international trade sanctions established under international law through the UN Security Council as well as under regional arrangements, but it does not specifically examine unilateral trade sanctions.

UN Commodity Sanctions.   Under Article 41, Chapter VII, of the UN Charter, the Security Council may impose restrictions on economic relations by UN members with targeted countries or groups "to maintain or restore international peace and security." Once this decision has been taken according to the voting rules of the Security Council, UN member states are obliged to accept and carry it out in accordance with the UN Charter (Article 25, Chapter V).

The implementation of sanctions is followed and assisted by Security Council–mandated sanctions committees, which solicit and review reports on measures that states take to implement sanctions, seek further information from states on implementation measures and violations, report periodically to the council on persons or entities reported in violation of sanctions, and recommend appropriate measures and promulgate guidelines to both the Security Council and states to facilitate the implementation of sanctions. Sanctions committees also deal with matters relating to the target list, administer the exceptions process, and assist the council in finding solutions for nontargeted states economically affected by sanctions (Article 50; Biersteker and others 2001). The breadth and effectiveness of the work of the sanctions committees have recently been enhanced by the creation of UN expert panels mandated by the Security Council to conduct independent investigations of sanctions violations.

The imposition of international trade sanctions on a multilateral basis under the aegis of the United Nations is a relatively new phenomenon. During the cold war, the ability of the five permanent members of the UN Security Council to veto any such resolution generally prevented these measures. The only clear exception over that period was sanctions imposed in 1966 against "the illegal racist [minority] régime in Southern Rhodesia" with a view to secure the "freedom and independence" of its population.[5] The UN economic sanctions against Iraq in 1990, aimed at securing Iraq's withdrawal from Kuwait and then disarmament of its weapons of mass destruction, opened a new era. Since then, UN sanctions or monitoring measures targeting natural resources have been imposed on nine occasions (table 6.2). Timber, oil, and precious gems have been the most frequently targeted resources. Sanctions have been imposed generally in an effort to curtail the financial means available to rebel factions or to entice these factions to sign or implement a peace agreement. When the commodity involved is already illegal on the international market, the Security Council has attempted to curtail items necessary for its production. For example, in the case of heroin in the Afghan conflict and international terrorism links, the Security Council attempted to curtail the provision of chemicals used in the production process.

Very few implementation measures have involved ground policing through military deployment by member states or UN peacekeeping missions. However, there have been at least two cases of military deployment. First, between 1966 and 1975, the British Navy attempted to enforce a naval blockade on the importation of oil by Rhodesia, mostly through the port of Beira. Although the high-profile blockade was ineffectual, the British government did not end it until Mozambique gained independence and assured the United Nations that no oil would reach Rhodesia through its territory (Mobley 2002). Second, immediately after the Iraqi invasion of Kuwait in 1990, the Security Council imposed a sanctions regime to block Iraqi oil exports. The Multinational Interception Force led by the U.S. Navy acts under Security Council Resolution 665 (1990) to interdict all maritime traffic to and from Iraq to ensure the strict implementation of sanctions. Iraqi oil exports declined 90 percent between 1990 and 1995, crippling its economy.[6] Yet Saddam Hussein proved sufficiently resilient and unconcerned by the plight of his population to withstand sanctions that were progressively eroded by the Oil-for-Food Program and smuggling.[7] By the late 1990s, oil smuggling brought in annual revenues in excess of

Table 6.2 UN Security Council Sanctions against Natural
Resource Exports

Year	Country	Resolution
1966	Southern Rhodesia	S/RES/232 (1966) and 253 (1968): all commodities
1990	Iraq	S/RES/661 (1990): all commodities; S/RES/665 (1990): calls for halting, inspecting, and verifying all maritime shipping in the Gulf area to ensure strict implementation of S/RES/661
1991	Yugoslavia	S/RES/757 (1991) and 787 (1992): all commodities
1992	Cambodia	S/RES/792 (1992): log exports; requests the adoption of an embargo on minerals and gems exports and the implementation measures by UN Transitional Authority in Cambodia
1993	Libya	S/RES/883 (1993): bans the provision to Libya of equipment for oil refining and transportation
1994	Haiti	S/RES/917 (1994): all commodities
1998	Angola	S/RES/1173 (1998): all diamonds outside government certificate-of-origin regime and the provision of mining equipment and services to areas not under government control; S/RES/1237 (1999): establishes an expert panel; S/RES/1295 (2000): establishes a mechanism for monitoring sanctions
2000	Afghanistan	S/RES/1333 (2000): bans the provision to Taliban-controlled areas of acetic anhydride used in heroin production
2000	Congo, Dem. Rep. of	S/PRST/2000/20: establishes an expert panel on the illegal exploitation of natural resources and other forms of wealth
2000	Sierra Leone	S/RES/1306 (2000): all rough diamonds pending an effective regime of government certificates of origin; creates an expert panel on the implementation of sanctions
2001	Liberia	S/RES/1343 (2001): all rough diamonds: establishes an expert panel; S/RES/1408 (2002): calls for establishment by the government of Liberia of transparent and internationally verifiable audit regimes on use of timber industry revenues

$500 million.[8] Major as well as minor oil purchasers and companies are involved. Nevertheless, there remains some potential for more effective enforcement of sanctions. The unique physical characteristics of oil fields and the availability of databases allow for identification of the oil transported to the international market (Myers 2000).

In addition to military deployment, civilian and peacekeeping forces can be involved in on-the-ground monitoring. Such monitoring by UN peacekeeping forces has been very limited:

• Military observers from the UN Transitional Authority in Cambodia were deployed at key cross-border points to monitor a ban on log exports.

• In the former Republic of Yugoslavia, border monitors from the UN Transitional Authority in Eastern Slavonia, Baranja, and Western Sirmium were deployed to supervise local police forces and customs officials—although this did not prevent the exportation of timber from Eastern Slavonia to Serbia for the benefit of local mafia groups.[9] Regional security organizations have also assisted in the monitoring of UN sanctions. For example, the Commission on Security and Cooperation in Europe deployed international border monitors to help seal the border of the former Republic of Yugoslavia and later on the transit from Serbia to Bosnia.

• Troops from the UN Mission in Sierra Leone occasionally contributed to conflict resolution in diamond-mining areas but did not play a major role in the enforcement of sanctions on diamond exports by the RUF, as they were mandated only "to coordinate with and assist, in *common areas of deployment,* the Sierra Leone law enforcement authorities in the discharge of their responsibilities" (Resolution S/RES/1289, emphasis added).[10] The suggestion by the Economic Community of West African States (ECOWAS) that UN monitors be deployed along Liberian borders to monitor the trade of natural resources was rejected, owing in part to the insecurity prevalent in border areas as well as the near-impossibility of effectively monitoring diamond trade across a land border.

The association of criminal organizations and terrorists directly targeting Western interests has reinforced the view within the United States that transnational crime could be kept in check more effectively through a global system of enforcement. A U.S. State Department official recently argued in favor of a new type of international law enforcement system composed of "UN inspection teams in ports and airports, with the authority to detain aircraft or ships or arrest people" but had no illusion that such a system could happen anytime soon (International Consortium of Investigative Journalists 2002b, p. 6).

Recent progress, however, has been made in terms of the international monitoring of UN sanctions through independent UN expert panels.

Mandated by the Security Council and reporting through the chair of the sanctions committees and the UN secretariat, these panels publicize their findings, thereby enabling a name-and-shame strategy, while their recommendations have included sanctions on complicit states or individuals. Experts do not work undercover and rely on voluntary testimonies; this makes their task more difficult than intelligence or police work. Greater cooperation from intelligence agencies and the financial sector is needed in this regard. Even if their most sweeping recommendations have not been implemented, UN expert panels have provided information that has significantly affected the operations of sanctions busters, by indirectly curtailing their access to financial credit and forcing them to change their logistical base or to seek protection in friendly countries. With staff hired on a consultant basis and budgets averaging $1 million for a typical team of five working over a six-month period, expert panels are relatively easy to set up and inexpensive to run in comparison to peacekeeping operations. Adding Interpol representatives also facilitates exchanges with police institutions worldwide. Although there is no coordinating facility between the different panels, several experts have worked on multiple panels, thereby maintaining an institutional memory. With peace in Angola and Sierra Leone, there is a risk that the use of expert panels will be greatly reduced. There is a need to reflect on this experience, notably to consolidate the future use of such instruments and to create a small permanent unit to track war economies and sanctions violators.

Economic sanctions have long been a tool of coercion and enforcement in international relations. There is a vast literature on their effectiveness and on the reasons and criteria for judging success or failure (see, for example, Heine-Ellison 2001; Mansfield 1995). Reviewing largely unilateral and comprehensive economic sanctions between 1914 and the 1990s, Hufbauer, Schott, and Elliot (1985) find that 34 percent of sanctions were at least partially successful.[11] Success depended on several factors:

- The sanction's goals were modest.
- The target was economically weak, politically unstable, and smaller than the country imposing sanctions.
- The sender and the target conducted substantial trade and were otherwise "friendly toward one another."
- Impact was maximized by imposing sanctions quickly and decisively.
- The sender avoided high costs to itself.

The argument that "sanctions work," however, is refuted by Robert Pape (1997), who finds only 5 percent effectiveness among the same sample. Pape argues that economic sanctions have not achieved major foreign policy goals, because there was no cooperation among sanctioning states and because modern nation-states are not "fragile" (Pape 1997, p. 106). A previous study by Knorr (1975), on a smaller sample of sanctions imposed between 1811 and 1974, also finds that sanctions were rarely effective.[12]

Examining 12 multilateral economic sanctions in the 1990s, Cortright and Lopez (2000) estimate that 36 percent were effective and blamed the failures on flaws in design, implementation, and enforcement rather than on the general principle of sanctions. In their view, both comprehensive and targeted sanctions can be effective, as long as member states are committed and effective in implementing and enforcing them strictly. However, they note that sanctions must remain a tool of coercive persuasion that assists in negotiation and bargaining and not become a form of punishment. They argue that combining positive incentives and sanctions can improve compliance on the part of targeted groups or states.

Looking at UN sanctions during the 1990s, Mack and Khan (2000) argue that sanctions have mostly failed to change the behavior of targets, but that they should not necessarily be considered as failures, especially in terms of stigmatizing and containing targets. In this perspective, sanctions can be effective as an instrument of policing and punishment. The counterargument is that economic sanctions, including targeted ones, can further aggravate conflicts by criminalizing targeted belligerents, making it more likely they will be less inclined to negotiate politically (Kopp 1996). Mark Duffield suggests that war economies need to be seen in a different light and that "transborder networks associated with organized violence have stimulated enterprise across large tracts of the South" (Duffield 2002, p. 160). Regulating these war economies through sanctions also means privileging some operators over others, with the risk of creating a climate in which criminal syndicates thrive, while more legitimate businesses, large and small, suffer.

The record of commodity sanctions in the 1990s is ambiguous. Since 1990, out of the 10 conflicts in which UN sanctions or monitoring regimes targeting resource exports were used, eight were resolved. But for five of these, resolution was mostly an outcome of military intervention (Afghanistan, Angola, Haiti, Sierra Leone, former Yugoslavia). Of the others, only Libya is a possible success in terms of the limited goal of extraditing two suspected terrorists in the bombing of a UTA airliner. In the case of sanctions on the Khmer Rouge, the United Nations was no longer enforcing them, and this relative success resulted instead from pressure by the nongovernmental organization Global Witness and donors on the Cambodian and Thai governments, as well as sustained, although not decisive, military action on the part of the Cambodian government. In the case of the Democratic Republic of Congo, no sanctions regime was imposed as such, only "naming and shaming" through UN expert panel reports, whereas negotiations and donor pressure were key to resolution of the conflict. The two unresolved "conflicts" are Iraq and Liberia. The case of sanctions on Iraq—a mixed regime including both comprehensive and targeted sanctions—is widely seen as a failure, although some analysts point to its success as a containment measure (see O'Sullivan 2002; "When Sanctions Don't Work" 2000). Some success has been registered in the case of Liberia, but the weakening of the government has further prolonged the conflict with a rebel movement (Liberians United for Reconciliation and Democracy), and President Taylor is alleged to remain involved in criminal activities.

Judging by the record in the 1990s, military interventions are more effective than commodity sanctions at ending conflicts. Advocates of sanctions point out, however, that they often weaken the targeted groups. In the case of Angola, following the killing of Jonas Savimbi in February 2002 and the end of the conflict, the highest-ranking UNITA official stated, "Sanctions weakened UNITA tremendously; they played a decisive role."[13] No such statement has come out of the RUF in Sierra Leone, although the UN expert panel on Liberia indicated that Taylor had limited some of its assistance to the rebel group as a result of targeted sanctions (Doyle 2002: United Nations 2000a). Successive sanctions have curtailed the purchasing power of targets for rearmament or deployment, addressed the economic motivation of belligerents, and created tensions within the chain of command of the targeted group as a result of financial and logistical difficulties. In Cambodia, the interdiction of transborder timber trade, which had sustained the Khmer Rouge during the early 1990s, contributed to the demise of the movement.

With regard to the institutional structure and practices of the United Nations, there are several barriers to more effective enforcement. The composition and voting rules of the Security Council and the powers it grants to its five permanent members at times have jeopardized the legitimacy of its decisions, leaving dissenting states to use inadequate or limited enforcement as a way to express their views and protect their interests.

Regarding state-level enforcement, while states may themselves be sanctioned for noncompliance, there is a general reluctance to multiply "secondary sanctions." Furthermore, the lack of adequate national legislation and enforcement by some governments has left many sanctions with a merely rhetorical effect. Such weak enforcement can favor criminal groups by forcing legitimate companies out of resource sectors, with potentially negative consequences for conflict prevention. Recognizing this dynamic in the context of sanctions against UNITA, the Security Council has urged "all States . . . to enforce, strengthen, or enact legislation making it a criminal offense under domestic law for their nationals or other individuals operating on their territory to violate the measures imposed by the Council."[14] A general model law resulting from the Interlaken II Process aims to facilitate the drafting of such legal measures.[15]

With regard to ground monitoring, border monitors deployed in Cambodia or the former Yugoslavia had limited impact. Monitors can be constrained by combatant forces or the forces and border patrols of allied neighboring states. Movement along the border is generally limited for security reasons—especially at night—leaving many smuggling routes open, and monitors generally lack the power of arrest or the mandate to seize goods, having to rely on local authorities. When the security concerns of monitors and high cost of implementation are included, ground monitoring is viable only when the resources targeted cannot be easily smuggled and trade is taking place in an area where local authorities support and can assist in the sanctions regime. In other cases, investigation of the trade by UN-mandated experts should be more effective. Even then, critics have argued that "naming people without shame" is ineffective and that, unless the authorities of countries where sanctions busters reside intervene judicially, little can be expected from such initiatives.[16]

To sum up, the following course of action can be recommended when natural resource revenues are suspected to contribute to an armed conflict:

- Creation of an expert panel by the UN Security Council to investigate the matter and possibly prohibit imports of the conflict resource by member states pending adequate national certification or international supervision of the resource sector (including humanitarian assessment of the potential effect of sanctions)
- Assessment of the potential role of UN peacekeeping deployments in targeted resource areas, especially if a mission is ongoing, by the Department of Peace Keeping Operations, Department of Political Affairs, or representative of the UN secretary general in liaison with the expert panel
- Review of legislation and practices in resource extraction and trading in neighboring countries and other areas identified as transit or importing countries by the expert panel

- An Interpol-sponsored regional meeting to exchange information on trade patterns and suspected resource brokers and assistance missions to relevant countries to effect potential UN Security Council sanctions as well as a compensation scheme and buffer (Article 50, UN Charter)
- Financial aid and technical assistance to targeted countries to facilitate compliance with international certification schemes and Security Council resolutions
- Criminal prosecution of sanctions busters using national and international legislation
- Potential use of diplomacy, aid conditionality, and sanctions to curtail the transit or importation of sanctioned resources.

Unilateral and Regional Trade Sanctions.   Individual countries and regional organizations have also imposed sanctions on commodity exports. In the United States, the federal administration, state governments, and even municipalities have imposed unilateral sanctions against countries or individuals—sometimes with extraterritorial reach, as through the Iran-Libya Sanctions Act (1996). Few of these sanctions, however, have been targeted at belligerents supported by resources. The U.S. government imposed sanctions against Iraq immediately after its invasion of Kuwait. It also targeted the military regime in Myanmar in 1995, through an investment moratorium affecting mostly U.S. energy companies. But that measure fell short of requiring divestment or even deterring reinvestment in existing projects. Because of growing and diversifying international trade flows, unilateral sanctions—even those imposed by the United States—are unlikely to have a significant impact on conflict trade except, of course, if the target country is utterly dependent on the sender country for exploitation technology, transport infrastructure, or market.

Regional organizations have also imposed commodity export sanctions. In Liberia, ECOWAS imposed economic sanctions on areas controlled by Charles Taylor's National Patriotic Front of Liberia (NPFL) in 1993, after its military arm, the ECOWAS Monitoring Group (ECOMOG), had organized a military blockade and takeover of Taylor's leading port in Buchanan, from which the NPFL imported arms and exported iron ore, rubber, and timber (Atkinson 1997). The sanctions regime suffered from the weakness of regional state institutions to perform their regulatory functions (Aning 2002). Sanctions were also imposed on Burundi in 1996 by the Central African states, but this regime was systematically violated not only by smugglers but also by participating states, allowing for the export of key commodities from Burundi, notably the smuggling of coffee (Mthembu-Salter 1999, pp. 18–19).

Many observers argued that the sanctions regime was not only ineffective but also counterproductive in humanitarian terms, with a vast amount of smuggling in both arms and commodities taking place, while humanitarian and development aid was impeded (Haq 1997).

In contrast to many unilateral sanctions imposed by a "distant" power attempting to control imports into its markets, regional sanctions may have been more capable of impeding conflict trade by intervening in both transport links and the exploitation of commodities. This intervention, however, may create significant vulnerability, as major local interests often can undermine the design and effective implementation of sanctions. Furthermore, the enforcement capacity of neighboring countries can be weak, especially when dealing with easily concealable commodities such as diamonds or gold.

Judicial Instruments

The judicial prosecution of sanctions busters and of resource companies and traders engaging with belligerents is in its infancy, both in terms of permanent international legislation—rather than ad hoc ones like UN resolutions—and in terms of institutions with international jurisdiction. The judicial prosecution of UN sanctions is also in a fledgling stage. As mentioned in the discussion of UN sanctions, many member states have failed to criminalize sanctions busting, and even fewer have acted on such legislation. So far there has been no arrest on charges of commodity sanctions busting, and only two individuals—one of them also a primary commodity trader—have faced charges for violating a UN arms embargo. In terms of judicial enforcement, national legislation and institutions remain key instruments of enforcement.

National Legislation. Although this chapter focuses on international instruments, national-level judicial instruments are highly relevant, starting with the implementation of legislation flowing from the imposition of UN sanctions. National-level instruments are used to target a wide range of "classic" criminal activities (such as money laundering) and other activities relevant to conflict trade (such as complicity in human rights abuses). This section examines two ways in which national-level enforcement instruments have been employed: to target rogue traders and to target multinational companies.

Since many national-level instruments are being applied in the context of armed conflicts, they constitute a potential instrument of enforcement. In general, though, these instruments have been deployed as a means of advocacy, redress, and deterrence rather than as a mechanism of enforcement to curtail conflict trade per se.

That national-level judicial instruments are, or could become, relevant to the regulation of conflict trade is demonstrated by the list of
individuals dealing in conflict resources who are facing criminal
charges—there are currently 10 individuals on this list in addition to
seven unnamed diamond traffickers. Judicial authorities in several
countries such as Belgium, France, and Switzerland have also initiated
judicial proceedings against named individuals dealing in conflict commodities. In these cases, the charges do not involve legislation specifically related to conflict commodities per se (which does not generally
exist with the exception of legislation to implement UN sanctions) but
rather related to criminal activities involving money laundering, tax
evasion, arms trafficking, forgery, or breach of trust.

In parallel to domestic charges against rogue traders involved in
conflict trade, extraterritorial lawsuits have also targeted multinational companies. In the United States, the Alien Tort Claims Act and
the Torture Victims Protection Act allow companies to be sued at
home for their behavior overseas and that of their business partners,
including host-government troops in charge of protecting staff and assets. The Alien Tort Claims Act grants "the district courts . . . original
jurisdiction in any civil action by an alien for a tort only, committed
in violation of the law of nations or a treaty of the United States."
The jurisdiction of the district courts to hear claims under this act is
limited by the constitutional requirements that the court obtain
proper personal jurisdiction over the defendant: the perpetrator of the
violation must be present within the territorial jurisdiction of the
court or be subject to the court's long-arm jurisdiction. Yet plaintiffs—
local people from production areas and supported by advocacy
groups—are increasingly using the Alien Tort Claims Act and the
Torture Victims Protection Act as judicial instruments for human
rights claims and corporate accountability. These initiatives are not
unique to the United States; a judicial case was opened recently in
France against a French company on allegations of using forced labor
in Myanmar.

Calls have been made to create more far-reaching and updated
legislation, in particular, the U.S. proposal for a Foreign Human Rights
Abuse Act (Saunders 2001). Although this act may in the future come
into being, some commentators have argued in favor of global, rather
than nationally specific, legislation. Although global-level, comprehensive legislation may in theory be more effective, there is disagreement
about how such global legislation could be designed and adequately
enforced. To date, most initiatives in this direction have been toward
voluntary regulation rather than mandatory legislation.

International Legislation and Judicial Instruments. Three major instruments can be identified, none of which has been designed or tested in relation to conflict trade. As such, they represent only potential enforcement instruments.

The first instrument is the International Criminal Court, which covers the actions of individuals, not companies. The crimes defined include seizing "the enemy's property unless such ... seizure be imperatively demanded by the necessities of war" and "pillaging a town or place."[17] Corporate liability—excluded from the statute—would allow victims to be compensated through the seizure of corporate assets (Carbonnier 2001). Accomplice liability on the part of economic actors facilitating the commission of crimes is covered but requires that such complicity be directed intentionally for the purpose of assisting others in committing a crime.[18] A broader definition of complicity—removing the dimension of personal intention while retaining the knowledge of the intention of the group to commit the crime—would make the statute more applicable to tackling conflict trade; this redefinition is likely to be too broad to be adopted. Another relevant point is that the international warrants that the International Criminal Court issues could complement UN Security Council resolutions, particularly for the purposes of identifying and legally defining individual actors for specific sanctions.

The second instrument is the International Convention for the Suppression of the Financing of Terrorism, which requires states to criminalize the provision or collection of funds for acts defined as offenses by previous antiterrorism conventions.[19] It also requires states to provide legal assistance with investigations and extradition regardless of their bank secrecy laws and for state parties to cooperate with one another in investigations and extraditions when these offenses are committed. Adopted at the UN General Assembly on December 9, 1999, the convention entered into force on April 10, 2002, following UN Security Council Resolution 1373 urging member states to ratify it. The convention could be relevant to conflict resources and in particular to resource businesses and financial institutions dealing financially with terrorists and war criminals.[20] Some rebel groups figure in the list of terrorists in major jurisdictions such as the European Union (EU) or the United States, and the definition of terrorism is very close to some war crimes, such as murders or physical violence perpetrated against noncombatants during wars.[21]

Resource businesses and financial institutions could be affected by this convention in three ways. First, financial institutions and other professions dealing with the finances of suspected terrorist groups come under measures from state parties "to utilize the most efficient measures available for the identification of their . . . customers . . . and report transactions suspected of stemming from criminal activities" (para. 18.b). Second, businesses come under obligation of cooperation with the judicial process as "State Parties may not refuse a request for mutual legal assistance on the ground of bank secrecy" (para. 12.2). Third, and most important, a business "commits an offence . . . if [it] by any means . . . provides or collects funds with the intention that they should be used . . . to carry out" acts of terrorism (para. 2.1). As such, a business providing funds—such as taxes or "protection fees"—to a combatant, with the knowledge that these funds are to be used to carry out acts of violence against civilians, could be subject to prosecution.[22] The renewed emphasis on fighting terrorism—including Osama Bin Laden, who had "legitimate" business interests and circulated large sums through formal financial networks—is certainly testing the application of this convention to the private commercial sector (Sallam 2000). It could be applied to diamond dealers allegedly linked to Al-Qaeda financing networks (Dietrich and Danssaert 2001; Farah 2001).

The third instrument is the UN Convention against Transnational Organized Crime. With its focus on the criminalization of the laundering of proceeds of crime (Article 6) and corruption (Article 8), this convention has the potential to cover the laundering of natural resource revenues obtained through criminal offenses defined domestically (such as armed rebellion or "grand corruption") or internationally (such as war crimes).[23] There is, however, no specific reference to this type of criminal activity or to natural resources within the text of the convention. Building on protocols already complementing the convention, such as protocols on arms and human trafficking, the possibility of a protocol specifically addressing the illicit exploitation of and trafficking in natural resources could be considered (Bayart, Ellis, and Hibou 1999; Berdal and Malone 2000).

Such a protocol is the Protocol against the Illicit Manufacturing of and Trafficking in Firearms, Their Parts and Components, and Ammunition, which provides both general provisions requesting a criminalization of offenses defined by the protocol and specific provisions relating to the prevention of offenses, including record keeping, marking of firearms, international trading licensing and authorization systems, and the registration and licensing of arms brokers.[24] The protocol on natural resources could cover a broad range of issues related to preventing and terminating conflicts, including financial complicity in war crimes, application of certification and sanctions regimes, legality of exploitation, record keeping and public access to import-export and revenue figures, and financial transparency of governments and the private sector. The experience and recommendations of the UN expert panels could prove useful in a negotiation process—in particular those of the Expert Panel on the Illegal Exploitation of Natural Resources and Other Forms of Wealth in the Democratic Republic of Congo. The impact of such a protocol on small-scale producers and traders, especially in developing countries, should be carefully assessed to avoid creating further economic imbalance to their disadvantage.

International Policing and Judicial Cooperation Organizations. International judicial and policing cooperation is essential to effective enforcement. Interpol provides a worldwide instrument of cooperation, crime analysis, and information dissemination, as well as forensic assistance between police forces.[25] Interpol has been active in the field of conflict resources by providing officers to UN expert panels, by participating in regional and international meetings, and by conducting its normal activities (for example, arms trafficking, money laundering). A specialized branch within Interpol deals with the laundering of funds derived from criminal activities (Fopac).[26] Although its focus has been on the laundering of drug proceeds, its activities could include proceeds from conflict resources. The decentralization of Interpol into subregional bureaus has enhanced regional cooperation, including on matters related to the smuggling of conflict resources such as the cooperation of Southern African police forces on diamond smuggling and armed conflicts through the Southern African Regional Police Chiefs Cooperation Organization and its Agreement on Co-operation and Mutual Assistance in the Field of Crime Combating, which allows for "police officers of the region to enter countries of other parties with the authority to do so, for the purpose of police investigations, seizure of exhibits, tracing and questioning of witnesses" (Msutu 2001).

Other policing and judicial cooperation organizations that can assist enforcement efforts include the Centre for International Crime Prevention, which can assist countries in their ratification and implementation of international criminal law conventions and protocols;[27] the UN Interregional Crime and Justice Research Institute, which concentrates on research, training, and field projects; as well as the World Customs Organization, which can assist in tracking the trade in conflict resources, in particular through its network of regional intelligence liaison offices. A mapping exercise, identifying the relevant enforcement agencies, their links, and avenues for progress, could prove valuable.

Certification Instruments

Like targeted sanctions, certification instruments set up a discriminatory regime allowing for selective access of resources to the market. Certification can be either mandatory or voluntary.

In the case of mandatory certification, or "verification," the primary goal is to restrict consumer access to legal products—however defined—by informing potential buyers and trade or customs authorities of the legal standing of the resources and to prevent or dissuade them from buying or licensing illegal resources. While resources certified as licit, even if originating in conflict-affected countries, can access legal markets, uncertified resources cannot and should thus be confined to the black markets with significant discounts for the seller.

In the case of voluntary certification, the idea is to help (and somehow create) the demand for products that meet or exceed specific criteria. Higher prices or specific demand for certified products are used as economic incentives to promote compliance by businesses. As such, voluntary certification is a type of "smart," rather than prescriptive, legislation, which seeks to create demand for "good" products rather than to curtail supply of "bad" ones. Yet as substantial profit margins result from certifying resources, there is also an incentive for certification authorities and traders to "launder" illicit resources through a fraudulent certification process. A study by World Wide Fund for Nature finds that out of a sample of 80 environmental claims put by companies on wood or paper products, only three could be partially substantiated.[28] The effectiveness of a certification regime thus depends on its independence and enforcement throughout the whole commodity chain, from the verification of exploitation criteria to the integrity of the commodity chain bringing the resource to consumers (for more details on custody chains, see chapter 4).

Certification regimes have been used according to criteria as diverse as consumer safety, quality, "fair" trading, or environmental friendliness. Accordingly, there is a wide diversity of institutional structures, from producer cooperatives to nongovernmental organizations, government agencies, and international agreements. So far, only one certification regime is designed specifically to prevent conflict resources from accessing legal markets: the Kimberley Certification Process Scheme for rough diamonds. Current certification schemes in the timber industry, such as the Forest Stewardship Council identification of wood harvested from sustainable sources, also provide an avenue to influence the trade of conflict and illegal timber.

The overall effectiveness of a certification scheme relies on a relative concentration of the industry, which allows companies or dependent countries to champion the scheme, on potential exposure of the resource to consumer pressure, and on ease of controls.

Diamond Certification: The Kimberley Certification Process.   The agreement on a Kimberley Certification Process Scheme seeks to rid the international rough diamonds trade of "conflict diamonds" by establishing a voluntary system of industry self-regulation. This system is based on a certification process requiring all participants:

- Not to trade in rough diamonds with any nonparticipant
- To accompany each shipment of rough diamond exports with a certificate and to require such a certificate on all imports
- To establish a system of internal controls and shipment eliminating conflict diamonds from any exports
- To collect and maintain statistical data on production, imports, and exports
- To cooperate and be transparent with other participants, including through external reviews and assistance to fulfill minimal requirements.

Launched in May 2000 in Kimberley, South Africa's first diamond town, by African diamond-producing countries eager to protect their trade, the Kimberley process consisted of a dozen international meetings, drawing together government officials from up to 38 countries as well as representatives of the diamonds industry and nongovernmental organizations. The dominant position of De Beers in the marketing chain, the existence of the Diamond High Council in the main trading center of Antwerp, and the creation in 2001 of the World Diamond Council, specifically tasked with eradicating the trade in conflict diamonds, facilitated the negotiation process, as did implementation of the country-specific certification scheme in Angola and Sierra Leone. The constructive, if at times tense, engagement between nongovernmental organizations, government, and industry was relatively innovative and succeeded in preserving the legitimate 80 to 96 percent of an economic sector that employs several hundred thousand people and is critical to the economies of many countries, including Botswana and Namibia.

The institutional structure of the Kimberley scheme comprises the following:

- Chair, nominated by participants (but without clear procedures for candidature, nomination, and duration) and in charge of chairing annual plenary meetings, collecting and disseminating information from and to participants, and liaising with participants
- Participants, governments, or regional economic integration organizations, for whom the certification is effective (fully open but without compulsory review of compliance to requirements of the scheme)
- Administrative support for the chair (but not in the form of a secretariat)

- Importing and exporting authority (or authorities) nominated by each participant and in charge of, respectively, issuing certificates and verifying their validity
- Independent auditors charged with helping government authorities to verify systems of warranties put in place by individual companies
- Review missions, which require the consent of concerned participants as to composition and conduct (in "an analytical, expert, and impartial manner")
- Observers, representatives of civil society, the diamond industry, international organizations, and nonparticipating governments, who are invited to take part in plenary meetings.

The participation criteria, as well as compliance and enforcement mechanisms, are weak and formulated on a voluntary basis. Review missions on compliance are to be conducted "with the consent of the Participant concerned and in consultation with all Participants." When an issue regarding compliance arises, "any concerned Participant may so inform the Chair, who is to inform all Participants without delay about the said concern and enter into *dialogue* on how to address it. Participants and Observers should make every effort to observe strict confidentiality regarding the issue and the discussions relating to any compliance matter." Finally, there is no explicit mention of an exclusion procedure for noncomplying participants.

The Kimberley scheme is complemented by self-regulatory measures on the part of the industry. As declared by the World Diamond Council's chairman, "The self-regulation . . . is vital . . . and the industry is committed to fulfilling its obligation in step with governments. Individuals or companies that fail to observe the new rules will pay a high price for that failure."[29] Critics point out that such declarations have not so far left anyone "paying a high price" in the industry, at least publicly, and self-regulation cannot be trusted. The scheme is also complemented by national legislation.

The Kimberley process was concluded in November 2002 and was to become effective on January 1, 2003, but this deadline had not been met at the time of writing. There is no means of asserting its effectiveness apart from the pilot certification projects conducted since 2001 in Sierra Leone and, to some extent, in Angola. In both cases, the projects did not completely stop the smuggling of diamonds, and, what is more important, their impact on the conflict could not be assessed given other external factors, such as military intervention and peacekeeping deployment. The Kimberley scheme came into effect after the conflicts in Angola and Sierra Leone had been officially declared over—largely due to military interventions—and the conflict in the Democratic Republic of Congo may be winding down. This does not mean that the scheme is now irrelevant. On the contrary, it is still of relevance to the situation in the Democratic Republic of Congo, to the possible financing of terrorism, and to the prevention of future conflicts.

Although the Kimberley scheme was implemented too late to apply to some of the conflicts it was originally designed to address, many observers argue that the process was rapid by international standards. However, in addition to being "too late," the Kimberley scheme instrument was also deemed too weak by advocacy nongovernmental organizations and has been described as a "watchdog without teeth."[30] The U.S. General Accounting Office released a critical report, also arguing that voluntary participation and self-regulated monitoring represent "significant challenges" to creating an effective system (U.S. General Accounting Office 2002, p. 16). This report also points out that, without "sound controls that meet basic accountability and transparency objectives . . . [the Kimberley scheme] risks the appearance of control, while still allowing conflict diamonds to enter the legitimate diamond trade and, as a result, continue to fuel conflict." Some critics even suggest that the scheme "will likely do little more than make conflict diamonds harder to detect as they move [across] borders" (Cambell 2002).

To sum up, the main obstacles to an effective certification regime result from the conjunction of the physical and economic characteristics of diamonds and the past tolerance of (illicit) practices within the industry, which make diamonds a highly valuable, easily concealed, and anonymous commodity. The Kimberley scheme in itself suffers from a number of weaknesses, including the following:

- A narrow definition of conflict diamonds and the exclusion of polished stones and jewelry from the certification process[31]
- The failure to establish sufficiently strong independent monitoring requirements, including the absence of an initial review to allow for participation or penalties for noncompliance (only strictly confidential "dialogue" between participants and possibly observers is prescribed)
- The failure to include a mechanism of direct regulation for individual companies, leaving this task to national authorities, while placing the threshold of compliance at the state level. This would prevent rapid penalties against offending companies that benefit from the complicity, complaisance, or incompetence of national authorities[32]
- The failure to regulate nonparticipating countries apart from excluding them from trading *rough diamonds* with participating countries. Some of these nonparticipating countries may continue smuggling illicit and conflict diamonds and may set up diamond-polishing and -cutting activities to short-circuit the markets for rough diamonds operating under the Kimberley scheme.

In response to these shortcomings, nongovernmental organizations that have initiated the "conflict campaign" are now seeking to establish a voluntary but independent monitoring scheme to complement the Kimberley scheme (Smillie 2002). If given more strength through widespread participation and tougher monitoring, this instrument could (a) deter large-scale investments in diamond mining in rebel-held territories (as seen in Angola prior to the UN sanctions on diamonds); (b) slightly increase the risks and possibly lower the profits for dealing in conflict and illicit diamonds; and (c) help to curb illicit trading and increase transparency in the trade, with the possibility of improving government and corporate accountability. It is too early in any case to assess the effectiveness of the Kimberley scheme, even with respect to these goals.

Forest Certification Schemes. As noted by Global Witness, in the absence of international legislation on illegal logging, "as soon as illegally obtained timber leaves the borders of the producer country, it is de facto immediately laundered into the legal timber trade" (Global Witness 2002, p. 10). According to studies by environmental groups, about half of the timber imported in Europe is illegal, as is a third of the timber imported by the G-8 and China (Friends of the Earth UK 2001; Toyne, O'Brien, and Nelson 2002). Illegal logging not only is associated with environmental damage, frequent disregard for local communities, and massive economic and tax revenue losses in exporting countries but also promotes a climate of corruption and impunity in the sector that comes to define its governance by authorities. Furthermore, the international impunity of illegal logging greatly facilitates the laundering of "conflict timber" benefiting rebel groups.

Among the measures needed to change this situation, certification could assist in guaranteeing minimum exploitation criteria (legality, financial transparency, community consultation, environmental impact) and chain of custody in domestic and international trade. The Forest Stewardship Council (FSC) scheme certifies sustainably harvested timber and incorporates legality requirements.[33] FSC is a global nongovernmental organization of civil society groups, industry, and forest product certification organizations. Its Principles and Criteria of Forest Stewardship serve as standards for the independent certification of well-managed forests. FSC also assists industry, governments, and civil society groups to define local guidelines to achieve these standards. FSC-accredited certification bodies are themselves evaluated and monitored to ensure their competence and credibility. The scheme has recently come under sharp criticism for allowing the certification of companies allegedly implicated in human rights abuses (Rainforest Foundation UK 2002). The scheme is voluntary, largely market driven, and still far from achieving a global change in the governance of forest resources. It has been criticized for being established as a "universal" standard and placed above intergovernmental and governmental regulatory instruments.

Other wood certification schemes promoted by national or regional authorities exist in this regard. Based on the criteria, indicators, and operational guidelines developed by the Ministerial Conference on the Protection of Forests in Europe, the Pan European Forest Certification Council (PEFC) also promotes independent third-party forest certification schemes within Europe.[34] Like the Forest Stewardship Council, PEFC relates to consumer markets through a logo for timber products from certified forests. PEFC, however, has been criticized by environmental nongovernmental organizations for its lack of consultation with civil society groups during the negotiation process and for controversial standards on logging practices.

In addition to these schemes, two complementary instruments can be noted: ISO 14001 certifies the quality of an organization's environmental management system, but not the standards of the output of the certification system, and EC Directive 84/450/EEC secures the integrity of certification schemes by prohibiting misleading advertising (for example, unsubstantiated claims to the sustainability of wood products).

While the Forest Stewardship Council and Pan European Forest Certification Council focus on sustainable forest management, some government, industry, and nongovernmental organizations have made efforts to address the more specific problem of illegal logging. The International Tropical Timber Organization is promoting legal and sustainable timber trade. In a joint effort with the Food and Agriculture Organization of the United Nations and the European Union, it is collecting statistics on imports and exports and investigating inconsistencies possibly indicating illegal trade. Commitments were made at the G-8 meeting in 1998 as well as a ministerial conference organized by the World Bank in September 2001 in Bali, which called for "immediate action to intensify national efforts and to strengthen bilateral, regional, and multilateral collaboration to address violations of forest law and forest crime, in particular illegal logging, associated illegal trade and corruption, and their negative effects on the rule of law." This led, for example, the European Union to set up a specific action plan on the legality of EU wood imports (Forest Law Enforcement, Governance, and Trade, FLEGT). From the perspective of importing countries (FLEGT 2002), challenges to effective instruments include:

- Creation of a mechanism for identifying the legality of wood production, tracking wood trade, and verifying legality
- Cooperation on customs and enforcement of rules of access to markets

- Policy coherence of international financial markets (aid, export credit agencies, banks) and government procurement to avoid promoting illegal practices
- Incentives and sanctions to ensure industry compliance along the commodity chain.

FLEGT is still being negotiated, and it is therefore not possible to assess its effectiveness.

Aid Conditionality and Economic Supervision

Aid conditionality and economic supervision schemes can provide a set of (dis)incentives and institutional mechanisms to influence resource governance and revenue allocation. Aid can provide an incentive and a source of support for reforms, but, as with sanctions, critics point out that developed countries, through their influence and voting power in international financial institutions, can also use aid conditionality to punish regimes they oppose.

International Aid Conditionality.   International aid can play several roles in relation to the enforcement of natural resource governance:

- It can assist communities, businesses, governments, or regional organizations to consolidate their own regulation and enforcement mechanisms through the provision of technical and legal expertise and training and through the funding of enforcement agencies. This role is particularly significant in the context of a peace process, when the availability of weapons and resources coupled with the opening up of market access and weak institutions during the transition period might lead to a criminalization of the natural resource sectors and thus prolong the conflict.[35] International organizations and key individuals in charge of transition processes—such as the UN Special Representative of the Secretary General or United Nations Development Programme— could give further attention to this problem (International Peace Academy 2002, p. 14).
- Aid may help to fund alternative livelihoods for persons reliant on the illegal exploitation of natural resources (Stein 1988).
- Aid conditionality can be used as an instrument of enforcement in itself, by acting as a dissuasive or coercive financial tool against targeted actors.

Examples of aid conditionality used as an instrument of enforcement in relation to conflict trade are considered below. The effectiveness of aid conditionality in regulating resource flows is highly dependent on the importance of the aid to the recipient as well as on the international standing and commercial relations it enjoys in relation to the country or institutions setting the conditions. Targeting the resource sectors themselves can also increase the leverage of aid conditionality as businesses lose support for infrastructure work, for example. The risk, however, is that aid conditionality may further resource exploitation as a revenue alternative and delay reforms.

Aid conditionality was used with some degree of success on Cambodia's neighbor to restrict the trade in illegal logging, which was fueling war in Cambodia.[36] Such pressure significantly contributed to the demise of the Khmer Rouge movement.

In 2000, following years of "quiet diplomacy" and aid commitment toward the Liberian government to improve human rights and regional stability, the EU suspended about $50 million in aid on evidence of government involvement in arms and diamond trading with the RUF. This suspension reportedly had little effect on the trade itself but was part and parcel of broader measures that convinced the RUF to lay down its arms.[37]

The Expert Panel on the Illegal Exploitation of Natural Resources in the Democratic Republic of Congo recommended the reduction of aid to noncompliant governments hosting individuals, companies, and financial institutions involved in such activities. It is too early to see if such aid conditionality will be uniformly imposed and achieve a lasting solution to the conflict in the region, especially given the large number of regional actors involved and vested interests.

It is difficult to assess the overall effectiveness of aid conditionality, as much will depend on the aid dependence of the target, its international trading environment, and the coordination and cohesion of the donor community. Success is probably more likely when it is possible to apply pressure on transit countries playing a crucial role in conflict trade, when the capacity for enforcement is relatively high, and when targeted countries have a comparatively high stake in maintaining good bilateral and multilateral relations.

In addition to these initiatives, and within the framework of the New Partnership for Africa's Development (NEPAD) and the G-8 Africa Action Plan (see box 6.2), the possibility of an agreement on a "partnership for transparency and accountability" among African, G-8, and Organisation for Economic Co-operation and Development (OECD) governments and companies should be examined, within the context of broader relevant agreements (for example, the Cotonou agreement). Such a partnership could cover issues such as corporate transparency on tax payments, banking disclosure and procedures for repatriation of embezzled funds, and customs declarations and be backed by access to export credit guarantees, assistance

Box 6.2 NEPAD and the G-8 Africa Action Plan

The New Partnership for Africa's Development (NEPAD), which met in Abuja in October 2001, represents a major initiative and commitment on the part of African governments to improve political and economic governance and create a context favorable to foreign investment and rapid economic growth. NEPAD specifically recognizes the vulnerability of African economies resulting from their dependence on primary production and resource-based sectors and their narrow base of exports. Beyond the need to diversify production and capture added value, NEPAD mentions a number of objectives and actions *indirectly* relevant to tackling conflict trade, including at an African level: (a) harmonize policies and regulations to ensure compliance with minimum levels of operational practices and (b) harmonize commitments to reduce the perceived investment risk in Africa.

More generally, in reference to promoting African exports, NEPAD also mentions that participation in the world trading system must enhance "transparency and predictability as preconditions for increased investment, in return for boosting supply capacity and enhancing the gains from existing market access."

The first NEPAD document did not specifically call for international action on conflict trade. In response to NEPAD, however, the G-8 designed an Africa Action Plan at its 2002 meeting, in which member states declared their willingness to work "with African governments, civil society, and others to address the linkage between armed conflict and the exploitation of natural resources, including by (i) supporting United Nations and other initiatives to monitor and address the illegal exploitation and international transfer of natural resources from Africa that fuel armed conflicts, including mineral resources, petroleum, timber, and water; (ii) supporting voluntary control efforts such as the Kimberley Process for diamonds and encouraging the adoption of voluntary principles of corporate social responsibility by those involved in developing Africa's national resources; and (iii) working to ensure better accountability and greater transparency with respect to those involved in the import or export of Africa's natural resources from areas of conflict" (G-8 Africa Action Plan, Group of Eight, Kananaskis, June 27, 2002).

programs in resource management, grants and loans, and peer-review mechanisms.

Economic Supervision.   Economic supervision to control the flow of resources and money could prove to be a powerful instrument for reducing conflict trade while fostering legitimate trade. Such instruments are likely to be resisted by governments and rebels, but cease-fire and peace agreements may provide an opportunity to use such measures. Analogous to the process of demobilization of soldiers and monitoring of elections attendant to most peace processes, a war economy could be "demobilized" and "monitored" by economic supervision. Too frequently, these periods of uncertainty and hope are used as mere breathing spaces for military reorganization and rearmament. The economic aspects of peace processes are generally neglected and too often placed under the initiative of belligerents jockeying for key economic positions within the new authority or simply embezzling funds to rearm. For example, the RUF leader, Foday Sankoh, either ignored the mineral commission he chaired following the Lomé agreement or used its legitimacy to advance his personal interests and to rearm his movement.[38] Similarly, while UNITA handed over to the government the control of its main diamond areas in late 1997, the rebel movement continued mining and purchasing weapons.

Beyond sanctions and global regulatory measures, it is thus imperative to set up practical regulatory frameworks that deprive belligerents of revenues that would allow them to follow a double agenda of peace transition and rearmament, as happened repeatedly in Angola, Cambodia, Colombia, Liberia, Sierra Leone, and Sri Lanka. Although economic activities, even illicit ones, often contribute to social peace by improving the well-being of the population and changing the focus of groups in conflict, they run the risk of fueling the continuation of war or future tensions.

Trade in conflict resources can at least be limited through internationally supervised tax collection and budgetary allocation using escrow funds (see figure 6.1), even if resources, like diamonds found in alluvial deposits, remain difficult to control.

Figure 6.1 Economic Supervision Scheme during Peace Processes

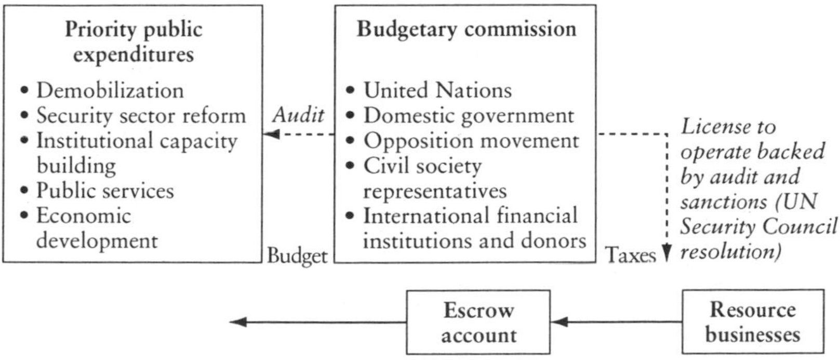

Source: Author.

In such a scheme, populations would benefit from tax transfers to social services, while the respective administrative and military structures of belligerents would receive monitored budgetary support to implement their effective integration into new government structures. Businesses themselves would be deterred from operating outside the scheme through a system of incentives, such as secure legal ownership, and deterrents, such as effective sanctions. If successful, and in the absence of alternative sources of support, opting out of a peace process would become a prohibitively costly alternative for belligerents. Several resource revenue-sharing schemes, such as those in Iraq, Angola, and Chad, include supervision mechanisms and provide a model in this regard.[39]

The Oil-for-Food Program, set up to assist in the implementation of UN sanctions against Iraq and lessen their humanitarian impact, represents an early example of such a scheme. Although this program was cumbersome and achieved only limited results, a UN expert panel has recommended a similar program to prevent the proceeds of the Liberian shipping and corporate registry from financing the busting of arms sanctions.[40] The UN Security Council has moved in this direction by calling on the government of Liberia to establish transparent and internationally verifiable regimes for auditing its use of revenues derived from its shipping and corporate registry, as well as the timber industry, to demonstrate that these are not used for busting sanctions but for "legitimate social, humanitarian, and development purposes."[41]

Although not described in these terms, the attempt by the International Monetary Fund (IMF) to audit the oil sector in Angola in 2000 and 2001 was also aimed, in part, at improving the accountability of public finances by a government at war (IMF 2002). Within the framework of a staff-monitored program including broader economic and institutional reforms, the IMF succeeded in obtaining this agreement from an Angolan government recently faced with minimal foreign reserves and growing pressure by international donors and advocacy groups. The resulting diagnostic study of the oil sector, conducted by an international audit firm, examined the channeling of oil revenues to the state treasury, not their subsequent allocation, as well as the conduct, honesty, and integrity of the management of the revenues. Furthermore, the findings of the audit were to be confidential. Human rights groups criticized the audit for its lack of transparency and retroactivity and for its limitations (Human Rights Watch 2001). With higher oil prices, a victory against UNITA, and continued support from the oil and private banking sectors, the Angolan government stopped its reform program, which led the IMF to close its program. A leaked IMF report estimated that about $4 billion had gone "missing" between

1997 and 2001 ("Measuring Corruption" 2002, p. 48). This episode in the long series of stalled reforms demonstrates the poor enforcement capacity of the IMF in the context of a resource-rich country.[42]

The World Bank has an indirect oversight role over the Chad-Cameroon Petroleum Development and Pipeline Project intended to prevent conflicts and prioritize the allocation of oil revenues to social sectors.[43] After nearly three decades of civil conflicts, negotiations between the northern-dominated government and the main southern rebellion in the mid-1990s made it feasible for oil companies to develop fields in southern Chad. The oil companies' consortium viewed the World Bank as the "centerpiece of its risk reduction strategy" by attracting institutional funding as well as assisting the government in its management of revenue and implementation of social and environmental programs (Horta 1997). To manage the estimated $1.5 billion in forecasted revenue over the next 28 years, the Chad Parliament placed this revenue into an offshore escrow account, allocated it to social and environmental priority sectors, and submitted it to a public auditing and an oversight committee.[44] However, President Déby, who came to power through a military coup in 1990, used $4 million from the oil development "signature bonus" to purchase weapons, triggering an outcry among nongovernmental organizations and leading the World Bank and the IMF to threaten exclusion from their debt relief program (World Bank 2001). As "moral guarantor" of the scheme, the World Bank also established an international advisory group to observe implementation of the project and make recommendations to both governments.[45] Although there remains a risk that the oil factor will bring about internal conflicts, the Chad-Cameroon project may provide a useful model and blueprint for similar arrangements in some resource-rich countries. With an ongoing war, rising oil revenues, and a viable peace process, Sudan also appears to be a strong candidate for a supervised mechanism for sharing wealth between the different parties and among the population.

The key to long-term success, however, is strong democratic control over resource revenues rather than weak external regulation.[46] An external supervision scheme poses risks, such as the resumption of conflict if the scheme dampens pressure for democratization and provides a façade of legitimacy through a partial control of the resource rents by a few select civil society representatives and foreign advisers.

The effectiveness of economic supervision, like many other enforcement mechanisms, appears to be highly relative. The economic situation of the target, the nature of the resource involved, the willingness of and compliance mechanisms on resource businesses, and the potential leverage of international authorities are key to its success. In any case, the complexity of the administration of such an instrument, its transaction cost, and the many possible loopholes should not be underestimated.

Corporate Conduct Instruments

Most resource businesses argue that they are neutral economic actors disengaged from the "business of war" (Bray 1997, p. 3). Businesses can have a positive influence in preventing or attenuating conflicts by generating economic and employment opportunities, raising standards in labor practices and social relations, and participating in political stability and even economic justice. Yet businesses can also have negative influences and exacerbate conflicts. If investment and commercial activities are essential to economic and human development, resource businesses need to recognize that they can produce—often unintentionally—a number of negative consequences, including the following:

• Increasing inequalities and economic rents amenable to factional control
• Sustaining poor governance by participating in the corruption and legitimization of unrepresentative and repressive authorities
• Contributing, either directly or indirectly, to human rights abuse by degrading local livelihoods and resource entitlements and turning a blind eye to forced or child labor or to the use of disproportionate force by security forces protecting their operations and staff
• Hindering peace processes by voluntarily or involuntarily bankrolling belligerents and thereby reducing the leverage of local populations, international institutions, and foreign powers (that is, commercially driven diplomacy).

Once a conflict has started, businesses often play the role of financial intermediary for belligerents. Although some businesses simply attempt to cope with a degrading political and security environment, others see in the situation an opportunity for competitive advantage. The complicity of businesses in conflicts varies from simple economic intermediaries to complex forms of influence, including political and military support. Operating in unstable areas, businesses are frequently able to act as financial supporters and brokers for arms deals. With a huge demand for arms and income from mineral resources, Angola, for example, became a prime target for savvy businesses juggling political relations, arms dealing, and natural resources brokering in the 1990s.

Countries in conflict also constitute a valuable "niche market" for businesses whose competitive advantage lies in their risk-taking approach, political savvy, or connections with security services. To access and secure resources in these markets, businesses often associate themselves with dubious regimes, rebel groups, arms brokers, or mercenaries. Opportunistic businesses have long "invested" in rebel factions in order to establish control over resource areas in the near term or in the future, counting on a rebel success. Western businesses supported Savimbi in Angola during the 1980s, not only to access diamonds in the short term but also to be on his side in case of victory. Some companies may even appear politically progressive as a result.

To date, most attention has been focused on the role of multinational corporations, notably the extractive industry. Other private sector actors who are deeply, if less visibly, involved include individual brokers, domestic or regional businesses operating without an international profile, and multinationals based in countries lacking strong civil societies. These firms often have few incentives to operate responsibly and face fewer sanctions for their activities. Whereas these firms may engage in questionable practices, their overall business strategy is still oriented toward legitimate ends. Still other companies specialize in, profit from, and may seek to prolong conflict. This is particularly true of businesses acting as fronts for laundering criminal proceeds.

In light of the recent literature on the issue of businesses and conflicts over the last three years, there is a clear need for a regulatory framework and instruments of enforcement to influence the behavior of businesses in relation to conflicts.[47] While voluntary and mandatory regulations have flourished in the fields of environmental and corporate labor practices, they are just beginning to emerge in relation to armed conflicts. So far, most efforts have been directed at the positive engagement and self-regulation of multinationals. One thorough review of the case for positive business engagement in conflict prevention identifies the following five principles:[48]

- Strategic commitment on the part of management, translated through explicit policies on human rights, corruption, and security
- Risk and impact assessment of the company's core business and social investment activities
- Dialogue and consultation with key stakeholder groups on a regular basis
- Partnership and collective action with other companies, government, and civil society organizations to address sensitive issues and to invest in practical projects
- Evaluation and accountability through performance indicators, independent verification, and public reporting.

With regard to enforcement instruments, few efforts have been made so far, and most regulatory initiatives remain voluntary or self-regulatory. Governments have refrained from imposing mandatory regulation on multinationals in the social and environmental realms, preferring voluntary rules (for example, OECD Guidelines for Multi-national Enterprises). Corporations have adopted self-regulation policies, in large part to reduce risks such as conflicts and costly government regulations, to protect or enhance their reputation in relation to social demands, and to respond to innovative concepts within the business community. Self-regulation has been most frequent within low-competition and high-asset-specificity industries, such as oligopolistic extractive sectors tied to fixed reserves and infrastructures (Haufler 2001, pp. 21–30).

Self-regulation is both reactive and proactive and can fill the regulatory gaps left by international and national regulations. But although this type of instrument can positively influence the behavior of some businesses, it often remains a limited one, both in scope and in accountability. While some see in it a way to explore and prepare future public regulation, others believe that it is becoming far too effective at retarding regulation. Few governments appear to be ready to impose strict regulation on businesses or individuals profiting from the trade in conflict resources (on mandatory investment screening and code of conduct in conflict-prone countries, see box 6.3). The consultation of governments on the issue of corporate complicity in war economies and human rights abuses by the UN expert panel on the Democratic Republic of Congo yielded no support or suggestion for meaningful measures to curb the trade among 11 transit countries. Out of 17 governments of end-user countries, only Belgium suggested the imposition of targeted sanctions against companies.[49]

The Global Mining Initiative and Other Reviews of Extractive Industries. The stated goal of the Global Mining Initiative, sponsored by nine of the world's largest mining and minerals companies, is to gain "a clearer definition and understanding of the positive part the mining and minerals industry can play in making the transition to sustainable patterns of economic development." It contracted an independent analysis of the industry in consultation with stakeholders—the Mining, Minerals, and Sustainable Development (MMSD) Project—that included a section on human rights violations and armed conflicts. Relevant recommendations of the report are in the following areas:

- Managing and distributing mineral wealth
- Increasing transparency in the management of mineral wealth
- Combating corruption
- Promoting and protecting human rights
- Preventing conflicts
- Providing information and collective stewardship in the value chain.

Box 6.3 Mandatory Conflict Impact Assessment and
Code of Conduct

The history of international trade relations is replete with practices
perpetuating human rights abuses, corrupt and coercive political rule, as
well as underdevelopment. To ensure that businesses and their home government are not contributing to human rights abuses and do not benefit
from such abuses, a number of initiatives have suggested that prospective
investments and commercial operations should be screened through a
mandatory conflict impact assessment and, once approved, should follow a mandatory code of conduct (see Gagnon, Macklin, and Simons
2003).

The collusion or incapacity of many local authorities means that a
legal framework at an international or home-country level should regulate dubious trade relations. Such regulation should focus on "conflict-
affected" or "conflict-prone" countries, a status to be decided by the
home government or an international institution such as the United
Nations Security Council. The conflict impact assessment as well as a
monitoring of the code of conduct could be conducted by a specific
agency or working group legally mandated by the home government or
international institution, such as the International Finance Corporation.
The assessment and recommendations of the screening agencies should
determine the availability of trade finance services provided by insurance and export credit domestic or international agencies. Although
such regulation is unlikely to have any impact on the most dubious
forms of conflict trade involving "resource-for-arms" brokers, it has the
potential to positively influence the impact of capital-intensive projects
on governance and conflict prevention. Acting as a potential form of
economic sanction, however, such an instrument should itself be subject
to careful independent scrutiny including by civil society representatives
from host countries in order to foster, rather than deter, investments
contributing to peace building.

The Global Mining Initiative was criticized by some mining specialists as being an "engineering engagement," and many critics of the
mining industry boycotted the initiative. The initiative resulted in the
creation of the International Council on Mining and Metals, which
had its first meeting in December 2002. Thus it is too early to evaluate
its effectiveness.

The oil and gas sector has also recently conducted an industry review of social issues relating to oil and gas projects (IPIECA and OGP
2002). The review was not independent of the sector; rather, it was
consultative and conducted through the International Association of
Oil and Gas Producers's Social Impact Assessment Task Force. Despite

its focus on social issues, the task force report does not address issues of human rights and conflict resolution, revenue management and transparency, and the role of governments, arguing that "these subjects are complex and have only emerged relatively recently as significant issues for the oil and gas industry and some of its stakeholders in some areas of the world" (IPIECA and OGP 2002, p. i).

The World Bank Group is conducting a major independent review and discussion of its role in the petroleum and mining sectors. Although the review is focusing on the role of the World Bank Group rather than on the activities and consequences of extractive sectors as a whole, its outcome (scheduled for September 2003) should include policies regarding the transparency and governance of financial and resource flows in these sectors. Already, the International Finance Corporation's Oil, Gas, Mining, and Chemical Department has been conducting specific consultation on the transparency and management of oil revenue.[50]

UN Global Compact.   Set up in 1999 by UN Secretary General Kofi Annan "to unite the powers of markets with the authority of universal ideals," the Global Compact is defined as a "value-based platform designed to promote institutional learning." The compact provides a set of nine nonbinding principles on labor, the environment, and human rights to be adopted on a voluntary basis by corporations. Participation is a function of willingness and ability to contribute to the advancement of the nine principles. Participating companies agree to share information regularly with the United Nations on best practices they have undertaken, to respect the principles, and to participate in policy dialogues with nongovernmental organizations, trade unions, and other relevant stakeholders.

The compact does not assess the performance of companies and has neither the mandate nor the capacity to audit them; instead it seeks to identify and promote good practices. However, to safeguard the initiative and to avoid potential abuse, the United Nations reserves the right not to accept participants, in particular for "complicity" in human rights abuses (a term not further defined). It can also cancel company participation if abuses take place. In the eyes of its detractors, however, this voluntary approach demonstrates the weakness of the United Nations in addressing the problem of corporate behavior. While supporting the initiative, the UN High Commissioner for Human Rights, for example, argues that the Global Compact should be complemented by a credible and independent monitoring and enforcement mechanism (UN Office of the High Commissioner for Human Rights 2000).

Begun in 2001, the first policy dialogue concerned the role of business in zones of conflict and included about 120 companies, international agencies, and civil society organizations. To date, four working groups have provided preliminary recommendations (on transparency, conflict impact assessment and risk management, multiple-stakeholder initia tives, and revenue-sharing regimes), but it is too early to assess the effectiveness of this instrument beyond its relative success in raising awareness among some businesses and facilitating dialogue.[51]

The Global Compact is not the only UN initiative dealing with corporate social responsibilities in terms of human rights. Most noticeable is a working group of the UN Subcommission on the Promotion and Protection of Human Rights, which is drafting an addendum to the UN Universal Declaration of Human Rights entitled Human Rights Principles and Responsibilities for Transnational Corporations and Other Business Enterprises. The draft text calls for business enterprises to be subject to independent, transparent, and open measures allowing for the verification of compliance.[52]

OECD Guidelines for Multinational Enterprises. The guidelines consist of voluntary principles and standards recommended by OECD governments to multinational enterprises operating in or from adhering countries (about 36) for their operations in any country, including through their supply chain. Of relevance to the issue of conflict resources and armed conflicts, this instrument recommends that enterprises conduct their affairs with transparency, refrain from discriminating among potential employees, refrain from paying bribes or making contributions to political parties (unless legally permissible), and "abstain from any improper involvement in local political activities." The guidelines also state that enterprises should "respect the human rights of those affected by their activities consistent with the host government's international obligations and commitments" (para. II.2).

While not legally binding, the guidelines represent a clear statement of public policy at the interministerial level and include a procedure of implementation with some similarities to a judicial process; they are binding on member states, but not on multinational enterprises (Howen 2001). With specific reference to enterprises operating in conflict-affected countries, an OECD background note invites enterprises to contribute by "improving management in the immediate vicinity of their operations (especially of security forces and resettlement operations); [and] participating in the search for long-term solutions to these countries' problems by helping them move toward healthier public governance (in particular by becoming more transparent in their financial relations with troubled host countries)" (OECD 2002, p. 13).

The guidelines have received support from the G-8's 2002 Africa Action Plan, which refers to their role in "intensifying support for the adoption and implementation of effective measures to combat corruption, bribery, and embezzlement," and from U.K. Prime Minister Tony Blair for their role in promoting responsible behavior on the part of multinational enterprises operating in conflict-affected areas of Africa. Yet the guidelines have also faced many comments and criticisms on the part of civil society organizations, which fear that they will become an alternative to a binding and enforceable instrument, including the following (Feeney 2002):

• Failure to incorporate "legal rights" for citizens and communities affected by corporate activities incorporating the direct liability of "foreign multinationals" and failure to respect the principle of "equality of arms" of appropriate complaints and judicial mechanisms

• Weakness of consensual nonadversarial means and unenforceable recommendations to be used by national contact points to address allegations of violations

• Restrictive demands put on civil society organizations to file complaints

• Low level of prioritization and staffing among many national contact points, including potential conflicts of interests because of their location within institutions primarily aimed at securing private sector profitability overseas

• No clearly specified time frames for dealing with complaints, so "flexibility" becomes a cover for inaction

• "Creeping bias" toward confidentiality protecting the interests of enterprises, with some national contact points demanding that nongovernmental organizations do not make public the complaints they file—possibly to win the confidence of enterprises

• Lack of separation between the promotional activities of the national contact points and the investigative and conflict resolution activities, which should be assigned to an independent legal office (for example, an ombudsman).

It is difficult to assess the effectiveness of these guidelines and the implementation mechanisms in part because of a lack of transparency and centralization of cases and in part because of the novelty of the compliance mechanism. Specific instances of application of the guidelines include the following:

• Complaints of forced labor in Myanmar by French enterprises involved in the petroleum sector were raised by French labor unions with the French national contact point, which led to consultations with some of these enterprises and (nothing more than) public recommendations by the national contact point on the practices that enterprises could take to contribute to the struggle against forced labor ("Recommendations du point de contact" 2002). The secretariat was asked to prepare a background note, entitled "Multinational Enterprises in Situations of Violent Conflict and Widespread Human Rights Abuses." This note recognized that "the influence of multinational enterprises in troubled societies, while often significant, does have limits" and suggested the following two areas of contribution for enterprises (OECD 2002):

• The threat of violent eviction of peasant farmers from a mining concession in Zambia was removed by the "timely intervention" of the Canadian national contact point after Oxfam Canada initially raised the issue (Feeney 2002).

• A report by a UN expert panel included a list of 85 multinational enterprises operating in the Democratic Republic of Congo that it considers in violation of the guidelines. According to the panel, home governments have "the obligation to ensure that enterprises in their jurisdiction do not abuse principles of conduct that they have adopted as a matter of law. They are complicit when they do not take remedial measures."[53] The panel also proposed the creation of a monitoring mechanism enabling the reporting of such enterprises to the OECD national contact points in the home government of these enterprises. Several national contact points have been contacted on this matter, some of which have approached the UN for more information but have received no reply (the mandate of the UN expert panel has not yet been renewed, and as such it does not officially exist at the moment).[54]

Overall, the guidelines are a more effective enforcement instrument than the Global Compact because of the compliance mechanism. This instrument, however, is lacking in global coverage (for example, Southeast Asian multinational enterprises) and is generally slow, ineffective, and, critics argue, biased toward the interests of the enterprises rather than those of the affected populations. This instrument could be strengthened if more countries adhered to the guidelines, the OECD Security Council strengthened its compliance mechanism, and national contact points increased their capacity (and will) to intervene more decisively.

Access to Markets, Corporate Reporting, and Transparency. The rules of access and trading on financial markets can provide useful instruments of enforcement in terms of reporting and financial accountability. The restrictions on access to capital markets as well as export credit guarantees and insurance can also complement commodity sanctions by curtailing investments or transactions. Current efforts by

governments and nongovernmental organizations in the field of corporate responsibility include the following (Adams 2002):

• Prescriptive legislation instituting mandatory disclosure and
"smart legislation" stimulating the demand for corporate social responsibility data
• Voluntary standards and principles, reporting guidelines, and
performance indexes
• Direct engagement with companies and industry associations
(high-level meetings, consumer pressure, independent monitoring).

These efforts have been directed mostly at the largest publicly listed
companies, which are generally dealing with governments rather than
groups or authorities.

Stock market regulations demand minimum levels of disclosure
from publicly listed companies on operations, risks, and finance; these
regulations can assist in the transparency and accountability of the
private sector. There is, as yet, no uniform reporting requirement on the
activities of the private sector. A voluntary initiative, the Global
Reporting Initiative, was established in 1997 to enhance the quality,
rigor, and utility of sustainability reporting on the economic, social, and
environmental performance of corporations and other organizations. It
is now a permanent institution, and more than 100 companies have
adopted its Sustainability Reporting Guidelines. To date, the guidelines
and associated documents do not make specific reference to the issue of
conflict resources, apart from a draft supplement for the mining sector
recommending questions on human rights violations. However, a member of the Global Reporting Initiative's board of directors, Roger
Adams, has suggested that the new guidelines should incorporate
"corporate accountability within war economies."[55]

Risks for investors continue to be the cornerstone of mandatory
reporting, rather than the risks facing affected populations where companies operate. The two are sometimes linked, however, for example,
through the reputation and security risks faced by companies. In the
United Kingdom, following recommendations from the Turnbull report, prescriptive legislation now requires companies listed on the
London Stock Exchange "to create systems to identify, evaluate, and
manage their risks and to make a statement on risk management in
their annual report" that accounts for business probity issues. Smart
legislation—the U.K. Pensions Act—requires pension funds to inform
customers about social policy commitments and to disclose ethical
considerations in their investment portfolio. This has created a demand for such data, which most listed companies now provide on
a voluntary basis. Such demand for social reporting is also created by

ethical investment and pension funds specifically integrating environmental or social responsibility as investment selection criteria. Like other ethically minded investors, these funds use their financial influence to encourage greater corporate social responsibility among the firms in which they have invested. Some advocacy groups have purchased shares only to be able to propose ethically driven resolutions. Specific indexes assessing the ethical responsibility of listed companies, such as the FSTE4Good Index or the Dow Jones Sustainability Index, also facilitate the choice of investors and could play a greater role in the future—although these indexes remain financially marginal and are criticized for requiring low ethical standards.

Several recent initiatives relate to the financial transparency of resource sectors in relation to armed conflicts. The G-8 promotes the transparency principle through its 2002 Africa Action Plan (box 6.2). U.K. Prime Minister Tony Blair launched at the World Summit on Sustainable Development meeting in Johannesburg the Extractive Industries Transparency Project, which is being backed by a number of governments and major companies and could lead to either a voluntary or a mandatory transparency instrument. A coalition of nongovernmental organizations led by George Soros and Global Witness is also seeking to improve the transparency of fiscal reporting through their Publish What You Pay campaign, which aims to make the disclosure of all payments by oil, gas, and mining companies to host governments a mandatory condition for being listed on international stock exchanges.[56] Because this measure would not affect unlisted companies, such as privately owned or state companies, the campaign also aims to set similar obligations of public disclosure under national or regional company law. A further loophole that will prove even more difficult to close concerns the regulation of international brokers registered in offshore jurisdictions and state companies in host countries. Such brokers specialize in carrying out the "dirty work" of obtaining resource concessions (often through corrupt deals), before selling them in a "clean" manner to resource companies. Local "sleeping partners" associated with the operations of resource companies, in the form of board directors or state companies in charge of some subcontracting operations, also act as vehicles for corruption by diverting large cash bonuses, commissions, or profit shares.[57] A system of mandatory disclosure, peer review, and industry certification associated with financial incentives and possibly market access thus needs to be extended to these types of companies.

There is a strong argument in favor of global and mandatory instruments given the financial confidentiality clauses imposed by many host governments on resource exploitation contracts and the competitive nature of trade. Mandatory legislation in home countries would provide the legal ground for overturning these financial confidentiality clauses. Applied globally, this would help to create a level playing field for all companies. More generally, these instruments would have the advantage of being relatively cheap to implement, since they would rely on available accounting data. Such legislation would avoid the charge of being "neocolonial," since it simply provides information to the public, without dictating the ways in which revenues should be allocated. Given these advantages, such measures should be promoted as an essential element of good governance of the global economy.

Disclosure rules, and their consequences for investment, can increase the social responsibility of companies; however, reporting is rarely specific enough to assist in the detection of complicity by companies in corruption or war economies. This could be improved by more specific and socially oriented disclosure requirements, such as social impact assessment in countries with a low Human Development Index, financial reporting at a country level, and links to more specific assessment reports. Many shareholders also complement company analysis by monitoring both the activities of the companies and the context in which they operate. This is particularly true of resource companies operating in politically volatile situations where risks are high. For most investors, however, the bottom line is more frequently defined by share value and dividends and less frequently by ethics. In this regard, the work of investigative journalists or advocacy nongovernmental organizations can provide fund managers with a detailed analysis of the practices of companies and their consequences and result in a general divestment movement. Such measures, however, require global action; many medium-size companies criticizing more stringent rules on the U.S. stock exchange following the Enron scandal threatened to withdraw to more lenient financial public markets or go private altogether.

Multilateral and national export credit and investment insurers, such as the World Bank's Multilateral Investment Guarantee Agency or the U.S. Overseas Private Investment Corporation, are not mandated to consider or reduce the impact of their clients on conflict-affected countries. Until recently, only the economic and political risk impinging on the ability of firms to perform contracts and the ability of the country to service its external debt were taken into consideration. Agencies nevertheless are becoming increasingly aware of the broader risks entailed by projects in conflict areas; by making their financial assistance conditional on criteria such as the OECD Guidelines for Multinational Enterprises, these agencies could provide a mechanism for applying enforcement instruments directed at conflict resources.

Advocacy groups and consumer watchdogs also monitor the activities of companies and the ethical standing of their products; these groups have some degree of influence on consumption patterns through consumer information campaigns and direct action. Targets of consumer boycotts have included banks alleged to be funding scientific research involving vivisection, oil companies perceived as having poor environmental records, and clothing manufacturers accused of exploiting workers in the developing world. Consumers, it is argued, want their preferred brands to reflect their social values, often prompting companies to adapt business practices and to adopt public relations countermeasures, including so-called "greenwash."[58] The threat of a consumer boycott of diamonds was a critical factor in motivating the diamond industry and the governments of producing countries to change their public policies and to engage in the Kimberley process; this demonstrates the effectiveness of a threat of consumer pressure.

Company Practices: The Case of Coltan.   Companies involved in the extraction and trade of coltan in eastern Democratic Republic of Congo have come under pressure to stop "fueling the war" through nongovernmental organization campaigning, nonregulatory governmental pressure, and naming and shaming from UN expert panels. UN expert panels reporting on the illegal exploitation of natural resources in the Democratic Republic of Congo named several companies directly or indirectly supporting rebel groups and their regional allies in the eastern part of the country. Much of the media attention also focused on the killing of endangered gorillas and environmental degradation by coltan diggers and militias operating in national parks.

The Tantalum-Niobium International Study Center reacted by calling on its member companies around the world "not to purchase raw materials from illegal or illegitimate sources . . . [and] to take great care in making purchases in the region of the Democratic Republic of the Congo [since] trade which causes harm, or threatens to cause harm, to local populations, to animals, or to the environment is not acceptable."[59] The world's largest manufacturer of tantalum capacitors informed its coltan suppliers about these policies and asked them to certify that they acted accordingly, although the company recognized that it could not trace the origin from the product itself.[60] The world's second-largest processor of coltan also declared—albeit in the midst of a glutted market—that it would not buy coltan from the Great Lakes region (Harden 2001). The Electronics Components, Assemblies, and Materials Association urged its members to avoid tantalum mined in environmentally protected areas of the Democratic Republic of Congo. Many electronics companies publicly rejected the

use of coltan from anywhere in Central Africa, relying instead largely
on Australian supplies (Delawala 2002). Investigations from the UN
expert panel suggest that leakages still occur and that considerable
incentives remain to use conflict coltan due to very low labor costs in
the Democratic Republic of Congo.

The relative success of these measures, in the context of falling
coltan prices, has led some international and local nongovernmental
organizations to question their humanitarian impact. The Congolese
POLE Institute—which included Congolese coltan traders—argued
that, despite the clear links between war and coltan as well as the need
to stop the illicit economy organized and controlled by armed groups,
"the people of the Kivu would not gain [from an embargo], but lose one
of their very few remaining sources of income" (POLE Institute 2001,
p. 4). The trade, however, appears to remain dominated by Rwandan
and Ugandan interests, with benefits apparently so low for the local
population that many have now abandoned this activity.[61]

U.S.-U.K. Voluntary Principles on Security and Human Rights.
Adopted in December 2000 by a number of (mostly resource-based)
companies and nongovernmental organizations at the initiative of the
U.S. and U.K. governments, this instrument defines voluntary principles to guide companies in maintaining the safety and security of their
operations within a framework that ensures respect for human rights
and fundamental freedoms.[62] Although not directly relevant to the
curtailment of conflict trade, this instrument provides a useful model
of collaboration between governments, resource companies, and
human rights groups. Continued dialogue between parties provides
the opportunity to review the principles and share experiences in
implementing them. The instrument is open to new parties and could
therefore set a global standard, although some companies operating in
conflict areas and most exposed to the problems of abusive and unaccountable security arrangements are not welcome for fear of bad
publicity. The principles cover risk assessment (the identification of
security risks, potential for violence, human rights records, rule of law,
conflict analysis, and equipment transfers) and interactions between
companies and public and private security entities (security arrangements, deployment and conduct, consultation and advice, responses to
human rights abuses).[63] Although voluntary and nonbinding, the
principles are based on international humanitarian and human rights
legislation as well as international principles on the use of force and
firearms by law enforcement officials. If featured in securing contracts,
however, the principles could become legally binding.

In terms of their effectiveness, participating companies themselves
have noted that there are practical barriers to the viability of the

principles, with significant delays and difficulties experienced in application. Because these principles, like most voluntary codes of conduct, lack compliance assessment by third parties, their efficacy pivots on the good will and priorities of individual managers as well as the operational context in which they have to make decisions; the profit motive, competitive pressures, and the practices of local security agencies constitute formidable countervailing forces.

The Role of Nongovernmental Organizations and the Media

Nongovernmental organizations and the media play a crucial role in investigating conflict trade and creating pressure on authorities, business intermediaries, and consumers through public information and lobbying. Early work by advocacy groups dates back at least to the slave trade and colonial period, when governments and companies were accused of plundering the colonies.[64] Nongovernmental organizations have also monitored breaches of sanctions regimes, such as the monitoring of oil tankers and shaming of companies "breaching" the voluntary oil embargo against South Africa.[65] Recent examples of campaigns targeting conflict trade include the following:

• Disinvestment campaigns targeting oil companies; campaigns and media focusing on the activities of petroleum companies in conflict-affected countries.

• The "fatal transactions" campaign against the laundering of conflict diamonds through legitimate trade. Orchestrated by a coalition of nongovernmental organizations led by Global Witness, the campaign launched a major international agreement and is generally assessed as effective, at least in terms of creating industry and international policy awareness.[66]

• The blockade of Liberian timber in a French port by Greenpeace activists on both environmental grounds and alleged connection of the Liberian timber trade with arms trafficking and conflict in the region (Mallet 2002). The blockade attracted some media attention but did not result in any major tangible outcome.

• The campaign on conflict timber emanating from Cambodia and more recently from Liberia by Global Witness, which included public information, pressure on regional governments and donors, as well as briefing documents to the United Nations.[67] The outcome was an effective ban by Thailand on Cambodian timber (exported by the Khmer Rouge), but little progress was made on Liberia.

Campaigns are generally led by human rights and environmental nongovernmental organizations specializing in advocacy work. Amnesty International, EarthRights International, Global Witness,

Human Rights Watch, and others have been at the forefront of investigative work, advocacy, and demands for regulatory improvements in the domain of resource flows to belligerents. Mainstream operational nongovernmental organizations and even intergovernmental agencies, which previously shunned such "politicized" activities, are increasingly involved, either through financial support to advocacy groups or through direct engagement. Development and humanitarian nongovernmental organizations, however, often face a serious dilemma and have to balance the risk of being expelled by host governments they criticize, the security of their local staff, and access to program beneficiaries.

In many cases, nongovernmental organizations have based the legitimacy of their engagement on universal principles of human rights, on the legislation of host countries, or on the contrast existing between the wealth generated by resources and the poverty of local populations. They employ a broad range of initiatives, including public information campaigns, direct action (for example, blockades), consumer boycotts, shareholder activism, institutional partnerships and negotiations, as well as litigation. While some nongovernmental organizations focus on corporate disinvestments, others seek constructive engagement. Most nongovernmental organizations working on the issue of conflict diamonds, for example, avoided a consumer boycott that would have been damaging to the populations of producing countries such as Botswana. Amnesty International never calls for sanctions against businesses or for their withdrawal, stressing instead the importance of a dialogue with businesses to promote the adoption of better practices. The Henri Dunant Centre for Humanitarian Dialogue established partnerships with oil companies in Aceh, Indonesia, to promote a cease-fire and in Myanmar to monitor human rights abuses. Several British nongovernmental organizations, including Christian Aid and Oxfam, have also engaged in investigations and dialogue with British Petroleum regarding its activities in Colombia. Overall, the engagement of nongovernmental organizations has become more constructive, leading to their participation in high-level negotiations with industries and governments.

The media have also played a major role, notably in disseminating the findings and arguments of nongovernmental organizations and campaigners but also in conducting their own investigations. For example, the links alleged by the *Washington Post*'s Douglas Farah between diamonds from RUF-controlled areas in Sierra Leone and the Al-Qaeda terrorist network lent further urgency to the Kimberley certification process (Farah 2001). The media attention devoted to the issue of conflict diamonds, however, is not guaranteed for other commodities involved in conflict trade—as stated by a campaigner, "Diamonds are more sexy than logs."[68] Articles on the roles of such obscure resources as coltan in both financing war and providing a source of livelihood to civilians, however, have demonstrated that the media cannot only disseminate news but can also add to the debate on conflict trade (Harden 2001).

The major strength of nongovernmental organizations, and to some extent the media, is their independence and their ability to engage with "politicized" issues and to challenge the status quo of "business as usual." Interventions by nongovernmental organizations and media are not without criticisms, however, which include the following:

• Campaigns mostly concentrate on Western multinationals: leaving other companies "off the hook" may lead more accountable companies to leave the country and worse ones to take their place.
• Campaigns often take a "piecemeal" approach: focusing on one country or one company may prove less effective in the long term than taking an issue-based approach.
• The media have a short attention span: advocacy campaigners may opt for "simple" arguments and solutions.
• Initiatives remain dominated by Western-based nongovernmental organizations: this raises the issue of legitimacy, even if it is useful for these organizations to protect local nongovernmental organizations by "taking the heat" on highly sensitive issues.

The effectiveness of interventions by nongovernmental organizations and the media remains highly dependent on the issue and the nongovernmental organizations involved, with a wide variety of track records. However, increased coalition building and professionalism among nongovernmental organizations, as well as greater legitimacy within (inter)governmental decisionmaking processes, are lending greater significance to their voice and values in current governance processes.

Transboundary Resource and Environmental Governance Instruments

Numerous transboundary resource and environmental governance instruments exist in state and nonstate areas. Instruments for the protection of biodiversity, the regulation of resource governance on the high seas, and cooperation in the management of transboundary rivers are well-known examples. Few of these instruments, however, are legally binding or have comprehensive monitoring mechanisms. The Convention on International Trade in Endangered Species of Fauna and Flora (CITES) is an exception in this regard. Another instrument, the UN Agreement on Fish Stock, is also examined briefly for its relevance to the enforcement of resource management in areas where there is no state sovereignty, the high seas.

License-Controlled Trade: The Case of CITES. CITES is one of the most comprehensive international agreements regulating trade for noneconomic purposes. First drafted in 1963, it entered into force in 1975. It now counts 160 parties and can be considered global in reach. CITES has direct relevance to this report, as wildlife constitutes a "natural resource," and endangered species are often exploited during armed conflicts due to the collapse of protection agencies. For example, there was a thriving trade in tiger skins and cubs in Cambodia during the early 1990s. Its greater relevance, however, arises from the enforcement mechanisms it employs and its relatively long-established record.

Adhesion to CITES is voluntary, but legally binding. Signatories that have ratified the treaty are subsequently required to reform their national laws in accordance with CITES, if necessary. CITES establishes a number of controls on the international trading of specimens of approximately 3,400 selected species; these controls include a licensing system for all import, export, reexport, and introduction from the sea of species covered by the convention. Three degrees of protection can be granted to species according to their vulnerability through a system of listing consisting of three appendixes to the convention. Species listed in Appendix I are threatened with extinction, and trade is allowed only in exceptional circumstances. Appendix II includes species not necessarily threatened with extinction, but in which trade must be controlled in order to avoid use incompatible with their survival. Appendix III contains species that are protected in at least one country, which has asked other CITES parties for assistance in controlling the trade. National scientific authorities assess the effects of trade on the status of species (which is decided during international meetings), and a system of import or export permits administered by national state management authorities enforces the convention.[69] Parties may import or export (or reexport) a specimen of a CITES-listed species only if the appropriate document has been obtained and presented for clearance at the port of entry or exit. This document, and the conditions attached to its delivery, varies according to the appendix in which the species is listed. There are two main relevant conditions: first, that the trade is not detrimental to the survival of the species and, second, that the specimen was legally obtained.

The core institution of the convention is the secretariat, which is empowered to study reports of the parties and to request any information it deems necessary to ensure the implementation of the convention and to focus the attention of the parties on any pertinent matter (Article XII, 2[d], 2[e]). The convention also provides for the secretariat to notify a party directly if it believes that the convention is not being effectively implemented, whereupon the party in question is to respond. (It may also request an inquiry, with information from the inquiry being furnished for the next meeting of the parties; Article X.) This makes CITES's secretariat possibly one of the more independent secretariats in the environmental field (Hajost and Shea n.d.).

According to its secretariat, the value of CITES has been demonstrated by the fact that "not one of the species protected by CITES has become extinct as a result of trade since the convention entered into force."[70] Yet criticisms of this instrument and its effectiveness continue to be made, which include the following:

- Absence of a supranational institution enforcing international obligations on individual states
- Poorly drafted sections of the convention that leave critical loopholes (for example, reservations by parties and other exemptions)
- Lack of financial commitment by some parties to enforce CITES at the domestic or international level and a poorly funded secretariat
- International-level instrument that does not affect domestic trade
- Listing system that puts the burden of proof on conservationists rather than traders
- Absence of a computerized database for enforcement agents (inspectors, customs)
- Vulnerability of the permit system to fraud resulting from the absence of a permit-tracking system and a uniform and tamper-proof permit form and registration of traders and transporters
- Potential for abuse in trade with nonparty countries and non-complying parties
- Absence of minimal training standards and an international corps of inspectors
- Lack of transparency on inspection reports
- Lack of economic incentives for legitimate trade
- Lack of criminal and civil liability for illegal wildlife trade among some parties.

The feasibility of applying similar instruments to *all* resources in order to prevent conflict trade appears to be limited, given the greater volume and greater difficulty in determining points of origin of regulated commodities (as opposed to the identification of threatened species). CITES nevertheless remains a valid model for the commodities most frequently involved in conflict trade, particularly those with highly specific or easily identified points of origin.

Resource Governance in Nonstate Areas: 1995 UN Fish Stock Agreement. The UN Agreement on Fish Stocks entered into force in December 2001.[71] Along with the Food and Agriculture Organization's Code of Conduct for Responsible Fisheries, this agreement outlines principles for good governance of fisheries in terms of maximum sustainable yield and applies a "precautionary approach" to the sector. The agreement provides a tough mechanism for monitoring and enforcement:

• Compliance and enforcement are ensured by the state in which the vessels are matriculated (flags), irrespective of where the violations occur. States will cooperate, either directly or through regional fisheries management mechanisms.
• States are granted boarding and inspection on vessels—including the right to use force "to the degree necessary to ensure the safety of the inspectors and where the inspectors are obstructed in the execution of their duties"—as well as the right to detain the vessel or otherwise incapacitate a vessel when there is sufficient evidence of an alleged violation.
• States are "liable in accordance with international law for damage or loss attributable to them in regard to this Agreement."
• States "shall take measures consistent with this Agreement and international law to deter the activities of vessels flying the flag of non-parties which undermine the effective implementation of this Agreement."

In terms of the resolution of disputes and sanctions, states have the obligation to resort to only peaceful means (for example, negotiation, inquiry, mediation, conciliation, arbitration, judicial settlement, referral to regional agencies or arrangements). The agreement recognizes the special requirements of developing states, including their frequent lack of inspection capacity, and calls on states and international agencies to assist in this regard; it also asks implementing states to consider the nutritional and subsistence needs of the populations of developing countries and the economic needs of workers in small-scale fisheries.

The effectiveness of the agreement, however, depends on the national or regional legislation passed, the quality of the data employed to determine quotas, as well as the enforcement capability of states. The agreement itself has been criticized for its engagement at the level of fish species rather than the ecosystem (MacGarvin 2001). Its exclusionary "relevancy rule," which confers governance status over the fish stock on relevant coastal states and on states having a "real interest in the fisheries concerned," has also been criticized as a significant departure from the inclusive constituency defined by the Law of the Sea Treaty (Admay 2000).

Given that it deals with resources located outside or beyond state sovereignty, the UN Agreement on Fish Stocks is somewhat relevant to the regulation of conflict resources in rebel-held territories; however, patrolling the high seas is undeniably distinct from monitoring and intervening in war-torn territories. Its relevance is therefore limited.

Challenges to Effective Enforcement

Drawing from a number of consultations and research conducted, in particular, by Global Witness, International Alert, the International Peace Academy, and the Overseas Development Institute, there is growing consensus that current international enforcement instruments are ineffective and insufficient.[72] Most of these consultations and research exercises have found that a dual-track strategy is required, involving improved identification, enforcement, and harmonization of relevant policies and institutional mechanisms and possibly the development of a new, inclusive, global regulatory framework.

The effective implementation of enforcement instruments for conflict-related natural resources faces major challenges, such as the following:

• Economic sectors are operated largely by private profit-driven actors coming under a variety of jurisdictions, and occasionally including international criminal outfits, that lack the will, incentives, or normative prescriptions to act to prevent or terminate conflict.

• Effective domestic enforcement in conflict-affected countries is extremely difficult. Such countries can provide a "safe haven" for other criminal activities, such as money laundering and terrorism; hence the reliance on international forces as well as regional or international enforcement mechanisms, with key transit countries and businesses acting as "market gatekeepers" against conflict trade as well as by industrial states to extend domestic regulation to the extraterritorial activities of multinationals and their subsidiaries.

• Lack of capacity and perverse incentives persist in police, customs, and judiciary systems in many developing countries, but also in industrial ones, notably because of the high volume of trading and the focus of regulatory agencies on drugs or terrorism.

• Private and public economic and strategic interests are protected by state apparatus (for example, corrupt interests of state officials, protection of multinational corporations, access to strategic commodities such as oil, international political alliances).

• Problems of consensus, coordination, and commitment by states and multilateral agencies at the national, regional, and international levels hinder effective enforcement (for example, absence or poor communication of both intelligence and public information, bureaucratic red tape, lack of financial resources, slow judicial procedures, and vested political interests).

• Uneven jurisdiction at the international level creates major loopholes (for example, offshore banking and incorporation).

Even if well implemented, international instruments of enforcement are unlikely to halt the mobilization of natural resources in armed conflicts. Nonetheless, by raising the production and transaction costs of belligerents and their accomplices, such instruments may be able to drastically reduce the trade in otherwise legal "conflict resources." Raising transaction costs for belligerents and their accomplices can only result from *effective* enforcement—even if simply by dissuading most potential buyers. Furthermore, production and transaction costs need to be sufficiently high to reflect the significant discounts that belligerents are often willing to make. Moreover, although profit making has been recently stressed as one of the motivations of belligerents, this is not always the case. Politically motivated belligerents will find ways to adapt their struggle to the difficult economic conditions resulting from effective enforcement measures. Belligerents are likely to accept noneconomic deals simply to increase their cash flow in the short term to achieve their goals. Raised costs must also reflect the low cost of appropriation or production by belligerents. Profit-motivated belligerents controlling or exploiting resources at significant discounts in comparison to normal authorities or businesses (for example, through theft, use of forced labor, or disregard for environmental standards or sustainability principles) are likely to accept significantly discounted buying prices.

Addressing these enforcement issues is complicated in the context of fragmented governance in which the designated enforcement agency and the most effective enforcement mechanism (self, soft, or hard) are difficult to identify. Moreover, little expertise exists to enable an evaluation of the effectiveness of enforcement instruments. Effectiveness can be assessed, for example, on the basis of the following:

• The priority and visibility of the policy agenda in international meetings or the media, but this does not guarantee effectiveness
• Expert knowledge within the industry or monitoring organizations
• The number of individuals arrested or "named and shamed" or the amount of resources and financial revenues seized, yet the impact on the rest of the trade and the course of the conflict may be difficult to assess
• The termination of the conflict itself, although many other factors frequently intervene.

The assessments at this point are very tentative. Furthermore, many of the instruments are recent or are still in the design phase. Given the apparent weakness of current enforcement instruments to date and the emergence of new ones, the assessment of enforcement is a critical issue for future research.

Drawing on this discussion, specific areas for additional research include the following:

• Information on resource businesses operating in conflict-affected countries. Much of the information currently available results from advocacy campaigns, limited investigative journalism, and UN expert panel reports. There is no global picture allowing a "profiling" of activities, the businesses involved, and regulatory efforts. Such information could assist not only in the design of policy tools but also in their enforcement.

• Mapping of the business intermediaries, authorities, and enforcement agencies intervening along the commodity chains. This could provide a clearer picture of areas where enforcement mechanisms can intervene, where loopholes are located, and in which collaborations and policies may be needed.

• Detailed examination of the decisionmaking and implementation processes involved, as well as the effect on the conflict and broad resource governance of enforcement mechanisms. Field-based investigation and a broad stakeholder consultation on a number of cases involving, for example, UN sanctions, the use of expert panels, advocacy campaigns, and company divestment could provide valuable information for the design of policy tools.

• Assessment of legal and political opportunities and constraints likely to shape a process of international agreement on resource governance. This could include the identification of applicable international norms as well as of design and implementing agencies; the definition of conflict resources, relevant offenses, and degree of complicity on the part of economic intermediaries and authorities; and the enforcement mechanisms and range of incentives and penalties.

Notes

1. Cited in interview of John Peleman, www.pbs.org.
2. An overview of these various means of financing conflict is provided in Le Billon, Sherman, and Hartwell (2002).
3. No correlation is found by Collier, Hoeffler, and Söderbom (2001), but most of the case study literature argues the contrary; see Ross (forthcoming).

4. Interview with the author, Cambodia, January 2001.

5. Security Council Resolution S/RES/232 (1966, para. 4 and 5).

6. Security Council Resolution S/RES/661 (1990); available at www.eia.doe.gov/emeu/cabs/iraq.html.

7. Oil exports represented 95 percent of Iraq's foreign earnings, and 60–80 percent of the food had to be imported; see Melby (1998, p. 115).

8. UN Security Council Resolution S/RES/665 (1990, para. 1); Recknagel (2000).

9. The author participated in border monitoring in 1996.

10. Interviews by the author in Sierra Leone, April 2001.

11. Their empirical study examines 115 cases and identifies 41 successes; see Hufbauer, Schott, and Elliot (1985).

12. Knorr's empirical study examines 22 cases; see Knorr (1975).

13. Secretary General Paulo Lukamba Gato, cited in United Nations (2002, p. 38).

14. Security Council Resolution S/RES/1295 (2000, para. 27).

15. See www.smartsanctions.ch/Papers/I2/2wg2a1.pdf.

16. Interview by the author with Ian Smillie, Ottawa, March 2002.

17. Article 8-b (XIII, XVI).

18. Article 25 (c,d).

19. See www.un.org/law/cod/finterr.htm.

20. Adopted at the UN General Assembly in December 1999 and in the process of being ratified by member states. See www.un.org/law/cod/finterr.htm.

21. The definition of the offense includes any act "intended to cause death or serious bodily injury to a civilian, or to any other person not taking an active part in the hostilities in a situation of armed conflict, when the purpose of such act . . . is to intimidate a population, or to compel a government or an international organization to do or to abstain from doing any act" (para. 2.1[b]).

22. With regard to jurisdiction, the convention does not apply if the business is from the state in which the offense is committed and is present in that state and no other state has a basis to exercise jurisdiction (para. 3).

23. According to the convention, an "'organized criminal group' shall mean a structured group of three or more persons, existing for a period of time and acting in concert with the aim of committing one or more serious crimes or offences established in accordance with this Convention, in order to obtain, directly or indirectly, a financial or other material benefit . . . [and a] 'Serious crime' shall mean conduct constituting an offence punishable by a maximum deprivation of liberty of at least four years or a more serious penalty" (Article 2).

24. Protocol supplementing the UN Convention against Transnational Organized Crime (Resolution of the UN General Assembly 55/255 on May 30, 2001).

25. See www.interpol.int/Public/Icpo/FactSheets/FS200101.asp. For the structure of Interpol, see www.interpol.int/Public/icpo/governance/default.asp.

26. See www.interpol.int/Public/FinancialCrime/FOPAC/default.asp.

27. See www.odccp.org/odccp/crime_cicp.html.

28. See www.fscoax.org/principal.htm.

29. Statement from World Diamond Council, press release, October 10, 2002, New York.

30. Ian Smillie, personal communication, Ottawa, March 2002.

31. See www.amnesty-usa.org/diamonds/update.html.

32. On the case of the South African Diamond Board, see International Consortium of Investigative Journalists (2002a).

33. About 29 million hectares of forests are currently certified under the Forest Stewardship Council scheme (for comparison, about 11 million hectares of forests are lost annually, according to the Food and Agriculture Organization).

34. With more than 43 million hectares, it is reportedly the world's largest certification system. See www.pefc.org/.

35. For the case of logging in Cambodia, see Le Billon (2000).

36. Lobbying accompanied the first report of Global Witness, *Forests, Famine, and War* (Global Witness 1995).

37. Interview by the author with Alex Vines, expert panel member, London, February 2001.

38. Report of the Panel of Experts Concerning Sierra Leone, dated December 13, 2000, S/2000/1195, para. 90-8.

39. For a review of some relevant revenue-sharing mechanisms, see Bennett (2002a).

40. Resolution S/2001/1015, para. 59.

41. UN Security Council Resolution S/RES/1408 (2002, Article 10).

42. On reforms and the political economy of Angola, see Hodges (2001).

43. The oil development involves the construction of a pipeline through Cameroon.

44. Article 1/PR/99 Concerning Oil Revenues Management, N'Djaména, January 11, 1999.

45. See www.worldbank.org/afr/ccproj/project/iag_tor_en.pdf.

46. Interview by the author with Charmian Gooch, Global Witness, London, June 2002.

47. A detailed review of this literature falls outside the scope of this report. See Avery (2000); Bennett (2002b); Carbonnier (2001); Clapham and Jerbi (2001); Frankental and House (2000); Howen (2001); International Council on Human Rights Policy (2002); Keen and Tickell (2000); Lilly and Le Billon (2002); Oloka-Onyango and Deepika (2000); Sherman (2001); Switzer (2001); Taylor (2002); Utting (2000); Williams (1999).

48. For a detailed review and analysis, see Nelson (2000).

49. Resolution S/2002/1146, p. 26.

50. Workshop on Petroleum Revenue Management, Washington D.C., October 23–24, 2002; see www.ifc.org/ogmc/petroleum.htm.

51. UN Global Compact (2002); for recommendations, see 65.214.34.30/un/gc/unweb.nsf/content/zones_conflict.htm.

52. See www.business-humanrights.org/UN-Sub-Commission.htm.

53. Resolution S/2002/1146, pp. 31–32.

54. Kathryn Gordon, OECD, personal communication, November 2002.

55. Comments from ACCA, dated May 27, 2002. See www.globalreporting.org/WorkingGroups/Revisions/Members/PublicComments2002/ACCAFurtherComments.pdf.

56. Publish What You Pay, press release, Global Witness, London, June 13, 2002.

57. For more details, see chapter 3, on the reporting of resource revenues.

58. On brands and corporate social responsibility, see Klein (2000). "Greenwash" can be defined as "the phenomenon of socially and environmentally destructive corporations attempting to preserve and expand their markets by posing as friends of the environment and leaders in the struggle to eradicate poverty"; see www.corpwatch.org.

59. Tantalum-Nobium International Study Center, press release (n.d.) and personal communication from official, November 2002.

60. Interview by the author with Kemet official, November 2002.

61. Field investigation by the author, April 2002; Jackson (2003).

62. The initial participants are British Petroleum, Chevron, Conoco, Freeport MacMoran, Rio Tinto, Shell, Texaco, Amnesty International, Fund for Peace, Human Rights Watch, International Alert, Lawyers Committee for Human Rights, Prince of Wales Business Leaders Forum, and the International Federation of Chemical, Energy, Mine, and General Workers Unions.

63. See www.state.gov/g/drl/rls/2931.htm.

64. For an account of the campaign against rubber exploitation in the Belgium Congo, see Hochschild (1999).

65. Monitoring was conducted by the Amsterdam-based Shipping Research Bureau; see Hengeveld and Rodenburg (1995).

66. See www.niza.nl/fataltransactions/.

67. See www.globalwitness.org.

68. Alex Yearsley, personal communication, 2002.

69. For more details, see www.cites.org/eng/disc/how.shtml.

70. See www.cites.org/eng/disc/what_is.shtml.

71. The United Nations Agreement on the Implementation of the Provisions of the UN Convention on the Law of the Sea of 10 December 1982 relating to the Conservation and Management of Straddling Fish Stocks and Highly Migratory Fish Stocks.

72. International Alert, stock-taking workshop on the regulation of the private sector in relation to armed conflicts, October 17, 2002; Sherman (2002).

References

The word "processed" describes informally produced works that may not be commonly available through libraries.

Adams, Roger. 2002. "The Case for Smart Legislation: The Detail Must Be Flexible." Paper presented to the seminar on the transparent company, Institute for Public Policy Research, London, March 20. Processed.

Admay, Catherine Adcock. 2000. "Rules of Relevancy in International Law: Straddling Stock Case Study." Paper presented at the environmental institutions colloquium, Duke Law School, Durham, N.C., April 20. Processed.

Aning, Emmanuel. 2002. *Regulating Illicit Trade in Natural Resources: The Role of Regional Actors in West Africa*. Accra: African Security Dialogue and Research.

Atkinson, Philippa. 1997. *The War Economy in Liberia: A Political Analysis*. RRN Paper 22. London: Overseas Development Institute, May.

Avery, Christopher L. 2000. *Business and Human Rights in a Time of Change*. London: Amnesty International UK.

Bayart, Jean-François, Stephen Ellis, and Beatrice Hibou. 1999. *The Criminalisation of the State in Africa*. Oxford: International African Institute in association with James Currey.

Bennett, Juliette. 2002a. "Conflict Prevention and Revenue-Sharing Regimes." UN Global Compact. Available at www.unglobalcompact.org/. Processed.

———. 2002b. "Multinational Corporations, Social Responsibility, and Conflict." *Journal of International Affairs* 55(2):393–410.

Berdal, Mats, and David Malone, eds. 2000. *Greed and Grievance: Economic Agendas in Civil War*. Boulder, Colo.: Lynne Rienner.

Biersteker, Thomas, Sue Eckert, Natalie Reid, and Peter Romaniuk. 2001. *Targeted Financial Sanctions: A Manual for Design and Implementation*. Providence, R.I.: Watson Institute for International Studies, Swiss Confederation, UN Secretariat.

Bray, John. 1997. *No Hiding Place: Business and the Politics of Pressure*. London: Control Risks Group.

Cambell, Greg. 2002. "Toward People-Friendly Diamonds." *Christian Science Monitor,* August 20.

Carbonnier, Gilles. 2001. "Corporate Responsibility and Humanitarian Action. What Relations between the Business and Humanitarian Worlds?" *IRRC* 83(December):844.

Clapham, Andrew, and Scott Jerbi. 2001. *Towards a Common Understanding of Business Complicity in Human Rights Abuses*. New York: UN Global Compact.

Collier, Paul, Anke Hoeffler, and Mans Söderbom. 2001. "On the Duration of Civil War." Policy Working Paper 2861. World Bank, Washington, D.C. Processed.

Cooper, Neil. 2001. "Conflict Goods: The Challenge for Peacekeeping and Conflict Prevention." *International Peacekeeping* 8(3):27.

Cortright, David, and George A. Lopez. 2000. *The Sanctions Decade: Assessing UN Strategies in the 1990s.* Boulder, Colo.: Lynne Rienner.

Delawala, Imtiyaz. 2002. "What Is Coltan? The Links between Your Cell Phone and Congo." *ABC News,* January 21. Available at abcnews.com.

Dietrich, Christian, and Peter Danssaert. 2001. "Antwerp Blamed, Again." International Peace Information Service and Diamond studies.com, Antwerp, November. Processed.

Doyle, Mark. 2002. "Liberia Sanctions Reviewed." *BBC News,* April 19.

Duffield, Mark. 2002. "War as a Network Enterprise: The New Security Terrain and Its Implications." *Cultural Values* 6(1-2):160.

Farah, Douglas. 2001. "Al-Qaeda Cash Tied to Diamond Trade." *Washington Post,* November 2, p. A-1.

Feeney, Patricia. 2002. "Making Companies Accountable: Rights and Accountability in Development." Paper prepared for the OECD nongovernmental organization Focal Point, October. Processed.

FLEGT (Forest Law Enforcement, Governance, and Trade). 2002. "International Workshop." Brussels, April 22–24. Available at europa.eu.int/comm/external_relations/flegt/. Processed.

Frankental, Peter, and Francis House. 2000. *Human Rights: Is It Any of Your Business?* London: Amnesty International, Prince of Wales Business Leaders Forum.

Friends of the Earth UK. 2001. "European League Table of Imports of Illegal Tropical Timber." August. Available at www.foe.co.uk/resource/briefings/euro_league_illegal_timber.pdf. Processed.

Gagnon, Georgette, Audrey Macklin, and Penelope Simons. 2003. *Deconstructing Engagement. Corporate Self-Regulation in Conflict Zones— Implications for Human Rights and Canadian Public Policy.* Toronto: Relationships in Transition.

Global Witness. 1995. *Forests, Famine, and War—The Key to Cambodia's Future.* London, March.

———. 2002. *The Logs of War: The Timber Trade and Armed Conflict.* Fafo Report 379. London: Fafo, March. Available at www.fafo.no/pub/rapp/379/379.pdf.

Hajost, Scott A., and Quinlan J. Shea III. n.d. "An Overview of Enforcement and Compliance Mechanisms in International Environmental Agreements." Available at www.inece.org/1stvol1/hajost.htm. Processed.

Haq, Farhan. 1997. "Politics: Regional Sanctions on Burundi Have Failed, UN Says." United Nations, New York, December 14. Processed.

Harden, Blain. 2001. "A Black Mud from Africa Helps Power the New Economy." *New York Times,* August 12.

Haufler, Virginia. 2001. *A Public Role for the Public Sector: Industry Self-Regulation in a Global Economy.* Washington, D.C.: Carnegie Endowment for International Peace.

Heine-Ellison, Sofia. 2001. "The Impact and Effectiveness of Multilateral Economic Sanctions: A Comparative Study." *International Journal of Human Rights* 5(1):81–112.

Hengeveld, Richard, and Jaap Rodenburg, eds. 1995. *Embargo: Apartheid's Oil Secrets Revealed.* Amsterdam: Amsterdam University Press.

Hochschild, Adam. 1999. *King Leopold's Ghost: A Story of Greed, Terror, and Heroism in Colonial Africa.* London: Macmillan.

Hodges, Tony. 2001. *Angola: From Afro-Stalinism to Petro-Diamond Capitalism.* Oxford: James Currey.

Horta, Korinna. 1997. "Questions Concerning the World Bank and Chad/Cameroon Oil and Pipeline Project." Environmental Defense Fund, New York, March. Processed.

Howen, Nick. 2001. *Business Wrongs and Rights: Human Rights and the Developing International Legal Obligations of Companies.* Geneva: International Council on Human Rights Policy.

Hufbauer, Gary C., Jeffrey J. Schott, and Kimberly A. Elliot. 1985. *Economic Sanctions Reconsidered: History and Current Policy.* Washington, D.C.: Institute for International Economics.

Human Rights Watch. 2001. "The Oil Diagnostic in Angola: An Update." New York, March. Processed.

IMF (International Monetary Fund). 2002. "Angola: Memorandum of Economic and Financial Policies." Washington, D.C., April 3. Available at www.imf.org/external/country/ago/. Processed.

International Consortium of Investigative Journalists. 2002a. "Conflict Diamonds Are Forever." In *Making a Killing: The Business of War,* part 6. Washington, D.C.: Center for Public Integrity, November 8.

———. 2002b. *Making a Killing: The Business of War.* Washington, D.C.: Center for Public Integrity. Available at www.public-i.org/dtaweb/report.asp?ReportID=469&L1=10&L2=10&L3=0&L4=0&L5=0.

International Council on Human Rights Policy. 2002. *Beyond Voluntarism: Human Rights and the Developing International Obligations of Companies.* Versoix, Switzerland.

International Peace Academy. 2002. "Policies and Practices for Regulating Resource Flows to Armed Conflict." Paper presented to the International Peace Academy conference, Bellagio, Italy, May 21–23. Processed.

IPIECA (International Petroleum Industry Environmental Conservation Association) and OGP (International Association of Oil and Gas Producers). 2002. *Key Questions in Managing Social Issues in Oil and Gas*

Projects. Report 2.85/332. London, October. Available on www.ogp. co.uk.

Jackson, Stephen. 2003. "Fortunes of War: Structure and Dynamics of the Coltan Trade in the Kivus." In Sarah Collinson, ed., *Understanding Someone Else's War: The Application of a Political Economy Approach to Humanitarian Action.* HPG Report. London: Overseas Development Institute.

Keen, David, and Sophia Tickell. 2000. "Business and the Humanitarian Imperative: The Humanitarian Responsibilities of Non-State Actors Operating in Conflict." Paper prepared for the Centre Henri Dunant, June. Processed.

Klein, Naomi. 2000. *No Logo.* London: Flamingo.

Knorr, Klaus. 1975. *The Power of Nations: The Political Economy of International Relations.* New York: Basic Books.

Kopp, Pierre. 1996. "Embargo et criminalisation de l'economie." In François Jean and Jean-C. Rufin, eds., *Economie des guerres civiles,* pp. 425–65. Paris: Hachette.

Le Billon, Philippe. 2000. "The Political Ecology of Transition in Cambodia 1989–1999: War, Peace, and Forest Exploitation." *Development and Change* 31(4):785–805.

Le Billon, Philippe, Jake Sherman, and Marcia Hartwell. 2002. *Controlling Illicit Resource Flows to Civil Wars: A Review and Analysis of Current Policies and Legal Instruments.* New York: International Peace Academy.

Lilly, D., and Philippe Le Billon. 2002. *Regulating Business in Zones of Conflict: A Synthesis of Strategies.* London: Overseas Development Institute.

MacGarvin, Malcolm. 2001. "Fisheries: Taking Stock." In *Late Lessons from Early Warnings: The Precautionary Principle 1896–2000.* Environmental Issue Report 22. Copenhagen: European Environment Agency.

Mack, Andrew, and Asif Khan. 2000. "The Efficacy of UN Sanctions." *Security Dialogue* 31(3): 279–92.

Malaquias, Assis. 2001. "Diamonds Are a Guerilla's Best Friend: The Impact of Illicit Wealth on Insurgency Strategy." *Third World Quarterly* 22(3): 311–25.

Mallet, Victor. 2002. "Liberia: Activists Stop Ship Unloading Timber in France." *Financial Times (London),* February 26.

Mansfield, Edward D. 1995. "International Institutions and Economic Sanctions." *World Politics* 47(4):575–605.

"Measuring Corruption." 2002. *The Economist,* October 26, p. 48.

Melby, Eric D. K. 1998. "Iraq." In Richard N. Haass, ed., *Economic Sanctions and American Diplomacy.* New York: Council on Foreign Relations.

Mobley, Richard. 2002. "The Beira Patrol, Britain's Broken Blockade against Rhodesia." *Naval War College Review* (Winter). Available at www.nwc. navy.mil/press/Review/2002/winter/art4-w02.htm.

Msutu, Frank. 2001. "Responses to Organised Crime in SADC: Interpol and SARPCCO." In Charles Goredema, ed., *Organized Crime in Southern*

Africa: Assessing Legislation. Monograph Series 56. Pretoria: Institute for Security Studies, June.

Mthembu-Salter, Gregory. 1999. *An Assessment of Sanctions against Burundi.* London: Action Aid.

Myers, Steven. 2000. "UN Concludes, Fining Shell, That Tanker Carried Iraq Oil." *New York Times,* April 26.

Nelson, Jane. 2000. *The Business of Peace: The Private Sector as a Partner in Conflict Prevention and Resolution.* London: International Alert, Council on Economic Priorities, Prince of Wales Business Leaders Forum.

OECD (Organisation for Economic Co-operation and Development). 2002. *OECD Guidelines for Multinational Enterprises: Annual Report 2002.* Paris.

Oloka-Onyango, J., and U. Deepika. 2000. *Globalization and Its Impact on the Full Enjoyment of Human Rights.* UN E/CN.4/Sub.2/2000/13. New York: UN Subcommission on the Promotion and Protection of Human Rights.

O'Sullivan, Meghan L. 2002. *Shrewd Sanctions: Economic Statecraft in an Age of Global Terrorism.* Washington, D.C.: Brookings Institution.

Pape, Robert A. 1997. "Why Economic Sanctions Do Not Work." *International Security* 22(2):106.

POLE Institute. 2001. "Coltan Phenomenon." Goma. Processed.

Rainforest Foundation UK. 2002. "Trading in Credibility: The Myth and Reality of the Forest Stewardship Council." London. Processed.

Recknagel, Charles. 2000. "Iraq: Oil Smuggling Produces High Profits." *Radio Free Europe/Radio Liberty,* June 21.

"Recommendations du point de contact national français à l'intention des entreprises au sujet de la question du travail forcé en Birmanie." 2002. Organisation for Economic Co-operation and Development, Paris, March 28. Available at www.minefi.gouv.fr/TRESOR/pcn/compcn280302.htm.

Ross, Michael. Forthcoming. "How Does Natural Resource Wealth Influence Civil War?" *Journal of Peace Research.*

Sallam, Ahmed. 2000. "Oussama Ben Laden: Le banquier du terrorisme international." *Renseignement et Opérations Spéciales* 5(July):131–36.

Saunders, Lucinda. 2001. "Rich and Rare Are the Gems They War: Holding De Beers Accountable for Trading Conflict Diamonds." *Fordham International Law Journal* 24(April):1402.

Sherman, Jake. 2001. *Private Sector Actors in Zones of Conflict: Research Challenges and Policy Responses. Summary Report.* New York: International Peace Academy.

———. 2002. "Policies and Practices for Regulating Resource Flows to Armed Conflicts." Paper presented to the International Peace Academy conference, Bellagio, Italy, May 21–23. Processed.

Smillie, Ian. 2002. *The Kimberley Process: The Case for Proper Monitoring.* Occasional Paper 5. Partnership Africa Canada and ReliefWeb.

Stein, Hansen. 1988. "Debt for Nature Swaps: Overview and Discussion of Key Issues." World Bank, Environment Department, Washington, D.C. Processed.

Switzer, Jason. 2001. *Conflict and Natural Resources: The Case of the Minerals Sector.* Report prepared by the International Institute for Sustainable Development for the Mining, Minerals, and Sustainable Development Project, July.

Taylor, Mark. 2002. *The Economies of Conflict: Private Sector Activity and Armed Conflicts.* Olso: Fafo.

Toyne, Paul, Cliona O'Brien, and Rod Nelson. 2002. *The Timber Footprint of the G-8 and China: Making the Case for Green Procurement by Government.* Gland: World Wildlife Fund International.

United Nations. 2000a. *Report of the UN Panel of Experts Concerning Sierra Leone.* S/2000/1195. United Nations, New York, December 13.

———. 2000b. *Report of the Panel of Experts on Violations of Security Council Sanctions against UNITA.* S/2000/203. New York: United Nations Secretariat.

———. 2002. *Report of the Monitoring Mechanism on Sanctions against UNITA.* S/2002/486. April 26. New York: United Nations Secretariat.

UN Global Compact. 2002. "Report on Progress and Activities." Global Compact Office, July. Available at 65.214.34.30/un/gc/unweb.nsf/. Processed.

UN Office of the High Commissioner for Human Rights. 2000. *Business and Human Rights: An Update.* Geneva.

U.S. General Accounting Office. 2002. *International Trade: Critical Issues Remain in Deterring Conflict Diamond Trade.* GAO-02-678. Washington, D.C., June.

Utting, Peter. 2000. *Business Responsibility for Sustainable Development.* Occasional Paper 2. Geneva: United Nations Research Institute for Social Development.

"When Sanctions Don't Work." 2000. *The Economist,* April 8–14.

Williams, Cynthia A. 1999. "The Securities and Exchange Commission and Corporate Social Transparency." *Harvard Law Review* 112:1197.

World Bank. 2001. "Note on the Use of Petroleum Bonus: The Chad-Cameroon Petroleum Development and Pipeline Project." Washington, D.C., June. Processed.

CHAPTER 7

Attracting Reputable Companies to Risky Environments: Petroleum and Mining Companies

John Bray

PETROLEUM AND MINING COMPANIES CONSIDER a wide range of technical and economic factors when assessing the commercial viability of a new project:

- What are the precise qualities of the mineral or petroleum deposit?
- How expensive is it to extract?
- How long will reserves last?
- What is the outlook for prices while the project is under way?
- How much will it cost to transport the product to market?

If there are no satisfactory answers to these questions, then there is little more to discuss. The mere existence of a mineral or petroleum deposit is far from guaranteeing its commercial viability.

This chapter focuses on the next level of inquiry. What other risk factors influence company decisions? In particular, what special factors must companies take into account when considering an investment in a zone of actual or potential conflict? How have their calculations changed in the last 10 years? And how far is it possible to encourage well-managed, responsible companies to invest in regions affected by conflict?

Part of the Problem or Part of the Solution?

At first sight, there are strong social and commercial disincentives for new investments in weak states with a history of political violence. In the 1990s and early 2000s mainstream Western companies have been stung by fierce controversy over their activities in resource-rich countries as diverse as Angola, Colombia, Indonesia, Myanmar, and Nigeria. Far from being seen as a blessing, mineral and petroleum resources are all too often seen as a curse to the countries that possess them—and international companies associated with these industries are tainted accordingly.

Petroleum and mining firms have been associated with poor governance and conflict in two ways. First, as discussed in other chapters, companies operating on or beyond the margins of the law have helped violent factions to raise money through the sale of natural resources such as "conflict diamonds" (chapter 5). Second, even mainstream international companies may—however unintentionally—contribute to conflict. All too often, income from natural resources has served to reinforce the powers of "predatory" states (see, for example, Fridthof Nansen Institute and Econ 2000). The wealth brought by mining or petroleum is often restricted to narrow social or political groups rather than being distributed more broadly. Income from natural resources has tempted governments to neglect other economic sectors such as agriculture. The resulting inequalities are a source of tension, unrest, and—in extreme cases—civil war (chapter 2).

Companies with existing investments have tended to resist pressure to leave when conflict breaks out or escalates. However, in the light of recent experience, it is much harder for companies that are sensitive to their reputations to justify new investments in conflict zones.

Equally, the petroleum and mining industries could—if properly managed—emerge as part of the solution to the problems of bad governance. Without balanced economic development, weak states are more likely to become failed states. For many African countries in particular, minerals and petroleum offer the most substantial and readily accessible sources of income. Foreign investment and expertise can help to develop these resources and thus finance the institutions needed to ensure stability.

The wider social and commercial case for investing in zones of conflict is outlined in reports such as the United Nations (UN) Global Compact's business guide for conflict impact assessment and risk management (UN Global Compact 2002). Political changes in the late 1980s and 1990s have opened up new markets to international business. Many of these are in developing countries that are exposed to conflict and might otherwise be considered unattractive. Nevertheless, as the business guide points out, these regions offer important opportunities: "It is in these areas of underdevelopment that we also find the highest potential for business growth due to untapped pools of human, social, and natural capital, unmet basic needs, unmet expansion opportunities, and lower operating costs."

Such arguments have particular resonance in the petroleum and mining sectors. These industries need to operate where geology dictates and not merely in the political or geographic regions that happen to be convenient. The "major" companies in both sectors need to build up new resources as existing reserves become depleted. The "junior" companies hope to make their fortunes by taking risks in regions where more established companies are reluctant to venture. The business case for exploration and investment in regions vulnerable to conflict is that it is possible to get ahead of competitors by going in early or when conditions appear difficult.

The central argument of this chapter is that investment by good, entrepreneurial companies can indeed be "part of the solution" to the problems of weak, post-conflict states. However, they cannot act effectively on their own—not least because they lack the legitimacy to intervene in matters that are often seen as "political."

The Investment Climate

The early 1990s was a period of expansion and relative optimism in both the mining and the petroleum sectors. Political changes in the former Soviet Union and other former socialist countries opened up new countries to foreign investment, and markets seemed favorable. By contrast, the investment climate in the early 2000s is more sober. This is partly because of the general economic downturn—which has hit mining more severely than petroleum—but also because of the lessons learned in the previous decade. Although the risk of outright expropriation is now rare, there are new forms of political risk—notably reputational risk—as well as the continuing hazards of substate conflict. This section examines the lessons learned in the past decade and the factors that influence the climate for extractive-industry investment in developing and transition economies.

From Optimism in the 1990s to Caution in the 2000s

Petroleum and mining companies are constantly looking for "elephants"—major new finds that will replenish old reserves and transform their fortunes. In the early to mid-1990s hopes were particularly high. Political changes in the former Soviet Union were echoed by a general trend toward economic liberalization in developing countries. In earlier decades the trend had been toward the nationalization of natural resources. Now, host countries were actively encouraging foreign investment.

As a senior Exxon economist points out, international capital had access to roughly 35 percent of the world's undiscovered oil and gas potential at the beginning of the decade (MacDonald 1998, pp. 120–23). By 1998, some 80 percent of potential reserves were open to private companies. Similar trends applied to the mining sector. In 1990 few African countries were open to foreign mining companies. By 1997, almost all had developed new mining codes to facilitate exploration and investment.

Technical advances reinforced the benefits of political change. Deepwater oil and gas technology developed in the Gulf of Mexico and the North Sea could now be applied to offshore fields in West Africa and Southeast Asia. Similarly, international mining companies were keen to apply new techniques to African and Asian countries that had been either partially explored several decades earlier or totally neglected.

There have been some significant success stories in both the petroleum and the mining industries. Central Asian oil and gas pipelines are beginning to come on stream. Mali and Tanzania (and before them Chile and Peru) provide cases where international investment has either transformed existing mines or helped to develop major new discoveries. However, few of the mineral exploration initiatives undertaken in Africa in the last decade have resulted in new mines. This is partly because of the long lead time—typically 10 years or more—between exploration and full-scale operations but also because of the general economic slowdown.

In 2001 and 2002 global flows of foreign direct investment declined sharply. Wider concerns included the downturn in the U.S. economy, heightened security concerns following the September 11 terrorist attacks, and the possibility of renewed conflict in Iraq.

Petroleum has fared better than mining. Short-term oil prices are notoriously volatile, but notwithstanding increased interest in renewable energy sources, there is little doubt of the continued need for hydrocarbons. To stay ahead of their competitors, the majors need new reserves to replenish stocks that have already been consumed. For example, in February 2003, British Petroleum announced that it would spend some $20 billion on developing new fields to build up its dwindling reserves ("BP to Spend $20 Billion" 2003). The broad rationale for new exploration and development therefore remains unchanged, and new petroleum developments in West Africa and Central Asia are pressing ahead.

However, as an international operator in Russia points out, as many as 83 countries are currently competing to offer oil and gas acreage to international investors. Against this background of competition for investors, host governments with promising petroleum reserves cannot afford to assume that international investors are automatically interested in what they have to offer.

The investment climate for new mining operations is much tougher. In a review of global markets in 2001, mining economist Philip Crowson reports that diversified mining companies achieved slightly higher returns than U.S. government bonds during the 1990s, but that these returns were "probably not high enough to offset their higher risk" (Crowson 2001). Low prices for base metals in the early 2000s have reinforced this pessimistic trend. The fall in zinc prices has been particularly painful—many working mines in developing countries have had to close down or are being maintained solely on a care-and-maintenance basis until prices rise to more profitable levels.

Gold has performed better than base metals. In February 2003 international gold prices rose to $380 per ounce, mainly because gold was regarded as a safe investment at a time when there was a risk of conflict in the Middle East. This represented a significant recovery from the historic lows—less than $280 per ounce—in the late 1990s. However, the long-term prospects even for gold are notoriously uncertain. The fact that investors generally are feeling risk averse means that there is less money for uncertain new ventures in possible conflict zones.

Market uncertainties and competition between rival host countries mean that investors can afford to—indeed are obliged to—look all the more closely at the political, security, and reputational risks involved in developing new prospects. Some of these risks are similar to those faced in the past. Others are relatively new.

Political Risks

In theory, the spread of economic liberalism to developing countries should mean that political risks are less significant than in earlier decades. Most governments now accept the need for foreign investment and expertise and, in principle, will do all they can to encourage them. The reality is more complex. Political leaders have to satisfy a variety of domestic interests to remain in power, and the task of improving conditions for foreign companies may not be at the top of their agenda. When asked what was the most important factor influencing investment, a senior executive from one of the oil majors discussed a variety of issues before summarizing them with a single sentence: "It's governance, stupid!"[1] He had in mind not only the risk of direct political intervention in business but also the failures of governance that lead to corruption, social unrest, and human rights abuses.

The overriding concern for would-be extractive-industry investors remains security of tenure and the extent to which this might be threatened by political unrest, legal uncertainties, changes in government policy, or expropriation. The extractive industries share with downstream energy companies the problem of the "obsolescing bargain."[2] Companies from these industries are obliged to make major capital investments before they can expect to reap any profit. These investments amount to a kind of "hostage." Once the companies have paid for multi-million-dollar fixed assets, they cannot lightly withdraw from the host country.

Security of tenure is essential because of the long time period—often well over a decade—between initial investment and payback. The long time frame, large capital investment, and typically high political risks mean that the companies feel justified in seeking high rates of return.

Paradoxically, these same high rates can raise political risks, rather than alleviate them, because they lead to charges that the company is "profiteering." Outright expropriation, the classic political risk of the 1960s and 1970s, is now unusual. However, companies may face forms of "creeping expropriation." In Russia there have been cases where local joint venture partners have unilaterally sold extra company shares to local purchasers, thus diluting the foreign partners' percentage stake without their knowledge. Elsewhere—for example, Papua New Guinea in the early 1990s—host governments have forced companies to renegotiate royalty agreements once mines came into profitable production.

Meanwhile, nationalism still manifests itself in government reluctance to lift restrictive regulations limiting foreign ownership. Despite more than a decade of debate—and a recent change of policy by President Gloria Macapagal-Arroyo—the Philippines has yet to reach consensus on foreign participation in the mining sector. A case challenging 100 percent foreign ownership of mines is still lying unresolved in the Supreme Court in Manila.

Uncertainties over security of tenure are all the greater in postsocialist transition or developing economies that are still in the process of developing the economic, legal, and fiscal regimes needed to attract private investment initiatives. Both in the former Soviet Union and in much of Africa, lack of confidence in the viability and transparency of legal reforms continues to discourage investors in major, long-term infrastructure projects.

Ultimately, security of tenure may depend less on legal formalities and more on intangible qualities of trust. Major energy and mining projects have little chance of long-term survival unless they are seen as being fair to stakeholders. Companies face the constant problem of arguing their case to host governments and local communities that are unfamiliar with the calculations made by international investors and therefore have different views of what constitutes "fairness." This task is likely to be all the more difficult in post-conflict regions that are new to international investment. The more that companies can do to build up a wide body of support among different sections of the host population, the safer their investments will be.

Security Risks

Meanwhile, companies operating in developing countries often have to operate against a background or a threat of conflict. The extractive industries are more exposed than other sectors: the vagaries of geological chance often take them to remote areas, they have large fixed assets that cannot be removed, and rival contestants for power may see control over their resources as a strategic objective. Conflict often reflects a history of poor governance, which in itself is a danger signal for business.

A survey conducted by PriceWaterhouseCoopers for the Mining, Minerals, and Sustainable Development (MMSD) Project in early 2001 found that 78 percent of the 32 mining majors surveyed had refrained from investing or withdrawn from an investment because of political instability, for example, armed conflict (PricewaterhouseCoopers 2001).

Nevertheless, the existence of a conflict in a host country does not necessarily deter new entrants. The questions include the potential economic value of oil or mineral deposits, the precise location of the conflict, and the possibility of a peace settlement. Junior companies, in particular, may see a competitive advantage in entering a region that has suffered from political violence and has a good chance of recovery. As one executive from a junior mining company comments, "It is often best to go in early, when there is still blood on the floor. If you succeed, you're regarded as a hero."[3] He cites as a favorable example Newmont's entry into Peru in the early 1990s, when the country was still suffering severely from the Sendero Luminoso (Shining Path) insurgency.

The Colombian state-owned company Ecopetrol uses a similar argument in a recent sponsored statement in the *Petroleum Economist*. Acknowledging that security is a concern for investors, the statement nevertheless argues that conditions are likely to improve: "If the situation improves dramatically, Colombia will be upgraded as an exploration region from an investment point of view. But by then, it might be too late. When is the timing perfect and when is it too late?

It may be appropriate to invest today, given that the perception of the security risk in the country might improve significantly in the future" (Ecopetrol 2002).

However, it will be harder to win financial backing for such investments at a time when the wider market has been influenced by fears of terrorism in the wake of the September 11 attacks and the threat of a Middle East conflict. The World Bank's Multilateral Investment Guarantee Agency's Foreign Direct Investment Survey published in January 2002 found that 85 percent of the companies surveyed were either "very concerned" or "somewhat concerned" about physical security (MIGA 2002).

Ethics and Reputation

The most significant new political risks since the 1990s relate to the risk of reputational damage to companies operating in regions with a record of human rights abuses or corruption. This is not completely new: companies operating in South Africa in the 1970s and 1980s faced the risk of boycott from activists in the West. Nevertheless, improvements in communication and especially the expansion of the Internet have made it much easier for nongovernmental organizations first to gather information about companies' international activities and then to mobilize effective campaigns (Bray 1997).

A symbolic turning point came in 1995 when Shell faced hostile campaigns first over the disposal of its Brent Spar offshore installation and then for its failure or inability to prevent the execution of Ogoni activist Ken Saro-Wiwa in Nigeria. As John Mitchell and his fellow authors point out in a recent study for the Royal Institute of International Affairs, companies now have to consider not only whether resources are *available,* but also whether they are *acceptable* to powerful constituencies in their home countries (Mitchell and others 2002). Investment can be problematic in countries where the host government is accused of extensive human rights abuses, democratic processes are absent or weak, or revenues are used for controversial purposes. As Mitchell comments, "To develop new supplies under these circumstances may not be acceptable for the companies concerned unless they can satisfy potential international critics that their intervention is serving the wider developmental purposes of promoting the expansion of freedom for the people affected" (Mitchell and others 2002, p. 270). ChevronTexaco Chairman Dave J. Reilly makes a similar point in a recent interview: "Success is no longer determined solely by traditional financial or operational metrics. Today we are held to new standards for corporate citizenship, human rights, and the environment that are no less rigorous than the financial requirements of the investment community" (Williams 2002, p. 28).

An example of how the new politics works in practice comes from Afghanistan in the late 1990s when the U.S. company Unocal aspired to build a pipeline linking gas reserves in Turkmenistan with potential markets in South Asia. The project involved significant security risks as well as the political and cultural difficulties of dealing with the Taliban government. However, the decisive factor in killing U.S. government support for the project came not from security concerns over Osama bin Laden, who was already operating in Afghanistan, but from U.S. women's advocates who called for a tough stance against the Taliban government out of solidarity with Afghan women (Rashid 2001, pp. 170–82). In Mitchell's terms, that particular project was clearly "unacceptable" to the U.S. domestic constituency.

Corruption. Corruption is one of the most sensitive ethical and reputational issues for international companies. A survey commissioned by Control Risks Group in late 2002 showed that more than half of the 23 oil, gas, and mining companies in the sample had put off an otherwise attractive investment on account of corruption (Control Risks Group 2002, p. 50).[4] The survey covered 250 companies in eight different sectors in Germany, Hong Kong (China), the Netherlands, Singapore, the United Kingdom, and the United States (table 7.1).

The PricewaterhouseCoopers survey came up with a similar result: 41 percent of the 32 "world-class" mining companies surveyed had refrained from investing or had withdrawn from an investment on account of corruption, for example, being asked for unofficial payments (PricewaterhouseCoopers 2001).[5]

Table 7.1 Companies Deterred from an Otherwise Attractive Investment by a Country's Reputation for Corruption, by Sector

Sector	Percent
Oil, gas, and mining	52.2
Public works, construction	44.2
Retail	42.9
Banking and finance	39.2
Power generation and transmission	37.5
Pharmaceuticals and medical care	35.7
Arms and defense	30.0
Telecommunications	27.3

Source: Control Risks Group (2002).

Companies in the extractive sectors are particularly vulnerable to corruption both because of the large sums of money involved—which increases the temptation for dishonest officials—and because of their frequent and regular interactions with government. High levels of corruption may have a direct practical impact: one oil executive interviewed for this report stated that his company was considering withdrawing from an investment in Central Asia because the arbitrary political environment combined with high levels of corruption made it impossible to get anything done or to be confident of the government's willingness to stick to an agreement.

Human Rights and "Constructive Engagement." Human rights emerged as a second major concern in the Control Risks Survey, although not on the same scale as corruption. Retail companies were more concerned about poor human rights, no doubt partly because they were more exposed to consumer boycotts. However, some 20 percent of oil, gas, and mining companies had put off an otherwise attractive investment on account of human rights concerns (table 7.2).

Again the results of the PriceWaterhouseCoopers survey were similar: 33 percent of the mining companies surveyed had either been deterred or withdrawn from investments because of human rights issues in the area or country. The Myanmar and Sudan case studies in appendix 7.1 illustrate how investment in those countries has led to reputational concerns for international companies operating there. One of the most sensitive issues concerns the companies' relationship with government security forces that are protecting their assets and may be associated with human rights abuses. Companies run the risk of being accused of complicity with such actions and—at least in the United States—facing legal action.

Table 7.2 Companies Deterred from an Otherwise Attractive Investment by a Country's Reputation for a Poor Human Rights Record, by Sector

Sector	Percent
Retail	28.6
Telecommunications	22.7
Oil, gas, and mining	21.7
Banking and finance	17.7
Arms and defense	16.7
Public works and construction	15.4
Pharmaceuticals and medical care	14.3
Power generation and transmission	12.5

Source: Control Risks Group (2002).

The fact that some companies are put off by such risks does not mean that all companies are deterred. A company's approach to human rights depends on its overall policies, and this theme is discussed below.

Corporate Social Responsibility

Pressure on ethical issues has contributed to the emergence of the new and still developing field of corporate social responsibility and a growing preoccupation with the principles of sustainable development.[6] Corporate social responsibility is—or should be—justifiable on ethical grounds alone, but it is linked to risk management in that companies deemed to be socially responsible are less likely to face reputational problems.

The larger oil and mining companies have responded to this agenda both by taking extra measures to ensure that their work forces are well treated (for example, mining companies have taken the lead in promoting AIDS prevention and treatment among their workers in South Africa) and by promoting links with local communities. Rio Tinto stresses that its community policies include "mutual respect, active partnership, and long-term commitment" (Rio Tinto 2001). Shell's report *People, Planet, and Profits* emphasizes the company's commercial objectives: "to engage efficiently, responsibly, and profitably" in its respective industries (Royal Dutch Shell 2001). However, it also points to the company's values and its concern for sustainable development, inclusiveness, and social investment.

Nevertheless, the scope and impact of corporate social responsibility are still widely contested on a variety of grounds:

• One concern is the extent to which corporate social responsibility is a preoccupation primarily of Northern, or even Northern European, companies.

• Skeptical nongovernmental organizations question the depth of companies' commitment to the principles of corporate social responsibility, arguing that it often amounts to a form of public relations "whitewash" or—in the case of environmental initiatives— "greenwash."

• Some business leaders argue that companies should concentrate on their prime commercial expertise rather than trespass into the domains of development agencies and government.

In line with this kind of thinking, ExxonMobil Executive Vice President Rene Dahan argues that a fundamental role of business is to create prosperity and that this limits its willingness to address broader social problems, particularly those brought on by conflicts: "Business enterprises are at base neither philanthropic nor peacekeeping organizations" (Williams 2002, pp. 28–29).

As is seen below, the extent to which company initiatives should overlap with, or replace, government programs is a particularly sensitive issue in zones of actual or potential conflict.

Constructive Engagement?

All reputable businesses acknowledge a responsibility to treat their work force fairly. Most now also acknowledge a wider duty to local communities. However, companies are generally unwilling to accept responsibility for the host government's use of the revenues they help to produce. Many activists contest this view. For example, Oxfam Policy Adviser Sophia Tickell argues, "A successful community program that benefits 100,000 people is important, but counts as nothing if the taxes you are paying keep in power a corrupt and dictatorial government" (cited in Ward 2000, p. 4).

As the Myanmar and Sudan case studies show, nongovernmental organizations have argued that foreign companies in those countries help to preserve illegitimate governments while giving them the financial resources to crack down on opposition movements. Companies are likely to face similar arguments in other conflict-affected regions ruled by controversial governments.

Company Policies on Risk

Individual companies adopt differing strategies on investment and conflict, and these depend both on their resources and on their attitudes to risk. The personalities of individual chief executive officers and boards of directors play an important role in deciding company policy. Other factors include size, stock market listing, and legal reform.

Defining Company Policy

The board of directors has overall responsibility for defining policies on investment risk and on ethical issues such as the company's policy on human rights. These policies depend both on the company's internal culture and on its market positioning.

Some companies have taken a deliberately robust approach to high-risk environments and informed their sponsors accordingly. These include the U.K. independent Premier (currently or recently active in Albania, Guinée Bissau, Indonesia, Myanmar, and Pakistan) and the Malaysian company Petronas (currently active in 15 international markets including Algeria, Iran, Myanmar, Sudan, and Turkmenistan). The French company TotalFinaElf claims to be ahead of its competitors because of its aggressive exploration policy, including in areas that might be considered high risk (Housego 2003).

The factors that influence company policy typically include the following:

- *The personality of the chief executive.* Almost by definition, chief executives tend to be strong, sometimes larger-than-life personalities. British Petroleum Chief Executive Lord (John) Browne has been his company's most prominent spokesman on its corporate responsibility policies. Jim Buckee, chief executive of the Canadian company Talisman, has become well known for his outspoken defense of his company's presence in Sudan. The projection of these companies' policies would have been different but for the part played by these individuals.

- *Nationality.* There is a perception that U.S. companies are likely to be less sensitive to human rights issues than their U.K. and Northern European equivalents. Companies from countries not in the Organisation for Economic Co-operation and Development (OECD) are even less likely to be exposed to the debate about company responsibilities for human rights or the issues surrounding constructive engagement with controversial regimes.

- *Past experience.* Senior Shell executives acknowledge that the 1995 protests against the company for its disposal of Brent Spar and its presence in Nigeria prompted it to rethink both its overall strategy and its communications with outsiders (for example, Herkströter 1996). Shell has not withdrawn from Nigeria, but it has sought to change how its activities are managed.

However, the most important influences on company strategy are size and market position, stock market listing, and regulatory reforms.

Implications of Size

Historically, junior companies have been more willing than major companies to take risks in countries that are vulnerable to conflict or have poor standards of governance. This fits in with their investment strategies as sold to their financial backers: high risks in the hope of high returns. It is generally understood that easy places are already taken, and thus the most cost-effective means for a small company to make an impact is to work in high-risk regions. The classic approach of a junior—whether in the mining or the petroleum industry—is to explore, develop a deposit until its commercial viability is proven, and then sell part or all of its stake to a major.

Cairn Energy, which discovered and developed the Sangu gas field in Bangladesh, is regarded as a positive—and profitable—example.

Cairn has now transferred the operation of its interests in two blocks in the field to Shell and signed production-sharing contracts with Shell in two further blocks.[7] Meanwhile, it is extending its offshore exploration activities to India.

An executive working for another petroleum junior explains his company's strategy: "We are a niche player. We look for places where there are good subsurface prospects combined with difficult surface risks. The geology is crucial: the rest we can manage."[8]

Surface risks may include an uncertain legal environment. Juniors are more likely than majors to begin exploration before a satisfactory legal framework is in place—indeed they may see a competitive advantage in doing so. While exploring, they may hope to establish a degree of influence with government officials, in the hope of encouraging them to institute more favorable legal regulations when the time comes to go into production.

The reputation of the whole junior mining sector suffered as a result of the 1997 Bre-X scandal when a Canadian company was found to be "salting" an Indonesian mine (falsifying geological data) in order to mislead investors. The Bre-X scandal, now combined with the general economic slowdown, has made it more difficult for juniors to raise funds either on the Canadian or on other stock markets.

Juniors typically have limited financial resources, and their survival often depends on the success or failure of one particular project. There may therefore be a greater temptation to take unacceptable shortcuts—whether by economizing on social programs or by paying bribes. At an MMSD seminar on armed conflict and natural resources, one participant commented that large mining companies were moving out of Papua New Guinea only to be replaced by smaller ones: "These are not the sort of guys who'll come and sit round a table like this" (MMSD 2001). The implication is that smaller companies are less likely to have the time or resources to discuss important social or ethical issues.

The juniors argue that they fulfill an important social as well as a commercial function by taking on the high-risk areas that the majors will not touch and thus promoting development in otherwise neglected areas. Like the majors, the juniors have become more sensitive to social issues in the last 10 years, and this is for self-interested reasons as well as altruism. It will be more difficult for them to sell the properties they have developed if these are associated with unresolved social controversies and even legal liabilities.

As is seen in the case studies in appendix 7.1, Premier and Talisman are examples of smaller companies that have responded to social and political controversy by investing in social programs in Myanmar and

Sudan, respectively. They have not succeeded in defusing the controversy, but they have demonstrated that concern with social issues may extend to juniors as well as majors.

Majors are more sensitive to their reputations than juniors because they have more to lose. By the fact of having a "big name," they are more exposed to public scrutiny, and their commercial health matters to more people. They generally are unwilling to jeopardize their reputations—and their share prices—through exposure to actual or potential zones of conflict.

This greater sensitivity to reputation has mixed implications. On the one hand, it means that majors are less likely to take on difficult projects in the first place. On the other hand, once they take on a project, they have greater financial and technical resources and are better placed to manage problems than are juniors. Their greater financial resources mean that they can play a long game, waiting for the right conditions to make major investments rather than being in a hurry to make quick returns.

One reason why juniors can afford to take greater risks is that they focus on the exploration and initial development stages of the investment cycle, and these require comparatively low capital sums. By contrast, world-class companies look for world-class deposits. As an executive from a major minerals company explained, this is likely to mean an open-pit mine that has a projected life of some 40 to 50 years.[9] If a company is to invest the tens or hundreds of millions of dollars needed to develop this kind of mine, it will need to be confident of a reasonably stable political and legal environment.

The same executive stated that his company would rarely consider a country that lacked a well-drafted mining code. High levels of corruption would be a major disincentive, and the company would not even look at a controversial country such as Myanmar. Low prices for metals mean that the company has a smaller exploration budget than before. It already has a portfolio of mining properties that are "ready to go" once prices rise again.

In cases where majors have become involved in conflict, this is often because violence has flared up after they have been operating in the country for many years. Shell's experience in Nigeria is an obvious example. As the company now acknowledges, it neglected the warning signs that led up to unrest in the Niger peninsula. It is now trying to apply the lessons both in Nigeria and elsewhere.

However, conflict is not an absolute deterrent even to majors, as long as the resources are attractive enough and they believe that they can manage the risks. Angola evidently qualifies on both counts, although the fact that the companies are able to operate offshore in comparative safety does not remove their exposure to the reputational risks of involvement with a controversial regime.

Implications of Stock Exchange Listing

Shareholders demand transparency from listed companies so that they can understand the potential risks to their investments. The overall trend is toward higher standards on a wide range of corporate governance issues—including open disclosure of the extra risks involved in investing in conflict regions or weak states.

Corporate Codes and Stock Exchange Regulations. In the United Kingdom the directors of companies listed on the London Stock Exchange are expected to comply with the risk guidelines outlined in the 1999 Turnbull report, officially known as *Internal Control: Guidance for Directors on the Combined Code* (Institute of Chartered Accountants of England and Wales 1999). Turnbull is the latest in a series of corporate governance reports. Its objectives are, first, to ensure that companies establish systems of internal control to assess and manage risks effectively and, second, to ensure that they publish regular reports. Similar guidelines have been issued in Canada, France, Germany, South Africa, and the United States.[10]

Turnbull does not encourage companies to avoid risks, but rather to understand what the risks involve, to manage them, and to give a public account of how they have done so. The report specifically includes reputational risks such as a company might incur from investing in a country with a poor human rights reputation. Again, it does not take a view on whether companies should or should not operate in such countries. Rather, the report aims to ensure that companies assess risks systematically, make appropriate choices in line with their overall strategies, and explain those choices to investors.

The Enron affair led to further pressure for corporate governance reforms on both sides of the Atlantic. The U.S. Sarbanes-Oxley Law, which was introduced as a result of the Enron scandal, imposes tighter corporate governance rules on all companies listed on U.S. stock exchanges, even if they are based outside the United States. The act requires a company that issues quarterly and annual reports to the U.S. Securities and Exchange Commission to have its principal executive and financial officers each certify financial and other information in the reports. In a similar spirit, in the United Kingdom the Higgs report, published in January 2003, tightens the requirements on nonexecutive directors to ensure that they are actively engaged in monitoring their company's activities (Higgs 2003).

Commenting on the Enron affair, British Petroleum Chief Executive Lord Browne points out: "The current crisis in corporate governance has involved only a small minority of companies, but it has damaged trust in the entire corporate world. Restoring trust must be the top priority for major businesses. . . . Transparency is the key to restoring trust" (Browne 2002, p. 34). The need for transparency applies to companies' activities both in developing countries and in Western markets.

Activist Shareholders and Socially Responsible Investment. The rise of the market for socially responsible investment since the 1990s has given greater weight to shareholders' ethical concerns, including human rights.

Early ethical investment funds in the 1980s tended to operate on the principle of screening out "unacceptable" companies, for example, those involved in the tobacco business. The current trend is more for ethical investment fund managers to engage with target companies and encourage them to improve their policies. Fund managers have argued that they have both a right and a duty to engage with companies whose policies—or lack of them—may incur ethical problems, which in turn may incur risks to their investments. The size of the funds' shareholdings gives them influence. One asset manager comments that companies may not welcome her calls, "but at least they pick up the phone."[11]

In December 2001 a group of eight fund management companies, who between them managed some £400 billion, issued a joint statement expressing concern about companies with investment in Burma (Myanmar).[12] Many of the issues raised apply to other countries as well. They included the possibility that "companies operating in unstable political climates can be exposed to loss of shareholder confidence, negative press and publicity campaigns, safety risks, and corruption." The statement did not call for divestment, but it did call on companies to establish "effective policies and procedures" to manage the risk, for example, by publishing verified social impact assessments.

A more recent initiative by ISIS (formerly Friends, Ivory, and Sime) includes the copublication of a report in July 2002 entitled *Changing Oil: Emerging Environmental Risks and Shareholder Value* in association with the World Resources Institute (ISIS and World Resources Institute 2002). The report argues that oil and gas companies are giving insufficient attention to their exposure to environmental risks and that this will result in diminished shareholder value over the next decade unless they take prompt action.

While the general trend among ethical investment funds is toward engagement rather than screening, managers retain the option of withdrawing investments from companies that are judged to fall below standard. In January 2003 Henderson Global Investors, which manages assets worth some £120 billion, withdrew its ethical investment funds from British Petroleum out of concern for the company's poor safety record in Alaska (Gumbel and Woolf 2003). Companies involved in major controversies in conflict zones could face similar pressure.

Shareholder interest in companies' performance on social issues has led to a demand for rating systems. The FTSE Group, which compiles stock exchange and other financial indexes, has responded by developing the FTSE4Good Socially Responsible Investment Index, which provides ratings assessing companies' performance in three areas: environmental sustainability, relationships with shareholders, and support for universal human rights.[13] The index has a limited number of exclusions, for example, companies working in the nuclear industry, but does include major petroleum and mining companies. In the human rights field, FTSE4Good assesses companies on their policy statement and their participation in initiatives such as the UN Global Compact.[14]

The index is still at an early stage in its development, but its emergence is a significant sign of the times. More and more investors in Western markets are looking for tools to help them integrate judgments on companies' social and environmental performance into their investment decisions.

Voluntary Codes

In assessing companies' social credentials, analysts look both at their voluntary internal policies and practices and at their compliance with external regulations.

The UN Global Compact, which was introduced by UN Secretary General Kofi Annan in 2000, is a high-profile example of a voluntary initiative designed to raise company standards. The compact calls on signatory companies to uphold nine broad principles in the areas of human rights, labor, and the environment. Other guidelines such as the OECD's Guidelines for Multinational Enterprises or the Global Sullivan Principles of Social Responsibility provide similar benchmarks of good corporate conduct.[15]

Most major international companies now have their own individual codes or statements of business principles. In 1997 Shell became the first large oil company to make a specific commitment to uphold human rights "in line with the legitimate role of business." Some 40 major companies now have their own codes referring to human rights.[16] Similarly, the Control Risks Group survey found that 94 percent of the U.K. companies and 92 percent of the U.S. companies surveyed now had codes that forbade the payment of bribes to obtain business (Control Risks Group 2002, p. 30).

The spread of corporate codes has led to a debate on the merits of voluntary guidelines versus regulation. Broadly, companies tend to prefer voluntary adherence to principles governing their international activities. They argue that legal regulations can lead to excessive bureaucracy and are hard to enforce. By contrast, nongovernmental organizations look for formal regulation, arguing that there is little reason to trust companies' commitment to voluntary principles. In this view, codes amount to little more than whitewash (or, in the case of the Global Compact, "bluewash"), giving companies an easy alibi without imposing any real pressure to change. A recently published report by three Canadian authors takes Talisman's operations in Sudan as an example and argues that international companies operating in conflict regions abroad "are not accountable under international law or in most home state jurisdictions for complicity in human rights abuses" (Gagnon, Macklin, and Simons 2003, p. 4).

Legislation and Regulation

Voluntary principles may in due course lead the way to regulation. So far, the international legal regime is much more highly developed with regard to corruption than to corporations' possible involvement in human rights abuses.

Anticorruption Laws

In 1977 the United States introduced the Foreign Corrupt Practices Act. The act makes it possible to prosecute U.S. companies in U.S. courts for paying bribes to foreign officials, even if the transaction takes place abroad.[17] The U.S. Department of Justice and the U.S. Securities and Exchange Commission have joint responsibility for enforcing the act, which applies to all companies listed on the New York Stock Exchange, whether they are based in the United States or not. The "books and records" sections of the act impose strict accounting requirements to prevent companies from disguising bribes under other headings. The United States actively enforces the Foreign Corrupt Practices Act—the Department of Justice has prosecuted 34 foreign bribery cases and pursued a further seven civil actions—and, although the number of prosecutions is relatively small, they serve as a deterrent to other companies.

For two decades, U.S. companies complained that the act put them at an unfair advantage when competing with foreign companies that were not bound by the same restrictions. These concerns were partially addressed in December 1997, when 29 OECD member states and five others signed the Convention on Combating Bribery of Foreign Public

Officials in International Business Transactions. Under the terms of the convention, which came into force in early 1999, signatories agreed to introduce legislation similar to the Foreign Corrupt Practices Act.[18]

In principle, companies from all the major industrial nations in the OECD are competing on the same terms as far as bribery is concerned. However, so far no prosecutions under the new laws have been introduced in other countries as a result of the convention. Their willingness to enforce the new laws therefore remains to be proven. The laws nevertheless establish a clear legal boundary that good companies respect.

International Human Rights Legislation. The international legal regime governing the human rights responsibilities of companies is poorly developed, although this may change. The nascent International Criminal Court is mainly concerned with governments and government employees. However, legal specialists suggest that it could ultimately extend jurisdiction over companies accused of complicity in human rights abuses.

Meanwhile, a U.S. legal expert is drawing up a draft set of human rights principles for business (with the official title Responsibilities of Transnational Corporations and Other Business Enterprises with Regard to Human Rights) for submission to the UN General Assembly. The most recent draft of the text was agreed by the Working Group on Transnational Corporations (of the UN Subcommission on the Promotion and Protection of Human Rights) when it met in late July and early August 2002. On August 14, 2002, the full UN subcommission decided to discuss the draft again at its next session in July-August 2003.

The principles will serve several roles. As with the OECD Guidelines for Multinational Enterprises, they will provide a basis for individual companies drawing up their own codes. They also will provide a reference point for international lawyers concerned with the human rights obligations of companies.

The U.S. Alien Torts Claims Act. The Alien Torts Claims Act is a U.S. law dating back to 1789 whose original purpose was to empower American courts to pass judgment on piracy committed on the high seas. Since 1996, human rights activists have made use of the law to bring cases against companies accused of complicity in human rights abuses committed outside the United States. So far, none of the cases has led to a conviction, but several are still outstanding, including cases against Unocal for its role in Myanmar and against Talisman for its role in Sudan (see the appendix).

The law applies only to companies that are connected to the United States either because they are registered there or because they are listed on U.S. stock exchanges. From an activist point of view, the cases have the merit of drawing public attention to alleged abuses and forcing companies to give detailed explanations of their actions. They impose a heavy cost on companies both in legal fees and in management time.

Publish What You Pay. In 2002 a coalition of nongovernmental organizations, with the backing of international financier George Soros, launched the Publish What You Pay campaign to encourage companies in the extractive sectors to make public disclosures of the signature bonuses as well as regular revenues paid to foreign governments.[19] They argue that this disclosure should be a mandatory requirement for companies listed on major stock exchanges. The U.K. government is currently leading a related initiative to seek international consensus on public disclosure of the payments that extractive industries make to governments.

Part of the motivation behind Publish What You Pay is concern about the nature of government expenditure in resource-rich states. In practice, much of the state's income tends to be spent on socially unproductive ends—such as financing weapons purchases or contributing to the personal enrichment of individual leaders. Having companies disclose their payments is the first step toward improving accountability in the government. Collective action is one of the principles underlying the campaign. Individual companies are likely to be penalized if they disclose revenue payments without authorization of the host government. Making disclosure a formal legal requirement would give them an "alibi."

The industry has responded somewhat cautiously. The International Association of Oil and Gas Producers has stated that it welcomes transparency but that this should allow for "protection of proprietary information and be within the laws of host countries as well as contractual obligations."[20] One of its particular concerns is to ensure consistency so as to avoid a situation where some, but not all, companies in a particular country (or even worldwide) might suffer an unfair competitive disadvantage.

Competition and the Costs of Compliance

The statement of the International Association of Oil and Gas Producers points to a wider concern about competitive pressures. New domestic and international laws, stock market regulations, and voluntary codes are intended to secure agreement on common standards. However, many companies worry that they may be at a disadvantage if they comply with those standards, but their competitors do not. This is more likely to be the case if the competitors are not covered by the same legislation, are not listed on the stock market (for example, if they are state-owned companies), or are simply less scrupulous.

Control Risks Group's 1999 and 2002 surveys on business attitudes to corruption (which is one aspect of a wider set of integrity problems that are likely to affect companies in weak states and conflict zones) show that international executives are still concerned about uneven levels of compliance between companies based in different countries. Respondents were asked to rate companies' likely compliance with the Foreign Corrupt Practices Act and similar anticorruption legislation according to the following four-point scale:

1. Companies have strict compliance.
2. Companies have generally high standards of compliance, but occasional lapses.
3. Companies prefer to comply but pay bribes if competitors are doing so.
4. Companies always pay bribes if it is customary to do so in the host country.

The results show a broad range of expectations (Control Risks Group 2002, p. 64). Companies from the leading OECD countries are perceived to have relatively high levels of compliance with anticorruption legislation (table 7.3). However, they now face competition from "new multinationals" based in a number of emerging markets. Among non-OECD countries, Singapore and, to a lesser extent, Hong Kong (China) rate highly, but respondents believe that companies from

Table 7.3 Standards of Compliance among Companies from Top-10 OECD Exporters, 1999 and 2002

Country	Average in 1999	Average in 2002
Canada	1.6	1.81
Germany	1.9	1.82
Netherlands	1.8	1.86
United Kingdom	1.7	1.95
United States	1.8	2.03
Belgium and Luxembourg	2.0	2.09
Japan	2.3	2.26
France	2.2	2.38
Italy	2.7	2.96
Korea, Rep. of	2.7	2.94

Source: Control Risks Group (2002).

Table 7.4 Standards of Compliance among Companies from Select Non-OECD Countries, 1999 and 2002

Country	Average in 1999	Average in 2002
Singapore	2.3	2.11
Hong Kong (China)	—	2.47
Malaysia	—	3.10
South Africa	2.6	3.10
China	2.9	3.19
India	—	3.29
Brazil	3.1	3.41

— Not available.
Source: Control Risks Group (2002).

other leading non-OECD economies are more likely to pay bribes if their competitors are doing so (table 7.4).

From a strategic point of view, large Western companies have no choice but to comply with domestic and international legislation (even if individual executives may fall short). Although there may be questions about implementation, these companies are in practice increasingly bound by voluntary ethical guidelines as well.

This does not mean that good companies are unable to operate in countries where such standards are not respected, but it may be more difficult. For example, through patient and persistent application, it may be possible to obtain a license honestly even if companies are normally expected to pay a bribe. However, the process is likely to take longer. Senior executives may decide that the high transaction costs— as measured in management time—are not justified, and the company will leave the field to smaller companies with lower standards.

Managing the Investment Cycle: What Companies Need

Extractive-industry companies face different risks at different stages of the investment cycle. This section analyzes the four main stages of a project's life—investment, construction, operation, and closure. It discusses the risks that companies face and what they need to make their projects successful. What companies most need is predictability. Effective government structures provide a framework for decisionmaking and a means of resolving disputes. However, particularly in zones of actual or potential conflict, commercial development is unlikely to be smooth. The next section analyzes the part played by different external actors in greater detail.

Exploration

Exploration involves several substages. The first takes place outside the country: the company undertakes a desktop review of all publicly available geological information to assess whether exploration is even worth considering. The next stage is to obtain an exploration license and carry out an initial geological survey. Initially, this may involve minimal disturbance—much of the information can be obtained through surveys from the air. Later on, the exploration teams may want to drill exploratory holes or to undertake seismic testing. By this point, the presence of the exploration team is highly visible in country.

The national government administers exploration licenses, and regional and local administrations may require further permits. Companies look to the government to ensure a safe operating environment, while taking responsibility for day-to-day security.

Exploration carries significant costs, particularly when it comes to drilling or seismic work, but these are much lower than the costs of development or operations. The financial stakes are higher for juniors, which are likely to have a limited number of projects in their portfolio and are more dependent on the success or failure of independent ventures.

Majors have a broader spread of assets. They expect no more than a limited number of explorations to lead to commercial discoveries. They can therefore more readily afford to abandon exploration ventures that, although somewhat promising, fall short of their requirements. At this stage, they have fewer financial hostages. Petroleum and mining companies, however, emphasize that relatively few explorations lead to commercial discoveries. At this stage, their prime concern is with geology rather than politics.

Their second concern is with physical safety. By the nature of their work, exploration teams need to travel to remote areas, often carrying expensive equipment. It may not be safe or practical to operate in regions that are affected by insurgency or political unrest. Smaller junior companies are often prepared to take greater risks than the majors.

For most companies, politics and social issues come third. Particularly among juniors, the prevailing view is "Let's deal with the geology first. The politics and the legal framework can come later—if we find anything." The majors tend to be more stringent. Some refuse even to enter countries with a reputation for high levels of corruption or political instability. The larger companies typically commission political risk assessments before they enter a country for the first time. Country-level political risk analysis is available through published sources or by subscription, for example, from the Economist Intelligence Unit, Political Risks Services, or Control Risks Group.

The physical impact of exploration is limited, but the quality of the exploration company's relationships with other interest groups has a critical impact on the future success of any project that may result. This issue is discussed in greater detail in the next section.

Construction

This is the time when the company decides whether to commit itself or not. It decides whether or not to go ahead on the basis of a feasibility report. The feasibility report also serves as a basis for negotiations with potential joint venture partners and financial backers. The report assesses the geological prospects, the commercial viability, and the political environment.

The company's environmental impact becomes more apparent during construction. At this stage, it is often necessary to build further roads and a camp for the construction force, and these need to be protected. The operators have to provide processing and waste-disposal facilities. They also need to consider how the product is going to be transported either to a smelter (in the case of metals) or to a refinery.

Companies look for predictability and security of tenure. If they cannot find these, they seek commercial agreements that provide greater compensation for what they regard as higher risks. The overall principle applies whether the company is paid through tax, royalties, or—as is becoming more common—a production-sharing agreement. Important considerations include the possibilities for arbitration in case of dispute.

This is the point at which risk assessment and planning are most important. The full impact of future operations is not yet apparent: it is still possible to take preemptive action to mitigate risks. Risk assessment therefore needs to take account not only of the current situation but also of how the project will change it.

Political and social analysis is often seen as a "soft" topic because it does not lend itself to precise measurement. The engineers who dominate the senior levels of the extractive industries tend to prefer dealing with objects that are—sometimes literally—more concrete. However, there is a general trend toward more systematic analysis, partly in the light of painful experience. Looking back at an earlier, uninformed decision to enter a conflict zone, a senior executive in a middle-size company recently commented: "Let's be honest. We just jumped into it."[21] The decision was taken on the basis of an overall assessment of the geological prospects combined with a misplaced confidence that the company's project partner would manage the political and social risks. He was not keen to repeat the experience.

Political risk forecasting is an art rather than a science: there are too many variables to make pinpoint predictions plausible. Scenario exercises help companies to assess the range of possibilities and plan for the unexpected. Royal Dutch Shell has been a leader in the scenario field.[22]

Environmental impact assessments are now an accepted part of the planning process, and they are often required by external lenders and insurers. There is also a growing demand for social impact assessments. This is a relatively new field, and it suffers from some of the same challenges as political risk analysis in that it does not lend itself to readily quantifiable predictions. However, particularly in light of the debate about the "natural resource curse," there is no doubt that it is needed. The International Association of Oil and Gas Producers and the International Petroleum Industry Environmental Conservation Association have recently produced a joint report on the management of social issues (IPIECA and OGP 2002).

Conflict risk assessment is also emerging as a separate subfield. From an aid sector perspective, the U.K. Department for International Development has recently produced a handbook on the issue (U.K. Department for International Development n.d.). The UN Global Compact (2002) has prepared a business guide for conflict impact assessment and risk management. Both texts provide overviews of the questions to ask rather than detailed manuals.[23] As with other aspects of risk analysis, the key questions include not only what is happening now but also how the petroleum or mining project will create new rivalries, tensions, and—in the worst case—pretexts for violence.

The management of the company's relationship with local communities is critical: mistakes made at this point may never be repaired. The key requirements are to secure the "informed" consent of the people who are most affected and to ensure compensation for those with land or customary rights to the area where the project will take place. Again, these issues are far from straightforward and are discussed in greater detail in the next section.

Operations

At the operations stage, both the "winners" and the "losers" are readily apparent. If all goes well, the project is producing revenue. Both the government and the company are profiting accordingly. The main "losers" are local people whose natural environment has changed radically and for the most part irrevocably. The environmental impact of the project is highly visible. This is particularly true of open-cast mines but also applies to oil and gas projects, especially on land. The flaring of unprofitable gas may cause air pollution. Damage to pipelines—whether caused by genuine accidents or by sabotage, as in Colombia—causes ground pollution. It is not surprising that the main conflicts occur at this stage.

The host government is the guarantor of the operating environment, but its interests may diverge from those of the company. The political risks are high, particularly if the government believes that the company's profits are "excessive."

The security risks also are higher than at any other point. The company will have to defend vulnerable fixed assets, and there is likely to be considerable movement to and from the site. As Colombia's experience shows, it is almost impossible to ensure full security to oil and gas pipelines. In such circumstances, companies concentrate on providing rapid repair services when pipelines are damaged.

The company's relationships with government security forces are particularly important and particularly sensitive. Companies have faced severe criticism when security forces are accused of human rights abuses while protecting their assets. Companies are typically held accountable even when—as is usually the case—the security forces are operating outside any kind of company control.

Large projects attract people looking for work, whether or not they find it. New roads may open up new parts of the country to settlement. And economic development attracts different kinds of rent seekers, whether these are corrupt officials hoping to take a share of government taxes or guerrillas seeking to levy their own "revolutionary taxes." Disputes over the proceeds of the development are common even if there was no conflict in the region in the first place. The combination of sensitive environmental issues, delicate political relationships, and security problems makes the company all the more vulnerable to criticism.

The financial risks to the company decline as income flows in, and it comes closer to payback. Once it reaches payback, it wants to benefit from the flow of profits for as long as possible, unless it receives a particularly good purchase offer. Normally, it withdraws only if the project becomes commercially unviable—for example, because of a fall in commodity prices—or the political and security situation becomes untenable because of a government takeover or a sustained threat to the lives of employees.

Closure

The main questions at this stage are environmental rehabilitation and the project's social legacy. It may not be possible to restore an open-cast mine site to its original pristine state, but the site should at least

be made safe. The prime outstanding risk to the company is reputational. The project is over, and the company wants to leave an acceptable legacy, not least so that it has a favorable chance of beginning new
projects in the same region.

From a social point of view, the main question is the future employment of people whose livelihoods have depended on the project
either directly or indirectly. That question is easier to answer if the
government and the operating company have helped to develop other
forms of employment, perhaps via a regional development plan or a
foundation. Best practice is to plan for the closure of the mine or oil
project, with this and other considerations in mind, from the inception
of the project.

Strategic Relationships: Helping and Hindering

The question of how much influence companies have, or should have,
on national and regional governments is an issue not only of power
but also of legitimacy. Business associations may lobby governments
over, for instance, tax policy. However, individual companies can
scarcely claim a mainstream political mandate. Few business people
point publicly to the deficiencies of government. Business arguably has
more legitimacy when its voice is raised in association with that of
other actors. This section discusses the part played by both formal and
informal actors, within the host country and abroad.

The National Government

The most important relationship is with the host government. Companies cannot operate without government approval, and governments
are responsible for the overall political, legal, and, to some extent,
social environment within which companies work.

After geological prospectivity and commercial viability, the quality
of a country's governance is therefore the single biggest factor in investment decisions. To the extent that governments can raise standards,
they automatically improve the environment for foreign business and
make it easier to negotiate investment from reputable companies on
more favorable terms.

Relative Bargaining Positions. The balance of power between
governments and companies is widely debated, with many nongovernmental organizations arguing that the largest multinationals have
greater resources than small or even medium-size governments. In
practice, the balance of power between them varies, but governments

enjoy what amounts to a trump card because they retain the ultimate sanction of withdrawing a company's license.

Companies are in a stronger position when the government believes that their services are essential rather than optional (as in Chad) or when they have access to sophisticated technology that is not readily available elsewhere (as may be the case in offshore West Africa). They are also in a stronger position before they make an investment, because at this stage they still retain the option of walking away. They lose this negotiating advantage once the investment is made and their costs are sunk in fixed assets.

Companies can afford to take a more relaxed view of governance issues at the exploration stage. If they find something, it takes several years for them to turn that discovery into a commercial project, and over that period the situation may improve. By contrast, the stakes, and the political risks, are much higher when they move into production.

The question of how much influence companies really enjoy has been an important part of the debate about the resource curse in Angola and the question of whether companies should publish what they pay to government. In principle, the companies are in a stronger position because relatively few firms have the skills to operate offshore. However, both in public and in private, company representatives constantly refer to the pressures of competition. If they antagonize the government, it may revoke their contract and invite a competitor to replace them. In practice, most governments hesitate to expel a mainstream Northern company in this way, but no company wants to call a government's bluff.

In making a deal with a foreign company, the government faces political risks of its own. Natural resources are part of a country's "patrimony." Selling those resources to foreigners can be portrayed as a betrayal. In practice, this kind of nationalism is often a form of protectionism put forward by the local commercial interests that have most to lose from foreign competition. This is at least one of the factors in the ongoing debate about the role of international mining companies in the Philippines.

Political leaders are conscious of the need to look after their domestic power bases if they are to retain their positions. Domestic realpolitik may or may not be consistent with liberal development strategies.

National or Personal Interests? Companies rightly point out that their commitment is to a country or to the government as a collective entity rather than to the party or individual who happens to be in power at any particular point. Rulers come and go, whereas the company aspires to stay for decades. Western companies operating in Nigeria emphasized this point in the face of calls to disinvest following Ken Saro-Wiwa's execution in 1995.

Their dilemma is that governments in developing countries are often dominated by personal or family interests. There may be little concept of the national interest, particularly long-term national interest. A representative of a major mining company recently discussed his frustrations from negotiating with an African government.[24] He argued that over a period of some 15 years or more the project would bring long-term benefit to the wider region through the construction of roads and other infrastructure. He felt that his counterparts were interested only in quick returns and personal benefits.

The overlap between personal and national concerns applied even to the relatively sophisticated government of Indonesia during the Suharto era. In that case, the Suharto family's personal interests were at least partially balanced by the planning skills of U.S.-trained economists—the so-called Berkeley Mafia. In the eyes of both local and international public opinion, it may be difficult for companies to dissociate themselves from sectional interests in their host countries.

The companies' dilemma is compounded when rulers fail to distribute the revenue derived from oil or mineral wealth equitably. In a series of interviews in October 2002, senior oil executives claimed little detailed knowledge of how governments actually spend resource revenues—the financial decisions of sovereign governments were outside their remit. However, they may suffer from the consequences of those decisions. If revenue distribution is perceived to be unfair, or to contribute to conflict, the companies are believed to share some of the blame. So, for example, nongovernmental organizations have accused foreign oil companies of helping to fuel the conflict in Sudan (see the appendix).

Provincial and Local Administrations

In the first instance, companies deal with national governments, but the quality of regional or local administrations is almost as important. If the regional government fails to give its consent, or is ineffective, the project may not be viable.

Regional administrations often argue that they receive little benefit from natural resources produced on their territory; this has been a constant theme in the strained relationship between successive provincial administrations in Baluchistan and the Pakistan national government in Islamabad. Relationships between the national and regional administrations are all the more complex when they are dominated by different ethnic groups.

In Nigeria the federal government sought to address accusations of neglect in the Niger Delta by establishing a Niger Delta Development Commission. The commission's mandate is to ensure that a proportion of oil revenue from the region is spent on local development. However, a recent report by Human Rights Watch finds that there is "virtually no control or proper audit over spending by state and local authorities" and that the commission has made little impact (Human Rights Watch 2002, p. 23). Human Rights Watch is critical both of the companies and of the government but points out: "Fundamentally, it is the failure of government to take up its responsibilities, including responsibilities to regulate corporate behavior, that has placed the oil companies in a position where they effectively substitute for government, with all the negative consequences that this report and others have illustrated" (Human Rights Watch 2002, p. 32).

If national or local governments do not deliver, then people may look to companies to fulfill some of their functions, for example, the provision of schools and medical care. However, this in itself creates problems. Companies argue that their expertise does not equip them to serve as development agencies. Also, if local people's expectations are unrealistic, they may resort to force to demand what they regard as their rights.

Local Communities

Experience underlines the need for a social "license to operate" from local communities. Again, governments often promise to look after this, but they cannot always deliver. Companies need to undertake their own consultations, but they may find it difficult to identify clear negotiating partners. For example, in the aboriginal societies of Australia decisions made by one leader may not be recognized by the community as a whole. Similarly, in the southern Philippines, Western Mining Corporation and its successors have had to deal with five subgroups of the indigenous Bla'an tribe rather than with a single entity.[25]

Current industry best practice emphasizes that good community relations are essential from the outset. For example, in a recent issue of the Rio Tinto *Review,* the company explains how it sets about diamond exploration in southern India (Morrisey 2002). Rio Tinto's exploration team made a point of visiting local villagers in advance to explain why they wanted to fly low over their fields "with two large objects that look like missiles suspended from their helicopter"—the "missiles" were special geological sensors. If people know what to expect, they are less likely to react with hostility.

The company cannot take it for granted that the government is looking after community relations, even if it promises to do so. A security manager working for an exploration company in Asia tells of a recent incident where reliance on the government proved to be a fatal mistake.[26] An exploration team was ambushed, and a geologist was killed. At first sight, it was not obvious where the attack came from. The company considered whether the ambush stemmed from a dispute between company employees who came from rival ethnic groups or was the work of refugee guerrillas from a neighboring country. It turned out that the attack had been ordered by a local tribal leader. He was not opposed to exploration per se, but he expected the company to pay due deference by coming to see him before it began to operate in his territory. The ambush was a demonstration of his power in his own territory.

During the construction period, the company will need to employ a substantial work force. Ideally, a large proportion of employees should be locals, but it is usually also necessary to import skilled labor from other parts of the country or abroad. It is important to provide them with adequate security, while minimizing the social tensions that may arise from their presence. In Papua New Guinea the presence of workers from other parts of the country—who are often regarded as "foreigners"—has been a major source of tension and has led to violence and blockades of mining sites. This is one of the factors that led to closure of the Bougainville copper mine in 1989, and it has been an issue at the Ok Tedi mine near the Papua New Guinea–Indonesian border.

Land rights also are a major concern, and again Papua New Guinea is a prominent example. It may be difficult to identify precisely who is genuinely entitled to customary land rights and therefore to compensation, particularly in a society where land rights belong to clans rather than to individuals. Customary land rights may not be formally registered, but people who believe their land rights have been infringed upon may react violently. Similar issues arise in Africa and in many other societies where access to land is the most important source of wealth and prestige. The company needs to ensure that it has addressed the concerns of everyone who has a genuine entitlement.

Some of the most sensitive community issues involve small-scale miners: local companies or individuals who use simple technology (picks and shovels) to exploit surface deposits. In many cases these may cause more environmental damage than more mainstream commercial mining, for example, when they use mercury—which then pollutes local water supplies—as part of the gold extraction process. Conflict is most likely to arise if the company claims exclusive mining rights and tries to dislodge small-scale miners from what they regard as their territory.

International Interests

Northern governments are a source of support for Northern companies in developing countries with poor governance but also present risks of their own. As with commercial companies, there may be questions about the extent to which external political influence is legitimate.

The greatest risk—particularly for U.S. companies—is the possibility that their "home" government may impose sanctions on the country where they are operating or hope to operate. The impetus for sanctions usually comes not so much from the executive branch of government as from members of Congress and their supporters. Diplomats are more likely to argue that sanctions create an unwelcome check on their freedom of maneuver.

Diplomatic representatives help companies by identifying people of influence in the host country and by giving guidance on how the local system works and the chances of success. They may also exercise political pressure to help their companies gain commercial advantage. In Control Risks Group's 2002 survey, there was a general perception that both the United States and other OECD countries resorted to this approach either "occasionally" or "regularly" (table 7.5; Control Risks Group 2002, p. 58).

Another issue is tied aid. In the past, Northern governments have linked development aid to commercial opportunities for their companies. They may do so by offering tied aid, where development funds are specifically designated for companies and experts from the donor country. Alternatively, they may offer the prospect of substantial aid grants in return for contracts in another sector. As Control Risks Group's survey shows, there is a widespread perception that both the U.S. and other OECD governments resort to such strategies either "occasionally" or

Table 7.5 How Often Do International Companies Use Political Pressure from Their Home Governments to Gain Business Advantage?
(percent)

Companies' home government	Never	Occasionally	Regularly	Nearly always	Don't know
United States	7.6	48.4	25.2	6.0	12.4
Other OECD countries	9.2	54.8	25.6	2.0	8.4

Source: Control Risks Group (2002).

Table 7.6 How Often Do International Companies
Use Tied Aid to Gain Business Advantage?
(percent)

Companies' home government	Never	Occasionally	Regularly	Nearly always	Don't know
United States	12.4	48.0	22.8	2.8	14.0
Other OECD countries	8.0	58.4	22.8	1.2	9.6

Source: Control Risks Group (2002).

"regularly" (table 7.6; Control Risks Group 2002, p. 58). Again, the legitimacy of such strategies is open to question—however effective they may be.

Improving governance is often an important component of bilateral aid programs. For example, in a recent speech to U.S. oil companies, U.S. Assistant Secretary Walter Kansteiner argues that the best way for the U.S. government to assist them in West Africa is by taking measures to curb corruption (Kansteiner 2002). Anticorruption initiatives are an increasingly important part not only of U.S. Agency for International Development programs but also of other bilateral programs, including those from Germany, Scandinavia, and the United Kingdom, and multilateral programs of international financial institutions, including the World Bank.

However, there are limits to the influence of any external agent unless there is a degree of local "buy-in." As Robert Ebel, energy program director of the Washington-based Center for Strategic and International Studies, comments with regard to West Africa, "Political jawboning and strong rhetoric can only go so far before some of the countries begin to resent the constant pressure to measure up to our standards" (cited in Vieth 2003, p. A1).

Finally, governments can also assist by helping to train host-government security forces. Currently, the most obvious example is Colombia, where U.S. armed forces are training Colombian troops to guard the Cano-Limón pipeline, which carries oil from fields developed by the U.S. company Occidental. U.S. assistance to the Colombian armed forces, however, is controversial, both in the country and abroad.

Multilateral agencies such as the World Bank or United Nations Development Programme (UNDP) face fewer political sensitivities than individual governments but nonetheless run the risk of unwarranted interference in the affairs of host governments. The International Monetary Fund (IMF), the World Bank, and UNDP all emphasize the importance of good governance in their country programs. In the long term, by enhancing governance these activities should improve the operating environment for business.

Finally, relationships between companies and nongovernmental organizations remain diverse and complex, with both sides often exhibiting a deep distrust of the other. Nevertheless, in recent years there has been greater interest on both sides in engagement and even partnership. The U.K.-based environmental group Living Earth is an example of a nongovernmental organization that has worked with Royal Dutch Shell in Nigeria—with difficulties and benefits on both sides (Heap 2000, pp. 192–213). Many other nongovernmental organizations and pressure groups continue to argue that any formal relationship with companies would compromise their independence.

Risk Sharing and Transfer

The task of the operator is to manage risks as effectively as possible on the ground, but it is obviously impossible to eliminate risks, and in any case the company may well need external sources of finance. The operators typically share or transfer risks to joint venture partners, external lenders, and insurers. Without the involvement of these parties, it may be difficult for the project to go ahead, but their participation raises new costs and demands. On the one hand, they have an interest in the financial success of the project and therefore wish to minimize costs and maximize returns. On the other hand, they may have their own standards—and face their own external pressures—on issues such as social and environmental responsibility. This section discusses the role of these third parties and the influence that they exercise.

Joint Venture Partnerships

Petroleum and mining companies enter joint venture partnerships for a variety of reasons. The first is that, in many jurisdictions, they are obliged to work with the state-owned oil or mining company. In some cases—as in the case of the Shell Petroleum Development Company in Nigeria—the state partner has majority ownership. In others, for example, Sudan, the state company may own no more than 5 percent. In either case, the participation of the state company enables the host government to maintain a higher degree of influence or control. The second main reason is that they need to raise finance and to spread the risks. Major operations in developing countries typically have two or three foreign partners. The operator is responsible for day-to-day management. External partners share the commercial risks and—as is seen in the case of Unocal in Myanmar—the reputational hazards. The third reason is that they want to gain access to technical expertise.

In all these cases, the participation of external partners can create reputational and political risks. An essential part of risk management is to conduct due diligence checks, both on potential partners' financial resources and on their reputation for integrity.

The involvement of state-owned partners is particularly likely to restrict the operator's freedom of maneuver, and the private company may be tainted by association with the host government, for example, if the latter is accused of human rights abuses. In extreme cases the state-owned partner may use its influence to take over control of the project.

The involvement of private partners also may lead to reputational risks that have to be managed. Companies seek joint venture partners that are well connected, often by virtue of senior executives' personal connections with political leaders. Those connections may backfire if the political leaders have a reputation for corruption or if the local partner takes advantage of local contacts to try to seize control of the venture.

Commercial codes of conduct now typically contain a phrase to the effect that the company will seek to ensure that its own standards are applied in joint venture operations. However, companies acknowledge that it is difficult to do more than influence projects where they do not have majority control.

Project Finance

Companies may raise external finance either from private financial institutions or from multilateral agencies such as the World Bank's private sector affiliate, the International Finance Corporation (IFC). As in the case of the Chad-Cameroon pipeline discussed in the appendix, companies value the involvement of influential multilateral agencies because they believe that host countries are less likely to back away from agreements involving institutions that give them valuable support in other areas. If the World Bank institutions are involved, projects must comply with their social and environmental guidelines.

The disadvantage of raising funds through project finance is that deals are often time-consuming, raise costs, and add complexity (MacDonald 1998). Companies regard them not so much as a panacea as one among several tools for mitigating risks.

Insurance

The combination of the global economic downturn with the aftermath of the September 11 terrorist attacks has led to a significant hardening of the insurance market. The global capacity of the main reinsurance companies has shrunk from some $800 billion to $600 billion.[27] In all classes of insurance, clients are asked to carry a higher proportion of potential losses than before; they are required to present more detailed evidence of measures taken to mitigate risks; and their policies are more tightly worded. Against this background, it is more difficult to obtain risk cover for projects in developing countries, particularly where there is a high risk of conflict.

Political risk insurance has traditionally focused on three main areas:

- Expropriation, including arbitrary governmental renegotiation of contracts as well as outright confiscation
- Currency transfer
- War and civil disturbances.

Insurance is not available for many other kinds of risk that might be classified as "political," for example, reputational damage arising from the campaigns of nongovernmental organizations.

Larger companies such as British Petroleum increasingly manage their own insurance requirements, either through captive companies or through some other financial provision. Other companies comment that political risk insurance is an extra cost that they prefer not to incur. However, they may be forced to do so by the demands of external lenders.[28]

Private Political Risk Insurance Market

Lloyd's of London provides the largest market for political risk insurance and services brokers acting for a wide variety of international clients. Political risk insurance is also available on U.S. markets, notably via the AIG Group.

The availability of insurance cover is often determined—somewhat arbitrarily—by the amount of capacity assigned to individual countries or classes of risk by insurers and reinsurers. However, a senior Lloyd's broker interviewed for this chapter insisted that there were "bags of capacity" for "good projects," including, for example, a well-designed oil or mining project in Africa. From an underwriter's point of view, the definition of a good project is often one that involves a well-known company with a favorable record. Typically this means a large Western firm. An application for insurance from a junior or less well-known company requires closer scrutiny. He added that insurers might influence the financial structure of a deal but seldom have the power to decide whether it goes ahead or not: "If a project is going to happen, it's going to happen."

Public Insurance Market

In the late 1990s, it was widely argued that there was now less need for
official insurance agencies because their role had been supplanted by
the private market. This is scarcely heard after September 11. It is now
generally accepted that public sector insurance has an important role in
supplementing the limited capacity of the private market. This is particularly important in, among other areas, insurance for new projects
in high-risk developing countries.

Corporate responsibility issues relating to the environment, corruption, and social impact are increasingly on the agendas of all the public
insurers, and they are passing on this concern to their clients.

Multilateral Investment Guarantee Agency.   The Multilateral Investment Guarantee Agency (MIGA) is the insurance arm of the World
Bank. Since its inception, it has issued more than 600 guarantees in
82 countries for a total of $11 billion in coverage and facilitated an
estimated $47 billion of foreign direct investment (*MIGA News,*
November 26, 2002). Companies say that applications to MIGA are
more complicated and time-consuming than working with the private
sector. However, as with the International Finance Corporation, they
value MIGA's involvement because of the extra political weight carried
by the World Bank Group.

MIGA typically offers longer coverage—15 to 20 years—than is
available on the private market. However, its particular value to its
commercial clients lies less in the actual amounts that it insures than in
the political influence that it exercises via the World Bank. It is understood that host countries are reluctant to antagonize the World Bank
by threatening MIGA-sponsored projects, and, throughout the organization's history, there has been only one claim. In other cases, MIGA
has mediated between its clients and host governments to resolve
problems that might otherwise have led to claims. MIGA actively promotes collaboration with private sector insurers, and these are generally more willing to insure projects once MIGA has taken the lead.

MIGA has played a role in promoting investment in post-conflict
regions—it is currently seeking to work with would-be investors in
Serbia. Among African countries, Mozambique is widely regarded as
a post-conflict "graduate," and MIGA is proud of its role in promoting investment there. The projects with which it is associated include
the $1.3 billion Mozal aluminum smelter, which is a joint venture of
South Africa's Industrial Development Corporation, BHP Billiton, and
Mitsubishi Corporation ("Encouraging FDI in Mozambique" 2002).
MIGA is providing $40 million in coverage for loan guarantees issued
by the Industrial Development Corporation. It has also extended

$70 million in guarantee coverage to Eskom, the South African electricity company, for new facilities supplying electricity to Mozal. The Mozal project has demonstrated a concern for corporate citizenship by setting up the Mozal Community Development Trust, a trust fund that supports communities around the smelter.

Some 9 percent of MIGA's portfolio goes to mining projects, and it has been particularly active in promoting new mining ventures in Africa, for example, by sponsoring investment conferences. MIGA's links with the mining sector have led to criticism from the U.S. wing of Friends of the Earth on the grounds of sponsoring industries that are environmentally damaging. MIGA has countered by pointing out that the mining sector was the most promising avenue for development in many African countries and emphasizing that it follows World Bank guidelines designed to mitigate social and environmental impact. MIGA's involvement may lead to higher standards being applied in these areas than would otherwise be the case.

MIGA is currently putting particular emphasis on promoting investment by small and medium-size enterprises and international companies based in developing countries. It is putting a particular focus on Africa.

African Trade Insurance Agency. The African Trade Insurance Agency came into existence in January 2001 and has its headquarters in Nairobi. Its purpose is to supplement the private sector by facilitating or providing political risk insurance for "trade, investments, and other productive activities" in African countries where it would otherwise be difficult to find cover. The risks it covers include war and civil disturbances as well as currency inconvertibility, expropriation, and other forms of government interference.

The agency is independent, but its startup expenses were covered by the International Development Agency and the European Union, as well as $105 million lent by the seven participating countries: Burundi, Kenya, Malawi, Rwanda, Tanzania, Uganda, and Zambia. The first layer of any losses will fall on the capital loaned to participating countries by the World Bank, and it is hoped that this will give them a strong incentive to prevent and mitigate the causes of claims.

The rationale for setting up the agency is to boost confidence among companies that see commercial opportunities in Africa but are worried about political risks. African Trade Insurance Agency Chairman Hakainde Hichilema has commented, "In Africa we realize that if we are to achieve the growth rates of 7 percent per annum over the next 10 to 15 years that will be required to achieve significant and sustainable poverty reduction, we need a vibrant private sector that is willing to invest in Africa's future" (Bolger 2001). The agency currently covers trade insurance rather than investment—it would be able to cover the risks of failure to pay for expensive equipment imported for a mine, but not the mine itself.

Export Credit Agencies. Most OECD countries have their own export credit agencies: the Export Credit Guarantee Department (ECGD) in the United Kingdom, Hermes in Germany, COFACE in France, the Overseas Private Investment Corporation in the United States, and Export Development Canada in Canada. The export credit agencies' relationships with their respective governments differ. For example, ECGD is partially privatized, whereas the Overseas Private Investment Corporation is still wholly owned by the U.S. government. However, the Overseas Private Investment Corporation expects to cover its costs through premiums and to that extent operates in the same way as a commercial corporation. There has often been tension between export credit agencies' dual role as quasi-commercial entities and official agencies whose activities are expected to reflect government policy.

Partly as a result of this tension, the role of export credit agencies has come under scrutiny from nongovernmental organizations and politicians in both Europe and North America: To what extent do they promote responsible businesses? Or are they more likely to be associated with companies that are corrupt or damage the environment? If so, are their activities acceptable for public bodies financed by taxpayers? They have responded by introducing codes of conduct and by imposing tighter requirements on client companies to ensure that they have not been involved in corruption and that they conduct proper environmental impact assessments.

Export Development Canada is widely considered to be a leader in this field. It has introduced strict requirements for companies to guarantee that they will not pay bribes to win contracts abroad, and it expects them to conduct detailed environmental impact assessments for major projects. Its concern for sustainable development also covers the social impact of projects. However, it is not quite so explicit in its requirements on social issues, possibly because the methodology for social, as distinct from environmental, impact assessments is less developed.

Similarly, ECGD in the United Kingdom has indicated that it will, "when considering support [for a project], look not only at the payment risks but also at the underlying quality of the project, including its environmental, social, and human rights impacts" (ECGD 2000). However, it will not take an absolutist approach. It goes on to say that ECGD's approach in determining whether to support a project will be "one of constructive engagement with a view to achieving necessary improvements in the project's impacts."

The export credit agencies are backed by the states in which they operate, but they function like private sector institutions in that they are expected to be self-financing. They are expected to insist on high social and environmental standards, but there may be tension between this role and the task of meeting their commercial objectives.

Incentives for Collective Action

The Sudan and Myanmar case studies offer discouraging lessons for Northern companies that are considering new investments in conflict-affected countries (see the appendix). Almost by definition, such countries are likely to have weak governments, and there is a high risk—particularly for oil or mining companies—of being caught in controversy over corruption, poor governance, or conflict. The current debate on the natural resource curse will lend weight to the controversy.

In late 2002 the British company Premier Oil announced plans to withdraw from Myanmar, and the Canadian company Talisman Energy said that it would sell its assets in Sudan. Both companies were able to claim that their ventures and their eventual sales had been profitable. However, Talisman explicitly pointed to the disproportionate impact of Sudan's high political risk rating on its share price. Both companies introduced community development programs, but these were not sufficient to defuse criticisms that the national impact of their presence—their contributions to supporting controversial regimes—was more important than any local impact that might or might not have been alleviated by their social programs.

The Chad-Cameroon case study is more hopeful, but its success remains unproven (see the appendix). If all goes well, it may prove to be a model for similar projects. However, it will be difficult to repeat some of the conditions that have allowed the project to take its present form. In particular, the World Bank gained greater leverage from the fact that the project was completely new and that Chad badly needed the income it would bring. ExxonMobil and its partners made clear that they would not proceed without Bank participation. This kind of leverage may not be available elsewhere, and in any case, the negotiating advantage that the World Bank and the companies now enjoy will diminish as the project proceeds. Ultimately, the success of the Chad-Cameroon project depends on the integrity and vision of the Chad government and, no doubt, its Cameroonian counterpart.

Collaborative Initiatives to Promote Best Practice

As the Chad, Myanmar, Sudan, and case studies show, it is difficult for international companies to justify their presence in countries with poor governance records unless they can demonstrate that they are a positive force for change. However, this raises questions about the extent to which companies have a mandate to influence host governments and societies beyond their immediate commercial responsibilities. Recent experience suggests that companies can play a valuable role in building up local technical and commercial capacity (see Nelson 2000). However, their role is most likely to be accepted if they work in partnership with other actors. There are now a number of examples of such collaboration.

The U.S.-U.K. Voluntary Principles on Security and Human Rights. One of the most important facets of governments is that they have convening power. The U.S.-U.K. voluntary principles provide an example.

The U.S. State Department and U.K. Foreign and Commonwealth Office together convened a series of meetings involving leading human rights nongovernmental organizations and companies in the extractive industries.[29] The participants agreed on a set of voluntary principles covering risk assessments and guidelines for company relationships with both government and private security forces. Among other undertakings, companies will inform the authorities of any "credible allegations of human rights abuses by public security" and use their influence to prevent any recurrences.

The two governments played a particularly important role in convening the meetings. Without their authority, it is questionable whether they would have taken place so quickly or so successfully. Some nongovernmental organizations have questioned the value of principles that are voluntary rather than statutory. However, they set an important benchmark, and it would have been difficult to secure agreement so quickly if they had not been voluntary.

The Dutch and Norwegian governments are participating in follow-up discussions, and Exxon has signed up to the principles. Now the most important challenge is to put the principles in practice and to secure the cooperation of host governments. The participants are focusing on Colombia, Indonesia, and Nigeria as test cases.

International Alert: Business Diversification in Azerbaijan. In 1999 International Alert, a London-based not-for-profit organization, began an initiative to engage multinational companies investing in Azerbaijan in a multiple-stakeholder dialogue (Killick n.d.). Azerbaijan is expected to receive some $10 billion of investment over the next few years, much of it in the oil and gas industry. Investment on this scale has the potential to stimulate social and economic growth but may also deepen inequalities and increase the risks of corruption. The dialogue is designed to find ways of preventing oil investment from triggering conflict.

One of the themes identified by the project is the need for business diversification so that the economy is not overly dependent on petroleum. Participants have set up the Business Development Alliance to promote the growth of the private sector. The Business Development Alliance is a network of international and local companies and business associations, government, international and local nongovernmental organizations, and international development agencies. It serves to enhance coordination between different initiatives, identify gaps in Azerbaijan's economic development, and develop strategies to address them.

The Business Development Alliance is keen to promote local entrepreneurship. Among other activities, it has set up a supplier database to provide an instant connection between buyers and sellers, and it is encouraging the creation of new institutions to increase the availability of credit to local companies.

Danish Industries: Capacity Building through Chambers of Commerce. A valuable example of a set of bilateral initiatives comes from Danish Industries, the Danish employers' federation, which has been working with its counterparts in China, Ghana, Lithuania, Tanzania, Uganda, and Zimbabwe to build up their technical capacity (Danish Industries 2001). Among other measures, Danish Industries has been advising its international counterparts on advocacy strategies. In turn, the local chambers have been advising their own governments on best practice, for example, on commercial law reform, an issue with important implications for the fight against corruption.

Statoil: Sponsorship of Judicial Training in Venezuela. In 1999 Statoil Venezuela, a subsidiary of the Norwegian company Statoil, formed a partnership with UNDP, the local branch of Amnesty International, and the Consejo de la Judicatura, which is the branch of the judiciary responsible for training and administration.[30] In the first phase of the project, which began in 1999, Statoil sponsored a series of training-the-trainers sessions on human rights issues. The sessions involved 24 specially selected judges and were conducted by Amnesty International in collaboration with the judiciary. In the second phase, which began after some delay in 2001, the original trainees conducted a series of follow-up training sessions for judges in two states.

Statoil's main contribution was financial, and it was not directly involved in the actual training. The course nevertheless demonstrated Statoil's commitment to human rights values and contributed to capacity building in the host country.

Policy Recommendations

So far the main participants in the debate about the natural resource curse have been large Northern companies, Northern governments, international nongovernmental organizations, and multilateral institutions such as the United Nations, United Nations Development Programme, and the World Bank. Given the high reputational risks, the companies that are most likely to work in conflict zones are juniors and Southern companies, which hope that their willingness to take high risks will enable them to catch up with the more established Northern majors. This underlines the need to involve a variety of different actors— including Southern governments and smaller companies from both North and South in the search for solutions to the problems of poor governance.

Engage Juniors and Southern Companies

A variety of levers can be used to influence both Northern juniors and Southern state-owned companies.

Juniors rarely have the resources to develop major finds. Sooner or later they seek partnerships with larger companies. They have less chance of finding the right partners if their project is caught up in controversy. As Talisman's experience shows, human rights controversies influence their stock market listings.

Companies that are wholly or partially state-owned are in principle free from the pressures of the stock market (although some are in the process of being wholly or partly privatized). However, they may be open to other forms of influence. Governments, like companies, should wish to avoid being implicated in human rights controversies.

One of the main arguments of this chapter concerns the importance of partnerships. It may be difficult to persuade nongovernmental organizations and even members of multilateral agencies to work with controversial companies. Apart from other considerations, they may well be concerned about the implications for their own reputations, and they may suspect the companies of trying to "buy" respectability.

It is not possible or practical to engage all types of companies. However, it will be difficult to make progress unless all parties are prepared to take on tough cases, including companies that have been involved in past controversies and even *causes celebres* but now wish to learn from their mistakes.

Engage Southern Governments

The U.S.-U.K. Voluntary Principles on Human Rights and Security involve Northern rather than Southern governments. The participants in the voluntary principles process are conscious of the need to involve their Southern counterparts, and there have been initiatives in this direction in Colombia, Indonesia, and Nigeria, but these are still at an early stage. Similar initiatives need to be pursued in other arenas.

Publicize the "Self-Interest" Argument

The role of business in conflict regions has moral and legal as well as very practical aspects. Bad practice—for example, the failure to consult local communities—often has direct, physical consequences that may make the project totally unviable as well as threaten the lives of company and government employees. Bougainville in Papua New Guinea is one of the starkest examples of a profitable project that has been forced to close down completely. This argument is powerful and still not widely understood. It may be one means of engaging Southern governments.

Develop Expertise in Social and Conflict Risk Assessment

Companies are familiar with geological, financial, and engineering risk assessments. However, the field of social impact assessment is much less well developed, partly because there are too many variables for assessments to lend themselves to pinpoint predictions.

Past failures to anticipate complex problems arising from extractive-industry developments demonstrate the need for more sophisticated social impact and conflict risk assessments. The UN Global Compact has made a beginning with its business guide to conflict impact assessment and risk management, and the International Association of Oil and Gas Producers and the International Petroleum Industry Environmental Conservation Association have recently published their report on managing social issues in oil and gas projects. However, there is a clear need for more work to refine expertise in this area. This developing field is one area where it would be worthwhile to engage Southern actors—companies, governments, academics, and nongovernmental organizations.

Involve the Insurance Sector

Export Development Canada and other export credit agencies are already requiring environmental and social impact assessments. They have an interest in developing effective tools to ensure that these are carried out effectively. Both the private and the public sectors should be more explicit in offering lower premiums to companies that carry out detailed risk assessments and take steps to mitigate the risks that are identified. MIGA is specifically promoting South-South investment. It should use its influence to promote high standards among the companies that it sponsors.

Promote Economic Diversification

One aspect of the resource curse is the lack of economic diversification, and this can lead to outright conflict as well as a distorted economy. The need for diversification is one of the issues that emerge from risk assessments. Companies, governments, and local civil society should work together to develop integrated regional development strategies.

Promote Transparency

There is now an emerging national and international legal regime covering companies that pay bribes outside their home countries. It is essential to ensure that laws are implemented in the North and to build capacity in the South. In particular, Northern governments need to demonstrate that they are meeting their side of the bargain by implementing the new anticorruption laws passed as a result of the 1997 OECD convention. This means publicizing the laws, distributing them to their own business constituencies (surveys by both Transparency International and Control Risks Group demonstrate high levels of ignorance and complacency about the new laws), and prosecuting offenders. So far, no country apart from the United States has prosecuted offenders under the new anticorruption laws. At the same time, it is important to help build government and judicial capacity in the South. Anticorruption initiatives are now an important feature of many multilateral and bilateral aid programs. This trend should continue.

Business people express concern that the Publish What You Pay transparency initiative is flawed because it does not cover all types of companies. However, this is not a sufficient reason not to promote the initiative. As with anticorruption legislation, it is useful for companies to have an "alibi" so that they can tell officials that they have no choice but to comply.

Local civil society organizations may play an important role in monitoring both public and private projects and identifying serious problems at an early stage. If they are to play this role effectively, they may need training to build up their expertise.

Promote Government and Public Understanding of Business

One by-product of greater transparency may be a greater public understanding of business risk. Companies frequently complain that government officials do not understand the principles of business. Both governments and companies have a role to play in explaining why and how companies make decisions.

Support the Refinement of Laws on Human Rights and Business

Many nongovernmental organizations and other observers point to the apparent contradiction that the legal principles covering transnational corruption are now well covered in international law, whereas there is much less clarity on the arguably more important (and diffuse) topic of business responsibility for human rights. Developing an international legal consensus is a complex process, but the draft UN document "Responsibilities of Transnational Corporations and Other Business Enterprises with Regard to Human Rights" is an important step.

Companies tend to resist new regulation. Trade ministries and business associations need to put greater emphasis on the argument that clear legal regulation strengthens rather than impedes good companies.

Work with Industry Groups

Industry associations and chambers of commerce have an important role in disseminating best practice. One disadvantage is a tendency—like armies—to proceed at the pace of their slowest members in the hope of achieving consensus.

An alternative approach is to set up ad hoc self-selected groups of best-of-class companies in the hope that they will pave the way for other companies in their sector. This kind of approach has had some success in international banks' development of the Wolfsberg principles against money laundering as well as the U.S.-U.K. voluntary principles. It would be helpful to set up a similar group, involving Southern companies from the start, to look at other conflict-related issues.

Involve Business in "Track 2" Post-Conflict Diplomacy

Companies do not have—and should not expect to have—a seat at post-conflict conference tables. That would rightly raise questions of political legitimacy. However, they may be able to play a role on the sidelines, giving technical advice on economic issues or, more broadly, opening up alternative visions of the future. Public sector actors should encourage this.

In the final stages of apartheid in South Africa, a mixed group of private, government, and opposition participants worked together to develop influential alternative scenarios of the future at Montfleur (near Cape Town), using scenario techniques refined by Shell. Similar processes and techniques may be applicable in other conflicts.

Take Time

Once mining and petroleum projects get under way, they take on a momentum of their own. Companies have put in large initial investments and are keen to get a return as soon as possible. Otherwise, they "might as well put their money in the bank" (a much-repeated cliché in the extractive sectors). However, people need time to absorb what may be momentous social and environmental change. It may be better to proceed slowly—and reduce the risk of conflict—than to press ahead rapidly and risk losing the project.

Appendix: Case Studies

Sudan

Sudan is the largest country in Africa and one of the poorest. International oil companies began exploration in the early 1980s, and oil first came on stream in the late 1990s. The country is understood to have substantial oil reserves that are as yet untapped. In principle, petroleum could provide the economic development needed to lift Sudan out of poverty.

However, Sudan has been divided by a fierce north-south civil war. The main oil reserves are in the south, but protected by the north, and both Sudanese opposition figures and international nongovernmental organizations have accused foreign oil companies of collusion with the Khartoum regime. There are two main concerns. The first is the extent to which international companies have been directly or indirectly associated with civil rights abuses in and around their main operating areas. The second is the accusation that oil is "fueling" the civil war by helping to finance purchases of military equipment.

The Canadian company Talisman faced particularly severe criticism, both in Canada and in the United States. Talisman vigorously defended its position, but in October 2002 it announced plans to sell its Sudan operations to an Indian company, ONGC Videsh. The Sudan case study illustrates both the controversies encountered by international companies operating in conflict zones and the contrasting exposure of Western and non-Western companies.

Opportunities. Sudan is classic territory for junior companies. There is general agreement both on its geological potential and on its currently high political risks. Companies that take the risk of operating there are well placed to make substantial profits if they can produce oil in difficult conditions and still better placed if the political situation improves.

Two international consortia are active in Sudan. The first is the Greater Nile Petroleum Operating Corporation, which consists of China National Petroleum Corporation (40 percent), Petronas (Malaysia, 25 percent), Talisman (Canada, 25 percent), and Sudapet (Sudan, 5 percent). The Greater Nile Petroleum Operating Corporation is producing oil in the Unity (Block 1) and Heglig (Block 4) fields and is exploring in Block 4. These are north of the Bahr-el-Ghazal. The consortium members operate the fields jointly and in 2001 produced a total of 32.1 million barrels of oil worth $674 million (Talisman Energy 2001, p. 26).

The second consortium consists of Lundin Petroleum (Sweden, 40 percent), OMV (Austria, 26 percent), Petronas (Malaysia, 26 percent), and Sudapet (Sudan, 5 percent); these operate in Block 5A, south of the Bahr el-Ghazal. Lundin, the operator, made a significant initial discovery in 1999 and sank two further appraisal wells in 2001. However, further exploration has been suspended since January 2002, as most of the block has been inaccessible for security reasons.

The French company TotalFinaElf has a stake in an exploration block in the south of the country, but this is currently in force majeure.

Political Context. Sudan's first north-south civil war broke out soon after independence in 1956 and continued until 1972. Fighting broke out again in 1983 and continues today. An estimated 2 million people are believed to have been killed as a result of the fighting. The social repercussions of the conflict include the widespread displacement of refugees, both in Sudan and in neighboring countries, as well as increased malnutrition and mortality from infectious diseases (see, for example, Médécins sans Frontières 2002).

The issues dividing north and south include religion, ethnicity, and the distribution of resources. Both halves of the country are ethnically diverse, but the north is predominantly Muslim, with close cultural links to North Africa and the Middle East. By contrast, most southerners are either Christian or animist and have closer cultural affinities with neighboring Sub-Saharan African countries to the south. Successive southern leaders have argued that their region has been marginalized by northern rulers.

The present Khartoum government came to power in 1989 as a result of a military coup and, particularly in its early years, adopted a strongly Islamist political stance. However, it is now keen to develop closer relations with Western countries.

The neighboring countries of Djibouti, Eritrea, Ethiopia, Kenya, and Uganda are taking part in the Inter-Governmental Authority on Development peace process under Kenya's chairmanship. In July 2002 negotiations between the Khartoum government and the southern-based Sudan People's Liberation Army (SPLA) led to the signing of the Machakos protocol. The protocol outlined provisional agreement on the south's right to self-determination. After the formal peace treaty is signed, there will be a transitional period of six years during which the states in the south will enjoy a degree of autonomy, followed by an internationally supervised referendum on the status of the south. This will include the option of independence. *Sharia* (Islamic law) will apply in the north, but not in the south. There have been further rounds of negotiations since July, but at the time of writing (February 2003), no final agreement.

The United States imposed commercial sanctions on Sudan in 1996 because of the country's reported links with international terrorists, and no U.S. companies operate in Sudan. However, in 2001 the U.S. government appointed former senator John C. Danforth to serve as a special envoy to promote the Sudan peace process. In October 2002 U.S. President George Bush signed the Sudan Peace Act, which commits the U.S. government to support the Sudan peace process but also to impose sanctions on the government if it "has not engaged in good faith negotiations to achieve a permanent, just, and equitable peace agreement or has unreasonably interfered with humanitarian efforts." Potential sanctions include a U.S. veto on loans to Sudan by international financial institutions, the downgrading of diplomatic ties with Sudan, and U.S. initiatives to seek a United Nations (UN) arms embargo against Sudan.

Norway and the United Kingdom have appointed their own special envoys, and France has announced plans to do so as well.

Oil Development. The conflict began before the discovery of oil in commercial quantities. Oil is therefore not a prime cause of the conflict, but the future distribution of oil revenue is one of the main outstanding issues in the Inter-Governmental Authority on Development peace negotiations.

Oil exploration in Sudan began in the late 1950s, but the first significant discoveries were made by the U.S. company Chevron in southern Sudan in the early 1980s. In 1984, soon after the resumption of the civil war, southern rebels kidnapped and killed three expatriate Chevron employees. The civil war prevented development of the newly discovered fields, and Chevron pulled out in 1990.

The most recent phase in the country's petroleum development began in 1997 following the signing of the Khartoum Peace Agreement between the government and six ethnic Nuer rebel groups who had broken away from the SPLA. The Khartoum agreement brought a temporary peace to the areas of Unity and Western Upper Nile Province immediately north and south of the Bahr-el-Ghazal River and made it possible to resume oil exploration. The Khartoum agreement brought no more than a temporary local peace, as some of the leaders who signed the agreement defected back to the SPLA.

Activism of Nongovernmental Organizations. Sudan attracts the attention of international nongovernmental organizations with a variety of mandates, including the following:

• *Secular aid and relief agencies.* Action Contre la Faim, CARE, German Agro-Aid, Médécins sans Frontières, Oxfam, Red Cross/Red Crescent, Save the Children Fund.

• *Church-related organizations.* Christian Aid, Christian Solidarity International, DanChurch Aid, Norwegian Church Aid, Pax Christi, Samaritan's Purse (United States), Sudan Focal Point (currently based in South Africa), Tear Fund, World Vision.

• *Human rights.* Amnesty International, Human Rights Watch, Justice Africa (antislavery organizations such as the American Anti-Slavery Group form an important subcategory of human rights groups).

• *Policy and conflict resolution.* International Crisis Group.

Sudan attracts attention first and foremost because of the humanitarian impact of the war. The churches in the south of the country have been able to build links and publicize their concerns via Christian organizations in Western Europe and North America. One of those concerns is the role of international petroleum companies.

The Campaign against International Oil Companies. International attention has focused on Talisman more than on any of the other companies. Talisman is listed on the Toronto and New York stock exchanges, and Sudan-related nongovernmental organizations are more active in Canada and the United States than in any of the other companies' home countries. Their campaign tactics have included calls on individuals and institutions to divest shares in the company, questions at the company's annual general meetings, and political pressure.

In 2000 the Canadian government published a formal inquiry on human security in Sudan, known after its chairman as the Harker report. The report was critical of Talisman's role in Sudan, but the government subsequently decided to take no formal action. In the United States, members of Congress called for the Sudan Peace Act to contain a clause banning companies active in Sudan from raising funds on the New York Stock Exchange. The final wording of the act left out this requirement. However, Talisman faced a class-action lawsuit under the Alien Torts Claims Act because of allegations that it asked the Sudanese government to remove villagers from the vicinity of its oil fields in 1999.

Talisman vigorously defended its record in Sudan but in October 2002 announced plans to sell its 25 percent stake in Greater Nile Petroleum Operating Corporation to the Indian company ONGC Videsh. Talisman chief executive officer Jim Buckee's comment on the sale was to reaffirm that the company's presence in Sudan had been a force for good—he alluded to the company's social projects—and to assert that the ongoing peace process raised hopes for the future. However, he also stated that controversy over the company's presence in the country had had a damaging impact on its share price: "Talisman's shares have continued to be discounted based on perceived political risk in-country and in North America to a degree that was unacceptable for 12 percent of our production. Shareholders have told me they were tired of continually having to monitor and analyze events relating to Sudan" (Talisman Energy 2002).

ONGC Videsh is a part state-owned company. Its proposed acquisition of Talisman's share in Sudan received Indian cabinet approval in line with New Delhi's strategic objective of improving access to vitally needed oil supplies (Watts 2002). In early 2003 Romanian and Turkish companies also expressed interest in entering the country (Kerr 2003; "Turkish Companies Interested" 2003).

Issues. The controversy over the presence of Western oil companies in Sudan, and Talisman's eventual sale, highlights many of the questions raised in this chapter. In particular, what is the extent of oil companies' responsibilities toward a sovereign government in a region of conflict?

After Chevron withdrew, Sudan was unable to attract any of the major companies despite its favorable geological prospects. The political, security, and reputational risks made the costs of entry too high. By contrast, the country was able to attract interest from smaller Northern companies and from Southern companies that are wholly or partially state-owned.

Of all the companies operating in Sudan, Talisman has attracted the most attention. Its listing on the U.S. and Canadian stock markets meant that it was more exposed to nongovernmental organization pressure and political activism in those countries. Canadian churches and other organizations were able to claim a special sense of responsibility because a company from their own country was involved in a war zone. Lundin and OMV have also faced criticism from churches and nongovernmental organizations in their own countries, but on a smaller scale.

The criticisms levied against the oil companies have been partly "local" and partly "national." At a local level, Talisman was accused of benefiting from military operations to depopulate the regions immediately surrounding the oil fields (see, for example, Christian Aid 2001). At the national level, the company was accused of helping to finance the conflict through the revenue that it produced.

In its report *Corporate Social Responsibility 2001,* Talisman pointed to its limited ability to influence the government on security issues. It had advocated the signing of a security agreement between the government and Greater Nile Petroleum Operating Corporation. Among other provisions, the draft agreement stipulated that the government would adhere to the UN Code of Conduct for Law Enforcement Officials and the UN Basic Principles on the Use of Force and Firearms by Law Enforcement Officials. However, the government rejected the draft agreement, arguing that "the provision of security is the prime responsibility and prerogative of governments and that these issues were not appropriate to be addressed by a company residing in and operating under the laws of Sudan" (Talisman Energy 2001, p. 17).

More positively, the company managed to secure the government's agreement to publish a summary of oil revenues and said that it would "continue to advocate for the expenditure of oil-related revenue for peaceful purposes" (Talisman Energy 2001, p. 26). However, it added that speaking to the government on its own was not enough to facilitate the desired changes; there must be involvement by other institutions, including international financial institutions.

In 2001 Talisman budgeted $2 million for community development projects: not all of it was spent, but the balance was put into trust to be allocated when appropriate projects were identified. Greater Nile Petroleum Operating Corporation as a collective entity spent $1.8 million on upstream community projects and a further $850,000 on downstream projects along the oil pipeline to Port Sudan. Talisman undertook to ensure the continuity of its own projects at least until 2005, whether the sale of its assets to ONGC Videsh went ahead or not. Community development projects may be good in themselves, but critics of the oil companies say that they are of little weight in the wider context of civil war.

Questions for the Future. The most important question is the outcome of the Sudan peace process. If the government and the SPLA are able to agree on a cease-fire and a political framework to decide the country's future, then many other problems will become much easier to solve. Reports of the negotiations in February 2003 were relatively optimistic (for example, Rosenberg 2003). Even if an agreement is signed, this will be the beginning of a new stage rather than the end of the peace process. Both sides will require years to build up the institutions needed to bring lasting stability.

Myanmar (Burma)

Myanmar has many issues in common with Sudan. Both countries have a history of conflict between an authoritarian regime and ethnic minorities, and in both cases petroleum is emerging as one of the prime sources of foreign exchange. Western petroleum companies have faced vigorous campaigns calling on them to withdraw, particularly in the United States and the United Kingdom. The U.S. company Unocal faces a long-standing legal case under the Alien Torts Claims Act on account of accusations that it is complicit in human rights abuses inflicted by the Myanmar army.

Opportunities. Commercial development of Myanmar's oil industry began during the British colonial period in the nineteenth century. However, from 1962 until 1988, the country's military regime adopted the so-called Burmese Path to Socialism. Foreign oil companies were nationalized, and Myanmar aspired to a policy of economic self-reliance. This policy changed in late 1988 following a series of bloody popular protests demanding democratic reform. These led to the seizure of power by a new military junta, the State Law and Order Restoration Council (SLORC), which began to open up the country to foreign investment once more.

International companies saw a combination of political and technical opportunity. In the late 1980s and early 1990s several international companies took advantage of the country's new economic policies to revive onshore oil and gas exploration. They hoped that new technology would enable them to find and develop reserves that had been neglected during the colonial period. Onshore exploration proved disappointing, but there have been significant offshore gas finds. The main market for the gas is in neighboring Thailand.

Currently, there are two offshore gas fields. The Yadana field is operated by the French company TotalFinaElf (31 percent), Unocal (United States, 28 percent), PTT Exploration and Production (Thailand, 26 percent), and Myanmar Oil and Gas Enterprise (15 percent). Investment in the field is on the order of $1.2 billion, and it is expected to bring the government annual royalties of some $100 million. The Yetagun field is operated by a joint venture of Petronas (Malaysia), Nippon-Mitsubishi Oil (Japan), and Myanmar Oil and Gas Enterprise. The field was originally operated by the U.S. company Texaco, which withdrew in 1998. Premier (United Kingdom) then took over, but itself withdrew in 2002.

Political Risks. International companies in Myanmar face a variety of risks arising from the country's unresolved political dilemmas. There are two overriding issues: the prospects for national democratic reform and the relationship between the majority Burman population and the country's many ethnic minorities, who together make up some 35 percent of the population. Political uncertainty will continue to hamper economic development until these issues are resolved.

SLORC promised to introduce democratic reform and held multiparty parliamentary elections in 1990. The opposition National League for Democracy won a sweeping majority. However, SLORC prevented the new Parliament from convening, and opposition leader Aung San Suu Kyi was placed under house arrest. More recently, intermittent talks have been taking place between Aung San Suu Kyi and the military leadership (now renamed the State Peace and Development Council). Both sides have expressed optimism that it will eventually be possible to achieve some kind of settlement but, at the time of writing (February 2003), there had been no breakthrough.

The unresolved national political debate creates risks for international companies at several levels. First, a future democratic regime may question agreements signed while the armed forces were in power. Second, the current government's arbitrary approach to the law has commercial as well as human rights implications: if there is a dispute, companies have no recourse to independent arbitration. Third, notwithstanding the government's promises of reform, the economy has far to go before it is truly liberalized. And fourth, international companies have come under varying degrees of pressure from nongovernmental organizations that argue that the profits they bring help to sustain an illegitimate regime. This argument has greater force in Myanmar than it might in other countries because gas sales are emerging as the country's prime source of foreign exchange.

Conflict between the national government and the ethnic minorities began soon after independence in 1948, and by the 1980s the country faced more than a dozen insurgencies. From 1989 onward, the military regime signed a series of cease-fires, first with the successor groups to the Burmese Communist Party in the north of the country and then with others along the eastern border with Thailand. However, sporadic fighting continues, notably with the Shan State Army and the Karen National Union.

The Yadana joint venture exports gas to Thailand by means of a pipeline that comes onshore in Tenasserim Division and then crosses some 39 miles of mainland Myanmar before reaching the Thai border. This region has been affected by insurgency from the Karen National Union, which is still active, and the New Mon State Party, which signed a cease-fire with the government in 1995. In March 1995, guerrillas attacked a TotalFinaElf survey team, killing five Myanmar employees and wounding 11. Apart from this, there have been no major security incidents. The pipeline nevertheless benefits from security provided by the armed forces, and this raises the issue of whether the operating companies are complicit in alleged human rights abuses committed by government forces. There are two main concerns: reports of the security forces' use of forced labor and claims that military action has forced local villagers to flee into Thailand.

International Pressures and Company Responses. Companies operating in Myanmar have faced pressure from several different sources and to varying degrees, depending on which country they come from. In 1997 the U.S. government imposed limited commercial sanctions on Myanmar, barring new investment by U.S. companies but allowing existing operations to continue. Texaco withdrew the following year; Unocal has retained its investment. In 1999 the U.K. government publicly called on Premier to withdraw, but stopped short of passing legislation to force it to do so. However, the most severe pressure has come not from governments but from nongovernmental organizations. These have been most effective in the United States, followed by the United Kingdom and, to a much lesser extent, France.

In the United States the Free Burma Campaign has been one of the pioneers of Internet activism, using websites and e-mails to coordinate the activities of hundreds of support groups, notably in colleges and universities across the country. The strategies of the Free Burma Campaign and its allies have included the following:

- *Shareholder activism.* Both individuals and pension funds have raised questions at company annual general meetings in the United States and threatened to withdraw their investments. In Europe, activist fund managers have put pressure on companies to adopt a set of minimum standards if they are to continue operating in Myanmar.
- *"Selective purchasing"campaigns.* U.S. activists called on city and state administrations to pass resolutions refusing to do business with companies active in Myanmar. The best known of these was the 1996 Massachusetts Burma Law, which said that any company doing business in Myanmar must pay a 10 percent surcharge when doing business with the state government. However, in 1998 the Tenth District Court struck down the law, arguing that it infringed on the U.S. government's ability to conduct its foreign affairs. The Supreme Court confirmed this ruling in 2000.
- *Legal action.* In 1996 lawyers acting on behalf of Myanmar refugees issued a legal case against Unocal under the Alien Torts Claims Act. The legal cases are supported by EarthRights International, the International Labor Rights Fund, and the Center for Constitutional Rights. The case is still outstanding. Whatever the outcome, the case will take up immense amounts of management time before it is resolved.

The companies have defended their position. First, they argue that their presence in Myanmar amounts to a form of constructive engagement: they are contributing to the country's social and economic development, and in the long run this is likely to prove the most effective agent of change. Second, they insist that they follow international standards in their employment practices: Myanmar employees receive higher-than-average wages, and there is no question of the companies using forced labor. Third, they argue that they bring wider economic and social benefits to people living in and around their projects through their social development programs. Premier has made a point of ensuring that its programs are audited by specialists from the Warwick Business School in the United Kingdom.

One of the main dilemmas facing companies operating in countries such as Myanmar concerns the extent to which they are responsible, directly or indirectly, for the activities of government security forces, which by definition operate under the command of the authorities and not the company. This is one of the key issues in the Alien Torts Claims Act legal case against Unocal. Lawyers acting on behalf of the plaintiffs argue that the company was aware of and benefited from the army's operations in the pipeline region. They maintain that this awareness amounted to a form of complicity. The companies do not accept this argument, but Premier acknowledges the importance of human rights in its code of conduct and has sponsored human rights training for members of the Myanmar armed forces and the police (Murray 2002).

Questions for the Future. In late 2002 Premier announced that it was selling its assets in Myanmar to Petronas. Its decision to sell was motivated by commercial considerations, and the sale fits the pattern whereby junior companies concentrate on exploration, develop projects to a certain stage, and then sell out to other countries at a suitable profit. Whatever the case, the company's withdrawal from Myanmar lifts a reputational burden. The outcome is similar to the Sudan case in that a Western junior has sold out to an Asian company that is far less exposed to pressure from nongovernmental organizations.

One question for the future concerns Petronas's continuing commitment to the social projects that Premier has started. Petronas's website affirms its commitment to community initiatives in its home country, and this experience should provide a good basis for a similar commitment in its international operations.

The wider questions concerning Myanmar's political future, and the role played by commercial constructive engagement, remain unresolved. It would, in any case, be unrealistic to expect companies to be prime movers. They may help or hinder, but the country's political leaders—whether civilian or military—will be the prime decisionmakers.

Chad-Cameroon Pipeline

The Chad-Cameroon Petroleum Development and Pipeline Project is one of the largest in Africa. It differs from the Sudan and Myanmar examples in that it has yet to come into production. Its sponsors hope that they will learn from the experience of other countries and avoid the problems associated with a sudden "resource boom." The project involves investment in the development of oil fields at Doba in southern Chad at a cost of $1.5 billion and the construction of a 1,070-kilometer pipeline to offshore oil-loading facilities on Cameroon's Atlantic coast at a cost of $2.2 billion (World Bank 2002). The project could earn as much as $2 billion in revenues for Chad (averaging some $80 million a year) and $500 million for Cameroon (averaging some $20 million a year).

The private sector participants in the project are ExxonMobil, with 40 percent of the private equity, Petronas (35 percent), and Chevron-Texaco (25 percent). The World Bank's International Finance Corporation (IFC) is cofinancing the project. Revenue from the project will be placed in special managed accounts, and priority will be given to sectors such as health and education. The Chad-Cameroon project is therefore a test case for international collaboration to defuse the "curse of resources" by ensuring that a broad section of the population benefits from oil revenue. The pipeline will begin to come on stream in late 2003 or early 2004.

The Opportunity. The first proposals by Exxon (now ExxonMobil) to develop the Doba fields date back to the 1980s. Exxon's initial partners were Royal Dutch Shell and Elf Aquitaine (now part of TotalFinaElf), but these companies withdrew in 1999. ExxonMobil operates the project under the name EssoChad.

Chad is one of the world's poorest countries, and there is a clear economic rationale for a project that will increase the country's revenue 45–50 percent once the oil comes on stream (World Bank 2002). The extra funds are to be used for investments in health, education, environment, infrastructure, and rural development. However, Chad's record of political instability has discouraged investment. The country has a record of north-south divisions and conflict. This is roughly analogous to Sudan in that the north has a history of cultural and religious links with North Africa and the Middle East, while the south is mainly Christian and has closer cultural affinities with neighboring Sub-Saharan African states. North-south tensions have not been as severe as in Sudan but have nonetheless led to the emergence of a series of southern rebel movements. These have now subsided, but tensions remain, and there is still a long-term risk of renewed conflict.

President Idris Déby came to power by means of a military coup in 1990 but has since emphasized the need for democratic reform. He led the way to democratic presidential elections in 1996 and again in 2001, returning to power each time. Despite some problems, the perception that Chad is now significantly more stable has helped to justify the expenditure needed to launch the Chad-Cameroon project. However, the political and social risks are far from eliminated.

Political Risks. The Chad-Cameroon negotiations illustrate the strong position that companies and external lenders typically enjoy at the outset of a major project. There was no doubt that Chad needed the revenues that the project would bring, and the government was willing to accept tough conditions, including requirements for international oversight that arguably impinge on the country's sovereignty. However, there is a risk that the politics of the "obsolescing bargain" will come into place as the project proceeds. Once the external participants have built the pipeline and other infrastructure, and therefore sunk their costs into fixed assets, the balance of power will shift in favor of the government.

In November 2000 the Chad government used part of a $25 million oil contract bonus to purchase $4.5 million worth of weapons. President Déby justified the purchases as being consistent with the demands of national security and the need to protect development. However, the episode raised concern over the possibility of further controversial decisions once the project gets under way and the government enjoys greater freedom of maneuver.

The involvement of the World Bank and other external lenders is part of a strategy to mitigate both the political and the social risks incurred by the project. The private sector partners are financing some $3 billion, or 81 percent of the project costs, from their own resources. The World Bank is providing $92.9 million in loans—$39.5 million to Chad's TOTCO (T'Chad Oil Transportation Company) and $53.4 million to Cameroon's COTCO (Cameroon Oil Transportation Company)—to help finance these countries' participation in the project (World Bank 2002). The IFC is providing loans of $14.5 million to TOTCO and $85.5 million to COTCO. The IFC's involvement has also mobilized another $100 million in commercial lending. The World Bank's participation, in turn, has made it easier to secure additional contributions of $41.5 million from the European Investment Bank, along with additional borrowing of $200 million from COFACE and $200 million from the U.S. Exim Bank.

In overall percentage terms, the contribution of the World Bank and the other public sector lenders is relatively small. However, their participation affords a degree of political risk protection because, at least in principle, the Chad and Cameroon governments will be reluctant to jeopardize their relationships with the international financial institutions given their indebtedness and reliance on foreign aid.

The World Bank insisted on an environmental impact assessment, and this includes a review of social issues linked to the project.[31] Ancillary projects have been designed to mitigate the environmental impact of oil development and to build local capacity, for example, by developing small and medium-size enterprises.

A combination of internal and external oversight is intended to ensure that revenue spending is consistent with the developmental objectives that, in principle, have been agreed by all parties. The 1998 Law

Governing the Management of Oil Revenue resulted in the creation of a revenue management plan (see Rosenblum 2002). The revenue management plan reserves 80 percent of oil revenue for spending on public health, social services, education, and rural development. It will be monitored by an independent body, the Committee for the Oversight and Monitoring of Oil Revenue, which, in turn, will be subject to the scrutiny of Chad's increasingly active civil society.

Meanwhile, an independent advisory group of five external experts will report to the World Bank on the implementation of the project. The group will meet twice a year, and its reports are publicly available on its website.[32]

The project has proved controversial among international nongovernmental organizations, which claim that it will prove socially and environmentally destructive, particularly in the forests along the pipeline route. They have little confidence in the willingness of Chad's government to abide by its promises and argue that there is a strong risk of continuing and deepening corruption as a result of the project. Much of their criticism and their lobbying has been directed against the World Bank rather than the companies.

Questions for the Future. The main outstanding concerns relate to the effectiveness of the project's oversight mechanisms. For example, Peter Rosenblum of the Harvard Law School Human Rights Program has questioned whether the oversight committee has as much independence from the government as it needs and called for measures to strengthen its authority, including the hiring of full-time staff and the acquisition of technical expertise (Rosenblum 2002). He also seeks a more permanent role for the independent advisory group so that it can interact with the local population continuously rather than only twice a year.

Although these measures would undoubtedly help, Rosenblum comes to the "inescapable conclusion" that the success of the Chad-Cameroon project "depends on the integrity of those in power and their willingness to engage in a truly transparent and politically open process." That remains a major challenge, but not a hopeless one.

Notes

1. Personal interview, January 2003.
2. For a discussion of the dynamics of the obsolescing bargain, see Moran (1998, pp. 7–14).
3. Personal interview, February 2003.

4. The survey results are available as a separate document on www. crg.com.

5. The proportion of companies deterred might have been smaller if the sample had included juniors.

6. For an overview of emerging trends, see Keay (2002).

7. See the company's website at www.cairn-energy.plc.uk.

8. Personal interview, January 2003.

9. Personal interview, January 2003.

10. For a summary of international corporate governance codes, see www. worldbank.org/html/fpd/privatesector/cg/codes.htm.

11. Personal interview, December 2001.

12. Institutional Investors (2001). The eight companies were Co-operative Insurance Society; Ethos Investment Foundation; Friends, Ivory, and Sime; Henderson Global Investors; Jupiter Asset Management; Morley Fund Management; PGGM; and the Universities Superannuation Scheme.

13. See www.ftse4good.com.

14. See www.unglobalcompact.org.

15. On the OECD Guidelines for Multinational Enterprises, see www. oecd.org. For the Global Sullivan Principles of Social Responsibility, see www. globalsullivanprinciples.org. Reverend Leon Sullivan played a prominent role in advising on the limits of U.S. corporate engagement with apartheid South Africa.

16. For samples, see www.business-humanrights.org.

17. For the historical background of the Foreign Corrupt Practices Act, see Noonan (1984).

18. For the background to the convention and a discussion of how it works in practice, see Control Risks Group (2002).

19. See www.publishwhatyoupay.org.

20. See www.ogp.co.uk.

21. Personal interview, November 2002.

22. On this topic, see Schwartz (1996). Schwartz is a former head of scenario planning at Shell.

23. The World Bank has developed a conflict analysis framework that allows country teams to consider factors affecting conflict when formulating development strategies, policies, and programs.

24. Personal interview, January 2003.

25. The case study of Western Mining Corporation is discussed in Amnesty International, Prince of Wales Business Leaders Forum (2000, pp. 98–101).

26. Personal interview, April 2002.

27. Interview with Swiss reinsurance broker, January 11, 2003.

28. Private interview, January, 2003.

29. The original participants were Amnesty International, British Petroleum, Business for Social Responsibility, Chevron, Freeport McMoRan, Human Rights

Watch, International Alert, International Business Leaders' Forum, Shell, and Texaco.

30. See www.wbcsd.org/casestud/statoil/index.htm.

31. See www.essochad.com/eaff/essochad/documentation/english/summary/index.html.

32. See www.gic-iag.org.

References

The word "processed" describes informally produced works that may not be commonly available through libraries.

Amnesty International, Prince of Wales Business Leaders Forum. 2000. *Human Rights: Is It Any of Your Business?* London.

Bolger, Andre. 2001. "African Insurance Initiative Aims to Boost Trade," *Financial Times,* August 7.

"BP to Spend $20 Billion to Replace Ageing Fields." 2003. *Financial Times,* February 12.

Bray, John. 1997. "Web of Influence." *The World Today* 53(8, August-September):206–08.

Browne, John. 2002. "BP's Browne: Transparency Key to Restoring Trust." *Oil and Gas Journal,* October 28.

Christian Aid. 2001. *The Scorched Earth: Oil and War in Sudan.* London. Available at www.christian-aid.org.uk.

Control Risks Group. 2002. *Facing up to Corruption.* London.

Crowson, Philip. 2001. "Mining in the Global Market." Paper presented at the Global Metals and Mining Conference, Toronto, June 13–15. Processed.

Danish Industries. 2001. "Capacity Building in Industrial Employers' Organizations." Copenhagen. Processed.

ECGD (Export Credit Guarantee Department). 2000. "Sustainable Development and Human Rights." Available at www.ecgd.gov.uk/graphic/debtdev/BusPrinSusDev&HR.asp. Processed.

Ecopetrol. 2002. "Short- to Medium-Term Exploration Map of Colombia: Is Now the Right Time to Invest?" *Petroleum Economist* (August).

"Encouraging FDI in Mozambique." 2002. *MIGA News* 10 (3), November 26.

Fridthof Nansen Institute and Econ. 2000. *Petro-States: Predatory or Developmental?* Oslo.

Gagnon, Georgette, Audrey Macklin, and Penelope Simons. 2003. *Deconstructing Engagement. Corporate Self-Regulation in Conflict Zones: Implications for Human Rights and Canadian Public Policy.* Relationships in

Transition. A Strategic Joint Initiative of the Social Sciences and Humanities Research Council and the Law Commission of Canada.

Gumbel, Andrew, and Marie Woolf. 2003. "Beyond Petroleum, or Beyond the Pale? BP Left out in the Cold." *Independent,* January 23.

Heap, Simon. 2000. "The Relationship between Living Earth and Shell: Emergence of a Progressive Partnership?" In Simon Heap, ed., *NGOs Engaging with Business,* pp. 192–213. Oxford: INTRAC (International NGO Training and Research Center).

Herkströter, Cor. 1996. "Dealing with Contradictory Expectations: The Dilemmas of the Multinationals." Speech made before the Shell International Ltd., Group External Affairs, Amsterdam, October 11. Processed.

Higgs, Derek. 2003. *Review of the Role and Effectiveness of Non-executive Directors.* London: Department of Trade and Industry. Available at www.dti.gov.uk/cld/non_exec_review/.

Housego, Kim. 2003. "TotalFinaElf Weathers the Storms." *Associated Press,* January 14.

Human Rights Watch. 2002. *The Niger Delta. No Democratic Dividend* 14(7A, October). New York.

Institute of Chartered Accountants of England and Wales. 1999. *Internal Control: Guidance for Directors on the Combined Code.* Also known as the Turnbull report. London. Available at www.icaew.co.uk.

Institutional Investors. 2001. "Business Involvement in Myanmar (Burma), a Statement from Institutional Investors." Available at www.burmainfo.org/econo/FMS.pdf. Processed.

IPIECA (International Petroleum Industry Environmental Conservation Association) and OGP (International Association of Oil and Gas Producers). 2002. *Key Questions in Managing Social Issues in Oil and Gas Projects.* Report 2.85/332. London. Available on www.ogp.co.uk.

ISIS (formerly Friends, Ivory, and Sime) and World Resources Institute. 2002. *Changing Oil: Emerging Environmental Risks and Shareholder Value.* July. Available at www.friendsis.com.

Kansteiner, Walter H. 2002. "Transcript of Assistant Secretary Walter H. Kansteiner's Speech to the Corporate Council on Africa's West Africa Oil and Gas Forum, Houston, Texas, November 19, 2002." Available at www.africacncl.com. Processed.

Keay, Malcolm. 2002. *Towards Global Corporate Social Responsibility.* Sustainable Development Program. Briefing Paper 3. London: Royal Institute of International Affairs, April.

Kerr, Simeon. 2003. "Sudan Sees Deals on Three Blocks End-Mar-Oil Min." *Dow Jones,* February 3.

Killick, Nick. n.d. *Oil and Gas Development, Azerbaijan.* Partnerships for Managing Social Issues in the Extractive Industries Case Study 4. London: Business Partners for Development Programme, Natural Resources Cluster.

Available at www.bpd-naturalresources.org/media/pdf/azer/azerbaijan_exec. pdf.

MacDonald, Andrea L. 1998. "Challenges in the Financing of International Oil Operations." In Theodore H. Moran, ed., *Managing International Political Risk*, pp. 120–23. Oxford: Blackwell.

Médécins sans Frontières. 2002. *Violence, Health, and Access to Aid in Unity State/Western Upper Nile*. n.p., April.

MIGA (Multilateral Investment Guarantee Agency). 2002. *Foreign Direct Investment Survey. A Study Conducted by the Multilateral Investment Guarantee Agency with the Assistance of Deloitte & Touche LLP*. Washington, D.C., January. Available at www.ipanet.net.

Mitchell, John, and others. 2002. *The New Economy of Oil*. London: Royal Institute of International Affairs and Earthscan.

MMSD (Mining, Minerals, and Sustainable Development). 2001. *Workshop Report on Armed Conflict and Natural Resources: The Case of the Minerals Sector*. London, July 11.

———. 2002. *Report of the Experts Meeting on Human Rights Issues in the Mining and Minerals Sector*. London.

Moran, Theodore H. 1998. "The Changing Nature of Political Risk." In Theodore H. Moran, ed., *Managing International Political Risk*. Oxford: Blackwell.

Morrisey, Chris. 2002. "Looking towards a Sustainable Future." *[Rio Tinto] Review* 64:4–11.

Murray, Sarah. 2002. "When Exploration Rights Meet Human Right." *Financial Times*, March 15.

Nelson, Jane. 2000. *The Business of Peace: The Private Sector as a Partner in Conflict Prevention and Resolution*. London: International Alert, Council on Economic Priorities, Prince of Wales Business Leaders Forum.

Noonan, John T. 1984. *Bribes: The Intellectual History of a Moral Idea*. Berkeley: University of California Press.

PricewaterhouseCoopers. 2001. *Mining, Minerals, and Sustainability Survey 2001*. Survey conducted for the Mining, Minerals, and Sustainability Development Project. Available at www.iied.org/mmsd/.

Rashid, Ahmed. 2001. *Taliban: The Story of the Afghan Warlords*, 2d ed. London: Pan Books.

Rio Tinto. 2001. *Community Relations, Global Business, Local Neighbor*. London.

Rosenberg, Mathew. 2003. "Sudanese Government and Rebels Agree to the Basics of a Wealth-Sharing Arrangement." *Associated Press*, February 6.

Rosenblum, Peter. 2002. "Analysis of Chad's Revenue Management Law." In *The Chad-Cameroon Oil and Pipeline Project. A Call for Accountability*. Chad: Association Tchadienne pour la Défense des Droits de l'Homme; Cameroon: Centre pour l'Envirronment et le Developpement, Cameroon;

USA: Environmental Defense, June. Available at www.eireview.org/
eir/eirhome.nsf/(DocLibrary)/3EB31D94A646FC2185256C4D007403C4/
$FILE/ONGs%20CCPP.pdf.

Ross, Michael. 2002. "Natural Resources and Civil War: An Overview with
Some Policy Options." Paper prepared for the governance of natural re-
sources conference, World Bank and Agence Francaise du Developpement,
Paris, December 9–10. Processed.

Royal Dutch Shell. 2001. *People, Planet, and Profits. The Shell Report 2001.*
Available in hard copy and on the company website at www.shell.com.

Schwartz, Peter. 1996. *The Art of the Long View: Paths to Strategic Insight for
Yourself and Your Company.* New York: Doubleday.

Talisman Energy. 2001. *Corporate Social Responsibility 2001.* Calgary. Available on www.talisman-energy.com/.

———. 2002. "Talisman to Sell Sudan Assets for C$1.2 Billion." Press state-
ment, October 30. Available at micro.newswire.ca/releases/October2002/
30/c6739.html/60728-0. Processed.

"Turkish Companies Interested in Oil Exploration, Production in Sudan."
2003. *Al-Anba,* January 17.

U.K. Department for International Development. n.d. *Conducting Conflict
Impact Assessments: Guidance Notes.* London.

UN Global Compact. 2002. *Global Compact Guide for Conflict Impact Assessment and Risk Management.* Available at www.unglobalcompact.org.

Vieth, Warren. 2003. "U.S. Quest for Oil in Africa Worries Analysts, Activists."
Los Angeles Times, January 13.

Ward, Halina. 2000. *Corporate Citizenship: International Perspectives on the
Emerging Agenda.* Conference report. London: Royal Institute of International Affairs, June.

Watts, Himangshu. 2002. "India Sees No Hitch in Sealing Sudan Oilfield
Deal." *Reuters,* June 19.

Williams, Bob. 2002. "Oil Industry Adapting to Evolving New Paradigm on
Corporate Governance, Accountability." *Oil and Gas Journal,* October 28.

World Bank. 2002. "Chad-Cameroon Petroleum Development and Pipeline
Project." Washington, D.C. Available at www.worldbank.org/afr/ccproj/
project/pro_overview.htm. Processed.

CHAPTER 8

Dampening Price Shocks

Patrick Guillaumont and Sylviane Guillaumont Jeanneney

THE INTEREST RECENTLY SHOWN IN GLOBAL policies on natural resources and raw materials in the effort to improve governance and reduce conflicts is shedding light once again on the long-standing problem of the international price fluctuations affecting developing countries. This renewal of interest comes after a lengthy period during which the very idea of a global policy for dealing with price shocks was out of favor because of measures that failed to take due account of market mechanisms. During this period, the magnitude of international price shocks did not diminish, and indeed increased, and a number of countries obviously remain vulnerable to them. In consequence, after two decades of market liberalization, the question of determining how the international community might contribute to dampening price shocks has once again come to the fore.

The purpose of this chapter is to examine global measures that might be taken efficiently in order to help developing countries overcome price shocks while avoiding past errors—that is, while respecting long-term market trends. We first review the reasons why dampening price shocks has once again become a reasonable objective of development cooperation policy. We then indicate why the measures taken previously proved inadequate. Finally, we examine the rationale for international mechanisms to provide insurance or guarantees against price shocks, perhaps in connection with external debt management.

Why Dampen Price Shocks?

It is difficult to design rational measures for dampening price shocks without inquiring about the reasons why such shocks can jeopardize development. There is clear evidence of the negative effects of export instability on growth (see, for example, Collier, Gunning, and Associates 2000; Combes and Guillaumont 2002; Dawe 1996; Fosu 1992; Guillaumont 1987, 1994; Guillaumont, Guillaumont Jeanneney, and Brun 1999).

On the microeconomic level and in the agricultural area, when international price instability is transmitted directly to agricultural producers, its effects are more damaging to agricultural supply when producers are poor and unable to obtain insurance. In such circumstances, farmers are inclined either to scale back their investment and innovation owing to their apprehension about using riskier techniques or, even in a period of price drops, to forgo educating their children, which is difficult to reverse.

Unstable international prices, because they lead to instability in export earnings, are also a factor in real exchange rate instability—that is, instability in the relative price of tradables and nontradables, which occurs regardless of the nature of the exchange arrangements in place. By disrupting signals about long-term market trends, this instability leads to poor resource allocation and hence to lower factor productivity.

Moreover, if a rise in export earnings leads to an appreciation of the real exchange rate in a boom period and a loss of competitiveness for the tradable goods sectors not benefiting from the boom (commonly referred to as the "Dutch disease"), a decline there does not necessarily have a symmetrical effect on the real exchange rate. In a fixed exchange arrangement, there may be less depreciation, with insufficient gains in competitiveness, while in a floating exchange arrangement, depreciation may be greater, perhaps at the cost of inflation triggered by nominal depreciation.

Third, the instability of export earnings induces a fiscal instability that generates serious problems. During an expansionary period, the growth of tax receipts, as well as the ease of recourse to external borrowing, leads to an increase in public expenditure. This triggers deficits during a period of declining prices. These deficits are difficult to absorb owing to the downward rigidity of expenditure, particularly in the case of wages and salaries. As a result, there is a chronic problem of inflation and public indebtedness.

While public investment constitutes a more flexible component of public expenditure, its instability, induced by that of exports, is a factor in lower average profitability (Guillaumont, Guillaumont Jeanneney, and Brun 1999).

Finally, the instability of export earnings, through the various effects referred to above and relative price instability in particular, is a factor in political instability, owing largely to the sudden changes it induces in absolute and relative incomes. Through this key channel, it undermines the sustainability of growth.

Recognizing the harmful nature of commodity price instability on the economies of exporting countries contributes toward justifying external assistance for such countries. Such aid is all the more justified in that, specifically in vulnerable countries (those subject to highly unstable world prices), aid has proven to be more effective in terms of growth than it has been in countries that are less vulnerable economically. As much as sound policy, vulnerability makes aid more effective, or, what amounts to the same thing, aid attenuates the negative consequences of the vulnerability (Chauvet and Guillaumont 2002; Guillaumont and Chauvet 2001). In particular, aid is marginally more effective when it is provided during periods of declining commodity prices (Collier and Dehn 2001). The various studies referred to here show both the negative effect of instability or price declines (an additive variable in econometric estimates) and the attenuation of this effect thanks to aid (multiplicative variable).

A rapid review of the various channels whereby international price instability affects development clearly reveals that dampening price shocks has both *microeconomic* implications (for economic agents in the sector affected by the international price change) and *macroeconomic* implications (through the central government budget, the real exchange rate, and political stability).

The expression "dampening price shocks" most often refers to dampening price drops. However, price shocks may be positive as well as negative. One clear lesson from the past 30 years is that rapid rises in international prices have drawn economies into situations that were particularly difficult to manage when prices later fell. Hence the occurrence of *positive and negative shocks in succession*—in other words, price instability—is at the root of the problem. It is illogical to devise a policy for dampening price drops that fails simultaneously to improve the management of export earnings booms.

An international commodity price shock calls for different responses depending on whether it is *temporary* or *permanent*. Only if the shock is permanent does it justify a reallocation of production factors, in other words, a change in the structure of production—that is, in specialization. The same does not hold in the case of temporary shocks, which are assumed to be reversible and are the shocks that are of interest for the concept of instability.

Why Have the Solutions Adopted Proven Inadequate?

Over 40 years of debate about the effects of export instability, various attempts have been made to deal with it. They have often proven inadequate, to such an extent that debate on the very advisability of new measures has been made more difficult, as they are regarded from the outset as a return to outdated positions. Four major categories of measures have been tried.

International Price Agreements

A first category of measures is intended to have a direct impact on international prices. This is the case of the international commodity agreements aimed at stabilizing the international price of a given commodity by involving both producer and consumer countries. The functioning of such agreements entails the use of a buffer stock or, in some cases, recourse to flexible production quotas. In 1976, at the height of the popularity enjoyed by such agreements, the resolution on the Integrated Programme for Commodities adopted at United Nations Conference on Trade and Development IV contemplated the introduction of such agreements for all (about 20) major commodities. A Common Fund for Commodities was even established with a view to financing this program. In any event, international commodity agreements of interest to the developing countries have remained limited in number (cocoa, coffee, sugar, tin, and natural rubber—the last being the only agreement concluded after 1976), and their effectiveness has been limited. Not only have such agreements been difficult to negotiate, but, more important, once agreements have been reached they have met with only temporary success in warding off major price spikes and, in particular, sharp drops. At present, none of these agreements is effectively being implemented.

The very principle of international price stabilization agreements has been the subject of a sizable body of critical literature (in particular, Newberry and Stiglitz 1981). Experience suggests that the main reason for their failure is that they limited their aims to price stabilization around the long-term market trend and, to one extent or another, ran up against that trend when attempting to affect it. It is symptomatic that the agreement that has best resisted this phenomenon is the agreement on natural rubber, specifically because the reference price used as the trigger for buffer stock intervention was regularly adjusted in terms of earlier prices. But in all cases it remains difficult to single out those aspects of international price movements that correspond to a trend and those that constitute a deviation from a trend and then to reach international agreement on financing the buffer stock required.

Stabilization Funds and Marketing Boards

In view of the high volatility of international commodity prices, and even before ineffective attempts were made to reduce this volatility by means of international agreements, many exporting countries, each at its own level, implemented internal price stabilization policies. The instruments of these policies are known by names such as stabilization fund and marketing board. While the use of such instruments has declined considerably, for many years it did ensure some stability in the prices paid to agricultural producers.

However, the effectiveness of this approach has been strongly contested for three main reasons. The first, but not the most general, reason is that these organizations have had a tendency to move well beyond the stabilization function and to become instruments for agricultural interventionism: after assuming responsibility for product marketing, the distribution of inputs and equipment, and agricultural credit and extension work, they often were inefficient and sometimes even predatory. The two other reasons are more general and fundamental. On the one hand, institutions of this kind were a way of taxing agriculture, with the surpluses recorded in periods of high prices largely being used to finance public expenditure. On the other, the price paid to producers was often stabilized without regard to the long-term market trend. As a consequence, when the long-term trend was downward, the gap between the international price and the corresponding producer price (taking transportation and marketing costs into account) gradually narrowed and then became negative, which led to a breakdown in the system owing to the lack of reserves or fiscal support. Like the commodity agreements, the stabilization funds ran aground on the long-term market trend.

Naturally, adjustment policies targeted the agricultural intervention agencies that were supported by stabilization funds as well as the excessive taxation of agriculture. At the same time, this led to the abandonment even of efforts to identify institutions that might be able to dampen price shocks domestically, while respecting market trends and sheltering their assets from being taken over by the public treasury.

Recourse to Forward Markets

To be sure, a partial response to the problem that international price instability raises for stakeholders in the sector concerned could be sought in having recourse to the forward market for export products. This solution is limited in scope, not only because such markets do not exist for all products and not all the developing countries concerned have the capacity to intervene in such markets but also because forward cover cannot generally exceed 12 to 18 months. Hence, although this approach makes it possible to cover price risk within a given year, it does not address the year-to-year instability that is at the root of the major difficulties. Work to develop the use of forward markets and promote the corresponding domestic insurance mechanisms is being carried out, at the initiative of the World Bank, in the context of the International Task Force on Commodity Risk Management in Developing Countries (see International Task Force on Commodity Risk Management in Developing Countries 1999).

Financial Compensation of Shocks: Compensatory Financing, Stabex

In light of the problems posed by any effort to affect international prices and of the financing requirements of any domestic effort to address price shocks, a third category of measures are international efforts to provide financial compensation to countries affected by such shocks. The two mechanisms in this area are compensatory and contingency financing, which was created by the International Monetary Fund (IMF) in 1963, and the export receipts stabilization system, or Stabex, which operated under the Lomé conventions for the period 1975–2000. While both aimed at compensating for drops in export earnings attributable to changes both in international prices and in the volume of exports, the two mechanisms are very different in design. Compensatory financing is a drawing on the International Monetary Fund authorized in the event of a decline in overall exports (or a price spike for imports) within the framework of a negotiated program. It is designed to help a country experiencing a balance of payments problem. Stabex was European assistance in the form of a grant or a loan, and subsequently grants only, provided to the African, Caribbean, and Pacific group of states in a manner initially planned to be automatic, so as to compensate for a decline in proceeds from agricultural exports to the European Community. Such agricultural exports were considered on a product-by-product basis for a certain number of eligible commodities.

These two mechanisms both evolved considerably over time and ultimately failed to fulfill the expectations they had initially raised. A common reason for this outcome is that, in order to make a genuine contribution to dampening shocks, compensatory financing should be automatic. Automaticity is necessary for payments to be rapid, and hence countercyclical, and to reduce the uncertainty associated with price instability that undermines the proper conduct of economic policy. Neither of these two approaches satisfied the principle of automaticity. While the conditionality was less rigorous for compensatory financing than for stand-by arrangements when it was first introduced, it ultimately became a simple adjunct to the IMF's other mechanisms for low-income countries and was subject to the same conditionality. As for Stabex, over time it increasingly suffered from a contradiction inherent in its two founding principles: the principle of automaticity and the targeting of compensation to the agricultural sector affected by the price decline. This is why, as one convention succeeded another, under pressure from the European countries the commission's supervisory function on the use of Stabex funds was strengthened at the cost of greater and greater delays in making payments, thereby eliminating any countercyclical use of such funds without guaranteeing that the farmers affected by the price decline would be genuinely compensated (see CERDI 1998; Collier and others 1999).

This loss of Stabex automaticity was reinforced by the fact that the resources allocated to the mechanism repeatedly fell short of the mark. This could perhaps be interpreted once again as the outgrowth of a poor understanding of the temporary and trend portions of drops in revenue: the method used to calculate drops vis-à-vis an arithmetic mean of past values led to an underestimation whenever the drops occurred following an upward trend (the most frequent situation in the 1970s) and an overestimation following a downward trend (as was the case for many products in the 1980s and even the 1990s).[1]

New Support for the Cotonou Agreement

Owing to the criticisms of the Stabex scheme, and despite the fact that these related more to its implementation modalities than its underlying principle, it was abandoned under the new Cotonou agreement. However, it has a successor in a new mechanism called "support in case of short-term fluctuations in export earnings." While the explanatory text does repeat a portion of the wording on Stabex in the Lomé conventions ("mitigate the adverse effects of any instability"), it clarifies the aim of the support: "to safeguard macroeconomic and sectoral reforms . . . that are at risk as a result of a drop in [export] revenue." The resulting modalities appear to be quite distinct from those of Stabex, since the support is conceived as budgetary support, for which the eligibility criteria are both a decline in the total export earnings of goods (or in some cases revenue from primary commodities as a whole) and a deterioration (of 10 percent) in the programmed fiscal deficit. More clearly than Stabex, the new mechanism appears to be budgetary support intended to ward off the macroeconomic consequences of the drop, but the mechanism could be used for sectoral purposes in order to dampen shocks incurred directly by stakeholders in the sector concerned. Moreover, agreement on the need to allocate funds is required. This requirement, of course, threatens to slow the procedure even though a system of advances is provided to overcome delays in the receipt of information on foreign trade statistics. Price drops are still calculated in relation to an average for previous years, which makes it impossible to distinguish between the temporary component and the trend component of the revenue decline and results in limiting the support to four successive years.

This brief review of the measures taken to dampen the international price shocks facing developing countries clearly shows their limits. If one excludes those measures, heretofore ineffective, aimed at reducing price instability upstream, the methods intended to dampen the effects of shocks are characterized by two major problems: they are associated with the consequences of price drops—that is, negative shocks—rather than with the consequences of instability, and insufficient efforts have been made to distinguish between permanent and temporary price shifts. Further, sometimes they seek to preserve the incomes of a particular category of stakeholders, and sometimes they seek to achieve macroeconomic stabilization, without reconciling these two objectives.

What Options Are Available to the International Community?

Although it may recognize the need to assist poor and vulnerable countries to address the price shocks that affect them, the international community may be tempted to skirt the issue in one of two ways. The first is to say that the main objective is to prevent instability. As there is little chance of doing so by means of agreements by commodity, the solution proposed is to diversify production and exports. But although diversification may be regarded as desirable, it is a long-term process, and speeding it up has its costs, particularly in small countries, namely, that of forgoing the advantages of specialization.

Another frequently heard proposal is to invite countries to manage the price shocks affecting their exports by means of exchange rate flexibility, allowing their exchange rate to depreciate in the event of price declines and to appreciate in the event of increases. Hence the change in export prices expressed in foreign currency terms would be offset by the change in the opposite direction of that currency's price expressed in domestic currency. This solution intrinsically entails variability of the real exchange rate (which governs the changes in relative prices of tradables and nontradables). Such variability has, in the long term, an unfavorable impact on macroeconomic stability and growth in developing economies. Oddly enough, in these circumstances, the solution consists of making the Dutch disease the appropriate response to an export receipts boom.

Offer a Guarantee Conditioned by Rules

The international community cannot content itself with stressing the importance of sound domestic macroeconomic management for purposes of dampening shocks, in that such shocks specifically make the conduct of economic policy more difficult. The role of the international community in response to shocks could be to act simultaneously to provide insurance and promote sound management. The general idea is that the international community could help to introduce automatic stabilization mechanisms by financing their costs subject to the adoption of agreed and controllable management rules. In short, the international community would offer a guarantee in exchange for a commitment as to rules. This principle can be applied on a macroeconomic scale and on a microeconomic or sectoral scale.

Adjust Debt Service in Response to Price Shocks

In the macroeconomic area, the principle whereby it is advisable to compensate for instability and not just price drops can be applied in a proposal to tie the way the debt is treated to developments in commodity export prices. Easing debt service when prices are low and raising it when prices are high exerts a countercyclical effect on public finances: the easing of external debt service makes it possible to maintain other domestic expenditure despite the decline in tax receipts induced by the drop in export earnings, while increasing debt service in a period of spiking prices prevents a destabilizing increase in public expenditure that would be difficult to reverse. Such a system could be put in place for any country that wanted it and would undertake to increase debt service in the event of commodity price rises. Naturally, implementation of this system raises a number of problems. First, there is the problem of defining a reference price level for triggering the mechanism. It seems logical to refer to a price corresponding to a trend value or to a price deemed reasonable by the major producers and consumers (oil at $20 a barrel, for example). A second problem to be resolved is the introduction of a financial mechanism making it possible to scale back debt service automatically while ensuring that creditors share the cost equitably. Conceivably, a multilateral rescheduling fund could be introduced to this end, which would be funded by the surplus debt service received from debtor countries benefiting from high prices as well as from an initial endowment from bilateral and multilateral donors and lenders. One important question that it is not possible to examine here concerns the modalities for modulating debt cost via interest payments or amortization payments.

Countries eligible for the Highly Indebted Poor Countries (HIPC) Initiative, which are particularly dependent on commodity exports, could find this new mechanism of interest even though they are benefiting from debt cancellation. The objective of the HIPC Initiative is to reduce the ratio of debt to exports to 150 percent when the completion point has been reached. However, the analysis of the sustainability of that debt level assumes that exports will expand at a given rate, without any explicit provision being made to adjust the debt and debt service levels in light of export price developments. Conceivably, the mechanism of the multilateral rescheduling fund could be applied to the remaining stock of debt. The advantage for highly indebted poor countries would depend crucially on the reference level for the export price. Indeed, for various products, the international price was relatively low when the completion point was reached and hence could not serve as a reference price.

Create a Special Fund for the Least Developed Countries

This type of proposal should not mask the reality that other countries, while not heavily indebted, remain extremely dependent on their commodity exports and subject to significant price shocks. It would be paradoxical for a new international initiative intended to address such shocks not to take such countries into account or to exclude them for the simple reason that they are not heavily indebted. The logical response would then be for automatic assistance in loan form to be extended to them in the event of price drops, subject to the condition that they undertake to repay the aid at a pace that itself depends on price developments.

As regards low-income countries, arrangements could be made for compensation to be paid in grant form beyond a certain threshold of price declines. In this spirit, a reasonable proposition would be to create a new mechanism for automatic assistance in the event of price declines that is reserved for least developed countries (LDCs), a category established by the United Nations with a view to ensuring differential treatment and based on criteria whereby they may be identified as particularly vulnerable and as poor countries.[2] In this connection, aid is even more effective for economic growth as a country is more vulnerable (Guillaumont and Chauvet 2001). This aid, extended in grant form, would be distinct from the International Monetary Fund's compensatory financing. It should correspond to partial compensation granted subject to the sole condition that the country first undertook to limit the growth of its public expenditure during periods of high prices. The country would thus be prompted to set aside a portion of the gains registered when prices are high in order to maintain its spending levels when prices decline to the extent such drops are not offset by the international community. This would thus play the role of insurance and constitute an incentive for self-insurance. It should be possible to mobilize the resources necessary for this mechanism insofar as it would be limited to the category of LDCs.[3]

Interconnect Macroeconomic and Sectoral Support

Since price instability has unfavorable effects on both the macroeconomic and sectoral levels, it is logical for the mechanisms to be designed in such a way as to remedy the effects of instability at each of these levels. Our focus here is on mechanisms aimed at attenuating the effects of price instability in the agricultural sector.

The intensity with which international price instability is transmitted to exporters and agricultural producers depends on the tax and parafiscal policies of the government as regards agricultural exports. In the absence of such levies, price changes are transmitted in their entirety, which does not preclude an influence on general tax receipts owing to the impact of price changes on national income. In the case of levies that are proportional to the value of exports and constant, the direct income gain or loss is shared by the government and the sector, which may result in greater producer price instability than international price instability if marketing costs are rigid. Naturally, by modifying its tax rates, the government changes the conditions under which gains or losses are divided between itself and the stakeholders in the sector. For this reason, the external support for a policy aimed at using insurance mechanisms to reduce the risks incurred by producers owing to price variability must ensure that it does not constitute a pretext for a greater transfer of risk from the government to producers. In other words, it must be accompanied by fiscal conditionality.

Establish Insurance Mechanisms or Guarantee Funds

First, the international community could assist with establishing insurance mechanisms for agricultural producers in low-income countries who currently find them out of reach owing to their cost.[4] Producers could then take out insurance at a modest price, in the form of an option to sell a given volume of their harvest. The price at which the option is exercised should be set in terms of the past trend for the international price. There would be no risk of adverse selection, but rather a beneficial selection, as it affects those with the greatest need, and there would be no moral hazard in that farmers, at least those producing export crops, cannot influence prices and the government's behavior is subject to conditionality. The external support should both cover a portion of the costs of managing the options and guarantee the financing of the possible gap between the option exercise price and the producer price corresponding to the international price at the time the export product is sold.

The advantage of this solution is that the sale of options could be managed by private operators. Moreover, it could be associated with insurance on the volume of harvests. To be sure, the ease with which this approach could be implemented would vary from country to country, depending on the scale, location, and dispersal of producing units. The major drawback is that it would dampen only negative shocks, as it is difficult to conceive of circumstances in which producers would undertake to pay back a portion of their earnings in the event of unusually high international prices.

This highlights the objective of reducing the variability of the prices paid to producers, notwithstanding the flaws in the operation of stabilization funds. Conceivably, the international community could provide its support to guarantee funds whose operation would meet a number of conditions. The two key conditions pertain to the flexibility of the reference price and the placement of the monetary assets involved.

The price guaranteed to the producer should be calculated on the basis of an international price that is gradually adjusted toward the international market trend and reflects normal marketing, transportation, and processing costs and perhaps a rate of public levies itself determined in light of the international trend price. This guaranteed price should be widely disseminated throughout the country by the media. The guarantee fund would be credited by the positive differentials between the effective international price and the trend price and be debited by the negative differentials.

The cash assets of the guarantee fund, built up both by contributions from producers during periods of high prices and by international assistance, should be managed by a body that is independent of the government and preferably has international status. These funds would thus be beyond the government's reach, which is necessary in order to ensure the credibility of the system and would make it possible to use them countercyclically.

The operation of such a guarantee is compatible with trade liberalization and can accommodate various forms of marketing, including those that give producers' associations an important role. In order to prevent differing systems in neighboring countries from favoring informal reexports to the country where the highest price is offered, it would be advisable to design the guarantee system in a regional context.

International community support for this kind of guarantee fund would be all the more justified should it cover products whose prices are structurally depressed and for which price variability is boosted by the subsidies that industrial countries pay to their own producers, in particular in the event of price declines.

Conclusion

Logical reasons, both theoretical and empirical, justify action by the international community to dampen the effects of price shocks on poor countries. Lessons have been drawn from the various efforts made over the past 40 years, and their failures stem largely from the fact that they did not take long-term market trends sufficiently into account. Solutions do exist that not only respect market trends but also are built on a contractual base involving the international community, governments, and producer groups. The common point of such solutions is to offer a guarantee in exchange for certain rules that make it possible to reconcile the macroeconomic management of shocks and the protection of poor producers. These solutions could be combined with the manner in which the external debt is treated, in a nonexclusive way, in particular for LDCs that are not heavily indebted. Considerable resources do not seem to be required for the implementation of such guarantees. Moreover, it should be possible to make use of existing mechanisms, such as an amended approach to the International Monetary Fund's compensatory financing or the support in cases of short-term fluctuations in export earnings provided for under the Cotonou agreement.

Notes

1. SYSMIN, a mechanism created under the second Lomé convention for mining products, is even less automatic.

2. On the method for identifying LDCs, see United Nations (2000).

3. It would not be out of the question to use in this way the "support in cases of short-term fluctuations in export earnings" provided under the Cotonou agreement to the African, Caribbean, Pacific (ACP) countries with, moreover, less rigorous eligibility criteria for the ACP countries that are members of the category of LDCs as defined by the United Nations.

4. This section is based on Collier and others (1999) and on Guillaumont and Guillaumont Jeanneney (1990).

References

Arcand, Jean-Louis. 2001. *Are Policy Reform and Growth in Africa Sustainable?* Études et Documents E 2001.05. Paris: Centre d'Études et de Recherches sur le Développement International.

CERDI (Centre d'Études et de Recherches sur le Développement International). 1998. "Evaluation globale du Stabex [Overall Appraisal of Stabex]." Report prepared at the request of the European Commission, Directorate General of Development, Brussels. Processed.

Chauvet, Lisa, and Patrick Guillaumont. 2002. "Aid and Growth Revisited: Policy, Economic Vulnerability, and Political Instability." Paper presented at the Annual World Bank Conference on Development Economics: Toward Pro-Poor Policies, Oslo. Processed.

Collier, Paul, and Jan Dehn. 2001. "Aid, Shocks, and Growth." Policy Research Working Paper 2688. World Bank, Washington, D.C. Processed.

Collier, Paul, J. W. Gunning, and Associates, eds. 2000. *Trade Shocks in Developing Countries.* Oxford: Clarendon Press.

Collier, Paul, Patrick Guillaumont, Sylviane Guillaumont Jeanneney, and J. W. Gunning. 1999. "Reforming Stabex." *The World Economy* 22(5):669–82.

Combes, Jean-Louis, and Patrick Guillaumont. 2002. "Commodity Price Volatility, Vulnerability, and Development." *Development Policy Review* 20(1):25–39.

Dawe, David. 1996. "A New Look at the Effects of Export Instability on Investment and Growth." *World Development* 24(12):1905–14.

Fosu, A. K. 1992. "Effect of Export Instability on Economic Growth in Africa." *Journal of Developing Areas* 26(3):323–32.

Guillaumont, Patrick. 1987. "From Export Instability Effect to International Stabilization Policies." *World Development* 15(5):633–43.

————. 1994. "Politique d'ouverture et croissance economique: Les effets de la croissance et de l'instabilité des exportations. [Opennness Policy and Economic Growth: The Effects of Growth and Export Instability]." *Revue d'Economie du Développement* 1:91–114.

Guillaumont, Patrick, and Lisa Chauvet. 2001. "Aid and Performance: A Reassessment." *Journal of Development Studies* 37(6):66–92.

Guillaumont, Patrick, and Syviane Guillaumont Jeanneney. 1990. "Why and How to Stabilize Producer Prices for Export Crops in Developing Countries." Occasional Paper 6. United Nations Development Programme and World Bank Trade Expansion Program.

Guillaumont Patrick, Syviane Guillaumont Jeanneney, and J. F. Brun. 1999. "How Instability Lowers Economic Growth." *Journal of African Economies* 8(1):87–102.

International Task Force on Commodity Risk Management in Developing Countries. 1999. *Dealing with Commodity Price Volatility in Developing Countries: A Proposal for a Market-Based Approach.* Discussion Paper. Washington, D.C.: World Bank, September.

Newberry, D. M. G., and Joseph Stiglitz. 1981. *Theory of Commodity Price Stabilization.* Oxford: Clarendon Press.

United Nations. 2000. *Poverty Amidst Riches: The Need for Change.* Report of the Committee for Development Policy on the second session, April 3–7. New York.

Index

Action Contre la Faim: activities in Sudan, 342

Adams, Roger: comments on Global Reporting Initiative, 264

Afghanistan: and Al-Qaeda, 170, 204; Taliban and Northern Alliance financing, 31, 169, 204–5; terrorism's role in sustained conflict, 170

Africa: booty futures, 32–33; Forest Law Enforcement and Governance Ministerial Process, 63; land rights issue, 318; minerals and petroleum as the most substantial and readily accessible sources of income, 288; new petroleum exploration and development, 290; off-budget revenue reporting, 52; resource-related conflicts, 17, 19; security of tenure concerns of businesses, 292. *See also specific countries*

African Trade Insurance Agency: coverage, 325–26; organizations covering startup expenses, 325; purpose, 325; rationale for setting up, 325

Agricultural sector: compensatory financing, 358–59; export receipts stabilization system (Stabex), 358–59; guarantee funds, 364–65; insurance mechanisms, 363–65; and marketing boards, 357; and negative effects of price shocks, 354; option to sell a given volume of the harvest, 364; and stabilization funds, 357; taxes on, 357, 363

AIG Group: political risk insurance, 323

Algeria: and booty futures, 37 n16; corrupt government link to civil war, 26; recent governance problems related to resource revenue, 90 n2

All the Presidents' Men, 50, 92 n35

Alluvial gemstones: difficulty of controlling, 253; ease of mining for, 25; and Kimberley Certification Process Scheme, 148. *See also specific types of gemstones*

Al-Qaeda: and Afghanistan, 170, 204–5; diamond smuggling, 201 n9; and illegal drug trafficking, 204–5; newspaper article alleging links between diamonds from RUF-controlled areas in Sierra Leone and the Al-Qaeda terrorist network, 270;

"Dutch disease," 82; resource revenue reporting case study, 82–84; revenue collection procedures, 82–83; use of resource extraction funds for government operations, 209 n6

Boycotts, 267, 280 n58

BP. See British Petroleum

Brazil: percentage of the cost of enforcement actions covered by fines, 157 n14

Bre-X: scandal regarding, 300

Bribery. See Corruption

British Petroleum: activities in Colombia, 270; new oil field development, 290; political risk insurance, 323; pressure from Angolan government to keep payments confidential, 49, 90 n3; preventive diplomacy efforts in West Papua, 29; U.S.-U.K. Voluntary Principles on Security and Human Rights participant, 348–49 n29; withdrawal of Henderson Global Investors's ethical investment funds from, 303–4

Browne, Lord John: chief executive role, 299; comments on the Enron scandal, 302–3

Buckee, Jim: chief executive role, 299; comments on the sale of Talisman Energy, 338

Burma. See Myanmar

Burundi: and African Trade Insurance Agency, 325; and economic sanctions, 238–39

Businesses. See Attracting reputable companies to risky environments; Corporate conduct enforcement measures; specific businesses and industries

Business for Social Responsibility: U.S.-U.K. Voluntary Principles on Security and Human Rights participant, 348–49 n29

Cairn Energy: junior company example, 299–300

Cambodia: and aid conditionality, 251; double agenda of peace transition and rearmament, 253; financing of the government by illicit commodities, 168; Forest Crimes Monitoring Unit, 180; Global Witness campaign on conflict timber, 269; intensification of fighting over log yards, 217; recent governance problems related to resource revenue, 90 n2; tax evasion by the forest sector, 137; UN border monitors, 237; United Nations Transitional Authority's log export monitoring, 233. See also Khmer Rouge

Cameroon: cooperative certification system, 118; projected revenue from the Chad-Cameroon Oil Development and Pipeline Project, 344–45. See also Chad-Cameroon Oil Development and Pipeline Project

Cameroon Oil Transportation Company: World Bank loans to, 346

Canada: Export Development Canada, 326; Harker Report inquiry on human security in Sudan, 338; Oxfam Canada's intervention on behalf of peasant farmers in Zambia, 263; use of resource extraction funds for government operations, 166, 209 n6

Cannabis: rebel group financing, 31

Capacity-building element of CTRs: and compliance and enforcement, 125–26; description, 101; developed country funding of programs in developing countries, 126; development of new enforcement tools, 132–33; equity issues, 132; and public education, 133; special enforcement units, 132;

Wal-Mart: child labor restrictions, 140

Weapons. *See* Firearms

"White list" of banks, 79, 194

WildAid: contraband trade route investigation, 130

Wildlife trade: differences between criminal constituencies, 135–36; EU's wildlife control legislation system, 107, 126; Kenya's Wildlife Service, 128; Trade Record Analysis of Flora and Fauna in Commerce's wildlife trade monitoring, 129–30; World Wildlife Fund, 129

Windfall funds, 53–54

Woicke, Peter: endorsement of the Publish What You Pay campaign, 76

Wolfsberg Group: antiterrorism principles, 187; correspondent principles for banking, 188–89; creation of additional guidelines, 199–200; Global Anti–Money Laundering Guidelines for Private Banking, 186–89; mandate extension, 187; membership, 162, 209 n3; model for action, 194; signatories to, 187; tracking structure, 190

Workshop on Petroleum Revenue Management, 280 n50

World Bank: and African Trade Insurance Agency, 325; and Cambodia's Forest Crimes Monitoring Unit, 180; Chad-Cameroon Petroleum Development and Pipeline Project oversight, 255, 327, 346; classification of "highly indebted poor countries" and civil wars, 21–22; collation of resource revenue information, 13; conflict analysis framework, 348–49 n23; Country Policy and Institutional Assessment ratings, 9; Economics of Civil Wars, Crime, and

Violence Project, 90 n12; expenditure reviews, 78–79; Financial Sector Assessment Program, 91 n14; Foreign Direct Investment Survey, 294; Forest Governance Program, 62; and forward markets, 358; global forest policy review, 142; Indonesian loan disbursement delay, 127; and interference in the affairs of host governments, 320–21; and International Finance Corporation, 322, 345; International Task Force on Commodity Risk Management in Developing Countries, 358; oversight conditions on Chad's resource revenue flows, 88; Petroleum Revenue Management workshop, 84, 87; position on illegal logging, 249; and price shock reduction, 10–11; report on the economic performance of countries with large mining sectors, 20; reports on the observance of standards and codes (ROSCs), 59–62; resource revenue reporting in developing countries, 47; role in setting up the State Oil Fund for the Azerbaijan Republic, 84; strengthening of anticorruption standards and norms, 181. *See also* Multilateral Investment Guarantee Agency

World Bank Group: review of role in the oil and mining sectors, 260. *See also* Multilateral Investment Guarantee Agency

World Business Council for Sustainable Development: and Mining, Minerals, and Sustainable Development Project, 72

World Conservation Monitoring Centre: logging restrictions, 150–51